The Bristol and Gloucestershire Archaeological Society
Gloucestershire Record Series

Hon. General Editor

Dr J. D. Hodsdon

Volume 27

Gloucestershire Feet of Fines
1360–1508

An example of a 'Divers Counties' foot of fine. It is abstracted below as no. 607. (Approximately half full size.)

ABSTRACTS OF FEET OF FINES
RELATING TO
GLOUCESTERSHIRE
1360–1508

Edited by C. R. Elrington

The Bristol and Gloucestershire Archaeological Society

2013

The Bristol and Gloucestershire Archaeological Society
Gloucestershire Record Series

ISBN 978 0 900197 82 6

British Library Cataloguing in Publication Data
A catalogue entry for this book is available from the British Library

Produced for the Society
by 4word Ltd, Bristol
Printed in Great Britain

CONTENTS

ACKNOWLEDGEMENTS

The help and advice of a number of people is gratefully acknowledged, and in particular of Dr Nicholas Herbert and Dr John Juřica, both formerly of the Victoria County History of Gloucestershire, of Dr Michael Roper, former Keeper of Public Records, and of Mr David Smith, former County and Diocesan Archivist and Hon. Secretary of the Bristol and Gloucestershire Archaeological Society. The staff of the Institute of Historical Research, University of London, of the National Archives, of the Gloucestershire Archives, and of Westminster Abbey Muniment Room and Library are also thanked for their assistance.

All the abstracts in this edition are from documents in the National Archives. Crown copyright material in the National Archives is reproduced by permission of the Controller of Her Majesty's Stationery Office.

C.R.E.

EDITORIAL NOTE

Christopher Elrington had largely completed the text of this, his third and final series of abstracts of Gloucestershire Feet of Fines, by 2004; he made minor adjustments to it in 2007, and on his untimely death in 2009 he left the work typeset and substantially in its present form. The only change of note has been the inclusion, as an Appendix, of a revised Bibliography of his works.

June 2013   J.D.H.

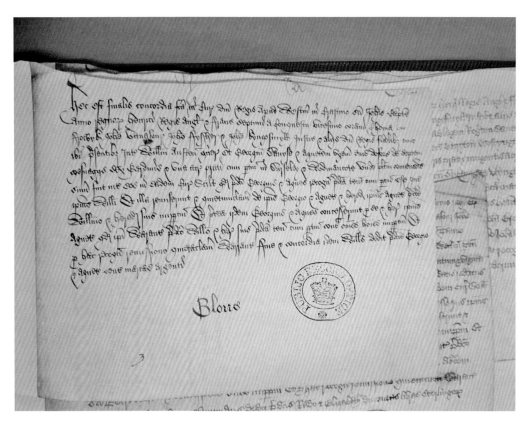

An example of a simple foot of fine. It is abstracted below as no. 843.
(Approximately two-thirds full size.)

LIST OF ABBREVIATIONS

B. & G. Trans.	*Transactions of the Bristol and Gloucestershire Archaeological Society*
Berkeley Castle Mun.	*Catalogue of the Medieval Muniments at Berkeley Castle*, 2 vols., Bristol and Gloucestershire Archaeological Society, Gloucestershire Record Series, vols. 17 and 18, 2004
Bristol Gt. Red Book	*Great Red Book of Bristol*, ed. E. W. W. Veale, Bristol Record Society, vol. ii, 1931
Cal. Inq. p.m.	*Calendar of Inquisitions post mortem*, 21 vols., Public Record Office, 1904–2002
Cal. Inq. p.m. (Rec. Com.)	*Calendar of Inquisitions post mortem*, 4 vols., Record Commission, 1806–28
Cornwall Fines, 1377–1461	*Cornwall Fines, 1377–1461*, Devon and Cornwall Record Society, 1950
def.	deforciant (i.e. defendant)
Dorset Fines, 1327–1485	*Full Abstracts of Feet of Fines relating to the County of Dorset* [1327–1485], Dorset Records, vol. x, 1910
Essex Fines, 1327–1422, 1423–1547	*Feet of Fines for Essex*, vols. iii and iv, Essex Archaeological Society, 1929–64 (vol. iii published in parts)
imp.	impedient (i.e. defendant)
Llanthony Priory Regs.	*A Calendar of the Registers of the Priory of Llanthony by Gloucester, 1457–1466, 1501–1525*, Bristol and Gloucestershire Archaeological Society, Gloucestershire Record Series, vol. 15, 2002
P.-N. Derb.	*The Place-Names of Derbyshire*, by K. Cameron, English Place-Name Society, vols. xxvii–xxix, 1959
P.-N.G.	*The Place-Names of Gloucestershire*, by A. H. Smith, English Place-Name Society, vols. xxxviii–xli, 1964–5
P.-N. Oxon.	*The Place-Names of Oxfordshire*, by Margaret Gelling, English Place-Name Society, vols. xxiii–xxiv, 1953–4
pet.	*petens* (demandant, i.e. plaintiff)
quer.	*querens* (complainant, i.e. plaintiff)
Som. Fines, 1347–99, 1399–1484	*Pedes Finium, commonly called Feet of Fines, for the County of Somerset, 1347–1399*, and Fourth Series, Somerset Record Society, vols. xvii, xxii, 1902, 1906

INTRODUCTION

The introduction to the first part of this edition of Feet of Fines relating to Gloucestershire, published in 2003 as Volume 16 of the Gloucestershire Record Series, serves in many respects as an introduction to the later parts.

The third part includes abstracts of fines granted and recorded between 1360 and 1508, completing the edition of fines for Gloucestershire in the Public Record Office in the class Feet of Fines, Series I (CP 25/1). The abstracts are taken from the following files:

Case	files	fines for	in regnal years
78	72–77	Gloucestershire	33–51 Edward III
78	78–82	Gloucestershire	1–18 Richard II
79	83	Gloucestershire	18–23 Richard II
79	84–85	Gloucestershire	1–13 Henry IV
79	86	Gloucestershire	1–10 Henry V
79	87–92	Gloucestershire	1–38 Henry VI
79	93–94	Gloucestershire	1–21 Edward IV
79	95	Gloucestershire	1–2 Richard III
79	96	Gloucestershire	1–24 Henry VII
288	46–48, 50	'Divers Counties'	32–51 Edward III
288	51	'Unknown and Various Counties'	1–49 Edward III
289	52–56	'Divers Counties'	1–17 Richard II
290	57–58	'Divers Counties'	17–22 Richard II
290	59–61	'Divers Counties'	1–11 Henry IV
291	62	'Divers Counties'	11–14 Henry IV
291	63–64	'Divers Counties'	1–10 Henry V
291	65	'Divers Counties'	1–5 Henry VI
292	66–69	'Divers Counties'	5–19 Henry VI
293	70–73	'Divers Counties'	19–37 Henry VI
294	74	'Divers Counties'	1–10 Edward IV
294	75	'Divers and Various Counties'	49 Henry VI
294	76	'Divers Counties'	12–17 Edward IV
294	77	'Divers and Various Counties'	1–22 Edward IV
294	78	'Divers and Various Counties'	1 Edward V and 1–3 Richard III
294	79–81	'Divers Counties'	1–24 Henry VII
294	82	Cities and Towns	1–24 Henry VII

The files of Gloucestershire feet of fines cease to include fines relating to Bristol after the city had, in 1377, become a county of itself. The surviving feet of fines relating to property in Bristol either relate also to property in other

counties and filed as 'Divers Counties' fines or are in the file for Cities and
Towns for Henry VII's reign. That file also contains fines for Gloucester and the
hundred of Dudstone and King's Barton, the inshire, which was made a distinct
county in 1483.

From 1360 fines came to be used less frequently than previously, at least partly,
it seems, because legislative change had rendered them ineffective as a way of
barring rival claims to an estate. The endorsement stating that a person not party
to the agreement had put in a claim ceases to appear, though there is a solitary
instance from 1361 (below, no. 19), presumably a superfluous repetition of
earlier practice. For Gloucestershire the average number of known fines declines
from nearly sixteen a year in the 60 years up to 1359 to fewer than six a year in
the 150 years from 1360.

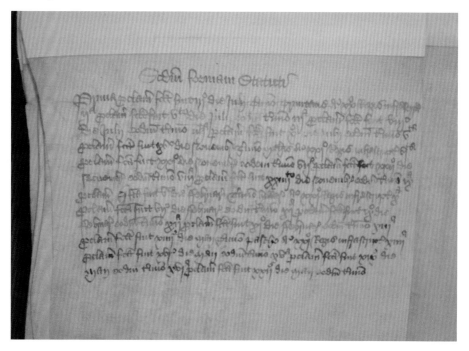

Endorsements of proclamations on the foot of fine abstracted below as no. 843.
(Approximately full size.)

The fifteenth-century feet of fines have two features that are not met earlier.
First, warranty instead of being against all men in general is in a few instances
said to be against a named possible claimant, particularly an abbot (of
Westminster, of Gloucester, of Cirencester) and his successors. Secondly, some of
the feet of fines of Henry VII are endorsed with a note that the fine was
proclaimed on specified days, four times in each of the four terms following the
granting of the fine; the earliest example below is from 1491 (no. 762).

The fines abstracted in the present volume tend to be less varied in form but longer and fuller in their content than those of earlier periods. The greater length resulted partly from the increasing use made of fines relating to more than one county: in the period 1300–59 'divers counties' fines constitute about 9 per cent of fines relating to Gloucestershire (83 out of 945), whereas in the period 1360–1508 the proportion was more than 18 per cent (159 out of 863). The growing practice of vesting property in groups of feoffees also tended to make the fines longer.[1]

From the mid 14th century to the 1490s the fines were invariably initiated by a plea of covenant, the parties being described as the querelants (the plaintiffs) and the deforciants (the defendants), but in the reign of Henry VII some fines were once again initiated by a plea of warranty of charter, as in the earlier 14th century. The earliest instance among the Gloucestershire fines is that abstracted below as no. 770, where the party who in the earlier period would have been described as the impedient is called the deforciant, as if the fine had been initiated by a plea of covenant. The parties in the fines abstracted below that were initiated by a plea of warranty of charter are variously described: in no. 795, as in no. 770, they are querelant and deforciant; in all the others the plaintiffs are described as demandants (in Latin *petentes*), while the defendants are called impedients in two instances (786, 787), defendants in two others (775, 791), tenants in three (781, 784, 785), and deforciants in the remaining four (773, 795, 797, 828).

---

[1] The fine illustrated above in the frontispiece is an example both of the greater length and of vesting in trustees.

COLLATION OF THE NUMBERS IN THE FILES WITH THE NUMBERS IN THE PRINTED TEXT

The full reference for each document begins with the class letters and number for Feet of Fines, series I, i.e. CP 25/1. To order a file those letters and that number need to be prefixed to the numbers of the case and file (the first two elements of the tripartite references given below and following each abstract in the text), and the number of the fine within the file (the last element in the tripartite reference) should be omitted.

number in file	number in text	regnal year	number in file	number in text	regnal year	number in file	number in text	regnal year
78/72/404	1	33 Edw. III	78/73/443	46	37 Edw. III	78/75/483	99	43 Edw. III
405	2	34 Edw. III	444	40	. . .	484	97	. . .
406	4	. . .	445	53	38 Edw. III	485	98	. . .
407	3	. . .	446	51	. . .	486(a)	100	. . .
408	5	. . .	447	59	. . .	486(b)	101	. . .
409	6	. . .	448	57	. . .	487	105	44 Edw. III
410A	8	35 Edw. III	449	62	39 Edw.III	488	106	. . .
410B	11	. . .	450	60	. . .	489	103	. . .
410C	13	. . .	78/74/451	64	40 Edw. III	490	110	. . .
411	15	. . .	452	65	. . .	491	107	. . .
412	14	. . .	453	63	. . .	492	102	. . .
413	12	. . .	454	74	41 Edw. III	493	104	. . .
414	16	. . .	455	75	. . .	494	109	. . .
415	17	. . .	456	76	. . .	495	108	. . .
416	19	. . .	457	77	. . .	496	101	43 Edw. III
417	22	36 Edw. III	458	73	. . .	497	111	44 Edw. III
418	30	. . .	459	67	. . .	498	112	. . .
419	27	. . .	460	68	. . .	499	124	45 Edw. III
420	23	. . .	461	69	. . .	500	125	. . .
421	28	. . .	462	72	. . .	78/76/501	118	. . .
422	20	. . .	463	70	. . .	502	126	. . .
423	21	. . .	464	71	. . .	503	130	. . .
424	29	. . .	464b	78	. . .	504	127	. . .
425	26	. . .	465	89	42 Edw. III	505	119	. . .
78/73/426	24	. . .	466	91	. . .	506	113	. . .
427	25	. . .	467	90	. . .	507	115	. . .
428	31	. . .	468	81	. . .	508	116	. . .
429	33	37 Edw. III	469	82	. . .	509	117	. . .
430	35	. . .	470	88	. . .	510	129	. . .
431	34	. . .	471	92	. . .	511	114	. . .
432	36	. . .	472	78	41 Edw. III	512	123	. . .
433	41	. . .	473	79	42 Edw. III	513	121	. . .
434	38	. . .	474	80	. . .	514	122	. . .
435	39	. . .	475	83	. . .	515	120	. . .
436	42	. . .	78/75/476	84	. . .	516	128	. . .
437	49	. . .	477	85	. . .	517	131	46 Edw. III
438	50	. . .	478	86	. . .	518	133	47 Edw. III
439	43	. . .	479	87	. . .	519	134	. . .
440	48	. . .	480	93	43 Edw. III	520	135	. . .
441	44	. . .	481	94	. . .	521	132	. . .
442	45	. . .	482	96	. . .	522	136	. . .

number in file	number in text	regnal year	number in file	number in text	regnal year	number in file	number in text	regnal year
78/76/523	137	47 Edw. III	78/79/28	188	3 Ric. II	78/81/79	248	11 Ric. II
524	141	48 Edw. III	29	183	. . .	80	253	12 Ric. II
525	138	. . .	30	186	. . .	81	257	. . .
78/77/526	140	. . .	31	184	. . .	82	258	. . .
527	142	. . .	32	195	4 Ric. II	83	251	. . .
528	149	49 Edw. III	33	200	. . .	84	252	. . .
529	143	. . .	34	196	. . .	85	255	. . .
530	144	. . .	35	199	. . .	86	254	. . .
531	145	. . .	36	201	. . .	87	256	. . .
532	146	. . .	37	197	. . .	88	259	13 Ric. II
533	147	. . .	38	205	5 Ric. II	89	264	. . .
534(a)	148	. . .	39	204	. . .	90	260	. . .
534(b)	150	. . .	40	202	. . .	91	266	14 Ric. II
535	157	50 Edw. III	41	203	. . .	92	271	. . .
536	155	. . .	42	206	. . .	93	270	. . .
537	159	. . .	43	207	. . .	94	268	. . .
538	150	49 Edw. III	44	208	. . .	95	265	. . .
539	151	50 Edw. III	45	216	6 Ric. II	96	277	15 Ric. II
540	152	. . .	46	211	. . .	97	282	. . .
541	153	. . .	47	215	. . .	98	276	. . .
542	154	. . .	48	213	. . .	99	281	. . .
543	160	51 Edw. III	49	210	. . .	78/82/100	273	. . .
544	161	. . .	50	214	. . .	101	279	. . .
545	162	. . .	78/80/51	212	. . .	102	274	. . .
78/78/1	170	1 Ric. II	52	217	7 Ric. II	103	272	. . .
2	166	. . .	53	218	. . .	104	287	16 Ric. II
3	167	. . .	54	223	8 Ric. II	105	284	. . .
4	168	. . .	55	224	. . .	106	285	. . .
5	169	. . .	56	221	. . .	107	288	. . .
6	163	. . .	57	220	. . .	108	283	. . .
7	164	. . .	58	219	. . .	109	289	17 Ric. II
8	180	2 Ric. II	59	233	9 Ric. II	110	291	. . .
9	181	. . .	60	227	. . .	111	294	. . .
10	178	. . .	61	232	. . .	112	292	. . .
11	177	. . .	62	228	. . .	113	293	. . .
12	179	. . .	63	229	. . .	114	295	. . .
13	171	. . .	64	230	. . .	115	296	. . .
14	175	. . .	65	226	. . .	116	290	. . .
15	176	. . .	66	225	. . .	117	297	. . .
16	172	. . .	67	231	. . .	118	298	. . .
17	173	. . .	68	238	10 Ric. II	119	301	18 Ric. II
18	174	. . .	69	239	. . .	120	302	. . .
19	187	3 Ric. II	70	246	. . .	121	300	. . .
20	182	. . .	71	237	. . .	122	303	. . .
21	190	. . .	72	240	. . .	123	305	. . .
22	191	. . .	73	241	. . .	124	306	. . .
23	192	. . .	74	242	. . .	125	307	. . .
24	193	. . .	75	243	. . .	79/83/126	308	. . .
25	194	. . .	78/81/76	244	. . .	127	309	. . .
78/79/26	189	. . .	77	236	. . .	128	310	. . .
27	185	. . .	78	247	11 Ric. II	129	311	. . .

number in file	number in text	regnal year	number in file	number in text	regnal year	number in file	number in text	regnal year
79/83/130	312	18 Ric. II	79/84/23	383	7 Hen. IV	79/86/11	444	3 Hen. V
131	313	19 Ric. II	24	384	. . .	12	446	4 Hen. V
132	322	. . .	25	385	. . .	13	447	5 Hen. V
133	314	. . .	79/85/26	386	. . .	14	448	. . .
134	317	. . .	27	379	. . .	15	449	6 Hen. V
135	319	. . .	28	387	8 Hen. IV	16	453	7 Hen. V
136	318	. . .	29	389	. . .	17	451	. . .
137	315	. . .	30	392	9 Hen. IV	18	452	. . .
138	316	. . .	31	393	. . .	19	457	8 Hen. V
139	320	. . .	32	391	. . .	20	456	. . .
140	321	. . .	33	390	. . .	21	458	. . .
141	329	20 Ric. II	34	401	10 Hen. IV	22	460	9 Hen. V
142	327	. . .	35	399	. . .	23	461	. . .
143	326	. . .	36	400	. . .	24	462	. . .
144	325	. . .	37	396	. . .	25	463	. . .
145	324	. . .	38	394	. . .	26	464	. . .
146	331	21 Ric. II	39	398	. . .	27	465	10 Hen. V
147	335	. . .	40	395	. . .	79/87/1	466	1 Hen. VI
148	336	. . .	41	402	11 Hen. IV	2	467	. . .
149	337	. . .	42	404	. . .	3	468	. . .
150	332	. . .	43	405	. . .	4	469	2 Hen. VI
79/83/151	330	. . .	44	406	. . .	5	470	. . .
152	333	. . .	45	407	. . .	6	471	. . .
153	338	22 Ric. II	46	409	12 Hen. IV	7	475	3 Hen. VI
154	339	. . .	47	408	. . .	8	476	. . .
155	341	. . .	48	412	. . .	9	474	. . .
156	343	. . .	49	411	. . .	10	478	4 Hen. VI
157	344	. . .	50	413	. . .	11	485	5 Hen. VI
158	345	23 Ric. II	51	416	13 Hen. IV	12	484	. . .
79/84/1	346	1 Hen. IV	52	415	. . .	13	482	. . .
2	353	2 Hen. IV	53	418	. . .	14	483	. . .
3	354	. . .	54	419	. . .	15	480	. . .
4	352	. . .	55	417	. . .	16	479	. . .
5	349	. . .	56	425	. . .	17	486	6 Hen. VI
6	350	. . .	57	426	. . .	18	490	7 Hen. VI
7	351	. . .	58	421	. . .	19	491	. . .
8	357	3 Hen. IV	59	422	. . .	20	489	. . .
9	360	. . .	60	423	. . .	21	492	. . .
10	368	4 Hen. IV	61	424	. . .	22	493	. . .
11	367	. . .	62	427	. . .	23	498	8 Hen. VI
12	362	. . .	63	428	. . .	24	494	. . .
13	364	. . .	79/86/1	430	1 Hen. V	25	496	. . .
14	366	. . .	2	437	. . .	79/88/26	495	. . .
15	369	5 Hen. IV	3	433	. . .	27	501	. . .
16	371	. . .	4	434	. . .	28	500	. . .
17	373	. . .	5	435	. . .	29	505	9 Hen. VI
18	377	6 Hen. IV	6	439	2 Hen. V	30	503	. . .
19	376	. . .	7	441	. . .	31	504	. . .
20	374	. . .	8	440	. . .	32	506	. . .
21	375	. . .	9	438	. . .	33	512	10 Hen. VI
22	382	7 Hen. IV	10	442	3 Hen. V	34	507	. . .

number in file	number in text	regnal year	number in file	number in text	regnal year	number in file	number in text	regnal year
79/88/35	508	10 Hen. VI	79/90/86	576	19 Hen. VI	79/92/137	645	35 Hen. VI
36	511	. . .	87	571	. . .	138	644	. . .
37	509	. . .	88	572	. . .	139	653	36 Hen. VI
38	510	. . .	89	574	. . .	140	654	. . .
39	524	11 Hen. VI	90	578	20 Hen. VI	141	650	. . .
40	523	. . .	91	580	21 Hen. VI	142	648	. . .
41	515	. . .	92	581	. . .	143	649	. . .
42	516	. . .	93	583	22 Hen. VI	144	647	. . .
43	513	. . .	94	584	. . .	145	651	. . .
44	517	. . .	95	586	. . .	146	656	37 Hen. VI
45	514	. . .	96	587	. . .	147	658	. . .
46	520	. . .	97	590	. . .	148	659	. . .
47	518	. . .	98	589	. . .	79/93/1	661	1 Edw. IV
48	519	. . .	99	588	. . .	2	662	. . .
49	527	12 Hen. VI	100	594	23 Hen. VI	3	660	. . .
50	528	. . .	79/91/101	591	. . .	4	664	3 Edw. IV
79/89/51	526	. . .	102	599	24 Hen. VI	5	665	. . .
52	525	. . .	103	596	. . .	6	666	4 Edw. IV
53	530	13 Hen. VI	104	597	. . .	7	667	. . .
54	533	. . .	105	598	. . .	8	668	. . .
55	532	. . .	106	601	25 Hen. VI	9	674	5 Edw. IV
56	534	. . .	107	602	. . .	10	672	. . .
57	538	14 Hen. VI	108	600	. . .	11	671	. . .
58	535	. . .	109	606	26 Hen. VI	12	680	6 Edw. IV
59	536	. . .	110	608	. . .	13	682	. . .
60	542	. . .	111	609	. . .	14	677	. . .
61	540	. . .	112	604	. . .	15	678	. . .
62	541	. . .	113	613	27 Hen. VI	16	679	. . .
63	544	15 Hen. VI	114	611	. . .	17	681	. . .
64	547	16 Hen. VI	115	616	28 Hen. VI	18	686	8 Edw. IV
65	545	. . .	116	615	. . .	19	685	. . .
66	549	. . .	117	620	29 Hen. VI	20	687	. . .
67	551	. . .	118	621	30 Hen. VI	21	689	9 Edw. IV
68	548	. . .	119	622	31 Hen. VI	22	690	. . .
69	550	. . .	120	624	. . .	23	697	. . .
70	546	. . .	121	625	. . .	24	692	. . .
71	553	17 Hen. VI	122	623	. . .	25	693	. . .
72	552	. . .	123	627	32 Hen. VI	79/94/26	696	. . .
73	554	. . .	124	626	. . .	27	695	. . .
74	556	. . .	125	629	. . .	28	703	12 Edw. IV
75	561	. . .	79/92/126	628	. . .	29	702	. . .
79/90/76	558	. . .	127	633	33 Hen. VI	30	704	13 Edw. IV
77	559	. . .	128	634	. . .	31	706	. . .
78	555	. . .	129	632	. . .	32	707	14 Edw. IV
79	562	18 Hen. VI	130	639	34 Hen. VI	33	710	. . .
80	563	. . .	131	640	. . .	34	708	. . .
81	568	. . .	132	637	. . .	35	709	. . .
82	570	. . .	133	642	. . .	36	714	15 Edw. IV
83	566	. . .	134	638	. . .	37	711	. . .
84	569	. . .	135	643	35 Hen. VI	38	715	. . .
85	565	. . .	136	646	. . .	39	716	16 Edw. IV

number in file	number in text	regnal year	number in file	number in text	regnal year	number in file	number in text	regnal year
79/94/40	718	16 Edw. IV	79/96/27	790	12 Hen. VII	287/45/539	54	38 Edw. III
41	721	17 Edw. IV	28	791	. . .	288/46/579	7	34 Edw. III
42	719	. . .	29	792	. . .	584	10	. . .
43	723	18 Edw. IV	30	793	. . .	596	18	35 Edw. III
44	722	. . .	31	794	. . .	288/47/603	9	. . .
45	725	. . .	32	798	13 Hen. VII	623	37	37 Edw. III
46	724	. . .	33	799	. . .	625	47	. . .
47	726	19 Edw. IV	34	800	. . .	630	32	. . .
48	731	20 Edw. IV	35	801	. . .	635	52	38 Edw. III
49	732	. . .	36	802	. . .	288/47/636	55	. . .
50	733	. . .	37	803	. . .	637	56	. . .
51	734	. . .	79/97/38	805	14 Hen. VII	639	58	. . .
52	727	. . .	39	808	. . .	646	61	39 Edw. III
53	728	. . .	40	809	. . .	288/48/668	66	40 Edw. III
54	729	. . .	41	810	. . .	692	95	43 Edw. III
55	735	. . .	42	811	. . .	288/50/757	139	48 Edw. III
56	730	. . .	43	812	. . .	794	156	50 Edw. III
57	737	21 Edw. IV	44	813	. . .	796	158	. . .
58	739	. . .	45	814	. . .	289/52/5	165	1 Ric. II
59	736	. . .	46	815	15 Hen. VII	47	198	4 Ric. II
60	738	. . .	47	816	. . .	289/53/58	209	5 Ric. II
79/95/1	744	1 Ric. III	48	819	. . .	289/54/120	222	8 Ric. II
2	742	. . .	49	820	. . .	146	234	9 Ric. II
3	743	. . .	50	822	. . .	148	235	10 Ric. II
4	745	2 Ric. III	51	824	16 Hen. VII	289/55/160	245	. . .
79/96/1	746	1 Hen. VII	52	825	. . .	175	249	11 Ric. II
2	748	. . .	53	826	. . .	177	250	12 Ric. II
3	751	3 Hen. VII	54	832	17 Hen. VII	198	261	13 Ric. II
4	752	. . .	55	833	. . .	289/56/202	262	. . .
5	753	. . .	56	837	18 Hen. VII	203	263	. . .
6	756	. . .	57	838	. . .	210	267	14 Ric. II
7	757	4 Hen. VII	58	839	19 Hen. VII	212	269	. . .
8	764	7 Hen. VII	59	840	. . .	218	275	15 Ric. II
9	765	. . .	60	841	. . .	225	278	. . .
10	768	8 Hen. VII	61	843	20 Hen. VII	235	280	. . .
11	769	. . .	62	844	. . .	241	286	16 Ric. II
12	770	. . .	63	845	21 Hen. VII	290/57/267	299	18 Ric. II
13	773	9 Hen. VII	64	846	. . .	270	304	. . .
14	775	. . .	65	849	. . .	296	323	20 Ric. II
15	776	. . .	66	850	. . .	290/58/302	328	. . .
16	777	. . .	67	852	. . .	309	334	21 Ric. II
17	778	. . .	68	853	. . .	319	340	22 Ric. II
18	779	10 Hen. VII	69	854	. . .	329	342	. . .
19	780	. . .	70	855	. . .	290/59/10	347	1 Hen. IV
20	781	. . .	71	856	. . .	11	348	. . .
21	783	11 Hen. VII	72	857	22 Hen. VII	29	355	2 Hen. IV
22	785	. . .	73	858	23 Hen. VII	32	356	. . .
23	786	. . .	74	859	. . .	44	358	3 Hen. IV
24	787	. . .	75	860	. . .	45	359	. . .
25	788	. . .	76	862	24 Hen. VII	50	361	. . .
26	789	12 Hen. VII	77	863	. . .	290/60/57	363	4 Hen. IV

number in file	number in text	regnal year	number in file	number in text	regnal year	number in file	number in text	regnal year
290/60/63	365	4 Hen. IV	292/69/250	575	19 Hen. VI	294/76/119	720	17 Edw. IV
70	370	5 Hen. IV	293/70/256	577	20 Hen. VI	294/77/137	740	21 Edw. IV
76	372	. . .	262	579	. . .	294/78/3	741	1 Edw. V
84	378	6 Hen. IV	272	582	21 Hen. VI	294/79/7	750	3 Hen. VII
94	380	7 Hen. IV	284	585	22 Hen. VI	9	754	. . .
95	381	. . .	295	592	23 Hen. VI	14	758	4 Hen. VII
290/61/113	388	8 Hen. IV	298	593	. . .	18	760	5 Hen. VII
133	397	10 Hen. IV	293/71/302	595	24 Hen. VI	25	762	6 Hen. VII
147	403	11 Hen. IV	318	603	25 Hen. VI	32	766	8 Hen. VII
291/62/159	410	12 Hen. IV	326	605	26 Hen. VI	33	767	. . .
162	414	. . .	330	607	. . .	294/80/63	795	12 Hen. VII
171	420	13 Hen. IV	333	610	. . .	67	796	. . .
184	429	14 Hen. IV	341	612	27 Hen. VI	70	797	. . .
291/63/4	431	1 Hen. V	347	614	28 Hen. VI	89	823	15 Hen. VII
6	432	. . .	293/72/352	617	. . .	97	827	16 Hen. VII
11	436	. . .	355	618	. . .	104	828	17 Hen. VII
31	443	3 Hen. V	359	619	29 Hen. VI	105	829	. . .
46	445	4 Hen. V	385	630	32 Hen. VI	106	830	. . .
291/64/79	450	7 Hen. V	386	631	. . .	294/81/116	835	18 Hen. VII
84	454	. . .	394	635	33 Hen. VI	129	842	20 Hen. VII
85	455	. . .	396	636	. . .	158	861	23 Hen. VII
98	459	8 Hen. V	293/73/406	641	34 Hen. VI	294/82/1	747	1 Hen. VII
291/65/22	472	2 Hen. VI	423	652	36 Hen. VI	2	749	2 Hen. VII
24	473	. . .	426	655	. . .	5	755	3 Hen. VII
45	477	4 Hen. VI	441	657	37 Hen. VI	7	759	4 Hen. VII
50	481	5 Hen. VI	294/74/9	663	2 Edw. IV	10	761	5 Hen. VII
292/66/79	487	6 Hen. VI	23	669	4 Edw. IV	11	763	6 Hen. VII
85	488	7 Hen. VI	25	670	. . .	17	771	8 Hen. VII
89	497	8 Hen. VI	30	673	5 Edw. IV	18	772	. . .
93	499	. . .	36	675	6 Edw. IV	19	774	9 Hen. VII
292/67/102	502	. . .	41	676	. . .	23	782	11 Hen. VII
135	521	11 Hen. VI	48	683	7 Edw. IV	24	784	. . .
136	522	. . .	49	684	. . .	25	804	14 Hen. VII
137	522	. . .	64	688	8 Edw. IV	26	806	. . .
292/68/160	529	13 Hen. VI	67	691	9 Edw. IV	27	807	. . .
161	531	. . .	71	694	. . .	29	817	15 Hen. VII
180	537	14 Hen. VI	74	698	. . .	30	818	. . .
186	539	. . .	294/75/1	699	49 Hen. VI	31	821	. . .
194	543	15 Hen. VI	11	700	. . .	34	831	17 Hen. VII
292/69/221	557	17 Hen. VI	294/76/83	701	12 Edw. IV	38	834	18 Hen. VII
223	560	. . .	92	705	13 Edw. IV	39	836	. . .
233	564	18 Hen. VI	100	712	15 Edw. IV	46	847	21 Hen. VII
238	567	. . .	103	713	. . .	47	848	. . .
246	573	19 Hen. VI	109	717	16 Edw. IV	48	851	. . .

ABSTRACTS
OF FEET OF FINES FOR
GLOUCESTERSHIRE

33 Edward III

1360

1.   One week [20 Jan.] from Hilary. (Made one week from St. Martin 30 Edward III [18 Nov. 1356].) William de Edington (*Edyndon*) bishop of Winchester quer.; Walter de Fretherne (*Frethorne*) def. The manor of Fretherne and the advowson of the church of Fretherne held by William Motoun 'chivaler' and Elizabeth his wife for term of Elizabeth's life of Walter's inheritance. Right of the bishop. Walter granted the remainder of the holding to the bishop and his heirs. (Warranty.) Cons. £100. [*Torn and stained.*]

78/72/404

[For William Motoun see *V.C.H. Glos.* x. 160. This fine and nearly all those in the file have been damaged apparently by damp and are missing the left-hand portion and in many instances the lower right-hand portion, the surviving edges being stained by damp.]

34 Edward III

1360

2.   Three weeks [26 April] from Easter. William Portland (*Portlond*) and Matilda his wife quer.; Geoffrey Martin (*Martyn*) and Beatrice his wife def. A messuage in the suburb of Bristol (*Bristoll'*). Right of William, as that which William and Matilda had by gift of Geoffrey and Beatrice. To hold to William and Matilda and William's heirs. (Warranty, specifying Geoffrey's heirs.) Cons. 10 marks. [*Torn and stained.*]

78/72/405

[Cf. *Bristol Gt. Red Book*, p. 239, no. 200.]

3.   Two weeks [14 June] from Trinity. John son of William de Cheltenham (*Chiltenham*) quer.; William de Cheltenham def. The manor of Woodcroft (*Wodecroft*). Grant to John. Render to him. To hold to John and his heirs in tail male, paying to William during William's life 20 marks a year at [. . .] and to William's heirs after his death a rose a year at St. John the Baptist and doing service to the chief lords. (Warranty.) Contingent remainder to William's heirs. Cons. [. . .]. [*Torn and stained.*]

78/72/407

4.   Two weeks [14 June] from Trinity. The abbot of Winchcombe (*Wy*[. . .]) quer.; William de [. . .]melesworth and Eleanor his wife def. Two messuages, 4 a. of land, 12d. rent, [and . . .] yardlands except 4 a. of land in Snowshill (*Snoweshull*) and Berry Wormington (*Parva Wormyngton*). Right of the abbot and his church. Render to him of a messuage and the said rent and yardlands. And grant to the abbot of the remainder of a messuage and 4 a. of land in Snowshill held by Juliana Fre[. . .] for term of her life, of William's inheritance. The abbot admitted William and Eleanor into all benefits [and prayers.] Cons. [. . . The abbot received] William's [heirs] into all benefits [and prayers]. [*Torn and stained.*]

78/72/406

[William was presumably William de Framelesworth: cf. below, no. 5.]

1

1360

5.   Two weeks [13 Oct.] from Michaelmas. (Made two weeks [14 June] from Trinity in the said year.) William de Dursley (*Dersleye*) chaplain and Richard Bushel (*Busshel*) quer. by Adam de Charlton (*Cherleton*) in William's place; William de Framelesworth and Eleanor his wife def. Three messuages and 2 yardlands in Alscot (*Alvescote*) [. . .]. Right of William de Dursley and Richard by gift of William de Framelesworth and Eleanor. (Warranty, specifying William de Framelesworth's heirs.) Cons. 20 marks. [*Torn.*]

78/72/408

6.   Two weeks [13 Oct.] from Michaelmas. Richard de Urdeley (*Urdele*) quer.; Thomas le Woodward (*Wodeward*) and Katherine his wife def. Two messuages, 8 a. of meadow, and ½ ploughland in [. . .]*ukesbury* [Hawkesbury *or* Tewkesbury?]. Right of Richard. Remise and quitclaim, specifying Katherine's heirs, to him. (Warranty.) Cons. 100 marks.

78/72/409

7.   Two weeks [13 Oct.] from Michaelmas. (Made two weeks from Michaelmas 33 Edw. III [13 Oct. 1359].) John Sage, Richard Dunmow (*Dunmouwe*), and John de Syde (*Side*) clerk quer.; Ellis Daubeney (*Daubeny*) and Agnes his wife def. A messuage, 1 ploughland, 1 a. of meadow, 10 a. of wood, and 30*s*. rent in Newent (*Newent*) and one third of the manor of Cromhall (*Cromhale*) and the advowson of the church of Cromhall, GLOS., and 4 messuages, 1 ploughland and 2 yardlands, 5 a. of meadow, and 6*s*. rent in Aston (*Aston*), HEREFS. Right of John de Syde, of which that John, John Sage, and Richard had one third and the advowson by gift of Ellis and Agnes. For this, grant back and render of the one third and the advowson to Ellis and Agnes. To hold during their lives. Grant also, specifying John de Syde's heirs, to Ellis and Agnes of the reversion of the said holdings, held by William de Matson (*Mattesdon*) and Matilda his wife for term of life, of John de Syde's inheritance. To hold as above. Remainder to Richard, elder son of Ellis and Agnes, and his heirs in tail. Contingent remainder to Richard's heirs. Cons. 200 marks. *Labelled* Glouc', Hereford'.

288/46/579

[The fine appears to be poorly drafted: the statement about the reversion refers to the said holdings rather than to the two thirds, and that about the remainder on the death of Ellis and Agnes is said to relate only to the one third and the advowson.]

35 Edward III

1361

8.   Two weeks [27 Jan.] from Hilary. Richard son of Nicholas le Hawker (*Haukere* [*reading uncertain*]) quer.; Thomas Horn' of Rutland (*Rotelond*) chaplain def. Three [messuages] and 2 shops in the suburb of Bristol (*Bristoll'*). Right of Richard by Thomas's gift. (Warranty.) Cons. 100 marks. [*Torn.*]

78/72/410A

[Cf. *Bristol Gt. Red Book*, p. 239, no. 201.]

9.   Two weeks [27 Jan.] from Hilary. Peter Cusaunce and Margaret his wife quer.; John de Burbage (*Burbache*) vicar of the church of Hilmarton (*Helmerton*), Walter de Fynamour chaplain, and William Punchon parson of the church of Hilmarton def. The manor of Down Ampney (*Dounamenee*), GLOS., and half of the manor of Silchester

1361

(*Chilchestre*), HANTS. Peter acknowledged the right of Walter, as those which Walter, John, and William had by Peter's gift. For this, grant and render to Peter and Margaret. To hold to them and Peter's heirs in tail. Contingent remainder of the said manor and western half of the said half to Peter's heirs, and of the other half of the half to Edmund Baynard and Eleanor his wife and Eleanor's heirs. *Labelled* Glouc', Sutht'.

288/47/603

10. Morrow [3 Feb.] of the Purification. John de Braose (*Breouse*) 'chivaler' and Elizabeth his wife quer.; Thomas de Braose 'chivaler' and Beatrice his wife def. The manor of Tetbury (*Tettebirs*), GLOS., the manor of Imworth (*Imeworth*) and half of the hundred of Elmbridge (*Emilbrigg*), SURREY, and the manor of Weaverthorpe (*Wyrthorp*), YORKS. Grant and render to John and Elizabeth. To hold to them and their heirs in tail male, the manors of Tetbury and Imworth and the half of the hundred of the king by the services belonging and the manor of Weaverthorpe of Thomas and Beatrice and Thomas's heirs, paying a rose a year at St. John the Baptist and doing service to the chief lords. (Warranty, specifying Thomas's heirs.) Contingent reversion of the manors of Tetbury and Imworth and the half hundred to Thomas and Beatrice and their heirs [*sic*] and of the manor of Weaverthorpe to Thomas and Beatrice and Thomas's heirs. Cons. 200 marks. Made, as to the manors of Tetbury and Imworth and the half of the hundred, by the king's order. *Labelled* Glouc', Surr', Ebor'.

288/46/584

11. Two weeks [11 April] from Easter. John Haxton (*Hakeston*) burgess of Bristol (*Bristoll*) quer. by John Whiteley (*Whitele*); John Thorp of Bristol 'mercer' and Margaret his wife def. A messuage in the suburb of Bristol. Right of John Haxton by gift of John Thorp and Margaret. (Warranty, specifying Margaret's heirs.) Cons. 10 marks.

78/72/410B

[Cf. *Bristol Gt. Red Book*, pp. 239–40, no. 202.]

12. Two weeks [11 April] from Easter. (Made two weeks [27 Jan.] from Hilary in the said year.) Robert Adam (*Ad'*) and Joan his wife quer.; Geoffrey Martin (*Martyn*) and Beatrice his wife def. A messuage in Berkeley (*Berkeley*). Right of Robert, as that which Robert and Joan had by gift of Geoffrey and Beatrice. (Warranty, specifying Beatrice's heirs.) Cons. 10 marks. [*Torn and stained.*]

78/72/413

13. Three weeks [18 April] from Easter. William Bulmyng and Agnes his wife quer.; Nicholas Wallsend (*Walsnede*) and Joan his wife def. A messuage, 6 a. of land, and 4 a. of meadow in Hasfield (*Hasfeld*). Right of William, as that which William and Agnes had by gift of Nicholas and Joan. Remise and quitclaim, specifying Joan's heirs, to William and Agnes and William's heirs. (Warranty.) Cons. 20 marks.

78/72/410C

14. One month [25 April] from Easter. Roger Chausy of North Nibley (*Nubbeleye*) quer.; Thomas Draysyde and Joan his wife def. Two messuages, 20 a. of land, and 3 a. of meadow in Wotton-under-Edge (*Wotton*) and Nibley. Right of Roger. For this, grant and

render to Thomas and Joan. To hold to them during their lives. Remainder to Richard son of Thomas and Joan and his heirs in tail. Successive contingent remainders to the heirs in tail of Thomas and Joan and to Joan's heirs. [*Torn and stained.*]

78/72/412

15. One week [6 Oct.] from Michaelmas. John Haxton (*Hakeston*) quer. by Richard Dorchester (*Dorchestre*); William Northen (*Northerne*) and Alice his wife def. A messuage in the suburb of Bristol (*Bristoll'*). Right of John. Remise and quitclaim, specifying Alice's heirs, to him. (Warranty.) Cons. 10 marks.

78/72/411

[Cf. *Bristol Gt. Red Book*, p. 240, no. 203.]

16. One week [6 Oct.] from Michaelmas. (Made two weeks from Hilary 34 Edward III [27 Jan. 1360].) William de Chesterton chaplain, Robert de Perle chaplain, and Walter de Perle quer.; Giles Freeman (*Freman*) chaplain def. A messuage, 3 yardlands, and 1 a. of meadow in Great Washbourne (*Wessebourn' Abbatis*) held by Adam le Porter and Sibyl his wife for term of Sibyl's life, of Giles's inheritance. Right of Robert. Grant of the reversion to William, Robert, and Walter and Robert's heirs. (Warranty.) Cons. 20 marks.

78/72/414

17. One week [6 Oct.] from Michaelmas. (Made three weeks [18 April] from Easter in the said year.) Thomas Moyne (*Moigne*) and Margery his wife quer.; John Moyne and Elizabeth his wife def. The manors of Kilcot (*Killecote*) and Little Taynton (*Parva Teyngton*). Right of Elizabeth, as those which John and Elizabeth had by gift of Thomas and Margery. For this, grant back and render to Thomas and Margery. To hold to them during their lives, of John and Elizabeth and Elizabeth's heirs, paying a rose a year at St. John the Baptist and doing service to the chief lords. Reversion to John and Elizabeth and Elizabeth's heirs. [*Torn and stained.*]

78/72/415

18. Three weeks [20 Oct.] from Michaelmas. Thomas de Beauchamp (*Bello Campo*) earl of Warwick (*Warr'*) quer.; John de Buckingham (*Bukyngham*), Ralph Basset of Sapcote, Richard de Pirton (*Piriton*), William Salwarpe (*Salwarp*), Richard de Sutton, and William de Gaddesby (*Gadesby*) def. The castle and shrievalty of Worcester (*Wygorn'*) with the hundreds, members, and other appurtenances, the manors of Elmley Lovett (*Elmeleye Lovet*), Yardley (*Yerdele*), Syntley (*Cyntele*), Abberley (*Abbedele*), and Hadzor (*Haddesore*), and half of a knight's fee in Redmarley D'Abitot (*Ridmarleye*), WORCS., the castle and manor of Beaudesert (*Beaudesert*), the manors of Whitchurch (*Whitchirche*), Wellesbourne Mountford (*Wellesbourn*), and Barford (*Bereford*), a knight's fee in Alcester (*Alicestre*), and 40 marks rent in Moreton Morrell (*Morton Daubeneye*), WARWS., the manors of Aberedw (*Abredough*) and Kilvey (*Kylvey*) in the marches of Wales, HEREFS., the manors of Childswickham (*Wykewane*), Chedworth (*Chedeworth*), and Lydney (*Lydeneye*) and the advowson of the church of Notgrove (*Nategrave*), GLOS., 10 marks rent in Longstanton (*Longa Staunton*), CAMBS., 2 messuages and the office of pesage (*pesagerie*) in Southampton (*Suthampton*), HANTS., the office of chamberlain and usher (*officio camerarie et hostiarie*) in the king's Exchequer, BUCKS., half a knight's fee in Woodborough (*Wodebergh*) and the advowson

1361

of the church of the same township, WILTS., the manor of Walthamstow (*Welcomstowe*), a knight's fee in Westbarrow (*Berghes*), and the advowsons of the churches of North Fambridge (*Fambrugge*) and Great Stambridge (*Stanbrugge*), ESSEX, the advowson of the church of Cranleigh (*Cranelee*), SURREY, the manors of Preston (*Preston*) and Uppingham (*Uppyngham*), RUTLAND, and the advowson of the priory of Shouldham (*Sholdham*), NORF. Right of John de Buckingham and the other def., of which they had all the premises except those specified below by the earl's gift. For this, grant back and render to the earl. To hold during his life, of the king. Also grant to the earl of the reversion of the castle and manor of Beaudesert, the manors of Whitchurch, Wellesbourne, Preston and Uppingham, held by Peter de Montfort (*Monte Forti*) for term of life, of the manor of Walthamstow, held by Matilda who was wife of Simon Francis (*Fraunceys*) for term of life, and of the manor of Hadzor, held by Thomas Cassy for term of life. To hold as above. Reversion to the earl's son Thomas and his heirs in tail male. Successive contingent remainders to Thomas's brother William and his heirs in tail male, to the earl's heirs in tale male, and to the earl's heirs. *Labelled* Wygorn', Warr', Glouc', Cantebr', Suth', Buk', Wyltes', Essex', Surr', Rotel', Norff'. [*Worn and stained.*]

288/46/596

[Cf. *Essex Fines, 1327–1422*, p. 132; *Warws. Fines, 1345–1509*, pp. 34–5, no. 2097; *Wilts. Fines, 1327–77*, pp. 119–20, no. 495.]

19. One month [27 Oct.] from Michaelmas. John Glover (*Glovere*) and John Mundham quer.; Henry Warner (*Warenner*) of Tetbury (*Tettebury*) and Isabel his wife def. A messuage, 1 ploughland, 6 a. of meadow, and 8s. rent in Lower Siddington (*Nether Sodynton*). Right of John Mundham, as those which John and John had by gift of Henry and Isabel. For this, grant back and render to Henry and Isabel. To hold to them and Isabel's heirs. *Endorsed* Thomas de Tresham and Joan his wife put in their claim.

78/72/416

36 Edward III

1362

20. One week [9 Feb.] of the Purification. John Bourdon of London chaplain quer.; Thomas de Thorney (*Thorneye*) and Joan his wife def. Three messuages and 8 shops in Gloucester (*Gloucestre*) and the suburb of the same town. Right of John by gift of Thomas and Joan. For this, grant back and render to Thomas and Joan. To hold to them and their heirs in tail. Contingent remainder to Joan's heirs. (Warranty.)

78/72/422

21. Morrow [27 May] of Ascension. Nicholas de Apperley (*Apperleye*) and Margaret his wife quer. by William de Westhall (*Westhale*) in Margaret's place; Walter Huk' of Mitcheldean (*Magna Dene*) and Katherine his wife def. Two messuages, 14 a. of land, 18½ a. of meadow, 10 a. of pasture, and 23s. 2½d. rent in Tirley (*Trynleye*) and Hasfield (*Hasfeld*). Right of Nicholas, as those which Nicholas and Margaret had by gift of Walter and Katherine. To hold to Nicholas and Margaret and Nicholas's heirs. (Warranty, specifying Katherine's heirs.) Cons. 20 marks.

78/72/423

1362

22. Two weeks [13 Oct.] from Michaelmas. Ralph Dunster (*Dunsterre*) of Bristol (*Bristoll'*) and Milicent his wife quer.; John Mursley (*Murslegh*) and Alice his wife def. A messuage in Bristol. Grant and render to Ralph and Milicent. To hold to them and their heirs in tail. Contingent remainder to Ralph's heirs. Cons. 10 marks. [Torn.]

78/72/417

[Cf. *Bristol Gt. Red Book*, p. 240, no. 204.]

23. Two weeks [13 Oct.] from Michaelmas. William Filberd quer.; John Goby def. A messuage in Bristol (*Bristoll'*). Right of William by John's gift. Remise and quitclaim to William. (Warranty.) Cons. 20 marks.

78/72/420

[Cf. *Bristol Gt. Red Book*, p. 241, no. 207.]

24. Two weeks [13 Oct.] from Michaelmas. John Drew (*Dreu*) of Pegglesworth (*Pekelesworthe*) quer.; Simon le Gambe of Pegglesworth and Isabel his wife def. A messuage, 1 yardland, 4 a. of meadow, and 6 a. of wood in Pegglesworth. Right of John by gift of Simon and Isabel. Remise and quitclaim, specifying Isabel's heirs, to John. (Warranty.) Cons. 100 marks.

78/73/426

25. Two weeks [13 Oct.] from Michaelmas. Walter Reyne of Lydney (*Lydeney*) and Joan his wife quer.; Walter Wilkins (*Willekyns*) of Lydney and Joan his wife def. A messuage in Lydney. Right of Walter Reyne. Remise and quitclaim, specifying the heirs of Joan wife Walter Wilkins, to Walter Reyne and Joan his wife and that Walter's heirs. (Warranty.) Cons. 20 marks. [*Torn.*]

78/73/427

26. One month [27 Oct.] from Michaelmas. Richard Sholl' quer.; John de Wightfield (*Whitefeld*) 'chivaler' def. The manor of Bromsberrow (*Brymmesbergh*) and the advowson of the church of the same manor. Right of John by Richard's gift. For this, grant back and render to Richard. (Warranty.) [*Torn.*]

78/72/425

27. Morrow [3 Nov.] of All Souls. John de Bath' of Bristol (*Bristoll*) quer.; Philip le Long (*Longe*) of Bristol and Alice his wife def. A messuage, 12 shops, and 20s. rent in the suburb of Bristol. Right of John by gift of Philip and Alice. Cons. 100 marks.

78/72/419

[Cf. *Bristol Gt. Red Book*, p. 241, no. 206.]

28. Morrow [3 Nov.] of All Souls. John de Haxton (*Hakeston*) of Bristol (*Bristoll'*) and Joan his wife quer.; Walter de Evesham chaplain and John de Wotton def. Nine messuages, 5 shops, 4 a. of land, 68s. 8d. rent in Bristol, the suburb of the same, and Blackswarth (*Blakesworth*). Right of Walter, of which Walter and John de Wotton had 5 messuages, the shops, the land, and the rent, and half of a messuage by gift of John de Haxton and Joan. For this, grant back and render to John de Haxton and Joan. To hold to John de Haxton and Joan and their heirs in tail. Contingent remainder to John de Haxton's heirs. And John de Haxton and Joan granted to Walter and John de Wotton the

1362

reversion of the residue, sc. of a messuage and half of a messuage held by John de Baltonsborough (*Baltesburgh*) for term of his life by the law of England [i.e. by the curtesy], and of 2 messuages held by Margery Cardiff (*Kerdif*) for term of her life, of Joan's inheritance in the said suburb. (Warranty.) [*Torn, stained, and holed.*]

78/72/421

[Cf. *Bristol Gt. Red Book*, pp. 241–2, no. 208.]

29. Morrow [12 Nov.] of St. Martin. Richard de Stafford knight the elder and Matilda his wife quer.; Hugh de Hopwas (*Hopewas*) chaplain, Henry de Tymmore chaplain, and Nicholas de Ivinghoe (*Yvyngho*) chaplain def. The manor of Aston Subedge (*Aston Underegge*). Right of Hugh, as that which Hugh, Henry, and Nicholas had by gift of Richard and Matilda. For this, grant back and render to Richard and Matilda. To hold to them and their heirs in tail male. Contingent remainder to Richard's heirs.

78/72/424

1363

30. One week [20 Jan.] from Hilary. John Reed (*Rede*) of Bristol (*Bristoll'*) quer.; William Dallaway (*Dalewey*) and Joan his wife def. Two messuages in the suburb of Bristol. Right of John. Remise and quitclaim, specifying Joan's heirs, to him. (Warranty.) Cons. 10 marks. [*Torn.*]

78/72/418

[Cf. *Bristol Gt. Red Book*, pp. 240–1, no. 205.]

31. One week [20 Jan.] from Hilary. John Foxcote and Margaret his wife quer.; Simon parson of the church of Digswell (*Dykyswell*) and John parson of the church of *Dyyette* [Ayot?] def. A messuage, 4 ploughlands, 20 a. of meadow, and 40*s*. rent in Turkdean (*Turkeden*), Foxcote (*Foxcote*), and Duntisbourne (*Duntisbourn*). John de Foxcote acknowledged the right of John the parson, as those which the same John and Simon had by John de Foxcote's gift. For this, grant and render to John de Foxcote and Margaret. To hold to them and their heirs in tail. Contingent remainder to John de Foxcote's heirs. [*Torn.*]

78/73/428

37 Edward III

1363

32. Two weeks [27 Jan.] from Hilary. (Made two weeks from Michaelmas 36 Edw. III [13 Oct. 1362].) John de Charlton (*Cherlton*) of Apley (*Apley*) knight quer.; John son of John de Trillowe knight and Joan his wife def. Seven eighths of the manor of Milcote (*Mulcote*), WARWS., and one eighth of the manor of Milcote, GLOS. Grant and render to John de Charlton. To hold during his life, of John and Joan and Joan's heirs, paying a rose a year at St. John the Baptist and doing service to the chief lords. Reversion to John and Joan and Joan's heirs. Cons. 200 marks (paid by John de Charlton). *Labelled* Warr', Glouc'.

288/47/630

[Cf. *Warws. Fines, 1345–1509*, p. 39, no. 2109.]

33. Two weeks [16 April] from Easter. William de Shareshill (*Shareshull*) 'chivaler' the elder, John de Baldon (*Baldyndon*), Robert de Whitehill (*Wyghthull*), Richard late vicar of

1363

the church of St. Mary Magdalene in the suburb of Oxford (*Oxon'*), William de Garsington (*Gersyndon*), and Roger Winstone (*Wynston*) chaplain quer. by John de Denton in their place; Richard Cavendish (*Cavendissh*) and Juliana his wife, John de Glemsford (*Glemesford*) and Beatrice his wife, and William Chamberlain (*Chamberlein*) and Cristina his wife def. The manor of Arlington (*Alurynton*), 60 a. of land, and 10 a. of meadow in Arlington. Right of Richard late vicar. Render to him and the other quer. To hold to them and that Richard's heirs. (Warranty, specifying Juliana's, Beatrice's, and Cristina's heirs.) Cons. 200 marks. [*Torn and stained.*]

78/73/429

34. Two weeks [16 April] from Easter. William Smalcombe quer.; Richard Phelps (*Phelpus*) and Agnes his wife def. A messuage 20 a. of land, 4 a. of meadow, and 3 a. of pasture in Wotton-under-Edge (*Wotton Underegge*). Right of William by gift of Richard and Agnes. Remise and quitclaim, specifying Agnes's heirs, to William. (Warranty.) Cons. 20 marks.

78/73/431

35. Three weeks [23 April] from Easter. Robert Gustard and Emma his wife quer.; William Henreys and Isabel his wife and Robert Heynes and Alice his wife def. Two thirds of a messuage and 2 yardlands in Woodlands (*Wodelond*) by Almondsbury (*Almondesbury*). Grant and render to Robert Gustard and Emma. To hold to them and their heirs in tail, of William and Isabel and Robert Heynes and Alice and Isabel's and Alice's heirs, paying a rose a year at St. John the Baptist and doing service to the chief lords. (Warranty.) Contingent reversion to William and Isabel and Robert Heynes and Alice and Isabel's and Alice's heirs. Cons. 10 marks. [*Torn and stained.*]

78/73/430

36. Three weeks [23 April] from Easter. Walter de Frampton (*Frompton*) quer.; John Bytheweye of Newent (*Newent*) and Alice his wife def. Two messuages in Bristol (*Bristoll'*). Right of Walter. Remise and quitclaim, specifying Alice's heirs, to him. (Warranty.) Cons. 20 marks. [*Torn and stained.*]

78/73/432

[Cf. *Bristol Gt. Red Book*, p. 242, no. 209.]

37. One week [4 June] from Trinity. (Made the morrow of Ascension [12 May] in the said year.) Richard de Pembridge (*Pembrugge*) 'chivaler' quer.; John de Verdon (*Verdoun*) 'chivaler' def. Half of the manors of Ditteridge (*Decherygge*), Fiddington (*Fifide*), and Market Lavington (*Lavynton*), WILTS., and half of the manors of Kilcot (*Killecote*) and Little Taynton (*Parva Teynton*), GLOS. Right of Richard. Render to him of half of the manor of Ditteridge. And grant to him of the reversion of half of the manors of Fiddington and Market Lavington, held by John Moyne (*Moigne*) for term of life, and of half of the manors of Kilcot and Little Taynton, held by Thomas Moyne for term of life, of John's inheritance. (Warranty.) Cons. 200 marks. *Labelled* Wiltes', Glouc'.

288/47/623

[Cf. *Wilts. Fines, 1327–77*, p. 124, no. 519.]

1363

38. Morrow [25 June] of St. John the Baptist. Richard de Stafford the elder knight and Matilda his wife quer.; John Golding (*Goldyng*) and Matilda his wife def. The manor of Charingworth (*Charyngworth*). Right of Richard. Remise and quitclaim, specifying the heirs of Matilda wife of John Golding, to Richard and Matilda his wife and Richard's heirs. (Warranty.) Cons. 100 marks. [*Torn and stained.*]

78/73/434

39. Morrow [25 June] of St. John the Baptist. Richard Leuward quer.; Richard Moltegras and Joan his wife def. A messuage, 50 a. of land, 3 a. of meadow, and 3*d.* rent in Frampton on Severn (*Frompton*), Slimbridge (*Slymbrugge*), and Coaley (*Coueleye*). Right of Richard Leuward by gift of Richard Moltegras and Joan. Cons. 100 marks. [*Torn and stained.*]

78/73/435

40. One week [6 Oct.] from Michaelmas. John Cheltenham (*Chiltenham*) 'bakere' and Agnes his wife quer.; Alexander Skarnynge and Katherine his wife def. A shop in Cirencester (*Cirencestre*). Right of John, as that which John and Agnes had by gift of Alexander and Katherine. To hold to John and Agnes and John's heirs. (Warranty, specifying Alexander's heirs.) Cons. 10 marks. [*Torn and stained.*]

78/73/444

41. Two weeks [13 Oct.] from Michaelmas. Walter Derby of Bristol (*Bristoll'*) quer.; John Gouys def. A messuage and 9*s.* 6*d.* rent in Bristol. Right of Walter by John's gift. Remise and quitclaim to Walter. (Warranty.). Cons 20 marks. [*Torn and stained.*]

78/73/433

[Cf. *Bristol Gt. Red Book*, p. 242, no. 210.]

42. Two weeks [13 Oct.] from Michaelmas. William Wellfed (*Welyfed*) of Tetbury (*Tettebury*) quer.; Robert Woodruff (*Woderove*) of Alderley (*Alreleye*) and Matilda his wife def. A messuage, 1½ a. of meadow, 4*s.* rent, and half of 1 yardland in Tetbury. Right of Matilda, as those which Robert and Matilda had by William's gift. For this, grant back and render to William. To hold during his life, of Robert and Matilda and Matilda's heirs, paying a rose a year at St. John the Baptist and doing service to the chief lords. (Warranty.) Reversion to Robert and Matilda and Matilda's heirs. [*Torn and stained.*]

78/73/436

43. Two weeks [13 Oct.] from Michaelmas. Thomas Moyne (*Moigne*) 'chivaler' quer.; Nicholas de Apperley (*Apperleye*) and Margaret his wife def. The manor of Coverdine (*Colverden*). Right of Thomas. Render to him. (Warranty, specifying Nicholas's heirs.) Cons. 100 marks. [*Stained.*]

78/73/439

44. Two weeks [13 Oct.] from Michaelmas. John de Compton quer.; Thomas Lymare of Gloucester (*Gloucestr'*) and Agnes his wife def. A messuage in the suburb of Gloucester. Right of John. Remise and quitclaim, specifying Agnes's heirs, to him. (Warranty.) Cons. 10 marks. [*Torn and stained.*]

78/73/441

1363

45. Two weeks [13 Oct.] from Michaelmas. William Griffin (*Griffyn*) of Gloucester (*Gloucestr'*) 'mercer' quer.; John Maggot (*Magote*) of Littledean (*Parva Dene*) and Sibyl his wife def. A messuage, 2 shops (*sopis*), and a toft in Gloucester. Right of William. Remise and quitclaim, specifying Sibyl's heirs, to him. Cons. 20 marks. [*Torn and stained.*]

78/73/442

46. Two weeks [13 Oct.] from Michaelmas. Peter le White (*Whyte*) clerk quer.; John Chaverey and Joan his wife def. A messuage, 12 a. of land, and 9½ a. of meadow in Maisemore (*Maysmor*). Right of Peter by gift of John and Joan. Remise and quitclaim, specifying Joan's heirs, to Peter. (Warranty.) Cons. 20 marks. [*Torn and stained.*]

78/73/443

47. Two weeks [13 Oct.] from Michaelmas. Edward de Cardiff (*Kerdyf*) and Joan his wife quer.; Henry de Empingham (*Impyngham*) of Tewkesbury (*Teukesbury*) 'parkere', Thomas Gefcok, John Baudripp and Elizabeth his wife, and Robert Underhill (*Underhull*) and Juetta his wife def. The manor of Walton Cardiff (*Walton Kerdyf*), GLOS., and the manor of Queenhill (*Quenhull*), WORCS. Right of Edward, as those which he and Joan had by gift of Henry, Thomas, John and Elizabeth, and Robert and Juetta. Remise and quitclaim, specifying Elizabeth's and Juetta's heirs, to Edward and Joan and Edward's heirs. (Warranty.) Cons. 200 marks. *Labelled* Glouc', Wygorn'.

288/47/625

48. Three weeks [20 Oct.] from Michaelmas. Geoffrey de Burches chaplain and Roger le Naylor (*Naillere*) quer.; Thomas Pury (*Purie*) and Margaret his wife def. A messuage in Gloucester (*Gloucestre*). Right of Geoffrey, as that which he and Roger had by gift of Thomas and Margaret. For this, grant back and render to Thomas and Margaret. To hold to them and Thomas's heirs. [*Torn and stained.*]

78/73/440

49. One month [27 Oct.] from Michaelmas. Robert de Perle clerk, John Sargent (*Sergeant*), Peter de Woodmancote (*Wodmancote*), and Robert Coule quer.; Walter Ragon and Joan his wife def. A messuage, 2 yardlands and 2 a. of meadow in Gupshill (*Goupeshull*) and Southwick (*Southewyk*). Right of Robert de Perle, as those which the same Robert, John, Peter, and Robert Coule had by gift of Walter and Joan. Remise and quitclaim, specifying Joan's heirs, to the quer. and Robert de Perle's heirs. (Warranty.) Cons. 10 marks. [*Torn and stained.*]

78/73/437

50. Morrow [3 Nov.] of All Souls. William la Zouche of Harringworth (*Haryngworth*) 'chivaler' quer.; Robert Corbet knight and Sibyl his wife def. the advowson of the church of Ebrington (*Ebryghton*). Right of William. Render to him. (Warranty, specifying Robert's heirs.) Cons. 100 marks. [*Torn and stained.*]

78/73/438

38 Edward III

1364

51. Two weeks [2 June] from Trinity. Ranulph in the Field (*in the Felde*) of Gloucester (*Gloucestr'*) 'sadeler' and Petronilla his wife quer.; Edward le Taverner def. A messauge in the suburb of Gloucester. Right of Edward by gift of Ranulph and Petronilla. For this, grant back and render to Ranulph and Petronilla. To hold to them and their heirs in tail. Contingent remainder to Ranulph's heirs. [*Torn and stained.*]

78/73/446

52. Two weeks [2 June] from Trinity. (Made two weeks [7 April] from Easter in the said year.) Thomas Crumme vicar of the church of St. Leonard, Bristol (*Bristoll'*), and Miles de Brislington (*Bristilton*) quer.; John Slo and Isabel his wife def. A messuage and 7*s.* rent in the suburb of Bristol, GLOS., and 3 messuages in the suburb of Bristol, SOM. Right of Thomas, as those which he and Miles had by gift of John and Isabel. For this, grant back and render to John and Isabel. To hold to them and their heirs in tail. Contingent remainder to Isabel's heirs. *Labelled* Glouc', Somers'.

288/47/635

[Cf. *Som. Fines, 1347–99*, pp. 187–8.]

53. Morrow [25 June] of St. John the Baptist. Richard Thornyng 'ferour' [*i.e. smith*] quer.; John atte Cellar (*Celer*) of Bristol (*Bristoll'*) 'burgeys' and Cecily his wife def. Two shops in Bristol. Right of Richard by gift of John and Cecily. Remise and quitclaim, specifying Cecily's heirs, to Richard. (Warranty.) Cons. 10 marks. [*Torn and stained.*]

78/73/445

[Cf. *Bristol Gt. Red Book*, p. 243, no. 211.]

54. One week [1 July] from St. John the Baptist. (Made the morrow of St. Martin 31 Edward III [12 Nov. 1357].) Robert de Sambourne chaplain, Henry de Tingewick (*Tyngewyk*) chaplain (dead by the time that the agreement was granted and recorded), and John de Coston chaplain quer.; John Mautravers of Lytchett Matravers (*Lychet*) (dead by the time that the agreement was granted and recorded) and Agnes his wife def. The manors of Coates (*Cotes*), Hill Deverill (*Hulle Deverel*), Winterbourne Stoke (*Wynterbournestoke*), and Great Somerford (*Somerford Mautravers*), WILTS., the manors of Philipston (*Phelpiston*), Wimborne St. Giles (*Upwynbourne*), Lytchett Matravers (*Lychet Mautravers*), Frome Whitfield (*Frome Whitefelde*), Langton Matravers (*Langeton in Purbyk*), Matravers (*Loderes*), and Wootton Fitzpaine (*Wodeton in Mersshwodeval*), and 2 ploughlands, 40 a. of meadow, 100 a. of pasture, and 10 a. of wood in Eggardon (*Egerdon*), Woolcombe (*Owelcombe*), and West Moors (*La More*), DORSET, and the manors of Woodchester (*Wodechestre*), Stonehouse (*Stonhouse*), and Shurdington (*Shurdyngton*) and 1 ploughland, 12 a. of meadow, and 100*s.* rent in Minchinhampton (*Munechenehampton*, GLOS. Right of Robert. Render to Robert, Henry and John de Coston except for rent of 66*s.* 4*d.*, 1 lb. of cumin, and 100 geese and 6½ knights' fees in the same manors of Somerford, Lytchett, Frome, Wootton, and Woodchester. And grant to Robert, Henry, and John de Coston of the rent and fees above excepted with all the homages and services of the abbot of Malmesbury (*Malmesbury*), the prior of Frampton (*Frompton*), John de Vere (*Veer*) earl of Oxford (*Oxon'*) and Matilda his wife, John de Bradenstoke 'chivaler', William FitzWarren (*Fitz Waryn*) 'chivaler', Thomas de Ramsbury (*Remmesbury*) 'chivaler', Edmund Everard 'chivaler', Thomas Cary

1364

'chivaler', Thomas de Hungerford and Eleanor his wife, John Waspal, John son of Roger de Kingston (*Kyngeston*), John Justice and Margery his wife, Robert Blake, Edward Russell, William Jordan (*Jurdan*), William de Bingham (*Byngham*), Peter atte Barrow (*Berue*), Robert de Bridport (*Brudeport*), John de Sunninghill (*Sunynghull*), William de Fifehead (*Fifhide*), Agnes Blake, William Gnat, William Fillol, William Gullifer (*Goloffre*), and Edmund Cailly (*Caylewey*) from all the holdings which they held of John de Mautravers and Agnes in the manors of Somerford, Lytchett, Frome, Wootton, and Woodchester. To hold to Robert, Henry, and John de Coston and Robert's heirs. (Warranty, specifying John de Mautravers's heirs.) Cons. 300 marks. *Labelled* Wiltes', Dors', Glouc'. [*Worn and stained.*]

287/45/539

[Cf. *Dorset Fines 1327–1485*, pp. 151–2; *Wilts. Fines, 1327–77*, p. 126, no. 529.]

55. One week [1 July] from St. John the Baptist. (Made one week from the Purification 33 Edw. III [9 Feb. 1359].) John Mautravers of Lytchett Matravers (*Lychet*) (dead by the time that the agreement was granted and recorded) and Agnes his wife quer.; Robert de Sambourne chaplain, Henry de Tingewick (*Tyngewyk*) chaplain (dead by the time that the agreement was granted and recorded), and John de Coston chaplain def. The manor of King's Stanley (*Kyngestanlegh*), GLOS., the manors of Sherrington (*Sharneton*) and Codford St. Peter (*Codeford*), half of the manor of Stapleford (*Stapelford*) except rent of 6*s*. 8*d*. and a pair of gilt spurs, and four and two thirds knights' fees in the said manors of Sherrington and Codford St. Peter, WILTS., the manors of East Moreton (*Estmordon*), Worth Matravers (*Worthe in Purbyk*), Witchampton (*Wychampton*), and Woolcombe (*Wolcombe*), DORSET, and the manor of Hendford (*Hyneford*) and 57*s*. rent in Yeovil (*Jevele*), SOM. John Mautravers acknowledged the manors of King's Stanley, Sherrington, Codford St. Peter, and East Moreton and the said half to be the right of Robert, Henry, and John de Coston, and the manors of Worth Matravers, Witchampton, Woolcombe and Hendford and the 57*s*. rent to be the right of Robert, of which he, Henry, and John de Coston had the said manors, except for rent of 39*s*. 4½*d*., 1 lb. of pepper, and 1¾ lb. of cumin and 10 and one third and one eighth knights' fees in the said manor of Sherrington and the half, by gift of John Mautravers. For this, grant to John and Agnes of the said manors, half, rent, and fees together with the homage and all the services of the abbot of Stoneleigh (*Stonlegh*), the abbot of Keynsham (*Caynesham*), the prior of Breamore (*Bremmore*) and of Hugh de Courtenay earl of Devon, Thomas Cray 'chivaler', Walter Scudamore (*Escudemor*) 'chivaler', John Gurney (*Gourney*) 'chivaler', John Giffard of Twyford (*Twyford*) 'chivaler', Walter Rodney (*Rodeney*) 'chivaler', Giles de Beauchamp (*de Bello Campo*) 'chivaler' and Katherine his wife, Robert de la Mare 'chivaler', Ellis de Filton, John de Edington (*Edyndon*) and Thomase his wife, Roger de Barley (*Berle*), John de Sherrington (*Sherneton*), William French (*Frenssh*), Edmund Cailly (*Caleway*), Robert de Wickford (*Wykford*) clerk, Walter atte Park (*Parke*), Roger Godfrey (*Godefrey*), Edith Fry (*Freye*), Thomas de Collingbourne (*Colyngbourn*) and Margery his wife, Thomas Andrew (*Andreu*) and Katherine his wife, Agnes de Longford (*Langeford*), Thomas Archibald (*Erchebaud*) chaplain, Thomas Stolle and Alice his wife, Nicholas Archibald, William de Bakeham (*Bakham*), Henry Fleming (*Flemyng*) and Joan his wife, Isabel de Wellington (*Welyngton*), and Richard de Tresham (*Tressham*) from the holdings which they held from Robert, Henry, and John de Coston in Sherrington and the half, and render to John

1364

de Mautravers and Agnes of the said manors of King's Stanley, Sherrington (*Sharnton*), Codford St. Peter, and East Moreton, the rent, and the half as aforesaid. To hold to John de Mautravers and Agnes and their heirs in tail, the manors of King's Stanley, Sherrington, Codford St. Peter, and East Moreton and the half of the king, and the 57*s.* rent of the chief lords. And grant to John de Mautravers and Agnes of the reversion of the manors of Hendford, Witchampton (*Wichampton*), and Woolcombe, held by Wentheliana who was wife of John Mautravers son of the said John Mautravers for term of life, and of the manor of Worth Mautravers, held by John de Vere (*Veer*) earl of Oxford (*Oxon'*) and Matilda his wife for term of Matilda's life. To hold as above, of the chief lords. Contingent remainder to John son of Richard [FitzAlan] earl of Arundel (*Arundell*) and Eleanor daughter of John son of John Mautravers and their heirs in tail, with further contingent remainder of the manor of King's Stanley to the heirs of John son of Richard, of the manors of Sherrington, Codford St. Peter, and East Moreton and the half to the heirs of John Mautravers, and of the manors of Worth Mautravers, Witchampton, Woolcombe, and Hendford and the rent successively to John de Buckland (*Boklond*) of Redlynch (*Radelynche*) 'chivaler' and his heirs in tail male, John son of John Mautravers of Crowell (*Crowelle*) and his heirs in tail male, and the heirs of John Mautravers of Lytchett Matravers. Made by the king's order as to the manors of King's Stanley, Sherrington, Codford St. Peter, and East Moreton and the half. *Labelled* Glouc', Wiltes', Dors', Somers'.

288/47/636

[Cf. *Dorset Fines, 1327–1485*, pp. 156–7; *Som. Fines, 1347–99*, pp. 188; *Wilts. Fines, 1327–77*, pp. 126–8, no. 30.]

56. One week [1 July] from St. John the Baptist. (Made one week from the Purification 33 Edw. III [9 Feb. 1359].) John Mautravers of Lytchett Matravers (*Lychet*) (dead by the time that the agreement was granted and recorded) and Agnes his wife quer.; Robert de Sambourne chaplain, Henry de Tingewick (*Tyngewyk*) chaplain (dead by the time that the agreement was granted and recorded), and John de Coston chaplain def. The manors of Philipston (*Phelpeston*), Wimborne St. Giles (*Upwymbourne*), Frome Whitfield (*Frome Whitefelde*), Langton Matravers (*Langeton in Purbyk'*), Matravers (*Lod. . .*), Wootton Fitzpaine (*Wodeton in Merssh'*), *Godeval* [Woodville?], and Lytchett Matravers (*Lychet Mautravers*) (except for a rent of 100 geese and 1½ knight's fee in the same manors of Lytchett Matravers and Wootton and the advowson of the church of the same manor of Lytchett Matravers) and 2 ploughlands, 40 a. of meadow, 100 a. of pasture, and 10 a. of wood in Woolcombe (*Owelcombe*) and West Moors (*la More*), DORSET, and the manors of Woodchester (*Wodechestre*), Stonehouse (*Stonhouse*), and Shurdington (*Shurdyngton*) and 1 ploughland, 12 a. of meadow, and 100s. rent in Minchinhampton (*Munechenehampton*), GLOS. Right of Robert, as those which Robert, Henry, and John de Coston had by gift of John Mautravers and Agnes, except for rents of 52*s.* 4*d.* and 1 lb. of cumin and 3½ fees in the same manors of Lytchett, Frome, Wootton, and Woodchester. For this, grant back and render to John Mautravers and Agnes of the said manors tenements, rent, and fees as aforesaid, together with the homages and all the services of the prior of Frampton (*Frompton*) and his successors, John de Vere (*Veer*) and Matilda his wife, Thomas de Ramsbury (*Remmesbury*) 'chivaler', William de Bingham (*Byngham*), Peter atte Berne, John de Sunninghill (*Sunynghull*), William de Fifehead (*Fifhide*), Agnes Blake, William Gnat, William Fillol,

1364

William Gullifer (*Golafre*), and Edmund de Cailly (*Caylewey*) and their heirs for all the tenements which they held of Robert, Henry, and John de Coston in the said manors. To hold to John Mautravers and Agnes and their heirs in tail. Contingent remainders to John son of Richard [FitzAlan] earl of Arundel (*Arundell*) and Eleanor his wife and their heirs in tail, and as to the holdings in Glos. to that Richard's heirs and as to the holdings in Dorset to John de Buckland (*Boklond*) of Redlynch (*Radelynche*) 'chivaler' and his heirs in tail male, to John Mautravers son of John Mautravers of Crowell (*Crowell*) and his heirs in tail male, and to the heirs of John Mautravers of Lytchett. *Labelled* Dors', Glouc'. [*Worn and stained.*]

288/47/637

[Cf. *Dorset Fines, 1327–1485*, pp. 157–8.]

57. Two weeks [13 Oct.] from Michaelmas. Peter son of Walter Marcolf of Newent (*Newent*) quer.; Richard de la Boure of Hereford (*Hereford*) and Agnes his wife. Three messuages and 1 yardland in Newent. Right of Peter. Remise and quitclaim, specifying Agnes's heirs, to him. (Warranty.) Cons. 100 marks. [*Torn and stained.*]

78/73/448

58. Two weeks [13 Oct.] from Michaelmas. Thomas de Berkeley (*Berkleye*) of Coberley (*Cobberleye*) 'chivaler' quer.; Edmund de Bridge (*Brugge*), Walter de Pirton (*Piriton*), John Philips parson of the church of Coberley, and William de Hardwicke (*Herdewyk*) parson of the church of *Adreston* [Adderstone?] def. The manor of Coberley, GLOS., and the manor of Eldersfield (*Eldresfeld*), WORCS. Right of Edmund, as those which Edmund, Walter, John, and William had by Thomas's gift. For this, grant back and render to Thomas. To hold during his life. Remainder to Thomas's son Thomas and Juliana his wife and to that Thomas's heirs in tail. Successive contingent remainders to that Thomas's brother John and his heirs in tail, to John's brother Nicholas and his heirs in tail, to Nicholas's brother Walter and his heirs in tail, and to the heirs of Thomas de Berkeley [the father]. *Labelled* Glouc', Wygorn'.

288/47/639

59. One week [18 Nov.] from St. Martin. Walter Ragon (*Ragoun*) and Joan his wife quer.; Mr. Peter de Woodmancote (*Wodemancote*) def. Three acres of land and half of a messuage in Tewkesbury (*Teukesbury*). Right of Mr. Peter by gift of Walter and Joan. For this grant back and render to Walter and Joan. To hold to them and their heirs in tail, of Mr. Peter, paying a rose a year at St. John the Baptist and doing service to the chief lords. Contingent reversion to Mr. Peter. [*Torn and stained.*]

78/73/447

39 Edward III

1365

60. Two weeks [27 Jan.] from Hilary. John Giffard of Weston Subedge (*Weston Underegge*) and Mary his wife quer.; William de Morton chaplain and Thomas Browning (*Brounyng*) of Weston Subedge def. The manors of Weston Subedge and Norton Subedge (*Norton Underegge*) and the advowson of the church of the same manor of Weston. John acknowledged the right of William, as those which William and Thomas had by John's

1365

gift. For this, grant and render of the manor and advowson of Weston to John and Mary. To hold during their lives. And grant back and render of the manor of Norton to John. To hold during his life. Remainder of both Weston and Norton to the heirs of John and Mary in tail male. Contingent remainder to John's heirs.

78/73/450

61. One week [15 June] from Trinity. (Made morrow [23 May] of Ascension in the said year.) John de Aylesford (*Eyllesford*) 'chivaler' quer.; Nicholas de Apperley (*Apperleye*) and Margaret his wife def. Two messuages, 3 ploughlands, 30 a. of meadow, 10 a. of wood, and 6 marks rent in Burghill (*Burghull*) and Howton (*Houton*) by Wormbridge (*Wormbrugg*), HEREFS., and a messuage, 2 ploughlands, 20 a. of meadow, and 30*s*. rent in Bulley (*Bolleye*) and Tibberton (*Tyberton*), GLOS. Grant to John. Remise and quitclaim to him of whatever right Nicholas and Margaret had during Margaret's life. Cons. 100 marks. *Labelled* Hereford', Glouc'.

288/47/646

62. Morrow [3 Nov.] of All Souls. Poncius son of Nicholas de Poyntz (*Pointz*) and William le Painter quer.; John de Poyntz 'chivaler' and Margery his wife def. A messuage, 2 ploughlands, 12 a. of meadow, 100 a. of wood, and half of a mill in Daglingworth (*Dagelyngworth*) and Cirencester (*Cirencestre*). Right of Poncius, as those which he and William had by gift of John and Margery. For this, grant back and render to John and Margery. To hold during their lives. Remainder to John's son Thomas and Alesia his wife and their heirs in tail. Contingent remainder to Margery's heirs.

78/73/449

40 Edward III

1366

63. Morrow [3 Feb.] of the Purification. William Hayberare (*Heyberare*) of Gloucester (*Gloucestre*) quer.; Gregory Courthose (*Courtheose*) and Joan his wife def. A messuage, 4 shops and half of a shop, and 18s. rent in Gloucester and the suburb of the same. Right of William by gift of Gregory and Joan. Remise and quitclaim, specifying Joan's heirs, to William. (Warranty.) Cons. 100 marks.

78/74/453

64. Two weeks [13 Oct.] from Michaelmas. Henry Walton and Alice his wife quer.; Thomas Moryn and Margaret his wife def. A messuage in Winchcombe (*Wynchecombe*). Right of Henry, as that which he and Alice had by gift of Thomas and Margaret. Remise and quitclaim, specifying Margaret's heirs, to Henry and Alice and Henry's heirs. (Warranty.) Cons. 10 marks.

78/74/451

65. Two weeks [13 Oct.] from Michaelmas. William de Chesterton chaplain, Walter de Herforton chaplain, and Peter de Wodemanton clerk quer.; John son of William Leach (*Lecche*) and Margery his wife def. A messuage, 1 ploughland, 12 a. of meadow, 18 a. of wood, and 9s. rent in Tewkesbury (*Tewkesbury*) and Twyning (*Twenyngg*). Right of Peter, as those which he, William, and Walter had by gift of John and Margery. To hold to

1366

William, Walter, and Peter and Peter's heirs. (Warranty, specifying John's heirs.) Cons. 200 marks.

78/74/452

66. Morrow [3 Nov.] of All Souls. William de Bughbrigge clerk and Walter de Campden (*Campeden*) clerk quer.; John [of Gaunt] duke of Lancaster (*Lancastr'*) and Blanche his wife def. The castles, lordships, and commotes of Kidwelly (*Kedwelly*), Carreg Cennen (*Karkennyn*), and Is Cennen (*Iskennyn*), the lordship and commote of Carnwyllion (*Karnwathlan*), and the manor of Ogmore (*Oggemore*), WALES, the manor of King's Somborne (*Somburne Regis*), HANTS., the castle and manor of Trowbridge (*Troubrigge*) and the manors of Aldbourne (*Aldebourne*), Collingbourne Ducis (*Colyngbourne*), Everleigh (*Everlee*), and Hungerford (*Hungerford*), WILTS., the manors of Poughley (*Poghlee*) and Standen (*Staundon*), BERKS., the manors of Rodley (*Rodelee*), Tibberton (*Tyberton*), and Minsterworth (*Menstreworth*), GLOS. and the manors of Gimingham (*Gymyngham*), Tunstead (*Tunstede*), Thetford (*Tefford*), and Methwold (*Methewold*), the hundreds of Gallow (*Galhowe*) and Brothercross (*Brothercros*), and the advowsons of the abbey of Marham (*Marham*) and the priory of the canons of Thetford, NORF. Right of William and Walter by gift of the duke and Blanche. For this, grant back and render to the duke and Blanche. To hold to them and their heirs in tail, of the king. Contingent remainder to Blanche's heirs. Made by the king's order. *Labelled* Hereford', Sutht', Wiltes', Berk', Glouc', Norff'.

288/48/668

[Cf. *Wilts. Fines, 1327–77*, p. 131, no. 548.]

41 Edward III

1367

67. Two weeks [2 May] from Easter. Mr. David Melksham (*Milkesham*) and John Oldland (*Oldelond*) parson of the church of King's Stanley (*Stanley Regis*) quer.; Walter le Glover (*Glovere*) of Wotton-under-Edge (*Wotton Underegge*) and Margaret his wife def. Four messuages in Wotton-under-Edge. Right of John, as those which he and Mr. David had by gift of Walter and Margaret. For this, grant back and render to Walter and Margaret. To hold to them during their lives, of Mr. David and John, paying a rose a year at St. John the Baptist and doing service to the chief lords. Reversion to Mr. David and John and John's heirs.

78/74/459

68. Two weeks [2 May] from Easter. Henry Holloway (*Holewey*) and Richard Heynes quer.; Robert atte Hall (*Halle*) and Elizabeth his wife def. Two messuages, 53 a. of land, and 1 a. and 3 roods of meadow in Shirehampton (*Sharnyhampton*), Compton Greenfield (*Compton Grenevylle*), and Tockington (*Tokynton*). Right of Henry, as those which Henry and Richard had by gift of Robert and Elizabeth. For this, grant back and render to Robert and Elizabeth. To hold to them and their heirs in tail. Contingent remainder to Elizabeth's heirs.

78/74/460

1367

69. Two weeks [2 May] from Easter. William Greville (*Gryvel*) quer.; William Willicote (*Wylicote*) and Isolda his wife def. A messuage in Chipping Campden (*Chepyngcaumpeden*). Right of William Greville by gift of William Willicote and Isolda. Remise and quitclaim, specifying Isolda's heirs, to William Greville. (Warranty.) Cons. 10 marks.

78/74/461

70. Two weeks [2 May] from Easter. William Crook (*Crok'*) burgess of the town of Gloucester (*Gloucestr'*) and Alice his wife quer.; William Avery (*Avereye*) chaplain def. Four messuages, 10 shops, and 9*s.* 6*d.* rent in Gloucester. Right of William Avery by gift of William Crook and Alice. For this, grant back and render to William Crook and Alice. To hold to them and their heirs in tail. Contingent remainder to Alice's heirs.

78/74/463

71. Two weeks [2 May] from Easter. John de Monmouth (*Monemuth'*) of Gloucester (*Gloucestr'*) quer.; William Warren (*Waryn*) of Gloucester 'tilare' and Margery his wife. Two messuages in the suburb of Gloucester. Right of John by gift of William and Margery. Remise and quitclaim, specifying Margery's heirs, to John. (Warranty.) Cons. 100 marks.

78/74/464

72. One week [20 June] from Trinity. (Made three weeks [9 May] from Easter in the said year.] John Bromwich (*Bromwych'*) 'chivaler' quer.; Thomas Pichard parson of the church of Sollers Hope (*Solershope*) def. The manor of Bromsberrow (*Brymmesbarwe*) and the advowson of the church of the same manor, held by Stephen de Cossington (*Cusyngton*) 'chivaler' and Constance his wife for term of Constance's life. Right of John. Grant to him of the reversion. (Warranty.) Cons. £100.

78/74/462

73. One week [6 Oct.] from Michaelmas. John de Everdon clerk and William de Weston quer.; Walter de Sherborne (*Shirborn*) and Alice his wife def. Four messuages, 1 ploughland, and 10 a. of meadow in Cirencester (*Cirencestre*), Baunton (*Baudynton*), and South Cerney (*Southcerneye*). Right of John, as those which he and William had by gift of Walter and Alice. To hold to John and William and John's heirs. (Warranty, specifying Alice's heirs.) Cons. 100 marks.

78/74/458

74. Two weeks [13 Oct.] from Michaelmas. Robert Walsh (*Walyssh*) parson of the church of Fretherne (*Frethorne*) and John Framilode (*Fremelode*) quer.; Peter le Webb (*Webbe*) of Wheatenhurst (*Whitenhurste*) and Matilda his wife and Henry Coleman of Abbots Morton (*Abbotes Morton*) and Agnes his wife def. Two messuages, 50 a. of land, 4 a. of meadow, and 5s. rent in Saul (*Salle*), Fretherne, Framilode, and Frampton on Severn (*Frempton*). Right of Robert, as those which he and John had by gift of Peter and Matilda and Henry and Agnes. To hold to Robert and John and Robert's heirs. (Warranty, specifying Agnes's heirs.) Cons. 100 marks.

78/74/454

[The warranty does not specify Matilda's heirs, perhaps in error.]

1367

75. Two weeks [13 Oct.] from Michaelmas. Thomas de Studley (*Stodeleye*) quer.; Richard de Morton and Joan his wife def. A messuage in Winchcombe (*Wynchecombe*) held by Agnes Janemon for term of her life. Right of Thomas. Grant to him of the reversion, of Joan's inheritance. (Warranty.) Cons. 10 marks.

78/74/455

76. Two weeks [13 Oct.] from Michaelmas. Adam parson of the church of Dowdeswell (*Doudeswelle*) and William Crounok' chaplain quer.; Ralph de Andoversford (*Auneford*) and Emma his wife def. Two messuages, a toft, 3 yardlands and 2 a. of land, and 11 a. of meadow in Dowdeswell, Andoversford, Whittington (*Whytyngton*), and Sevenhampton (*Sevenhampton*). Right of Adam, as those which he and William had by gift of Ralph and Emma. For this, grant back and render to Ralph and Emma. To hold to them during their lives. Remainder to John de Andoversford.

78/74/456

77. Two weeks [13 Oct.] from Michaelmas. Thomas Shaw (*Shauwhe*) and Matilda his wife quer.; Ralph de Andoversford (*Auneford*) and Emma his wife def. A messuage and 1 ploughland in North Cerney (*Nothcerneye*) and Woodmancote (*Wodemancote*). Right of Thomas, as those which Thomas and Matilda had by gift of Ralph and Emma. To hold to Thomas and Matilda and Thomas's heirs. (Warranty, specifying Emma's heirs.) Cons. 100 marks.

78/74/457

1368

78. One week [20 Jan.] from Hilary. (Made the morrow of All Souls in the said year [3 Nov. 1368].) Ralph Waleys and William Smalcombe quer.; John de Clifford and Erneburga his wife def. A messuage, 1 yardland, and 3 a. of meadow in North Nibley (*Nubbeleye*) and Alkington (*Alkynton*). Right of William, as those which he and Ralph had by gift of John and Erneburga. Remise and quitclaim, specifying Erneburga's heirs, to Ralph and William and William's heirs. (Warranty.) Cons. 20 marks.

78/74/464b (formerly 78/74/472)

42 Edward III

1368

79. Two weeks [27 Jan.] from Hilary. Nicholas Birdlip (*Bridlep*) of Gloucester (*Gloucestre*) quer.; William Griffin (*Griffyn*) burgess of Gloucester (*Gloucestr'*) and Amice his wife def. A messuage in Gloucester. Right of Nicholas by gift of William and Amice. (Warranty, specifying Amice's heirs.) Cons. 10 marks.

78/74/473

80. Two weeks [27 Jan.] from Hilary. Nicholas Birdlip (*Bridlep*) of Gloucester (*Gloucestre*) quer.; John Maggot (*Magot*) of Littledean (*Parva Dene*) and Sibyl his wife def. A messuage in Gloucester. Right of Nicholas by gift of John and Sibyl. (Warranty, specifying Sibyl's heirs.) Cons. 10 marks.

78/74/474

1368

81. Two weeks [23 April] from Easter. William Howes (*Houwes*) quer.; William Cat and Edith his wife def. A messuage in Chipping Sodbury (*Chepyng Sobbury*). Right of William Howes by gift of William Cat and Edith. Remise and quitclaim, specifying William Cat's heirs, to William Howes. (Warranty.) Cons. 10 marks.

78/74/468

82. Two weeks [23 April] from Easter. Richard Spicer of Bristol (*Bristoll'*) quer.; Richard son of Roger de Cubbington (*Cobyngdon*) def. Eight messuages, 30 shops, a cellar, 10 a. of land, and 23*s*. rent in Bristol and the suburb of the same town. Right of Richard Spicer. Remise and quitclaim to him. (Warranty.) Cons. 200 marks.

78/74/469

[Cf. *Bristol Gt. Red Book*, p. 243, no. 212.]

83. Two weeks [23 April] from Easter. (Made two weeks from Michaelmas 41 Edward III [13 Oct. 1367].) Thomas Gayner of Aylburton (*Aylberton*) quer.; Richard Bruton (*Brutton*) and Joan his wife and John Wauncy and Alice his wife def. A messuage, 1 ploughland, 3 a. of meadow, 8 a. of pasture, and 17*s*. rent in Aylburton by Lydney (*Lydeneye*). Right of Thomas. Remise and quitclaim, specifying Joan's and Alice's heirs, to Thomas of the holdings [sc. the messuage, ploughland, meadow, and pasture]. And grant to Thomas of the rent together with the homage and services of Agnes Crowder (*Croudar'*), Juliana and Agnes [sic] sisters of the same Agnes, Richard Foxley (*Foxlegh*), John Ragon, John Gawayn, Robert Gawayn, John Boter, Richard Pulesdon, Ralph Bokerych', John Clerk, Thomas Shipman (*Shupman*), John Edy, Philip Edy, Eleanor Shipman, John King (*Kyng*), John Gayner, and Philip Millward (*Muleward*) for all the holdings formerly held by Richard and Joan and John and Alice in the said town. (Warranty, specifying Joan's and Alice's heirs.) Cons. 20 marks. [*Worn*.]

78/74/475

[The initial letter of the name Gawayn is in each instance a yogh.]

84. Two weeks [23 April] from Easter. William de Bridgemere (*Briddesmere*) and Alice his wife quer.; Isabel daughter of John Gille def. A messuage and 1 ploughland in Great Bentham (*Magna Bentham*). Right of Isabel by gift of William and Alice. For this, grant and render to William and Alice. To hold during their lives, of Isabel, paying a rose a year at St. John the Baptist and doing service to the chief lords. Reversion to Isabel. [*Worn*.]

78/75/476

85. Two weeks [23 April] from Easter. John de Morehalle, Alexander de Besford, and John Asselyn chaplain quer.; John Trillowe the younger 'chivaler' and Joan his wife def. Eighteen messuages, a mill, a dovecot, 14 yardlands and 24 a. of land, and 20*s*. rent in Weston-on-Avon (*Weston Maudit*). Right of John de Morehalle, as those which the same John, Alexander, and John Asselyn had by gift of John Trillowe and Joan. Remise and quitclaim, specifying Joan's heirs, to John de Morehalle, Alexander, and John Asselyn and John de Morehalle's heirs. (Warranty.) Cons. 200 marks.

78/75/477

86. Two weeks [23 April] from Easter. John Chapman (*Chapmon*) of Minchinhampton (*Munechenehampton*) quer.; Robert atte Mill (*Mulle*) and Edith his wife def. A messuage

1368

and 4 a. of land in Minchinhampton. Right of John by gift of Robert and Edith. Remise and quitclaim, specifying Edith's heirs, to John. (Warranty.) Cons. 10 marks.

78/75/478

87. Two weeks [23 April] from Easter. John de Shardlow (*Shardelowe*) and Agnes his wife quer.; Richard de Hay (*Heye*) chaplain def. A messuage, 36 a. of land, and 1 rood of meadow in Newent (*Newent*) and Elmore (*Elmor*). Right of Richard by gift of John and Agnes. For this, grant back and render to John and Agnes. To hold to them and John's heirs.

78/75/479

88. Morrow [19 May] of Ascension. William Cheddar (*Cheddre*) and William Draper 'chapelleyn' quer.; Richard Arthur and Isabel his wife def. Two messuages and 4 a. of land in the suburb of Bristol (*Bristoll'*). Right of William Draper, as those which the same William and William Cheddar had by gift of Richard and Isabel. To hold to William Draper and William Cheddar and William Draper's heirs. (Warranty, specifying Isabel's heirs.) Cons. 100 marks.

78/74/470

[Cf. *Bristol Gt. Red Book*, p. 243, no. 213.]

89. One week [6 Oct.] from Michaelmas. (Made two weeks [23 April] from Easter in the said year.) William de Chedworth (*Cheddeworth*) chaplain quer.; Thomas Kenn (*Kynne*) and Agnes his wife def. Fourteen messuages, 1 ploughland and 20 a. of land, 4 a. of meadow, 1 a. of wood, 18*s*. 6*d*. rent, and half of a messuage in Minchinhampton (*Munechenehampton*), Avening (*Avenynge*), Aston (*Astone*), Rodborough (*Rodberwe*), and Frampton Mansell (*Frompton Maunsel*). Right of William, of which he had 2 messuages, 12*s*. 4*d*. rent, two-thirds of the 4 a. of meadow and 1 a. of wood, and half of the ploughland in the township of Minchinhampton by gift of Thomas and Agnes. And Thomas and Agnes granted to William the reversion of 6 messuages, 20 a. of land and half of the other half of the ploughland, and the half of a messuage held by Agnes who was wife of Robert Kenn for term of her life; of a messuage, 6*s*. 2*d*. rent, half of half of the ploughland, and one third of the 4 a. of meadow and 1 a. of wood in Minchinhampton held by the same Agnes in dower; of a messuage in Minchinhampton held by Thomas Toller and Cristina his wife for term of life; of a messuage in the same township held by Alice Jenkins (*Jankyns*) for term of life; of a messuage in the same township held by Robert Allesley (*Alsleye*) for term of life; of a messuage in the same township held by Agnes Frere (*Frer'*) for term of life; and of a messuage in the same township held by Robert Sende for term of life, all of Thomas Kenn's inheritance. (Warranty.) Cons. 200 marks. [*Worn*.]

78/74/465

90. One week [6 Oct.] from Michaelmas. (Made one month [7 May] from Easter in the said year.) John Whitewenche quer.; John de Stanshawe and Isabel his wife def. A messuage in Chipping Sodbury (*Chepyngsobbury*). Right of John Whitewenche by gift of John de Stanshawe and Isabel. Remise and quitclaim, specifying John de Stanshawe's heirs, to John Whitewenche. (Warranty.) Cons. 10 marks.

78/74/467

1368

91. Two weeks [13 Oct.] from Michaelmas. (Made the morrow of the Purification 41 Edward III [3 Feb. 1367].) Laurence Dolman quer.; Roger Duryard def. A messuage, 1½ yardlands, 4 a. of meadow, and 16 a. of wood in Over Lypiatt (*Overlupgate*) and Nether Lypiatt (*Netherlupgate*). Right of Laurence. Grant to him of the reversion of half of the ½ yardland held by Joan who was wife of Henry Duryard in dower, and all of the residue, sc. the messuage, 1 yardland, the meadow, the wood, and the other half of the ½ yardland, held by the same Joan for term of life, of Roger's inheritance. (Warranty.) Cons. 100 marks.

78/74/466

[The letter g in *Overlupgate* and *Netherlupgate* is in each instance a yogh.]

92. Two weeks [13 Oct.] from Michaelmas. Walter de Frampton (*Frompton*) quer.; John atte Cellar (*Celer*) and Cecily his wife def. A messuage in Bristol (*Bristoll'*). Right of Walter. Render to him. (Warranty, specifying John's heirs.) Cons. 10 marks.

78/74/471

[Cf. *Bristol Gt. Red Book*, p. 244, no. 214.]

43 Edward III

1369

93. Two weeks [15 April] from Easter. John Coleseye quer.; Thomas atte Lowe (*Loue*) and Asselina his wife def. A messuage, 20 a. of land, 5 a. of meadow, and 6*s.* 8*d.* rent in Apperley (*Appurleye*). Right of John by gift of Thomas and Asselina. Remise and quitclaim, specifying Asselina's heirs, to him. (Warranty.) Cons. 20 marks.

78/75/480

94. Two weeks [15 April] from Easter. William Warthewyke quer.; Hugh Warthewyke and Joan his wife def. Seven messuages, 1 ploughland and 26 a. of land, 12 a. of meadow, 50 a. of pasture, 60 a. of wood, and 3*s.* rent in Badgeworth (*Beggeworth*). Right of William. Remise and quitclaim, specifying Joan's heirs, to him. (Warranty.) Cons. 100 marks.

78/75/481

95. Two weeks [15 April] from Easter. Richard le Cook of Winterbourne (*Wynterborn*) and Juliana his wife and Henry Baker (*Bakere*) quer.; John Foliot (*Folyot*) of Bristol (*Bristoll'*) and Lucy his wife def. A messuage, 1 yardland, and 8 a. of meadow in Frenchay (*Fromshawe*) and Hambrook (*Hambrok*), GLOS., and a messuage, 1 yardland, and 10 a. of meadow in Hinton Blewett (*Henton Bluet*), SOM. Right of Richard. Remise and quitclaim, specifying Lucy's heirs, to Richard and Juliana and Henry and Richard's heirs. (Warranty.) Cons. 100 marks. *Labelled* Glouc', Somers'.

288/48/692

[Cf. *Som. Fines, 1347–99*, p. 191.]

96. Morrow [11 May] of Ascension. Roger de Charlton (*Cherleton*) and Elizabeth his wife quer.; John de Stoke and William de Hereford of Ludlow (*Lodelowe*). The manor of Eyford (*Eyforde*). Right of John, as that which John and William had by gift of Roger and Elizabeth. For this, grant and render to Roger.

78/75/482

[The fine is unusual in that Roger and Elizabeth are jointly conusors but the grant and render are to Roger alone.]

1369

97. One week [11 May] from Trinity. Lewis [Charlton] bishop of Hereford (*Hereford*), William de Charlton (*Charleton*), and Thomas de Bushbury (*Bysshebury*) quer.; John Billing (*Byllyng*) and Margery his wife def. One acre of land in Westbury on Severn (*Westbury*) by Newnham (*Newenham*) and one third of one third of the advowson of the church of the same township of Westbury. Right of the bishop. Render to him and William and Thomas. To hold to them and the bishop's heirs. (Warranty, specifying Margery's heirs.) Cons. 100 marks.

78/75/484

98. One week [11 May] from Trinity. Richard Spicer burgess of the town of Bristol (*Bristoll'*) quer.; Roger Cornish (*Cornyssh*) and Alice his wife def. Four shops and half of 1 a. of land in the suburb of Bristol. Right of Richard. Remise and quitclaim, specifying Alice's heirs, to him. (Warranty.) Cons. 20 marks.

78/75/485

[Cf. *Bristol Gt. Red Book*, p. 244, no. 215.]

99. Two weeks [10 June] from Trinity. William Blunt (*Blount*) chaplain and Richard de Calverton chaplain quer.; Robert Palet and Katherine his wife and William de Winchcombe (*Wynchecombe*) and Isolda his wife def. Two messuages and 1 ploughland and 2 yardlands in Trewsbury (*Trusebury*) and Coates (*Cotes*) by Cirencester (*Cirencestre*). Right of William Blunt. Remise and quitclaim, specifying Katherine's and Isolda's heirs, to William and Richard and William's heirs. (Warranty.) Cons. 200 marks.

78/75/483

100. Two weeks [13 Oct.] from Michaelmas. Edward Fort quer.; William Cheyney (*Cheny*) and Joan his wife def. A messuage in Bristol (*Bristowe*). Right of Edward. Render to him. Cons. 20 marks.

78/75/486(a)

[Cf. *Bristol Gt. Red Book*, p. 244, no. 216.]

1370

101. One week [20 Jan.] from Hilary. (Made one week from St. Martin in the said year [18 Nov. 1369].) William Hardhead (*Hardhed*) quer.; John Morris (*Moris*) of Aust (*Auste*) and Joan his wife def. A messuage, a toft, 28 a. of land, and 6 a. of meadow in Aust. Right of William by gift of John and Joan. (Warranty, specifying Joan's heirs.) Cons. 20 marks.

78/75/486(b), formerly 78/75/496

44 Edward III

1370

102. Morrow [25 June] of St. John the Baptist. Robert Swayneshey quer.; Philip Alleron and Margaret his wife def. A messuage and 2 tofts in Gloucester (*Gloucestre*). Right of Robert by gift of Philip and Margaret. Remise and quitclaim, specifying Margaret's heirs, to Robert. (Warranty.) Cons. 20 marks.

78/75/492

1370

103. One week [6 Oct.] from Michaelmas. Thomas Pendelesford chaplain and Peter de Tiverton (*Tyverton*) chaplain quer.; Richard Fowey 'mason' and Agnes his wife def. A messuage in the suburb of Bristol (*Bristoll'*). Right of Thomas, as that which Thomas and Peter had by gift of Richard and Agnes. Remise and quitclaim, specifying Agnes's heirs, to Thomas and Peter and Thomas's heirs. (Warranty.) Cons. 20 marks.

78/75/489

[Cf. *Bristol Gt. Red Book*, p. 245, no. 219.]

104. One week [6 Oct.] from Michaelmas. Richard Cook of Winterbourne (*Wynterbourn*) and Juliana his wife and Henry Baker quer.; John Honypyn and Cristina his wife def. A messuage and 34 a. of land in Winterbourne, Frenchay (*Fremshaw*), Hambrook (*Hambrok*), and Harry Stoke (*Stoke Henrey*). Right of Richard. Render to him, Juliana, and Henry of the messuage and 29 a. of land. To hold to them and Richard's heirs. And John and Cristina, for themselves and Cristina's heirs, granted to Richard, Juliana, Henry and Richard's heirs the reversion of the remaining 5 a. of land, held by Adam atte Green (*Grene*) for term of life in the said townships, of Cristina's inheritance. (Warranty.) Cons. 20 marks.

78/75/493

105. Two weeks [13 Oct.] from Michaelmas. Walter de Frampton (*Frompton*) of Bristol (*Bristoll'*) merchant and Isabel his wife quer.; Roger Cornish (*Cornyssh*) and Alice his wife def. A messuage and a garden in Bristol. Right of Walter, as those which Walter and Isabel had by gift Roger and Alice. Remise and quitclaim, specifying Alice's heirs, to Walter and Isabel and Walter's heirs. (Warranty.) Cons. 20 marks.

78/75/487

[Cf. *Bristol Gt. Red Book*, pp. 244–5, no. 217.]

106. Two weeks [13 Oct.] from Michaelmas. Walter de Frampton (*Frompton*) of Bristol (*Bristoll'*) merchant and Isabel his wife quer.; Richard Fowey (*Fowy*) and Agnes his wife def. A messuage in Bristol. Right of Walter, as that which Walter and Isabel had by gift of Richard and Agnes. Remise and quitclaim, specifying Agnes's heirs, to Walter and Isabel and Walter's heirs. (Warranty.) Cons. 10 marks.

78/75/488

[Cf. *Bristol Gt. Red Book*, p. 245, no. 218.]

107. Two weeks [13 Oct.] from Michaelmas. Robert Swayneshey (*Swyneseye*) and Sarah his wife and John Madeley (*Maddeleye*) and Clemency his wife quer.; Nicholas Ampney (*Awemeneye*) clerk and Ralph Sherborne (*Shirburn*) clerk def. A messuage and 2 tofts in Gloucester (*Gloucestre*). Right of Nicholas, as those which Nicholas and Ralph had by gift of Robert and Sarah and John and Clemency. Remise and quitclaim, specifying Clemency's heirs, to Nicholas and Ralph and Nicholas's heirs. (Warranty.) Cons. 20 marks.

78/75/491

[It is surprising that neither the remise and quitclaim nor the warranty specifies Sarah's heirs.]

108. Three weeks [20 Oct.] from Michaelmas. John Lucy quer.; Robert Croust and Edith his wife def. A messuage in Cirencester (*Cirencestre*). Right of John. Render to him. (Warranty, specifying Edith's heirs.) Cons. 10 marks.

78/75/495

1370

109. Morrow [12 Nov.] of St. Martin. Thomas Cole of Tewkesbury (*Teukesbury*) quer.; John Sargent (*Serjaunt*) of Cirencester (*Cirencestre*) and Isabel his wife def. A messuage in Tewkesbury. Right of Thomas by gift of John and Isabel. Remise and quitclaim, specifying Isabel's heirs, to Thomas. (Warranty.) Cons. 100*s*.

78/75/494

110. One week [18 Nov.] from St. Martin. John [de Berwick] prior of Bath (*Bathon'*) quer.; Hugh Leygrave and Joan his wife def. Two messuages and 2 shops in Bristol (*Bristoll'*). Right of the prior and his church of the apostles Peter and Paul of Bath. Remise and quitclaim, specifying Joan's heirs, to the prior. Cons. 20 marks.

78/75/490

[Cf. *Bristol Gt. Red Book*, pp. 245–6, no. 220.]

1371

111. One week [20 Jan.] from Hilary. (Made two weeks from Michaelmas in the said year [13 Oct. 1370].) Ralph Waleys and John Allen (*Aleyn*) quer.; John de Lorridge (*Lorewynge*) and Margery his wife def. A messuage, 1 ploughland, 15 a. of meadow, 8 a. of wood, and 7*s*. 8*d*. rent in Wick (*Wyke*), Lorridge, Walgaston (*Walmegarston*), Berkeley (*Berkele*), Ham (*Hamme*), Alkington (*Alkynton*), and Halmore (*Halmare*). Right of Ralph. Remise and quitclaim, specifying Margery's heirs, of the holdings to Ralph and John Allen and Ralph's heirs. And grant to Ralph and John Allen of the rent with the homages and all the services of John Sargent (*Sergeaunt*) of Monmouth (*Mynnemouth*), John Frigg, and William chaplain of Newport (*Neuport*) and their heirs from the holdings which they held of John de Lorridge and Margery in the said townships. To hold to Ralph and John Allen and Ralph's heirs. (Warranty.) Cons. 100 marks.

78/75/497

112. One week [20 Jan.] from Hilary. John Somerville (*Somerwill*) of Bristol (*Bristoll'*) quer.; Nicholas Davy and Margaret his wife def. A messuage and 2 shops in Bristol and the suburb of the same town. Right of John by gift of Nicholas and Margaret. Remise and quitclaim, specifying Margaret's heirs, to John. (Warranty.) Cons. 10 marks.

78/74/498

[Cf. *Bristol Gt. Red Book*, p. 246, no. 221.]

45 Edward III

1371

113. Two weeks [20 April] from Easter. Richard Cook of Winterbourne (*Wynterbourn*) and Juliana his wife and Henry Baker (*Bakere*) quer.; William Carpenter burgess of the town of Bristol (*Bristoll'*) and Elena his wife def. A messuage, 12 a. of land, and 2 a. of meadow in Hambrook (*Hambrok*). Right of Richard, as those which Richard, Juliana and Henry had by gift of William and Elena. Remise and quitclaim, specifying Elena's heirs, to Richard, Juliana and Henry and Richard's heirs. (Warranty.) Cons. 20 marks.

78/76/506

114. Two weeks [20 April] from Easter. John Moul of *Aylburton* [Aylburton or Elberton] quer.; Richard Bruton and Joan his wife. A messuage, 3 a. of land, and 3 acres of meadow

1371

in *Aylburton*. Right of John by gift of Richard and Joan. Remise and quitclaim, specifying Joan's heirs, to John. (Warranty.) Cons. 10 marks.

78/76/511

115. Three weeks [27 April] from Easter. Adam parson of the church of Dowdeswell (*Dodeswell*) and Thomas Francis (*Fraunceys*) parson of the church of Shipton Oliffe (*Shipton Olyve*) quer.; John atte Forthey and Juliana his wife def. A messuage, 2 yardlands, 8 a. of meadow, 6 a. of pasture, and 3 a. of wood in Boddington (*Botynton*). Right of Adam, as those which Adam and Thomas had by gift of John and Juliana. Remise and quitclaim, specifying Juliana's heirs, to Adam and Thomas and Adam's heirs. (Warranty.) Cons. 100 marks.

78/76/507

116. Three weeks [27 April] from Easter. John le Eyre (*Heyr*) and John Witt (*Wyt*) of Brinkworth (*Brenkworthe*) quer.; Richard Churchey of Stroud (*Strode*) and Joan his wife def. A messuage and 50 a. of land in Winstone (*Wynston*). Right of John Witt, as those which the same John and John le Eyre had by gift of Richard and Joan. Remise and quitclaim, specifying Joan's heirs, to John and John and John Witt's heirs. (Warranty.) Cons. 20 marks.

78/76/508

117. Three weeks [27 April] from Easter. William Hayberare (*Heyberere*) quer.; Thomas Birdlip (*Bridelep*) and Petronilla his wife def. A messuage in Tewkesbury (*Teukesbury*). Right of William by gift of Thomas and Petronilla. Remise and quitclaim, specifying Petronilla's heirs, to William. (Warranty.) Cons. 10 marks.

78/76/509

118. One month [4 May] from Easter. Ellis Spelly of Bristol (*Bristoll'*) quer.; Hugh Leygrave and Joan his wife def. A messuage in the suburb of Bristol. Right of Ellis by gift of Hugh and Joan. Remise and quitclaim, specifying Joan's heirs, to him. (Warranty.) Cons. 10 marks.

78/76/501

[Cf. *Bristol Great Red Bk.* p. 247, no. 224.]

119. One month [4 May] from Easter. John Browning (*Brounyng*) and John vicar of the church of Down Hatherley (*Hatherleye*) quer.; Walter Browning and Elizabeth his wife def. A messuage, 16 tofts, 5 ploughlands, 12 a. of meadow, 20 a. of pasture, 5 a. of wood, and 6*s.* rent in *Piryton* [Parton or Pirton] by Churchdown (*Churchedon*). Right of John Browning, as those which the same John and John the vicar had by gift of Walter and Elizabeth. For this, grant back and render to Walter and Elizabeth. To hold during their lives. Remainder to William de Warthewyke (*Warthewyk*) and Alice his wife and their heirs in tail. Contingent remainder to Walter's heirs.

78/76/505

120. Morrow [16 May] of Ascension. John de Salisbury (*Salesbury*) the elder and Elena his wife quer.; Thomas de Salisbury and John son of John de Tenbury (*Temedebury*)

1371

'bakere' def. Seven messuages and 4 shops in Gloucester (*Gloucestr'*) and the suburb of the same town. Right of Thomas, as those which Thomas and John son of John had by gift of John de Salisbury and Elena. For this, grant back and render to John de Salisbury and Elena. To hold to them and their heirs in tail. Contingent remainder to Roger Bigod (*Bygot*).

78/76/515

121. One week [8 June] from Trinity. (Made the morrow [16 May] of Ascension in the said year.) Thomas Stewart (*Stiward*) quer. by Robert de Ketford; John Salisbury (*Salesbury*) and Elena his wife def. A messuage in the suburb of Gloucester (*Gloucestr'*). Right of Thomas. Remise and quitclaim, specifying Elena's heirs, to him. (Warranty.) Cons. 10 marks.

78/76/513

122. One week [8 June] from Trinity. (Made the morrow [16 May] of Ascension in the said year.) John Anlep quer. by Robert de Ketford; John Salisbury (*Salesbury*) and Elena his wife def. A messuage in Gloucester (*Gloucestr'*) held by William Wightfield (*Wyghtfeld*) and Agnes his wife for term of Agnes's life, of Elena's inheritance. Right of John Anlep. Grant, specifying Elena's heirs, of the reversion to him. (Warranty.) Cons. 20 marks.

78/76/514

123. Two weeks [15 June] from Trinity. Emma who was wife of Henry atte More quer.; John Renger and Emma his wife def. A messuage, 1 ploughland, 10 a. of meadow, 4 a. of wood, 60*s.* rent, and half of a mill in Lawrence Weston (*Weston Sancti Laurencii*). Right of Emma who was wife of Henry. Remise and quitclaim, specifying the heirs of Emma wife of John, to Emma who was wife of Henry. (Warranty.) Cons. 100 marks.

78/76/512

124. One week [6 Oct.] from Michaelmas. (Made one week from Hilary 44 Edward III [20 Jan. 1371].) John Hanham quer.; John son of Philip Toryton of Bristol (*Bristoll'*) def. A messuage in the suburb of Bristol held by Richard Hooper (*Hoper*) for term of life, of the inheritance of John son of Philip. Right of John Hanham. Grant of the reversion to him. (Warranty.) Cons. 20 marks.

78/75/499

[Cf. *Bristol Gt. Red Book*, p. 246, no. 222.]

125. Two weeks [13 Oct.] from Michaelmas. William Somerville (*Somerwelle*) of Bristol (*Bristoll'*) quer.; John Bath (*Bathe*) of Bristol 'boucher' and Alice his wife def. A messuage in Bristol. Right of William. Remise and quitclaim, specifying John's heirs, to William. (Warranty.) Cons. 10 marks.

78/75/500

[Cf. *Bristol Gt. Red Book*, p. 246, no. 223.]

126. Two weeks [13 Oct.] from Michaelmas. John de Everdon clerk and William de Weston of Cirencester (*Cirencestre*) quer.; Richard de Tenbury (*Temedebury*) and Isabel his wife def. One third of 2 messuages, 1 ploughland, and 9 a. of meadow in Cirencester,

1371

Baunton (*Baudynton*), and South Cerney (*South Cerneye*). Right of William. Remise and quitclaim, specifying Isabel's heirs, to John and William and William's heirs. Cons. 100 marks.

78/76/502

127. Three weeks [20 Oct.] from Michaelmas. Walter de Aust quer.; Thomas Smith (*Smyth*) of Blakeney (*Blakeney*) and Joan his wife def. A messuage and 18 a. of land in Purton (*Pyryton*) by Lydney (*Lydeneye*). Right of Walter by gift of Thomas and Joan. Remise and quitclaim, specifying Joan's heirs, to Walter. (Warranty.) Cons. 20 marks.

78/76/504

128. Three weeks [20 Oct.] from Michaelmas. William Draper (*Drapere*) parson of the church of Haselbury (*Haselbere*) and John Burgoyne (*Borgoyne*) parson of the church of Thornfalcon (*Thorne Faucon*) quer.; Richard de Acton 'chivaler' def. Two messuages, 1 ploughland and 1 yardland, 45 a. of meadow, 25 a. of pasture, and 6 a. of wood in Cote (*Cotes*), Elberton (*Ailberton*), and Iron Acton (*Irenacton*) and half of the manor of Aust (*Aust*). Right of William, as those which William and John had by Richard's gift. Remise and quitclaim to them and William's heirs. (Warranty.) Cons. £200.

78/76/516

129. One month [27 Oct.] from Michaelmas. Geoffrey Smith (*Smyth*) of Tewkesbury (*Teukesbury*) and Cristina his wife quer.; John Roger (*Rogger*) and Joan his wife def. A messuage in Tewkesbury. Grant and render to Geoffrey and Cristina. To hold during their lives, of John and Joan and Joan's heirs, paying a rose a year at St. John the Baptist and doing service to the chief lords. Reversion to John and Joan and Joan's heirs. Cons. 10 marks.

78/76/510

130. Morrow [12 Nov.] of St. Martin. Richard atte Bridge (*Brugge*) quer.; John de Stanshawe and Isabel his wife def. A messuage and 6 a. of land in Chipping Sodbury (*Chepyngsobbury*). Right of Richard. Remise and quitclaim, specifying John's heirs, to him. (Warranty.) Cons. 100*s*.

78/76/503

46 Edward III

1372

131. One week [30 May] from Trinity. Thomas Tailor (*Taylour*) of Burford (*Borford*) chaplain quer.; John Bedford of North Newington (*Northnewenton*) and Cristina his wife def. A messuage in Bristol (*Bristoll'*). Right of Thomas by gift of John and Cristina. Remise and quitclaim, specifying Cristina's heirs, to him. Cons. 20 marks.

78/76/517

[Cf. *Bristol Great Red Bk*. p. 247, no. 225.]

47 Edward III

1373

132. Three weeks [8 May] from Easter. Nicholas Poynter (*Ponyter*) of Cirencester (*Cirencestre*) and John Lucy quer. by Robert de Charlton (*Cherlton*) in John's place;

1373

Henry Warner (*Warenner*) and Isabel his wife def. A messuage, 3 yardlands, and 22 a. of meadow in Lower Siddington (*Nether Sodyngton*) and Upper Siddington (*Over Sodyngton*). Right of Nicholas, as those which Nicholas and John had by gift of Henry and Isabel. Remise and quitclaim, specifying Isabel's heirs, to Nicholas and John and Nicholas's heirs. (Warranty.) Cons. 20 marks.

78/76/521

133. One week [6 Oct.] from Michaelmas. Thomas Botener of Bristol (*Bristoll'*) quer.; and Thomas Tailor (*Taylour*) of Burford (*Boreford*) chaplain def. A messuage in Bristol. Right of Thomas Botener by gift of Thomas Tailor. Remise and quitclaim to Thomas Botener. Cons. 100 marks.

78/76/518

[Cf. *Bristol Great Red Bk*. p. 247, no. 226. The consideration is unusually large for an urban messuage.]

134. One week [6 Oct.] from Michaelmas. (Made two weeks [26 June] from Trinity in the said year.) John Browning (*Brounyng*) and Robert Ketford quer.; Gilbert Giffard 'chivaler' and Elizabeth his wife def. The manors of Kingsholm (*Kyngeshome*), Matson (*Mattesdon*), and Cromhall (*Cromhale*) and the advowson of the church of Cromhall. As to the manor of Kingsholm, right of John and Robert, and as to the manors of Matson and Cromhall and the advowson, right of John, as those which John and Robert had by gift of Gilbert and Elizabeth. For this, grant back and render of the manor of Kingsholm to Gilbert and Elizabeth. To hold to them and their heirs [in tail], of the king. And grant back and render to them of the manors of Matson and Cromhall and the advowson. To hold to them and their heirs in tail, of the chief lords. Contingent remainder to Gilbert's heirs. Made as to the manor of Kingsholm by the king's order.

78/76/519

[That the manors and advowson were to hold to Gilbert and Elizabeth and their heirs *in tail* is not stated in the relevant clause but is clear from the provision for contingent remainder.]

135. One week [6 Oct.] from Michaelmas. (Made one week [19 June] from Trinity in the said year.) Edward le Despenser 'chivaler' quer.; William le Carter (*Cartere*) of Great Rissington (*Broderysyndon*) and Alice his wife def. One third of the manor of Whittington (*Whytynton*) and the advowson of one third of the church of the same manor, held by Alice who was wife of Edmund Hakluyt (*Hakeluyt*) knight for term of life, of the inheritance of Alice wife of William. Right of Edward. Grant to him of the reversion. (Warranty.) Cons. 100 marks.

78/76/520

136. One week [6 Oct.] from Michaelmas. Henry Warde and Alice his wife quer.; Roger le Marshal of Oldberrow (*Ulbarewe*) and Alice his wife def. A messuage, 2 yardlands, and 6 a. of meadow in Lower Lemington (*Lemynton Hennemersh*). Right of Henry, as those which Henry and Alice had by gift of Roger and Alice. Remise and quitclaim, specifying Roger's heirs, to Henry and Alice and Henry's heirs. (Warranty.) Cons. 20 marks.

78/76/522

1373

137. One week [6 Oct.] from Michaelmas. (Made two weeks [26 June] from Trinity in the said year.) Thomas Frary of Down Ampney (*Dounameney*) and Alice his wife quer. by John Dymock (*Dymmok*) in Alice's place; John Bedale of Down Ampney and Juliana his wife def. Half of a messuage and of 3 yardlands in Down Ampney. Right of Thomas, as that which Thomas and Alice had by gift of John and Juliana. Remise and quitclaim, specifying Juliana's heirs, to Thomas and Alice and Thomas's heirs. (Warranty.) Cons. 10 marks.

78/76/523

48 Edward III

1374

138. Two weeks [11 June] from Trinity. John Roper (*Ropere*) of Yanworth (*Yaneworth*) and Agnes his wife quer. by John Stanburn in Agnes's place; Richard Whitchurch (*Whytchurche*) and Margaret his wife def. A messuage in Cirencester (*Cirencestre*). Right of John, as that which John and Agnes had by gift of Richard and Margaret. Remise and quitclaim, specifying Margaret's heirs, to John and Agnes and John's heirs. (Warranty.) Cons. 10 marks.

78/76/525

139. Two weeks [11 June] from Trinity. Mr. Alexander Neville (*Nevill*), Thomas Cheyney (*Cheyne*), William Cheyney, and John de Deddington (*Dadyngton*) quer.; John Cheyney and Margaret his wife def. The manor of Langar (*Langar*), NOTTS., the manor of Edmondthorpe (*Thorpe Edmere*), LEICS., and the manor of Oxenton (*Oxendon*), GLOS. Grant to Mr. Alexander, Thomas, William, and John de Deddington and remise and quitclaim to them and Mr. Alexander's heirs of whatever John Cheyney and Margaret had in the said manors for term of Margaret's life. (Warranty.) Cons. 300 marks. *Labelled* Notingh', Leyc', Glouc'.

288/50/757

140. One week [1 July] from St. John the Baptist. John Clifford the elder quer.; James Clifford and Margaret his wife def. The manor of Stowell (*Stowelle*). Right of John. Render to him. (Warranty, specifying Margaret's heirs.) Cons. 200 marks.

78/77/526

141. One week [6 Oct.] from Michaelmas. Richard Rook of Westminster (*Westm'*) quer.; John Fowke (*Fouk*) of Long Marston (*Dryemerston*) and Joan his wife def. Two messuages and 3 yardlands in Long Marston. Right of Richard by gift of John and Joan. Remise and quitclaim, specifying John's heirs, to Richard. (Warranty.) Cons. 10 marks.

78/76/524

1375

142. One week [20 Jan.] from Hilary. (Made one week from St. Martin in the said year [18 Nov. 1374].) Walter Oldland (*Oldeland*) and Margaret his wife quer.; Robert de Ketford and Robert atte Mead (*Mede*) def. Three messuages, 1 ploughland and 3 yardlands, and 16 a. of meadow in Berkeley (*Berkele*) and Cam (*Camme*). Right of Robert de Ketford, of which he and Robert atte Mead had a messuage, the ploughland,

1375

and 8 a. of meadow by gift of Walter and Margaret. For this, grant back and render to Walter and Margaret. To hold to them and Margaret's heirs. And grant to them and Margaret's heirs of the reversion of a messuage, 1½ yardlands, and 6 a. of meadow held by William Bicknor (*Bykenore*) and Agnes his wife for term of life and of a messuage, 1½ yardlands, and 2 a. of meadow held by John Bond and Edith his wife for term of life, of the inheritance of Robert de Ketford. [*Worn.*]

78/77/527

49 Edward III

1375

143. Two weeks [6 May] from Easter. William de Chesterton clerk and Peter de Woodmancote (*Wodmancote*) quer. by Robert de Ketford in William's place; Henry Placy and Joan his wife def. A messuage and a shop in Tewkesbury (*Teukesbury*) held by John Strensham (*Strengesham*) the elder and Alice his wife and Cristina their daughter for term of life. Right of Peter. Grant to William and Peter and Peter's heirs of the reversion, of Joan's inheritance. (Warranty.) Cons. 20 marks.

78/77/529

144. Two weeks [6 May] from Easter. Peter de Woodmancote (*Wodmancote*) and Richard Vynt clerk quer. by Robert de Ketford in Richard's place; Henry Leigh (*Leg'*) of Tewkesbury (*Teukesbury*) and Isabel his wife def. A messuage in Tewkesbury. Right of Peter. Render to him and Richard. To hold to Peter and Richard and Peter's heirs. (Warranty, specifying Isabel's heirs.) Cons. 20 marks.

78/77/530

145. Two weeks [6 May] from Easter. John Compton of Gloucester (*Gloucestr'*) quer.; John Scaward and Alice his wife def. A messuage in Gloucester. Right of John Compton by gift of John Scaward and Alice. Remise and quitclaim, specifying Alice's heirs, to John Compton. (Warranty.) Cons. 20 marks.

78/77/531

146. Two weeks [6 May] from Easter. John Anlep of Gloucester (*Gloucestr'*) quer.; William Wightfield (*Wyghtfeld*) and Agnes his wife def. A messuage in Gloucester. Grant to John. Remise and quitclaim to him of whatever William and Alice had in the messuage for term of Agnes's life. (Warranty.) Cons. 20 marks.

78/77/532

147. One week [24 June] from Trinity. (Made two weeks [6 May] from Easter in the said year.) Richard Lydbrook (*Loudbrok*) clerk and Henry Birch (*Burch*) quer.; Edward White and Joan his wife def. Two messuages, 30 a. of land, 4 a. of meadow, and 10*s*. rent and one third of a messuage, 10 a. of land, and 6 a. of meadow in Newland (*Newelonde in Foresta de Dene*). Right of Richard, of which Richard and Henry had the holdings [other than the one third] by gift of Edward and Joan. To hold to Richard and Henry and Richard's heirs. And grant to them and Richard's heirs of the reversion of the one third, held by Joan who was wife of Henry Prat for term of life, of the inheritance of Joan wife of Edward. (Warranty.) Cons. 100 marks.

78/77/533

1375

148. Two weeks [1 July] from Trinity. John Sparrow (*Sparwe*) and William his son quer. by John Stanborough (*Stanburgh*) in William's place; Alexander Chapman (*Chepman*) and Margery his wife def. Two messuages in Tetbury (*Tettebury*). Right of John, as those which John and William had by gift of Alexander and Margery. Remise and quitclaim, specifying Margery's heirs, to John and William and John's heirs. (Warranty.) Cons. 20 marks.

78/77/534(a)

149. Two weeks [13 Oct.] from Michaelmas. William Hayberare (*Heyberere*) and Simon Parker of Gloucester (*Gloucestre*) chaplain quer. by the said William in Simon's place; John Forthey and Juliana his wife def. Two messuages, a toft, 2 yardlands, 6 a. of land and ½ yardland, 6 a. of meadow, and 10*s.* rent in Charlton Kings (*Cherleton Regis*) and Naunton (*Newenton*) by Cheltenham (*Chiltenham*). Right of William. Render of the holdings to him and Simon. Grant to them of the rent with the homage and all the services of Robert atte Style from the holdings which he held from John and Juliana in the said townships. To hold to William and Simon and William's heirs. (Warranty, specifying Juliana's heirs.) Cons. 20 marks.

78/77/528

1376

150. One week [20 Jan.] from Hilary. (Made the morrow of St. Martin in the said year [12 Nov. 1375].) Richard Crese quer.; Stephen Clement of Queenhill (*Quenehull*) and Agnes his wife def. Two messuages, 2 tofts, 63 a. of land, and 1 a. of meadow in Alderton (*Aldryngton*) and Gretton (*Gretton*). Right of Richard, of which Richard had a messuage, 40 a. of land, and the meadow by gift of Stephen and Agnes. Remise and quitclaim, specifying Agnes's heirs, to Richard. And grant to Richard of the reversion of a messuage and 10 a. of land held by Henry Webb (*Webbe*), of 4 a. of land held by John Webb, of 2 a. of land held by Amice Bedewoman, of a croft and 4 a. of land held by John Smith (*Smyth*), of 2 a. of land held by Robert Hayward and Edith his wife, and of a toft and 1 a. of land held by Juliana Laverok and Sabina her sister, all in Alderton and held for term of life (Robert and Edith's for term of Edith's life), of Agnes's inheritance. (Warranty.) Cons. 100 marks.

78/77/534(b), formerly 78/77/538

50 Edward III

1376

151. One week [15 June] from Trinity. Thomas son of John Hard and Juliana his wife quer. by Richard Ivie guardian of Thomas and Juliana; John Hard and Margaret his wife def. Two messuages and 1 ploughland in Dymock (*Dymmok*). Grant and render to Thomas and Juliana. To hold to them and Thomas's heirs in tail, of John and Margaret and Margaret's heirs, paying during John's and Margaret's life 20*s.* a year, at Michaelmas and Easter, and to Margaret's heirs a rose a year at St. John the Baptist and doing service to the chief lords. (Warranty.) Contingent reversion to John and Margaret and Margaret's heirs. Cons. 100 marks. [*Worn.*]

78/77/539

[Richard Ivie is said to be in place of Thomas and Juliana only for winning (*ad lucrandum*), not for winning or losing (*ad lucrandum vel perdendum*), the usual phrase.]

1376

152. Two weeks [8 July] from St. John the Baptist. (Made two weeks from St. John the Baptist 49 Edward III [8 July 1375].) John de Dauntsey (*Daundeseye*) 'chivaler' quer.; Nicholas Waker def. Two thirds of the manor Whittington (*Whityngton*) and the advowson of two thirds of the church of the same manor, held by William Barndhurst and Alice his wife for term of Alice's life. Right of John. Grant to him of the reversion, of Nicholas's inheritance. Cons. 100 marks.

78/77/540

153. Two weeks [8 July] from St. John the Baptist. John Bromsgrove (*Bremesgrove*) of Murcot (*Morcote*) quer.; Walter Bromsgrove of Murcot def. Two messuages, 1 ploughland, 8 a. of meadow, pasture for 8 oxen, and 2*s*. 2*d*. rent in Childswickham (*Wykewane*) and Murcot. Right of John by Walter's gift. Remise and quitclaim to John. (Warranty.) Cons. 100 marks.

78/77/541

154. Two weeks [8 July] from St. John the Baptist. William Gille clerk quer.; John Blundel of Adlestrop (*Tatlesthrop*) and Margaret his wife def. Two messuages, 9 tofts, 7½ yardlands, 20½ a. of meadow, and 6 a. of pasture in Adlestrop. Right of William by gift of John and Margaret. Remise and quitclaim, specifying Margaret's heirs, to William. (Warranty.) Cons. 100 marks.

78/77/542

155. One week [6 Oct.] from Michaelmas. (Made the morrow [25 June] of St. John the Baptist in the said year.) William Purlewent and Katherine his wife quer. Amaury le Butler (*Botiller*) clerk def. The manor of Brawn (*la Brewerne*) by Gloucester (*Glouc'*). Grant and render to William and Katherine and their heirs in tail, of Amaury, paying a rose a year at St. John the Baptist and doing service to the chief lords. Contingent remainder to John le Butler of Tidenham (*Tudenham*) and his heirs in tail. Contingent reversion to Amaury. Cons. 100 marks. [*Worn.*]

78/77/536

156. Two weeks [13 Oct.] from Michaelmas. John White (*Whyte*) and Richard Ivie quer.; Andrew Hurley (*Herle*) and Juliana his wife def. The manor of Harescombe (*Harsecumb*), GLOS., and one third of the manor of Newbury (*Newebury*), BERKS. Grant and render to John and Richard. To hold during their lives, of Andrew and Juliana and Juliana's heirs, paying a rose a year at St. John the Baptist and doing service to the chief lords. Remainder to Matilda who was wife of Thomas Rouse (*Rous*) and her heirs by Thomas in tail. To hold as above. Contingent reversion to Andrew and Juliana and Juliana's heirs. Cons. 200 marks. *Labelled* Glouc', Berk'.

288/50/794

157. Morrow [12 Nov] of St. Martin. Robert de Kendal (*Kendale*) and Matilda his wife quer.; Andrew Hurley (*Herle*) and Juliana his wife def. The manor of Duntisbourne Rouse (*Dontesborne Rous*) except for 30 a. of wood in the same manor. Grant and render to Robert and Matilda. To hold during Matilda's life, of Andrew and Juliana, paying a rose a year at St. John the Baptist and doing service to the chief lords. Reversion to Andrew and Juliana and Juliana's heirs. Cons. 100 marks.

78/77/535

1376

158. One week [18 Nov.] from St. Martin. Roger Lestrange, Philip vicar of the church of Wellesbourne (*Wellesburne*), and William Offechurch clerk quer.; John Lestrange of Walton (*Walton*) and Mabel his wife def. Eight messuages, 4 tofts, 12 yardlands, 6 a. of meadow, and 6*s*. 8*d*. rent in Alkerton (*Alcrynton*), Balscott (*Balscote*), and Wroxton (*Wroxton*), OXON., a messuage, 4 yardlands, and 4 a. of meadow in Shenington (*Shenyndon*), GLOS., and 2 messuages, 5 tofts, 9 yardlands, and 14 a. of meadow in Evesham (*Evesham*), *Totebache*, Bradley (*Bradle*), and *Goldcote*, WORCS. Right of Philip. Remise and quitclaim, specifying John's heirs, to Roger, Philip, and William and Philip's heirs. Cons. 200 marks. *Labelled* Oxon', Glouc', Wygorn'.

288/50/796

159. One week [18 Nov.] from St. Martin. Katherine who was wife of Thomas de Berkeley (*Berkele*) of Berkeley quer.; John Newburgh (*Nyweborgh*) and Margaret his wife and John Barre and Avice his wife def. The manor of Tockington (*Tokynton*). Right of Katherine. Remise and quitclaim, specifying Margaret's and Avice's heirs, to her. (Warranty.) Cons. £100.

78/77/537

51 Edward III

1377

160. One week [9 Feb.] from the Purification. Thomas Adynet quer.; Robert Hammond (*Hamond*) and Alice his wife def. Five messuages, 9 tofts, 1 ploughland, 4 yardlands, 30 a., and one third of a yardland of land, 44 a. of meadow, 50 a. of pasture, 12 a. of wood, and 11*s*. 6*d*. rent in Dowdeswell (*Doudeswell*). Right of Thomas by gift of Robert and Alice. Remise and quitclaim, specifying Robert's heirs, to Thomas. (Warranty.) Cons. 200 marks.

78/77/543

161. One week [31 May] from Trinity. (Made the morrow [8 May] of Ascension in the said year. John Stanshawe quer.; Walter Wombourn (*Womborn*) and Joan his wife and Walter Avis (*Avyce*) and Matilda his wife def. A messuage, a toft, 1 ploughland, 10 a. of meadow, 10 a. of pasture, and 6 a. of wood in Siston (*Cyston*). Right of John. Remise and quitclaim, specifying Joan's and Matilda's heirs, to him. Cons. 100 marks.

78/77/544

162. One week [31 May] from Trinity. (Made the morrow [8 May] of Ascension in the said year. Nicholas Adams (*Adames*) chaplain and John Stanshawe quer.; Walter Wombourn (*Womborn*) and Joan his wife def. A messuage, 1 yardland, 10 a. of meadow, 4 a. of pasture, and 4 a. of wood in Old Sodbury (*Magna Sobbury*). Right of John, as those which John and Nicholas had by gift of Walter and Joan. Remise and quitclaim, specifying Joan's heirs, to John and Nicholas and John's heirs. (Warranty.) Cons. 20 marks.

78/77/545

1 Richard II

1377

163. One week [18 Nov.] from St. Martin. (Made two weeks from Trinity 51 Edw. III [7 June 1377].) Nicholas Adams (*Adames*) chaplain and Cradoc de Penho clerk quer.; John Stafford of Gloucester (*Gloucestr'*) 'cardemaker' and Petronilla his wife def. A messuage in Gloucester. Right of Nicholas, as that which Nicholas and Cradoc had by gift of John and Petronilla. Remise and quitclaim, specifying Petronilla's heirs, to Nicholas and Cradoc and Nicholas's heirs. (Warranty.) Cons. 10 marks.

78/78/6

164. One week [18 Nov.] from St. Martin. (Made two weeks from Trinity 51 Edw. III [7 June 1377].) John Burbage (*Burbache*) of Malmesbury (*Malmesbury*) and Elena his wife quer.; Henry Warner (*Warener*) of Charfield (*Charfeld*) and Isabel his wife def. A messuage in Tetbury (*Tettebury*). Right of Henry. For this, grant back and render by Henry and Isabel to John and Elena. To hold to them and John's heirs. (Warranty, specifying Henry's heirs.)

78/78/7

165. One week [18 Nov.] from St. Martin. (Made one week from Trinity 51 Edw. III [31 May 1377].) Robert vicar of the church of Overbury (*Overbury*) and Robert de Carrant (*Carent*) quer.; John Pullen (*Poleyn*) and Alice his wife def. Two messuages, a toft, and 20*s*. rent in Tewkesbury (*Teukesbury*) and Aston on Carrant (*Aston super Carent*), GLOS., and a messuage and 2 yardlands in Overbury, WORCS. Right of Robert de Carrant, as those which the same Robert and Robert the vicar had by gift of John and Alice. Remise and quitclaim, specifying Alice's heirs, to Robert and Robert and Robert de Carrant's heirs. (Warranty.) Cons. 100 marks. *Labelled* Glouc', Wygorn'.

289/52/5

1378

166. One month [16 May] from Easter. John Mayde quer.; Thomas Walters (*Waltres*) and Lucy his wife and Robert Skinner (*Skynnere*) and Emma his wife def. A messuage in Tetbury (*Tettebury*). Right of John by gift of Thomas, Lucy, Robert, and Emma. Remise and quitclaim, specifying Lucy's and Emma's heirs, to John. (Warranty.) Cons. 10 marks.

78/78/2

167. One month [16 May] from Easter. Robert de Carrant (*Carent*), Walter Galeys, Adam Apperley (*Appurle*), Thomas Cole, and William Scott (*Scot*) quer.; Richard Goose (*Gos*) of Tewkesbury (*Teukesbury*), and Isabel his wife def. Two messuages and 1 a. of land in Tewkesbury. Right of Adam, as those which Robert and the other quer. by gift of Richard and Isabel. Remise and quitclaim, specifying Isabel's heirs, to Robert and the other quer. To hold to them and Adam's heirs. (Warranty.) Cons. 20 marks.

78/78/3

168. One month [16 May] from Easter. Henry Borch clerk and Edward White (*Whyte*) quer.; John Joce of Newland (*Neulond*) and Isabel his wife def. Five messuages, 2 mills, 6 ploughlands, 36 a. of meadow, 60 a. of pasture, 46 a. of wood, and 45 marks rent in Newland, Staunton (*Staunton*), English Bicknor (*Englissh Bykenore*), and the township of

1378

St. Briavels (*de Sancto Briavello*). Right of Henry, as those which Henry and Edward had by gift of John and Isabel. For this, grant back and render to John and Isabel. To hold to them and their heirs in tail, of Henry and Edward, paying a rose a year at St. John the Baptist and doing service to the chief lords. Contingent reversion to Henry and Edward and Henry's heirs.

78/78/4

169. One month [16 May] from Easter. Robert Cheddar (*Cheddre*), William Cheddar of Bristol (*Bristoll'*) the elder, and Walter Laurence quer.; Richard de Acton knight and Richard de Callaughton (*Calweton*) def. Two messuages, 2 ploughlands and 1 yardland, 46 a. of meadow, 6 a. of wood, and 20 a. of pasture in Cote (*Cotes*) by Aust (*Aust*), Elberton (*Aylberton*), and Iron Acton (*Ireneacton*) and half of the manor of Aust. Right of Richard de Acton, of which Richard and Richard had a messuage, 1 ploughland and 1 yardland, 26 a. of meadow, 10 a. of pasture and the half of the manor by gift of Robert, William, and Walter. For this, grant back and render to Robert, William, and Walter. To hold to them and William's heirs. And Richard and Richard granted to Robert, William, and Walter the reversion of the other messuage, 1 ploughland, 20 a. of meadow, 6 a. of wood, and 10 a. of pasture in Iron Acton, held by Robert de Stinchcombe (*Stintescomb*) and Edith his wife for term of life, of the inheritance of Richard de Acton. To hold as above. (Warranty.) [*Worn*.]

78/78/5

170. Two weeks [27 June] from Trinity. Nicholas Hawley (*Haweleye*) of Childswickham (*Childeswykewane*) chaplain quer.; John Kembe of Childswickham and Agnes his wife def. Two messuages, 1 yardland, and 4 a. of meadow in Childswickham. Right of Nicholas by gift of John and Agnes. For this, grant back and render to Nicholas and Agnes. To hold to them and their heirs in tail. Contingent remainder to John's heirs.

78/78/1

[The return day, two weeks from Trinity 1 Richard II, fell in fact in the regnal year 2 Richard II, the regnal year beginning on 22 June. In 1377 Trinity fell on 24 May, so that two weeks from Trinity was before the end of Edward III's reign.]

2 Richard II

1379

171. One week [20 Jan.] from Hilary. Richard de Stafford 'chivaler' and Matilda his wife quer.; John de Withington (*Wytynton*) parson of the church of Naunton (*Newynton de la Wolde*) and Richard de Drayton parson of the church of Seckington (*Sekynton*), Warws., def. Half of the manor of Chipping Campden (*Caumpeden*) and half of the advowson of the chapel of the same manor. Right of John and Richard de Drayton by gift of Richard de Stafford. For this, grant and render to Richard de Stafford and Matilda. To hold to them and their heirs in tail male, of the king. Contingent remainder to the heirs of Richard de Stafford. Made by the king's order.

78/78/13, formerly 78/78/15

172. One week [20 Jan.] from Hilary. (Made one week from St. Martin in the said year [18 Nov. 1378].) John Priver and Katherine his wife quer.; Thomas Rodley (*Rodeley*) and Agnes his wife def. A messuage and 5 a. of land in Lydney (*Lydeney*). Right of John, as

1379

those which John and Katherine had by gift of Thomas and Agnes. To hold to John and Katherine and John's heirs. (Warranty, specifying Thomas's heirs.) Cons. 20 marks.

78/78/16, formerly 78/78/18

173. One week [20 Jan.] from Hilary. Ivo de Sandhurst quer.; Nicholas Porter and Margery his wife def. Three messuages, a toft, 28 a. of land, 7 a. of meadow, 2 a. of pasture, 3½ a. of wood, and 2s. rent in Sandhurst (*Sandhurst*). Right of Ivo. Render to him. (Warranty, specifying Margery's heirs.) Cons. 100 marks.

78/78/17, formerly 78/78/19

174. One week [20 Jan.] from Hilary. Roger Pirton (*Piryton*) quer.; Walter Browning (*Brounyng*) and Elizabeth his wife def. A messuage and 1 yardland in Churchdown (*Chircheton*). Right of Elizabeth, as those which Walter and Elizabeth had by Roger's gift. For this, grant back and render to Walter. To hold to Roger and his heirs in tail, of Walter and Elizabeth, paying a rose a year at St. John the Baptist and doing services to the chief lords. Contingent reversion to Walter and Elizabeth and Elizabeth's heirs.

78/78/18, formerly 78/78/20

175. Two weeks [27 Jan.] from Hilary. Elena daughter of John Draper of Gloucester (*Gloucestr'*) and Peter de Londe 'mercer' quer.; William Tyryngton and Joan his wife def. A messuage, 8 shops, and 2s. 5d. rent in Gloucester. Right of Elena, as those which Elena and Peter had by gift of William and Joan. Remise and quitclaim, specifying Joan's heirs, to Elena and Peter and Elena's heirs. (Warranty.) Cons. 100 marks.

78/78/14, formerly 78/78/16

176. Two weeks [27 Jan.] from Hilary. Thomas Maynston quer.; Edmund Toky and Joan his wife def. One third of the manor of Ruardean (*Ruardyn*). Grant to Thomas and render to him of whatever Edmund and Joan had therein for term of Joan's life. To hold to Thomas and his heirs during Joan's life. (Warranty.) Cons. 100 marks.

78/78/15, formerly 78/78/17

177. Two weeks [27 Jan.] from Hilary. Richard Micheldevere quer.; John Walden (*Waldene*) clerk def. Three messuages, 1 ploughland and 16½ a. of land, 5 a. of meadow, 8 a. of wood, and 11s. 8d. rent in Compton Abdale (*Magna Compton*) and Cassey Compton (*Parva Compton*). Right of Richard, of which he had a messuage, 1 ploughland, the meadow, the wood, and the rent by John's gift. For this, grant back and render to John. To hold during his life, of Richard, paying a rose a year at St. John the Baptist and doing service to the chief lords. Reversion to Richard. And John granted to Richard the reversion of a messuage and 1 a. of land held by Thomas atte Hill (*Hulle*) and Margery his wife for term of life, of a messuage and 7 a. of land held by John atte Hill and Alice his wife for term of life, of 6 a. of land held by John Hurrel (*Hurel*) and Margaret his wife for term of life, of 2 a. of land held by William Perkins (*Perkyns*) of Compton Abdale for term of life, and of ½ a. of land held by Walter de Marcle (*Marclee*) for term of life, all of John Walden's inheritance in the said townships. To hold as above.

78/78/11, formerly 78/78/13

1379

178. Two weeks [24 April] from Easter. William de Barwell (*Barewell*) quer.; Walter de Luddington (*Lodyngton*) of Alcester (*Alyncestre*) and Margery his wife def. A messuage, 1 ploughland, and 6 a. of meadow in Alscot (*Alscote*) and Preston on Stour (*Preston super Stoure*). Right of William by gift of Walter and Margery. Remise and quitclaim, specifying Margery's heirs, to William. (Warranty.) Cons. 100 marks.

78/78/10, formerly 78/78/12

179. Two weeks [24 April] from Easter. (Made two weeks [27 Jan.] from Hilary in the same year.) John Sargent (*Sergeaunt*) and Ralph Waleys quer.; Robert Mareys and Cristina his wife def. A toft, 11 a. of land, 16 a. of meadow, and 2 a. of wood in Tockington (*Tokyngton*). Right of John and Ralph. Render to them of the toft, the land, 12 a. of meadow, and the wood. To hold to John and Ralph and Ralph's heirs, paying to Robert and Cristina 13s. 4d. a year, at Easter, St. John the Baptist, Michaelmas, and Christmas, during the lives of Robert and Cristina, with right of distraint for non-payment, and rent-free after their death. And Robert and Cristina granted to John and Ralph the reversion of 4 a. of meadow held by Nicholas Oakley (*Akkeleye*) for term of life, of Christina's inheritance. To hold as above. (Warranty.) Cons. 20 marks. [*Worn.*]

78/78/12, formerly 78/78/14

180. Two weeks [19 June] from Trinity. Ralph Waleys quer.; Richard Clevedon (*Clyvedon*) and Agnes his wife def. The manor of Hinton (*Henton*) by Dyrham (*Durham*). Right of Ralph by gift of Richard and Agnes. Remise and quitclaim, specifying Agnes's heirs, to Ralph. (Warranty.) Cons. 100 marks.

78/78/8, formerly 78/78/10

181. Two weeks [19 June] from Trinity. Ralph Waleys and Peter Yeovilton (*Yevelton*) quer.; Richard Clevedon (*Clyvedon*) and Agnes his wife def. The manor of Sturden (*Stourdon*) and a mill in Barton Regis (*Bertona*) by Bristol (*Bristoll'*). Right of Ralph, as those which Ralph and Peter had by gift of Richard and Agnes. Remise and quitclaim, specifying Agnes's heirs, to Ralph and Peter and Ralph's heirs. (Warranty.) Cons. 200 marks.

78/78/9, formerly 78/78/11

3 Richard II

1379

182. Two weeks [8 July] from St. John the Baptist. Thomas de Broadwell (*Bradewell*) quer.; William Carter (*Cartere*) of Great Rissington (*Broderysyndon*) and Alice his wife def. A messuage, 1 ploughland, and 30s. rent in Great Rissington. Right of Thomas by gift of William and Alice. For this, grant back and render to William and Alice. To hold to them during their lives, of Thomas, paying a rose a year at St. John the Baptist and doing service to the chief lords. Reversion to Thomas. [*Worn.*]

78/78/20 (formerly 78/78/9)

183. Two weeks [13 Oct.] from Michaelmas. Edmund Blunt (*Blount*) quer.; Roger Marmion (*Marmyoun*) and Agnes his wife def. One acre of land in Bitton (*Button*). Right of Edmund by gift of Roger and Agnes. Remise and quitclaim, specifying Agnes's heirs, to Edmund. (Warranty.). Cons. 20s.

78/79/29

[Cf. *Berkeley Castle Mun.* ii, p. 842, E1/1/40 (counterpart).]

1379

184. Two weeks [13 Oct.] from Michaelmas. John Head (*Hede*) and Thomas Cumberworth quer.; William Griffith (*Griffyth*) and Amice his wife def. Five messuages, 2 shops, and 7*s.* rent in Gloucester (*Gloucestre*). Grant and render to John and Thomas. To hold to them and Thomas's heirs. (Warranty, specifying Amice's heirs.) Cons. 100 marks.

78/79/31

185. Morrow [3 Nov.] of All Souls. John Stockton (*Stoghton*) of Tewkesbury (*Teukesbury*) 'taverner' quer.; Thomas Conyng of Tewkesbury def. Four messuages and 16 shops in Tewkesbury. Right of John by Thomas's gift. (Warranty.) Cons. 100 marks.

78/79/27

186. Morrow [3 Nov.] of All Souls. John Childrey (*Chelrey*) clerk quer.; John de Arundel (*Darundell*) 'chivaler' and Eleanor his wife def. The manors of Woodchester (*Wydechestre*) and King's Stanley (*Kyngestanleye*). Right of John Childrey by gift of John de Arundel and Eleanor. For this, grant back and render to John de Arundel and Eleanor. To hold during John de Arundel's life. Remainder to his son John and Elizabeth his wife and their heirs in tail. Contingent remainder to John de Arundel's heirs.

78/79/30

187. Morrow [12 Nov.] of St. Martin. (Made one week from Trinity 2 Ric. II [12 June 1379].) Peter de Woodmancote (*Wodemancote*) clerk, Henry West, Richard Alderton (*Aldryngton*), William Chamber (*Chaumbre*), John Corse (*Cors*) chaplain and William Mansell (*Maunsel*) quer. by Richard de Welford (*Welneford*) in place of Peter, William, John, and William; Robert Underhill (*Undurhull*) and Juette his wife def. Half of the manor of Walton Cardiff (*Walton Keardyf*) held by Henry Greyndor (*Grendor*) and Joan his wife for term of Joan's life, of Juette's inheritance. Right of Henry West. Grant of the reversion on Joan's death to Peter and the other quer. and Henry's heirs. (Warranty.) Cons. 100 marks. [*Worn.*]

78/78/19 (formerly 78/78/8)

188. Morrow [12 Nov.] of St. Martin. William Hardhead (*Hardhed*) quer.; John Morris (*Morys*) of Aust (*Auste*) and Joan his wife def. A messuage and a moiety of 1 yardland in Aust. Right of William by gift of John and Joan. Remise and quitclaim, specifying Joan's heirs, to William. (Warranty.) Cons. 20 marks.

78/79/28

1380

189. Three weeks [15 April] from Easter. Elizabeth who was wife of Edward le Despenser knight quer.; John Dauntsey (*Daundeseye*) 'chivaler' def. Two thirds of the manor of Whittington (*Whityngton*) and the advowson of two thirds of the church of the same manor, held by William Barndhurst and Alice his wife for term of Alice's life, of John's inheritance. John granted the reversion to Elizabeth. To hold during her life. Reversion to Edward's son Thomas. Cons. 200 marks.

78/79/26

1380

190. Two weeks [3 June] from Trinity. Nicholas Poynter quer.; Walter Restot and Matilda his wife def. One acre of meadow in Bagendon (*Bagyngden*). Right of Nicholas by gift of Walter and Matilda. Remise and quitclaim, specifying Matilda's heirs, to Nicholas. (Warranty.) Cons. 20*s*.

78/78/21

191. Two weeks [3 June] from Trinity. Robert Playn and John Boys quer.; Walter Restot and Matilda his wife def. The manor of Bagendon (*Bagyngden*). Right of Robert, as that which Robert and John had by gift of Walter and Matilda. Remise and quitclaim, specifying Matilda's heirs, to Robert and John and Robert's heirs. (Warranty.) Cons. £100.

78/78/22

192. Two weeks [3 June] from Trinity. Richard Harborough (*Harbergh'*) chaplain, Richard Tirley (*Trilleye*) chaplain, and Henry Rose chaplain quer.; Peter de Evenlode and Katherine his wife def. The manor of Sezincote (*Shesnecote*) and the advowson of the church of the same manor. Right of Richard Harborough, as those which Richard, Richard, and Henry had by gift of Peter and Katherine. Remise and quitclaim, specifying Peter's heirs, to Richard, Richard, and Henry and Richard Harborough's heirs. (Warranty.) Cons. 200 marks.

78/78/23

193. Two weeks [3 June] from Trinity. William Briddesmere quer.; Walter Denyas and Margery his wife def. A messuage and 1 ploughland in Witcombe (*Wydecombe*), Great Bentham (*Magna Bentham*), Little Bentham (*Parva Bentham*), and Great Shurdington (*Magna Shurdyngton*). Right of William. Remise and quitclaim, specifying Margery's heirs, to him. (Warranty.) Cons. 100 marks.

78/78/24

194. Two weeks [3 June] from Trinity. Edmund Blunt (*Blount*) quer.; Thomas FitzNichol 'chivaler' and Margery his wife def. The manors of Filton (*Filton*) and Harry Stoke (*Stokehenry*) and the advowson of the church of Filton. Right of Edmund. Render to him. To hold of the chief lords, paying 18 marks a year, at St. John the Baptist, Michaelmas, Christmas, and the Annunciation, to Thomas and Margery and Margery's heirs, with right of distraint for non-payment. (Warranty.) Cons. £200.

78/78/25

4 Richard II

1380

195. Morrow [25 June] of St. John the Baptist. Thomas Bisley (*Biseley*) and John Hazleton (*Hasulton*) quer.; John Bisley and Margery his wife def. Six messuages, 5 shops, a toft, and 12s. rent in Gloucester (*Gloucestre*). Right of Thomas, as those which Thomas and John Hazleton had by gift of John Bisley and Margery. For this, grant back and render to John Bisley and Margery. To hold to them and their heirs in tail. Contingent remainder to Margery's heirs.

78/79/32

1380

196. Three weeks [20 Oct.] from Michaelmas. Richard Cook of Hambrook (*Hambrok*) and Henry Baker (*Bakere*) of Hambrook quer.; Richard Clevedon (*Clyvedon*) and Agnes his wife def. A messuage, 80 a. of land, 4 a. of meadow, 20 a. of pasture, and 4 a. of wood in Frenchay (*Fromshawe*). Right of Richard Cook by gift of Richard Clevedon and Agnes to Richard Cook and Henry. Remise and quitclaim, specifying Agnes's heirs, to Richard Cook and Henry and Richard Cook's heirs. (Warranty.) Cons. 100 marks.

78/79/34

197. Three weeks [20 Oct.] from Michaelmas. Thomas Prayers (*Preyers*) of Great Dorsington (*Magna Dersyngton*) quer.; Robert Villein (*Vyleyne*) and Isabel his wife def. A messuage, a mill, and half of 1 yardland and 1 a. of meadow in Great Rissington (*Magna Rysyngdon*). Right of Thomas by gift of Robert and Isabel. Remise and quitclaim, specifying Isabel's heirs, to Thomas. (Warranty.) Cons. 100 marks.

78/79/37

198. On month [27 Oct.] from Michaelmas. Robert Cheddar (*Cheddre*), William Cheddar the younger, Roger Seward, and William Draper clerk quer.; Richard Clevedon (*Clyvedon*) and Agnes his wife def. Eight messuages, 2 yardlands, and 20 a. of meadow in Sandford (*Sandford*) by Banwell (*Banewell*), SOM., and a messuage, a toft, 1 a. of land, 5 a. of pasture, and 22*s.* rent in Bristol (*Bristoll'*) and its suburb and the advowson of the church of St. Laurence, Bristol. Right of William Cheddar, as those which William, Robert, Roger, and William Draper had by gift of Richard and Agnes. Remise and quitclaim, specifying Agnes's heirs, to them and William Cheddar's heirs. (Warranty.) Cons. 100 marks. *Labelled* Somers', Bristoll'.

289/52/47

[Cf. *Som. Fines, 1347–99*, p. 198.]

199. Morrow [12 Nov.] of St. Martin. Walter Galeys quer.; Vincent de Alcester (*Alcestre*) and Joan his wife def. A messuage in Tewkesbury (*Teukesbury*). Right of Walter. For this, grant and render to Vincent and Joan. To hold to them and their heirs in tail. Contingent remainder to Joan's heirs.

78/79/35

1381

200. Two weeks [28 April] from Easter. (Made two weeks [27 Jan.] from Hilary in the said year.) John Anlep' of Gloucester (*Gloucestr'*) quer.; William Griffin (*Griffyn*) and Amice his wife def. Two shops in Gloucester. Right of John. Render to him. (Warranty, specifying Amice's heirs.) Cons. 20 marks.

78/79/33

201. Two weeks [28 April] from Easter. (Made one week from the Purification 1 Ric. II [9 Feb. 1378].) William Worfton quer.; Peter de Besilles def. The manor of Didmarton (*Dudemerton*) and the advowson of the church of the same manor, held by Thomas de Besilles for term of life, of Peter's inheritance. Right of William. Grant to him of the reversion. (Warranty.) Cons. 100 marks.

78/79/36

5 Richard II

1382

202. One week [20 Jan.] from Hilary. Walter Shipton (*Chipton*) quer.; Thomas Compton and Joan his wife def. Twelve shops, 2 tofts, 28*s.* 8*d.* rent and rent of 1 lb. of pepper in Gloucester (*Gloucestr'*) and the suburb of the same town. Right of Walter by gift of Thomas and Joan. Remise and quitclaim, specifying Joan's heirs, to Walter. (Warranty.) Cons. 100 marks.

78/79/40

[Cf. *Berkeley Castle Mun.* i, p. 467, A2/24/33 (copy).]

203. One week [20 Jan.] from Hilary. John Compton and Isabel his wife quer.; Thomas Compton and Joan his wife def. A messuage and a garden in Gloucester (*Gloucestr'*). Right of Thomas. For this, grant and render to John and Isabel. To hold to them during their lives, of Thomas and Joan and Thomas's heirs, paying a rose a year at St. John the Baptist and doing service to the chief lords. (Warranty.) Reversion to Thomas and Joan and Thomas's heirs.

78/79/41

204. Two weeks [20 April] from Easter. (Made one week [8 Feb.] from the Purification in the said year.) John Apperley (*Appurley*) and Margaret his wife quer.; William atte Nash (*Nassh*) and Elena his wife def. Half of the manor of Postlip (*Potteslepe*). Grant and render to John and Margaret of half of the half. To hold to them and their heirs in tail. And grant to them of the reversion of the other half of the half, held by Gerard Vaughan (*Vaghan*) for term of life, of Elena's inheritance. To hold as above. Contingent remainder to Margaret's heirs. (Warranty.) Cons. 100 marks.

78/79/39

205. One week [8 June] from Trinity. (Made the morrow [16 April] of Ascension in the said year.) William Chesterton (*Chesturton*), John Apperley (*Appurley*), and Henry West quer.; Henry Greyndor and Joan his wife def. The manor of Walton Cardiff (*Walton Keardyf*). Grant and render to William, John, and Henry West. To hold to them and Henry West's heirs during Joan's life, paying £34 a year to Henry Greyndor and Joan, at Michaelmas and Easter, with right of distraint for non-payment, and after Joan's death rent-free. (Warranty.) Cons. £100.

78/79/38

[The *habendum* clause appears to limit the tenure to Joan's lifetime, but the clauses relating to the rent indicate that the tenure was not so limited. The warranty is by Henry Greyndor and Joan alone, with no mention of heirs.]

206. One week [8 June] from Trinity. (Made the morrow [16 April] of Ascension in the said year.) Thomas Cadel quer.; Robert Forstal and Isabel his wife def. A messuage, 30 a. of land, and 2 a. of meadow in Framilode (*Frameloode*). Right of Thomas by gift of Robert and Isabel. Remise and quitclaim, specifying Isabel's heirs, to Thomas. (Warranty.) Cons. 20 marks.

78/79/42

207. One week [8 June] from Trinity. (Made the morrow [16 April] of Ascension in the said year.) William Wellfed (*Welifed'*) of Tetbury (*Tettebury*) quer.; Robert Woodruff (*Woderove*) and Matilda his wife def. A messuage, 20 a. of land, 1 a. and 1 rod of

1382

meadow, and 4*s*. rent in Tetbury and Charlton (*Cherleton*) by Beverston (*Beverston*). Right of William by gift of Robert and Matilda. Remise and quitclaim, specifying Matilda's heirs, to William. (Warranty.) Cons. 20 marks.

78/79/43

208. Two weeks [15 June] from Trinity. (Made the morrow [16 April] of Ascension in the said year.) Thomas Cole quer.; Richard Goose (*Goos*) of Tewkesbury (*Teukesbury*) and Isabel his wife def. A messuage in Tewkesbury. Right of Thomas. Render to him. (Warranty, specifying Isabel's heirs.) Cons. 10 marks.

78/79/44

209. One week [18 Nov.] from St. Martin. Thomas de Bridge (*Brugge*) and Elizabeth his wife quer.; Roger Dore and Joan his wife, def. A messuage, 3 a. of meadow, 60*s*. rent, and half of 1 ploughland in Lea (*Lee*), and the bailiwick of the forest of Dean (*forestaria de Dene*), GLOS., and 2 a. of meadow, 20*s*. rent, and half of 1 ploughland in Walton (*Walton*) and Lea, HEREFS. Grant and render to Thomas and Elizabeth. To hold to them and Thomas's heirs in tail. Contingent remainder to Richard de Burley 'chivaler'. (Warranty, specifying Joan's heirs.) Cons. 100 marks. *Labelled* Glouc', Hereford'.

289/53/58

6 Richard II

1382

210. Morrow [25 June] of St. John the Baptist. John de la Mare knight, William de Fulbourn (*Fulburn*) clerk, Thomas Catewy, and John Lucy quer.; Richard de Seymour (*de Sancto Mauro*) knight def. The manor of Meysey Hampton (*Hampton Meysy*). Right of John de la Mare, as that which John, William, Thomas, and John had by Richard's gift. Remise and quitclaim to John, William, Thomas, and John and John de la Mare's heirs. (Warranty.) Cons. 200 marks.

78/79/49

211. One week [6 Oct.] from Michaelmas. (Made one week from St. John the Baptist 3 Ric. II [1 July 1379].) John Adams quer.; John Dengard the younger and Alice his wife def. A messuage and 18 a. of land in Wick Rissington (*Wykerysendon*) by Stow-on-the-Wold (*Stowe*). Right of John Adams by gift of John Dengard and Alice. Remise and quitclaim, specifying Alice's heirs, to John Adams. (Warranty.) Cons. 20 marks.

78/79/46

212. One week [6 Oct.] from Michaelmas. (Made two weeks from Easter 5 Ric. II [20 April 1382].) Thomas Edmund of Gloucester (*Gloucestr'*) 'dier' and Agatha his wife quer.; Richard son of Walter Underhill (*Underhull*) of Longdon (*Langedon*) and Joan his wife def. A messuage and 2*s*. 6*d*. rent in Gloucester and the suburb of Gloucester. Right of Thomas, as those which Thomas and Agatha had by gift of Richard and Joan. To hold to Thomas and Agatha and Thomas's heirs. (Warranty, specifying Joan's heirs.) Cons. £20.

78/80/51

1382

213. One month [27 Oct.] from Michaelmas. John Harper (*Harpour*) and Juliana his wife quer.; Richard atte Mill (*Mulle*) and Thomas atte Mill def. Three messuages, 60 a. of land, 10 a. of wood, and half of a messuage in Littledean (*Parva Dene*). Right of Richard, as those which Richard and Thomas had by gift of John and Juliana. Remise and quitclaim, specifying Juliana's heirs, to Richard and Thomas and Richard's heirs. (Warranty.) Cons. 40 marks.

78/79/48

214. One month [27 Oct.] from Michaelmas. Richard Wotton quer.; Thomas Lovecock (*Lovecok*) and Cecily his wife def. Three messuages and 2 a. of land in Tewkesbury (*Teukesbury*) and Southwick (*Southwyk*). Right of Richard by gift of Thomas and Cecily. (Warranty, specifying Cecily's heirs.) Cons. 20 marks.

78/79/50

215. One week [18 Nov.] from St. Martin. William Brayn of Newnham (*Newenham*) quer.; John son of John le Fletcher (*Flecchere*) of Ley (*la Lee*) and Joan his wife def. Half of 1 ploughland and of a fishery in the water of Severn (*aqua Sabrine*) called Hedesrewe in Rodley (*Rodele*). Right of William by gift of John and Joan. (Warranty, specifying Joan's heirs.) Cons. 20 marks.

78/79/47

1383

216. Two weeks [31 May] from Trinity. Thomas Cadel (*Cadul*) of Framilode (*Fromlode*) quer.; Robert Forstal (*Forestall'*) and Isabel his wife def. Seventy-five acres of land and 5 a. of meadow in Fretherne (*Frethorne*). Right of Thomas. Remise and quitclaim, specifying Robert's heirs, to Thomas. (Warranty.) Cons. 20 marks.

78/79/45

7 Richard II

1383

217. Morrow [12 Nov.] of St. Martin. (Made the morrow [25 June] of St. John the Baptist in the said year.) William Hayberare (*Heyberer*), John Head (*Hede*), and Simon Parker chaplain quer.; Edward St. John (*Seint Johan*) of Stopham (*Stopham*) 'chivaler' and Joan his wife def. The manor of Haresfield (*Harsefeld*) which was Matthew FitzHerbert (*fitz Herberd*)'s in Haresfield, except 1 a. of land in the same manor. Right of William, John, and Simon. Render to them, except for 20*s.* rent in the same manor. And grant to William, John, and Simon of the same rent together with the homage and all the services of John Stanshawe and Isabel his wife from all the tenements which they held of Edward and Joan in the said manor. To hold of the king, paying to Edward and Joan £11 a year during Edward's life and to Joan after Edward's death £10 a year during her life, with right of distraint in the manor for non-payment. (Warranty.) Cons. £200. Made by the king's order.

78/80/52

1384

218. One week [12 June] from Trinity. (Made the morrow of St. John the Baptist 6 Ric. II [25 June 1382].) Thomas Adynet quer.; William Naylor (*Naylere*) of Burford (*Burford*) and Matilda his wife def. Three tofts, a dovecot, 1 ploughland, 2 yardlands, and 2 a. of land, and 6 a. of meadow in Notgrove (*Nategrave*). Right of Thomas, of which he had 2 tofts, the dovecot, the ploughland and 2 a. of land, and the meadow by gift of William and Matilda. Remise and quitclaim, specifying Matilda's heirs, to Thomas. And grant to Thomas of the reversion of a toft and 2 yardlands held by Alice who was wife of Richard Warde and John Warde for term of life, of Matilda's inheritance. (Warranty.) Cons. 100 marks.

78/80/53

8 Richard II

1384

219. One week [1 July] from St. John the Baptist. John Banbury (*Bannebury*) and Cristina his wife quer.; John Perry (*Pyrye*) def. Thirteen messuages, 1 yardland, 2 a. of meadow, and a fishery in the water of Severn (*aqua Sabrine*) in Longney (*Longgeneye*). Right of John Banbury. Render to him and Cristina. To hold to them and John Banbury's heirs. (Warranty.) Cons. 100 marks.

78/80/58

220. One week [6 Oct.] from Michaelmas. (Made one week from St. Martin 6 Ric. II [18 Nov. 1382].) Gilbert Denis (*Deneys*) and Margaret his wife quer.; William Denis and Robert Daldene def. The manors of Alveston (*Alveston)*, Earthcott (*Erdecote*), and Siston (*Ciston*) and the hundred of Langley (*Langele*). As to the manors of Alveston and Earthcott and the hundred, right of William and Robert, and as to the manor of Siston, right of William, of which they had one third of the manors of Alveston and Earthcott and of the hundred by gift of Gilbert and Margaret. To hold of the king. And grant of the reversion of the manor of Siston and two thirds of the manors of Alveston and Earthcott and of the hundred, held by William Cannings (*Canyngns*) as a free tenement by grant of William Cheddar (*Cheddre*) the elder and John Cannings the younger by virtue of a recognizance made to them before Walter Frampton (*Frompton*) late mayor of the staple of the town of Bristol (*Bristoll'*) by William Corbet, brother of the said Margaret whose heir she is, of £320 until that sum with damages and expenses be fully satisfied, of Margaret's inheritance, the reversion becoming effective on the satisfaction of the debt, sc. the two thirds to William and Robert and their heirs [*unspecified*] and the manor of Siston to William and Robert and William's heirs. To hold the two thirds of the king and the manor of Siston of the chief lords. (Warranty.) Cons. 200 marks. Made as to Alveston, Earthcott, and the hundred by the king's order. [*Worn.*]

78/80/57

1385

221. Two weeks [27 Jan.] from Hilary. Walter Wellfed (*Welifed*) burgess of the town of Gloucester (*Gloucestr'*) quer.; Robert Scotard' citizen of London (*London'*) and Cristiana his wife def. Four messuages in Gloucester and the suburb of the same town. Right of Walter. Remise and quitclaim, specifying Cristiana's heirs, to Walter. Cons. £200.

78/80/56

1385

222. Two weeks [16 April] from Easter. (Made one week [20 Jan.] from Hilary in the said year.) William Thurning (*Thernyng*), Robert Isham, Robert Hemington (*Hemyngton*) and John de Aldwinkle (*Aldewyncle*) quer.; Henry Green (*Grene*) knight and Matilda his wife def. The manor of Grately (*Gratelee*), HANTS., the manor of Buckworth (*Bukworth*), HUNTS., half of the manors of Taynton (*Teyngton*) and Kilcot (*Kyldecote*), GLOS., and half of the manor of Market Lavington (*Lavynton*), WILTS. Right of Robert Isham, of which the same Robert, William, Robert Hemington, and John had the manor of Grately and the halves by gift of Henry and Matilda. For this, grant back and render to Henry and Matilda. To hold to them and their heirs in tail. And grant to them and their said heirs of the reversion of the manor of Buckworth, held by Joan who was wife of Thomas Mauduit (*Mauduyt*) for term of life, of Robert Isham's inheritance. To hold as above. Contingent remainder to Matilda's heirs. *Labelled* Sutht', Hunt', Glouc', Wiltes'.

289/54/120

[Cf. *Wilts. Fines, 1377–1509*, pp. 15–16, no. 74. For the identity of Lavington, *V.C.H. Wilts.* x. 94.]

223. Three weeks [23 April] from Easter. Robert de Charlton (*Cherlton*), Richard de Charlton, and John Weston quer.; Robert Oughtred and Joan his wife def. Two messuages, 3 tofts, 1 ploughland, 3 a. of meadow, 12*d*. rent, and half of a messuage and a garden in Avening (*Avenyngge*) and Minchinhampton (*Munchenehampton*). Right of Robert de Charlton. Render to him and Richard and John. To hold to them and Robert de Charlton's heirs. (Warranty, specifying Joan's heirs.) Cons. 100 marks.

78/80/54

224. Three weeks [23 April] from Easter. Robert de Charlton (*Cherlton*), Henry Warner of Charfield (*Charefeld*), and William Smalcombe the elder quer.; Robert Oughtred and Joan his wife def. Half of 2 tofts, 60 a. of land, and 6 a. of meadow in Beverston (*Beverston*). Right of Robert de Charlton. Render to him and Henry and William. To hold to them and Robert de Charlton's heirs. (Warranty, specifying Joan's heirs.) Cons. £20.

78/80/55

9 Richard II

1385

225. Morrow [3 Nov.] of All Souls. William de Wykeham bishop of Winchester (*Wynton*), William Walworth (*Walleworth*) knight, John de Buckingham (*Bukyngham*) clerk, John de Campden (*Campeden*) clerk, and Robert de Charlton (*Cherleton*) quer.; Maurice Russell son and heir of Ralph Russell def. Rent of £10 issuing from the manor of Aust (*Auste*). Grant of the rent, to be paid every year during the life of Maurice's wife Isabel, at Easter and Michaelmas, at Maurice's hands, to the bishop, William, John, John, and Robert and Robert de Buckingham's heirs, with right of distraint for non-payment. Cons. 100 marks.

78/80/66

226. One week [18 Nov.] from St. Martin. William Greville (*Grevel*) of Campden (*Caumpedene*) and John his son quer.; Walter Brown (*Broun*) and Margaret his wife def. The manor of Lasborough (*Lassebergh'*) and the advowson of the church of Lasborough. Right of William, as those which William and John had by gift of Walter and Margaret.

1385

Remise and quitclaim, specifying Margaret's heirs, to William and John and William's heirs. (Warranty.) Cons. 100 marks.

78/80/65

1386

227. Two weeks [6 May] from Easter. John Webb (*Webbe*) of Tockington (*Tokyngton*) quer.; Thomas Alkeleye and Matilda his wife def. A messuage, 1 yardland, and 10 a. of meadow in Tockington. Right of John. Remise and quitclaim, specifying Matilda's heirs, to him. (Warranty.) Cons. 20 marks.

78/80/60

228. Three weeks [13 May] from Easter. John Davy vicar of the church of Diddlebury (*Dodelbury*) and Walter de Whittingslow (*Whittyngeslowe*) chaplain quer.; Richard de Chelmick (*Chelmeswick*) and Margaret his wife def. The manor of Stantway (*Steyntewey*) and 8 yardlands and 60*s.* rent in Arlingham (*Erlyngham*) and Slimbridge (*Slymbrigge*). Right of Walter, as those which Walter and John had by gift of Richard and Margaret. Remise and quitclaim, specifying Margaret's heirs, to John and Walter and Walter's heirs. (Warranty.) Cons. 200 marks.

78/80/62

229. One month [20 May] from Easter. John Cassy, Walter Perham, Richard Harborough (*Harbergh*) parson of the church of Wolston (*Wolston*), and Richard Tirley (*Trilley*) chaplain quer.; Edmund Toky of Gloucester (*Gloucestr'*) and Joan his wife def. A messuage, a toft, 1 ploughland, and 13 a. of meadow in Wightfield (*Wyghtfeld*) and Apperley (*Appurley*). Right of John, as those which John, Walter, Richard, and Richard had by gift of Edmund and Joan. Remise and quitclaim, specifying Joan's heirs, to John, Walter, Richard, and Richard and John's heirs. (Warranty.) Cons. 100 marks.

78/80/63

230. One month [20 May] from Easter. Philip Rodborough (*Rodberwe*) quer.; James de Charlton (*Charleton*) of Tibberton (*Tyburton*) and Agnes his wife and William Pirk of Tibberton and Alice his wife def. A messuage and 30 a. of land in Stroud (*Strode*). Right of Philip. Remise and quitclaim, specifying Agnes's and Alice's heirs, to Philip. (Warranty.) Cons. 20 marks.

78/80/64

231. One month [20 May] from Easter. John Walour of Gloucester (*Gloucestr'*) quer.; Thomas Paty of Gloucester and Agnes his wife def. Two messuages and 5 shops in the suburb of the town of Gloucester. Right of John. Remise and quitclaim, specifying Agnes's heirs, to John. (Warranty.) Cons. £20.

78/80/67

232. Morrow [1 June] of Ascension. John Ponger quer.; John atte Wood (*Wode*) def. The manor of Eycot (*Eycote*). Right of John atte Wood by gift of John Ponger. For this, grant back and render to John Ponger. (Warranty.)

78/80/61

1386

233. One week [24 June] from Trinity. John Didmarton (*Dodmerton*) chaplain, William Plant (*Plonte*) chaplain, John Sheet (*Sheote*), and William Ricardes quer.; Robert Chamberlain (*Chaumberlayn*) of Tortworth (*Torteworth*) and Edith his wife def. Five messuages, 2 tofts, 1½ yardland and 87½ a. of land, 10 a. of meadow, 2 a. of pasture, 16½ a. of wood, and 3*s*. 8*d*. rent in Olveston (*Olveston*). Right of William Plant. Remise and quitclaim, specifying Edith's heirs, to John, William, John, and William and William Plant's heirs. (Warranty.) Cons. 200 marks.

78/80/59

[For the date of this fine see note to no. 234, below.]

234. One week [24 June] from Trinity. John Ponger quer.; Thomas de Beerton of Eycot (*Eycote*) def. The manor of Eycot, GLOS., and 2 messuages, 2 ploughlands, 80 a. of meadow, and 10 a. of wood in Purton (*Puriton*), WILTS. Right of Thomas by John's gift. For this, grant back and render to John. (Warranty.) *Labelled* Glouc', Wiltes'.

289/54/146

[Cf. *Wilts. Fines, 1377–1509*, p. 19, no. 90. The return day, the octave of Trinity 9 Richard II, fell in fact in the regnal year 10 Richard II, the regnal year beginning on 22 June.]

10 Richard II

1386

235. One week [1 July] from St. John the Baptist. John Ponger quer.; Richard de Norton and Juliana his wife def. The manor of Eycot (*Eycote*), GLOS., and 2 messuages, 2 ploughlands, 80 a. of meadow, and 10 a. of wood in Purton (*Puriton*), WILTS. Right of Juliana, as those which Richard and Juliana had by John's gift. For this, grant back and render to John. (Warranty.) *Labelled* Glouc', Wiltes'.

289/54/148

[Cf. *Wilts. Fines, 1377–1509*, p. 19, no. 92.]

236. One week [1 July] from St. John the Baptist. Ralph Waleys and John Sargent (*Sergeaunt*) quer.; Robert Chamberlain (*Chaumberleyn*) of Tortworth (*Torteworth*) and Edith his wife def. A toft, 16 a. of land, 16 a. of meadow, and 2 a. of wood in Tockington (*Tokynton*). Right of Ralph. Remise and quitclaim (specifying Edith's heirs) to Ralph and John and Ralph's heirs. (Warranty.) Cons. £20.

78/81/77

237. One week [6 Oct.] from Michaelmas. (Made two weeks from Easter 49 Edw. III [6 May 1375]. Robert Cockrup (*Cokthorp'*) vicar of the church of Coln St. Aldwyn (*Colun Aylwyn*) and John Tanner chaplain quer.; John Tanner of Berkhampstead (*Berkhamstede*) and Agnes his wife def. Half of a messuage and 12 a. of land in Fairford (*Fayreford*) held by John Campden (*Campeden'*) and Emma his wife for term of Emma's life, of Agnes's inheritance. Right of John Tanner chaplain. Grant of the reversion to Robert and John Tanner chaplain and that John's heirs. (Warranty). Cons. 20 marks. [*Worn.*]

78/80/71

238. Two weeks [13 Oct.] from Michaelmas. Thomas de Berkeley (*Barkeley*) knight, Ralph Waleys, John Babington (*Babyngton*), and John Chese quer.; John Weston of Ingst (*Inste*) and Margaret his wife def. Eight messsuages, 5 ploughlands, 40 a. of

1386

meadow, 20 a. of pasture, and 12 a. of wood in Olveston (*Olveston*), Winterbourne (*Wynturbourne*), Ingst, Henbury (*Hembury*), Earthcott (*Erdecote*), and Alveston (*Alveston*). Right of Ralph. Render to Ralph, Thomas, John, and John. To hold to them and Ralph's heirs. (Warranty, specifying John Weston's heirs.)

78/80/68

239. Two weeks [10 Oct.] from Michaelmas. Edith who was wife of John de Thorndon, Nicholas de Thorndon, and Robert de Charlton quer.; Walter Tandy clerk and Thomas Bruet clerk def. The manor of Tetbury Upton (*Upton*) by Avening (*Avenyngge*), 12 messuages, 9 tofts, 21 yardlands, and 10s. rent in Upton, Tetbury (*Tettebury*), and Doughton (*Doughton*). Right of Thomas, as those which Thomas and Walter had by gift of Edith, John, Nicholas, and Robert. For this, grant and render to Edith. To hold during her life. Remainder to Robert and Katherine his wife during their lives. Remainder to Walter son of Robert and Katherine during Nicholas's life. Remainder on Nicholas's death to Edith's heirs in tail. Contingent remainder to Robert's heirs.

78/80/69

240. Two weeks [10 Oct.] from Michaelmas. Thomas de Bridge (*Brugge*) quer.; John Caneros and Margery his wife def. Rent of 10s. in Parton (*Parton*). Right of Thomas by gift of John and Margery. Remise and quitclaim, specifying Margery's heirs, to Thomas. (Warranty.) Cons. 10 marks.

78/80/72

241. Two weeks [10 Oct.] from Michaelmas. William Greville (*Grevel*) of Chipping Campden (*Chepyng Caumpedene*) quer.; Walter Perham and Matilda his wife def. A messuage, 2 ploughlands, and 24 a. of meadow in Sezincote (*Shesencote*). Right of William by gift of Walter and Matilda. Remise and quitclaim, specifying Matilda's heirs, to William. Cons. 100 marks.

78/80/73

1387

242. Two weeks [21 April] from Easter. John Herdman chaplain, Thomas Gamage, and Philip Hook quer.; William Watkins (*Watkyns*) and Elizabeth his wife def. A messuage, a toft, 1 ploughland and 11 a. of land, 14 a. of meadow, 20 a. of wood, and 40s. rent in Ley (*Leye*) and Boseley (*Boseleye*). Right of John. Remise and quitclaim, specifying Elizabeth's heirs, to John of the messuage, the ploughland, 13 a. of meadow, and the rent. For this, John, Thomas, and Philip granted and rendered to William and Elizabeth the residue, sc. the toft, 11 a. of land, and 1 a. of meadow. To hold during the lives of William and Elizabeth, of John, Thomas, and Philip and John's heirs, paying a rose a year at St. John the Baptist and doing service to the chief lords. Reversion to John, Thomas, and Philip and John's heirs. [*Worn.*]

78/80/74

[The 20 a. of wood included in the initial description of the holding are mentioned neither in what was remised and quitclaimed to John nor in what was granted and rendered to William and Elizabeth.]

1387

243. Three weeks [28 April] from Easter. Nicholas de Apperley (*Appurleye*) quer.; John Chapman of Prestbury (*Prestbury*) and Alice his wife and John Upcote and Isabel his wife def. Two thirds of a messuage, 40 a. of land, 8 a. of meadow, and 15*s.* rent in Corse (*Cors*) and Hasfield (*Hasfeld*) and of the bailiwick of keeping the wood of the abbot of Westminster (*Westmonasterii*) in the chase of Corse. Right of Nicholas by gift of John and Alice and John and Isabel. (Warranty, specifying Alice's and Isabel's heirs.) Cons. £20.

78/80/75

244. One month [5 May] from Easter. Nicholas Poynter and William Boughton (*Boueton*) clerk quer.; Thomas Shogghe and Matilda his wife def. A messuage and 4 yardlands in North Cerney (*North Sarneye*) and Woodmancote (*Wodemancote*). Right of Nicholas, as those which Nicholas and William had by gift of Thomas and Matilda. To hold to Nicholas and William and Nicholas's heirs. (Warranty, specifying Matilda's heirs.) Cons. £20.

78/81/76

245. Morrow [17 May] of Ascension. Richard Nash (*Nasshe*) and Hugh Haresfield (*Haresfeld*) quer.; John Bromwich (*Bromwiche*) knight and Katherine his wife def. The manors of Credenhill (*Credenhull*) and Eaton Tregose (*Eton Tregoos)* and the advowson of the chapel of Eaton (except the advowson of the church of Credenhill in the said manor of Credenhill), HEREFS.; and the manor of Bromsberrow (*Brymmesbergh'*) and the advowson of the church of Bromsberrow, GLOS. Right of Richard, as those which Richard and Hugh had by gift of John and Katherine. For this, grant back and render to John and Katherine. To hold to them and their heirs in tail. Contingent remainder to John's heirs. *Labelled* Hereford', Glouc'.

289/55/160

246. Two weeks [16 June] from Trinity. Philip Hook (*Hoke*) quer.; Walter de Thurlocushope and Joan his wife def. A toft and 12 a. of land in Littledean (*Parva Dene*). Right of Philip by gift of Walter and Joan. (Warranty, specifying Joan's heirs.) Cons. 10 marks.

78/80/70

11 Richard II

1388

247. Three weeks [19 April] from Easter. (Made one week from St. John the Baptist in the said year [1 July 1387].) Richard Ryhall (*Ruyhale*) the younger and Elizabeth his wife quer.; Roger Northwood (*Northwode*) 'chivaler' and Alice his wife def. One third of two thirds and one third of one third of the manor of Dymock (*Dymmok*). Roger and Alice granted and rendered to Richard and Elizabeth the one third of the two thirds. To hold to Richard and Elizabeth and their heirs in tail. And Roger and Alice granted to Richard and Elizabeth the reversion of the one third of the one third, held in dower by Margaret who was wife of Thomas Grandison (*Graunson*) knight, of Alice's inheritance. To hold as above. Contingent remainder to Richard's heirs. (Warranty.) Cons. £100. [*Stained.*]

78/81/78

1388

248. One month [26 April] from Easter. Walter Wheeler (*Whelere*) of Hempstead (*Heyhamstede*) by Gloucester (*Gloucestre*) quer.; Walter Oadby (*Oudeby*) and Margery his wife def. A shop in Gloucester. Right of Walter Wheeler. Remise and quitclaim (specifying Margery's heirs) to him. (Warranty.) Cons. 10 marks.

78/81/79

249. One week [31 May] from Trinity. Edmund Love and Thomas Crump (*Crompe*) quer.; Richard de Marden (*Maurdyn*) and Edith his wife def. The manor of Little Sodbury (*Parva Sobbury*) and the advowson of the church of the same manor, GLOS.; and the manor of Great Durnford (*Magna Derneford*) and 6 messuages, 3 ploughlands, 10 a. of meadow, and 42*s.* 6*d.* rent in Great Woodford (*Magna Wodeford*) and Stratford sub Castle (*Stratford*) by Old Sarum (*Vetus Sar'*) and the bailiwick of the bedelry of the hundred of Underditch (*Wonderdich*), WILTS. Right of Thomas. Render to Thomas and Edmund. To hold to Edmund and Thomas and Thomas's heirs. (Warranty, specifying Edith's heirs.) Cons. 200 marks. *Labelled* Glouc', Wiltes'.

289/55/175

[Cf. *Wilts. Fines, 1377–1509*, p. 23, no. 112.]

12 Richard II

1388

250. Morrow [25 June] of St. John the Baptist. (Made two weeks from Easter 11 Ric. II [12 April 1388].) Thomas Brooke (*Broke*) knight and Joan his wife quer.; Ralph Percival (*Perseval*) and Henry Bokerell (*Bokerel*) def. The manor of Avill (*Avele*) by Dunster (*Dunsterre*) and 31 messuages, a mill, 8 ploughlands, 160 a. of meadow, 200 a. of pasture, 10 a. of wood, and 70*s.* rent in Huntspill (*Honyspull*), Alston Sutton (*Alleston*), Lympsham (*Lymplesham*), Cheddar (*Cheddre*), Axbridge (*Axebrigge*), Cocklake (*Cokelake*), Clewer (*Clywere*), Wedmore (*Wedmore*), Nyland (*Nye*), Sandford (*Sandford*), Max Mill (*Makkesmulle*), Winscombe (*Wynscombe*), Winterhead (*Wyntred*), Barton (*Barton*), Woodborough (*Wodeburgh*), Compton Bishop (*Compton Epsicopi*), Draycott (*Draycote*), Bruton (*Brutton*), Rolstone (*Rolleston*), and Rowberrow (*Rouberugh*), and the advowson of the chantry of St. Mary in the church of St. Andrew of Cheddar, SOM.; and the manor of Down Hatherley (*Dounhatherley*), GLOS. Grant and render to Ralph and Henry, with the homages and all services of the abbot of St. Augustine's, Bristol, and his successors, John Warren (*Waryn*) parson of the church of Cheddar, and Isabel Cripps (*Crips*). To hold to Ralph and Henry and Ralph's heirs. (Warranty, specifying Joan's heirs.) Cons £500. *Labelled* Somers', Glouc'.

289/55/177

[Cf. *Som. Fines, 1347–99*, p. 204.]

1389

251. Morrow [3 Feb.] of the Purification. John Adynet of Burford (*Burford*) quer.; John Pindrup (*Pyndrop*) and Agnes his wife def. A messuage in Northleach (*Northlech*). Right of John Adynet. Remise and quitclaim (specifying Agnes's heirs) to him. (Warranty.) Cons. 10 marks.

78/81/83

1389

252. Morrow [3 Feb.] of the Purification. John Colas of Northleach (*Northlech*) and Alice his wife quer.; John Pindrup (*Pyndrop*) and Agnes his wife def. Two messuages in Northleach. Right of John Colas. Remise and quitclaim (specifying Agnes's heirs) to John Colas and Alice and John Colas's heirs. (Warranty.) Cons. 20 marks.

78/81/84

253. One week [9 Feb.] from the Purification. Hugh Stephens (*Stephenes*) of Worcester (*Wygorn'*) and Margery his wife quer.; Richard de la Field (*Felde*) clerk, John Clive (*Clyve*) clerk, and William Freeman (*Freman*) clerk def. Eight messuages in Gloucester (*Gloucestr'*) and the suburb of the same. Right of John, as those which Richard, John, and William had by gift of Hugh and Margery. For this, grant back and render to Hugh and Margery. To hold to them and their heirs in tail. Contingent remainder to Margery's heirs.

78/81/80

254. Two weeks [2 May] from Easter. John Ferrer (*Ferrour*) of Newland (*Neulonde*) quer.; Edward Ferrer of Gloucester (*Gloucestr'*) and Isolda his wife def. A messuage, a toft, 6 a. of land, and 2 a. of meadow in Newland (*Neulond*). Right of John by gift of Edward and Isolda. Remise and quitclaim (specifying Isolda's heir) to him. (Warranty.) Cons. 10 marks.

78/81/86

255. One month [16 May] from Easter. John Eynsford (*Eynesford*) knight, William Huntelowe clerk, and Richard Ash (*Ayssh*) of Hereford (*Hereford*) quer.; John Greyndor of Abenhall (*Abenhale*) def. The manor of Bulley (*Bolley*) and 12 a. of meadow in Tibberton (*Tebirton*). Right of Richard. Remise and quitclaim to John Eynsford, William, and Richard and Richard's heirs. Cons. £100.

78/81/85

256. One month [16 May] from Easter. Thomas de Bridge (*Brugge*) quer.; Henry Palmer (*Palmere*) and Cristina his wife def. A messuage, 4 a. of meadow, and 3 a. of pasture in Tirley (*Trynleye*). Right of Thomas by gift of Henry and Cristina. Remise and quitclaim (specifying Cristina's heirs) to him. (Warranty.) Cons. 20 marks.

78/81/87

257. One week [20 June] from Trinity. (Made one month [16 May] from Easter in the said year.) William Harley quer.; Hugh Stephens (*Stevenes*) and Margery his wife def. Two messuages and a dovecot in Gloucester (*Gloucestre*). Right of William by gift of Hugh and Margery. Remise and quitclaim (specifying Margery's heirs) to him. (Warranty.) Cons. 20 marks.

78/81/81

258. One week [20 June] from Trinity. (Made the morrow [28 May] of Ascension in the said year.) John Godeston and Thomas Horwood (*Horwode*) quer.; Thomas Tailor (*Taylour*) of Chipping Sodbury (*Chepyngsobbury*) and Margaret his wife def. A messuage, 2 a. of land, and ½ a. of meadow in Chipping Sodbury. Grant and render to John and Thomas Horwood. To hold to them and John's heirs. (Warranty, specifying Margaret's heirs.) Cons. 20 marks.

78/81/82

13 Richard II

1389

259. Three weeks [20 Oct.] from Michaelmas. Richard de Wotton quer.; Walter Galeys of Tewkesbury (*Teukesbury*) and Cristina his wife def. One acre of land and three quarters of a messuage in Tewkesbury. Right of Richard by gift of Walter and Cristina. Remise and quitclaim (specifying Cristina's heirs) to him. (Warranty.) Cons. 10 marks.

78/81/88

260. Three weeks [20 Oct.] from Michaelmas. Nicholas Apperley (*Appurley*) quer.; John Chapman of Prestbury (*Prestbury*) and Alice his wife def. A messuage, 40 a. of land, 8 a. of meadow, and 13*s.* 4*d.* rent in Corse (*Cors*) and Tirley (*Trynleye*). Right of Nicholas by gift of John and Alice. Remise and quitclaim (specifying Alice's heirs) to Nicholas. (Warranty.) Cons. 20 marks.

78/81/90

1390

261. One month [1 May] from Easter. Henry Hussey (*Huse*) of Harting (*Hertyng*) knight and William de Lee quer.; Thomas de Lee and Joan his wife def. The manor of Great Rissington (*Broderysyngden*) except 2 a. of land in the same manor, GLOS.; the manor of Standen (*Staunden*) except 100 a. of land, 10 a. of meadow, 20 a. of pasture, 40 a. of wood, and 100*s.* rent in the same manor, BERKS.; and 100 a. of land, 10 a. of meadow, 20 a.. of pasture, 40 a. of wood, and 100*s.* rent in Standen, WILTS. Right of Henry, as those which Henry and William had by gift of Thomas and Joan. For this, grant back and render to Thomas and Joan. To hold during their lives, of Henry and William and Henry's heirs, paying a rose a year at St. John the Baptist and doing service to the chief lords. Reversion to Henry and William and Henry's heirs. *Labelled* Glouc', Berk', Wiltes'.

289/55/198

[Cf. *Wilts. Fines, 1377–1509*, p. 26, no. 127.]

262. One week [5 June] from Trinity. John de Tibbay clerk and John de Lund chaplain quer.; Stephen le Scrope (*Lescrop*) 'chivaler' the younger and Milicent his wife def. The manor of Castle Combe (*Castelcombe*) and the advowson of the church of the same manor, WILTS., the manors of Wyton (*Wyghton*), Bentley (*Benteley*), and Hampsthwaite (*Hamthwayt*) and the advowson of the church of Arksey (*Arkesey*), YORKS., and the manor of Oxenton (*Oxendon*), GLOS. Right of John de Lund, as those which the same John and John de Tibbay had by gift of Stephen and Milicent. For this, grant back and render to Stephen and Milicent. To hold to them and their heirs in tail. Contingent remainder to Milicent's heirs. *Labelled* Wiltes', Ebor', Glouc'.

289/56/202

[Cf. *Wilts. Fines, 1377–1509*, p. 26, no. 129.]

263. One week [5 June] from Trinity. Henry Bokerell and John Canterbury (*Caunterbury*) of Bristol (*Bristoll'*) quer.; Edward Buckland (*Bokelond*) of Bristol and Agnes his wife def. A messuage and 2 shops in the suburb of Bristol, county of BRISTOL, and 2 messuages, 16 a. of land, and 3 a. of meadow in Wraxall (*Wroxale*), Tickenham (*Tykenham*), and Hele (*Hele*), SOM. Right of Henry, as those which Henry and John had

1390

by gift of Edward and Agnes. For this, grant back to Edward and Agnes. To hold to them and their heirs in tail. Contingent remainder to Agnes's heirs. *Labelled* Bristoll', Somers'.

289/56/203

[Cf. *Som. Fines, 1347–99*, p. 205.]

264. Two weeks [12 June] from Trinity. John Browning (*Brounyng*) the elder and Alice his wife and John Browning the younger and Agnes his wife quer.; Robert Reynold (*Reynald*) and Elizabeth his wife def. A messuage, 1 ploughland, 4 a. of meadow, and 4 a. of pasture in Staverton (*Staverton*), Boddington (*Bodynton*), Evington (*Yevynton*), and Leigh (*Leghe*). Grant to John and Alice and John and Agnes. Remise and quitclaim of whatever Robert and Elizabeth had in the holdings for term of life to John and Alice and John and Agnes and Agnes's heirs. Cons. 20 marks.

78/81/89

14 Richard II

1390

265. Two weeks [13 Oct.] from Michaelmas. (Made the morrow [25 June] of St. John the Baptist in the said year.) John atte Brooke (*Broke*) of Bromsberrow (*Bremesbergh*) quer.; Robert Clement and Alice his wife and Robert More and Joan his wife def. A messuage, 10 a. of land, and 2 a. of meadow in Bromsberrow. Right of John by gift of Robert and Alice and Robert and Joan. Remise and quitclaim (specifying Alice's and Joan's heirs) to John. (Warranty.) Cons. 10 marks.

78/81/95

266. One week [18 Nov.] from St. Martin. Thomas de Bridge (*Brugge*) quer.; Thomas de Clifton and Joan his wife def. A messuage, 1 ploughland, 12 a. of meadow, and 6*s.* 8*d.* rent in Tirley (*Trynleye*) and Hasfield (*Hasfeld*). Right of Thomas de Bridge. Remise and quitclaim (specifying Joan's heirs) to him. (Warranty.) Cons. 100 marks.

78/81/91

267. One week [18 Nov.] from St. Martin. John Clifford (*Clyfford*) parson of the church of Shenington (*Shenyndon*) and John Erre vicar of the church of Crowell (*Croule*) quer.; Thomas Huddington (*Hodyngton*) and Joan his wife daughter of Richard Thurgrym def. The manor of Huddington and a salt-boilery of six leaden vessels (*bullar' sex plumborum aque salse*) in Droitwich (*Wyche*), WORCS., 14 messuages, 6 tofts, 5 ploughlands, 44 a. of meadow, 20 a. of pasture, rents of a root of ginger, 2 lb. of pepper, and 50*s.*, and the advowson of the church of Batsford (*Bacchesore*) in Broad Campden (*Brodecampedene*), Batsford, and Moreton-in-Marsh (*Morton*), GLOS., and 8 messuages, a mill, 1 ploughland, 15 a. of meadow, 20 a. of pasture, 10 a. of wood, and 20*s.* rent in Little Tarrington (*Parva Tatynton*), HEREFS. Thomas acknowledged the right of John Clifford, as those which the same John and John Erre had by Thomas's gift. For this, grant and render to Thomas and Joan. To hold to them and their heirs in tail. Successive contingent remainders to Thomas's heirs in tail, to Thomas son of Alexander de Besford by Thomas [Huddington]'s sister Margaret and his heirs in tail male, to Thomas son of John Morraunt by the said Margaret and his heirs in tail male, and to Thomas Huddington's heirs. (Warranty, specifying John Clifford's heirs.) *Labelled* Wygorn', Glouc', Hereford'.

289/56/210

1391

268. One week [20 Jan.] from Hilary. (Made the morrow of St. Martin in the said year [12 Nov. 1390].) John Lucy and Katherine his wife quer.; Roger White (*Wyght*) and Alice his wife def. One third of a mill and 3 a. of land in Lower Siddington (*Nethersodyntone*). John acknowledged the right of Alice. For this, Roger and Alice granted and rendered to John and Katherine two thirds of the one third of the mill and the one third of the land. To hold to John and Katherine and John's heirs. And they granted to John and Katherine the reversion of one third of the one third of the mill, held by Robert Wick (*Wyke*) and Katherine his wife in Katherine's dower, of Alice's inheritance. To hold as above. (Warranty.)

78/81/94

269. Morrow [3 Feb.] of the Purification. William Bylon and William Bulkington (*Bolkynton*) quer.; John Fry (*Frye*) and Agnes his wife def. Five messuages, a toft, 6 yardlands, 12 a. of meadow, and rents of 12*s*. and 1 lb. of pepper in Chedglow (*Chigelewe*) and Hankerton (*Hankynton*), WILTS., and 2 messuages, 60 a. of land, and 10 a. of meadow in Minchinhampton (*Munchenehampton*) and Rodborough (*Rodbergh*), GLOS. Right of William Bylon, as those which the same William and William Bulkington had by gift of John and Agnes. For this, grant back and render to John and Agnes. To hold to them and Agnes's heirs. *Labelled* Wiltes', Glouc'.

289/56/212

[Cf. *Wilts. Fines, 1377–1509*, p. 27, no. 134.]

270. Two weeks [9 April] from Easter. (Made the morrow of St. John the Baptist in the said year [25 June 1390].) John de Alderley (*Alderlegh*) quer.; John Addurwyne of Winchcombe (*Wynchecombe*) def. A messuage, a toft, 110 a. of land, 12 a. of meadow, 16 a. of wood, and 12*s*. rent in Horton (*Horton*), Hawkesbury (*Haukesbury*), Wickwar (*Wykewarre*), and Yate (*Yate*). Right of John de Alderley, of which he had the messuage, 94 a. of land, the meadow, the wood, and the rent by John Addurwyne's gift. And John Addurwyne granted to him the reversion of the toft and 16 a. of land, held by William Aylward (*Ailleward*) for term of his life, of John Addurwyne's inheritance. (Warranty.) Cons. 100 marks. [*Stained.*]

78/81/93

271. One week [28 May] from Trinity. (Made one month [23 April] from Easter in the said year.) William son of John Power and Philippa his wife quer.; John Power of Whichford (*Wychenford*) and Eleanor his wife def. Four messuages, 3 yardlands, 9 a. of meadow, and pasture for 11 oxen and a horse in Slaughter (*Sloughtre*), held by John Giffard (*Gyfford*) for term of life, of Eleanor's inheritance. John and Eleanor granted the reversion to William and Philippa and their heirs in tail, to hold of John and Eleanor and Eleanor's heirs, paying a rose a year at St. John the Baptist and doing service to the chief lords. Contingent remainder to John and Eleanor and Eleanor's heirs. Cons. 100 marks.

78/81/92

15 Richard II

1391

272. Morrow [25 June] of St. John the Baptist. John de Alderley (*Alderlegh*) quer.; John Redrys of Bristol (*Bristoll'*) 'skynnere' and Margery his wife def. Half of a messuage, 100 a. of land, 12 a. of meadow, 16 a. of wood, and 12*s*. rent in Horton (*Horton*), Hawkesbury (*Haukesbury*), Wickwar (*Wykewarre*), and Yate (*Yate*). Right of John de Alderley. Remise and quitclaim, specifying Margery's heirs, to him. (Warranty.) Cons. 100 marks.

78/82/103

273. One week [1 July] from St. John the Baptist. Richard Leckhampton (*Lekhampton*) chaplain, John Tims (*Tymmes*) chaplain, and John Baker (*Bakere*) of Cheltenham (*Cheltenham*) quer.; Thomas Pope and Leticia his wife def. Ten messuages, 9 shops, a toft, 27 a. of land, 10 a. of meadow, 4 a. of wood, and 7*d*. rent in Maisemore (*Mayesmore*) and Gloucester (*Gloucestr'*) and the suburb of the same town of Gloucester. Right of John Baker, of which he, Richard and John Tims had the messuages, 8 shops, the toft, the land, the meadow, the wood, and the rent by gift of Thomas and Leticia. Remise and quitclaim, specifying Leticia's heirs, to Richard, John, and John and John Baker's heirs. And grant to them of the reversion of a shop in Gloucester held by Isabel Fers for term of her life, of Leticia's inheritance. (Warranty.) Cons. 100 marks.

78/81/100

274. One week [1 July] from St. John the Baptist. Richard Leckhampton (*Lekhampton*) chaplain, John Tims (*Tymmes*) chaplain, and John Baker (*Bakere*) of Cheltenham (*Cheltenham*) quer.; Thomas Pope and Leticia his wife def. Five messuages and 8 shops in Maisemore (*Mayesmore*) and Gloucester (*Gloucestr'*) and the suburb of the same town of Gloucester. Grant to Richard, John, and John, and render to them of whatever Thomas and Leticia had in the holdings for term of Leticia's life. To hold to Richard, John, and John and John Baker's heirs during Leticia's life. (Warranty.) Cons. 100 marks.

78/82/102

275. One week [6 Oct.] from Michaelmas. (Made the morrow of Ascension 14 Richard II [5 May 1391].) Ralph Percival (*Perceval*) and Edmund Pyne quer.; Thomas Brooke (*Brook*) 'chivaler' and Joan his wife def. The manor of Thornfalcon (*Thornfaucon*), 1 ploughland, 6 a. of meadow, 4 a. of pasture, 4 a. of wood, and rents of 1*d*., 1 lb. of pepper, and 1 lb. of cumin in Compton Dando (*Compton Dando*) and half of the manors of Winsford (*Wynsford*) and Tarnock (*Tornok*), SOM., and 2 messuages, 2 ploughlands and 1 yardland, 46 a. of meadow, 20 a. of pasture, and 6 a. of wood in Cote (*Cotes*) by Aust (*Aust*), Elberton (*Ailberton*), and Iron Acton (*Ireneacton*) and half of the manor of Aust, GLOS. Right of Edmund. Render to Edmund and Ralph of the holdings, rents, and halves. To hold to Edmund and Ralph and Edmund's heirs. And grant to them of the reversion of the manor [of Thornfalcon], held by Margaret who was wife of Richard de Acton knight for term of life, of Joan's inheritance. To hold as above. (Warranty.) Cons. £200. *Labelled* Somers', Glouc'.

289/56/218

[Cf. *Som. Fines, 1347–99*, p. 206.]

1391

276. Two weeks [13 Oct.] from Michaelmas. Robert Hawkins (*Haukyns*) of Thornbury (*Thornbury*) quer.; Thomas Laurence of Iron Acton (*Irenacton*) and Amice his wife def. A messuage and a garden in Thornbury. Right of Robert by gift of Thomas and Amice. Remise and quitclaim, specifying Amice's heirs, to Robert. (Warranty.) Cons. 10 marks.

78/81/98

277. Morrow [3 Nov.] of All Souls. (Made two weeks [8 July] from St. John the Baptist in the said year.) John Lucy and Katherine his wife quer.; Roger White (*Wyght*) and Alice his wife def. One third of 5 tofts, a mill, a dovecot, 2 ploughlands, 3 yardlands, and 14 a. of land, 15 a. of meadow, 60 a. of wood, 16*s*. rent, and ½ yardland in Great Taynton (*Magna Teynton*), Bagendon (*Bagyndene*), Baunton (*Baudynton*), Daglingworth (*Daglyngworth*), Stroud (*Strode*), and Stratton (*Stratton*) by Cirencester (*Cirencestre*). Right of John. Render to John and Katherine of two thirds of the one third of 4 tofts, the mill, 3 yardlands and 14 a. of land, 7 a. of meadow, and the ½ yardland in Bagendon, Daglingworth, Stroud, and Stratton. And grant to John and Katherine of the reversion of the third of a toft, the dovecot, the 2 ploughlands, 8 a. of meadow, the wood, and the rent in Great Taynton, held by Robert Wick (*Wike*) and Katherine his wife for term of that Katherine's life, and of the third of one third of 4 tofts, the mill, 3 yardlands and 14 a. of land, 7 a. of meadow, and the said ½ yardland in Bagendon, Baunton, Daglingworth, Stroud, and Stratton, held by the same Robert and Katherine in Katherine's dower, all of Alice's inheritance. To hold to John and Katherine and John's heirs. (Warranty.) Cons. £20. [*Stained and illegible in part.*]

78/81/96

278. Morrow [3 Nov.] of All Souls. Robert [Braybrooke] bishop of London (*London'*), Reynold Grey of Ruthin (*Ruthyn*) knight, John Markham, Hugh de Holes, and John Woodruff (*Woderove*) quer.; Roger Hillary knight and Margaret his wife def. Half of the manors of Ford (*Fordeshome*) and Newport (*Neuport*) and one third of the manor of Edgmond (*Egemundon*), SALOP., half of the manors of West Raddon (*Westraddon*), George Nympton (*Nymet Sancti Georgii*), and Newton Tracey (*Neuton juxta Barnestaple*), of one quarter of the manor of Kilmington (*Kylmynton*), and of 6*s*. rent in East Anstey (*Estansty*) and West Anstey (*Westansty*) and half of the advowson of the church of Newton, DEVON, half of one half of the manor of Badgeworth (*Begeworth*), GLOS., half of one half of the manors of Broughton Gifford (*Broghton*) and Ashton Giffard (*Aston Giffard*) and half of the advowson of the church of Codford (*Codeford*), WILTS., and one third of the manors of Dilwyn (*Dillewe*) and Monnington on Wye (*Monyton super Waiam*), HEREFS., held by Elizabeth who was wife of Nicholas de Audley (*Audele*) for term of life, of Margaret's inheritance. Right of Hugh. Grant of the reversion to the bishop, Reynold, John Markham, Hugh, and John Woodruff. To hold to them and Hugh's heirs. (Warranty, specifying Margaret's heirs.) Cons. 500 marks. *Labelled* Salop', Devon', Glouc', Wiltes', Hereford'. [*Stained.*]

289/56/225

[Cf. *Wilts. Fines, 1377–1509*, p. 29, no. 142.]

1392

279. One week [20 Jan.] from Hilary. (Made the morrow of St. Martin in the said year [12 Nov. 1391].) Robert Butte and Margery his wife quer.; John atte Nelme and Isolda his wife def. A messuage and a shop in Gloucester (*Gloucestre*). Right of Robert, as those which Robert and Margery had by gift of John and Isolda. Remise and quitclaim, specifying Isolda's heirs, to Robert and Margery and Robert's heirs. (Warranty.) Cons. 10 marks.

78/82/101

280. Morrow [3 Feb.] of the Purification. John Moyne (*Moigne*) knight and William Forthey (*Forthay*) chaplain quer.; John Bache and Joan his wife def. Half of the manor and one quarter of the hundred of Westbury (*Westbury*), one quarter of the manors of Imber (*Immer*) and Hilperton (*Hilperton*), and the advowson of one quarter of the church of the same manor of Hilperton, WILTS., and one third of the manor of Clifton (*Clyfton*) and the advowson of one third of the church of the same manor, GLOS. Right of William, as those which John Moyne and William had by gift of John Bache and Joan. For this, grant back and render to John Bache and Joan. To hold to them and Joan's heirs. *Labelled* Wiltes', Glouc'.

289/56/235

[Cf. *Wilts. Fines, 1377–1509*, p. 31, no. 149.]

281. Two weeks [28 April] from Easter. (Made one week [9 Feb.] from the Purification in the said year.) Thomas Norton chaplain and William Shaw (*Shawe*) chaplain quer.; Edmund Ford (*Forde*) and Joan his wife def. Nine messuages, a toft, 2 ploughlands and 100 a. of land, 24 a. of meadow, 15 a. of pasture, 10 a. of wood, 40*s.* rent, and half of a toft in Stone (*Stone*), Ham (*Hamme*), Alkington (*Alkynton*), Wanswell (*Waneswell*), Falfield (*Falefeld*), and North Nibley (*Nubbeley*), and the advowson of the chantry at the altar of St. Mary in the chapel of Stone. Right of Thomas, of which he and William had a messuage, the toft, the 2 ploughlands, 12 a. of meadow, 7 a. of pasture, the 10 a. of wood, and the advowson by gift of Edmund and Joan. And grant to Thomas and William of the rent with the homage and all the services of John Galyene and Denise his wife, Richard Galyene, John Morris (*Morys*), Nicholas Huggins (*Huguns*), Thomas Heaven (*Hevene*) and Joan his wife, John Purlewent (*Porlewent*), John atte Hearne (*Hurne*), Matilda Oldland (*Oldelond*), and Cristina Smith (*Smyth*). To hold to Thomas and William and Thomas's heirs. And grant to Thomas and William of the reversion of a messuage, 20 a. of land, 2 a. of meadow, and 2 a. of pasture, held by John Hill (*Hulle*) and Elena his wife for term of life, of a messuage, 3 a. of land, and ½ a. of meadow, held by John Badcock (*Badecocke*) for term of life, of a messuage and 7 a. of land, held by William Smith and Edith his wife for term of life, of a messuage, 10 a. of land, and 1 a. of meadow, held by William Chapman (*Chepman*) for term of life, of a messuage, 3 a. of land, and ½ a. of meadow, held by Gilbert Whiting (*Wytynge*) for term of life, of 2 a. of land, held by John Walker (*Walkere*) and Agnes his wife for term of life, of 2 a. of land, held by Joseph Walker and Margaret his wife for term of life, of 3 a. of land, held by John Packer (*Pakkere*) and Agnes his wife for term of life, of a messuage, 15 a. of land, 3 a. of meadow, and 1 a. of pasture, held by William Mayowe and Thomas his son for term of life, of a messuage, 16 a. of land, 2 a. of meadow, and 2 a. of pasture, held by William Standen (*Stondon*) and Nichola his wife for term of life, of a messuage and 1 a. of land, held by Walter Carter (*Cartere*) for term of life, and of 18 a. of land, 3 a. of meadow, 3 a. of pasture, and half of

1392

a toft, held by William Smalcombe and Edith his wife for term of life, all of Joan's inheritance. To hold as above. (Warranty.) Cons. £100.

78/81/99

[Cf. *Berkeley Castle Mun.* i, p. 204, A1/24/177 (copy).]

282. Three weeks [5 May] from Easter. John Northriding (*Northridyng*) quer.; Robert Chamberlain (*Chaumberleyn*) and Edith his wife def. A moiety of 2 messuages, a toft, 120 a. of land, and 12 a. of meadow in Tockington (*Tokynton*). Right of John. Remise and quitclaim, specifying Edith's heirs, to him. (Warranty.) Cons. 10 marks.

79/81/97

16 Richard II

1392

283. York. Morrow [25 June] of St. John the Baptist. (Made Westminster, three weeks from Easter 15 Richard II [5 May 1392].) John Adynet of Burford (*Boreford*) quer.; Thomas Sollers (*Solers*) of Northleach (*Northlecche*) and Alice his wife def. A messuage in Northleach. Right of John by gift of Thomas and Alice. Remise and quitclaim, specifying Alice's heirs, to John. (Warranty.) Cons. 10 marks.

78/82/108

284. York. One week [6 Oct.] from Michaelmas. Richard Goodfellow (*Godefelagh*) and Roger Merry (*Myry*) quer.; William Baxter (*Bakester*) of Lydney (*Lydeney*) and Joan his wife def. The manor of Nass (*Nasse*) and 6 messuages, 2 mills, and 30*s.* rent in Lydney and Newerne (*Nywarne*). Right of Richard, as those which Richard and Roger had by gift of William and Joan. Remise and quitclaim, specifying Joan's heirs, to Richard and Roger and Richard's heirs. (Warranty.) Cons. £100.

78/82/105

285. York. One week [6 Oct.] from Michaelmas. William Tanner (*Tannere*) of Cirencester (*Cirencestre*) and Joan his wife quer.; Roger White (*Wyght*) and Alice his wife def. Eight messuages, 80 a. of land, and 200 a. of pasture in Cirencester and Wiggold (*Wyggewolde*). Grant and render to William and Joan. To hold during their lives, of Roger and Alice and Alice's heirs, paying 20*s.* a year, at the Annunciation and Michaelmas, and doing service to the chief lords. (Warranty.) Reversion to Roger and Alice and Alice's heirs. Cons. 100 marks.

78/82/106

286. Morrow [3 Nov.] of All Souls. John Woodruff (*Woderove*), Richard Bank, and William Mirfield (*Mirfeld*) clerk quer.; Thomas Saville (*Sayvyll*) and Katherine his wife def. The manor of Aldenham (*Aldenham*), the bailiwick of the hay of Shirlett (*Shirlet*), and one quarter of the manor of Chirbury (*Chibury*), SALOP., the manor of Aspley (*Aspeley*), STAFFS., the manor of *Murcote* [Murcot or Murcott], GLOS., and the manor of *Hide*, HEREFS. Right of John, as those which he, Richard, and William had by gift of Thomas and Katherine. For this, grant back and render to Thomas and Katherine. To hold to them and Katherine's heirs. *Labelled* Salop', Staff', Glouc', Heref'.

289/56/241

[Cf. *Staffs. Fines, 1327–1547*, p. 208.]

1393

287. One week [8 June] from Trinity. (Made one week from the Purification 13 Richard II [9 Feb. 1390].) John Lovel 'chivaler', Richard Abberbury 'chivaler', and John Gernon (*Gernoun*) clerk quer.; Thomas Broadwell (*Bradewell*) def. A messuage, 1 ploughland and 1 yardland, 10 a. of meadow, and 36*s*. 8*d*. rent in Great Rissington (*Broderysyndon*). Right of John Lovel. Grant to John Lovel, Richard, and John Gernon of 6*s*. 8*d*. rent of the above, together with the homage and all the services of William Wormington (*Wormynton*) from all the holdings which he held of Thomas in the said township. To hold to John, Richard, and John and John Lovel's heirs. And grant to them of the reversion of the holdings and 30*s*. rent, held by William Carter (*Cartere*) and Alice his wife for term of life, of Thomas's inheritance. To hold as above. Cons. 100 marks.

78/82/104

288. One week [8 June] from Trinity. (Made one week from the Purification 14 Richard II [9 Feb. 1391].) Robert Cricklade (*Crekkelade*) quer.; Roger de White (*Wyght*) and Alice his wife def. One third of 1 a. in South Cerney (*Southcerneye*). Right of Robert. Render to him of two thirds of the third. And grant to him of the reversion of the third of the third, held by Robert Wick (*Wyke*) and Katherine his wife in Katherine's dower, of Alice's inheritance. (Warranty.) Cons. 10 marks.

78/82/107

17 Richard II

1393

289. Morrow [25 June] of St. John the Baptist. Peter Woodmancote (*Wodemancote*) clerk and Adam Apperley (*Appurleye*) of Tewkesbury (*Teukesbury*) quer.; Reynold Gow (*Goue*) of Cirencester (*Cirencestre*) 'spicer' and Juliana his wife def. A messuage in Tewkesbury. Right of Adam, as that which Adam and Peter had by gift of Reynold and Juliana. Remise and quitclaim, specifying Juliana's heirs, to Peter and Adam and Adam's heirs. Cons. 10 marks.

78/82/109

290. One week [1 July] from St. John the Baptist. William Warthewyk of Birdlip (*Brydlep*) quer.; Thomas Watts (*Wattes*) of Birdlip and Juliana his wife def. A messuage, 4 tofts, 3 yardlands, 6 a. of meadow, and 6 a. of wood in Brimpsfield (*Brymesfeld*). Right of William by gift of Thomas and Juliana. Remise and quitclaim, specifying Juliana's heirs, to William. (Warranty.) Cons. £20.

78/82/116

291. One week [6 Oct.] from Michaelmas. (Made one week [1 July] from St. John the Baptist in the said year.) Thomas de Bridge (*Brugge*) of Tewkesbury (*Teukesbury*) and Isabel his wife quer.; Walter Gough (*Gugge*) and Thomas Twyning (*Twenyng*) of Tewkesbury def. Four messuages in Tewkesbury. Right of Walter, as those which Walter and Thomas Twyning had by gift of Thomas de Bridge and Isabel. For this, grant back and render to Thomas de Bridge and Isabel of three messuages of the above. To hold to them and their heirs in tail. Successive contingent remainders to Isabel's heirs in tail and to her heirs. Grant and render of the fourth messuage to Thomas de Bridge. To hold to him and his heirs in tail. Contingent remainder to Isabel.

78/82/110

1393

292. Morrow [12 Nov.] of St. Martin. (Made the morrow of Ascension 15 Richard II [24 May 1392].) John Cassy of Wightfield (*Wyghtfeld*) quer.; Roger Burley brother and heir of Richard Burley 'chivaler' def. One quarter of the manors of Little Taynton (*Parva Teynton*) and Kilcot (*Kylcote*), held by Hugh Waterton (*Watirton*) 'chivaler' for term of the life of Beatrice who was wife of the said Richard. Right of John. Grant to him of the reversion, of Roger's inheritance. (Warranty.) Cons. 200 marks.

78/82/112

293. Morrow [12 Nov.] of St. Martin. James Clifford quer.; John atte Water (*Watre*) and Alice his wife def. A messuage in the suburb of Gloucester (*Glouc'*). Right of James by gift of John and Alice. Remise and quitclaim, specifying Alice's heirs, to James. (Warranty.) Cons. 10 marks.

78/82/113

294. One week [18 Nov.] from St. Martin. David Ewyas chaplain quer.; John Paunton and Joan his wife def. Rent of 6 marks issuing from the manor of Brinsham (*Brunsham*). Grant and render to David. To be paid every year during David's life by the hand of John and Joan and Joan's heirs, at Christmas, the Annunciation, St. John the Baptist, and Michaelmas, with right of distraint in the said manor for non-payment. Cons. 100 marks.

78/82/111

1394

295. Two weeks [3 May] from Easter. (Made one week [9 Feb.] from the Purification in the said year.) Mr. John Snapp clerk and Henry Tellisford (*Telesford*) clerk quer.; Thomas Hungerford knight def. The manor of Down Ampney (*Dounamneneye*) and a toft and 2 ploughlands in Wick (*Wyke*) by Meysey Hampton (*Hampton Meysy*). Right of Mr. John, as those which he and Henry had by Thomas's gift. For this, grant back and render to Thomas. To hold during his life. Remainder to Thomas's son Walter and his heirs in tail. Successive contingent remainders to Walter's brother John and his heirs in tail and to Thomas's heirs. [*Worn.*]

78/82/114

296. Two weeks [3 May] from Easter. (Made York, one week from Michaelmas 16 Richard II [6 Oct. 1392].) Richard Blackhead (*Blakheed*) of Kempley (*Kempeleye*) quer.; Thomas Power of Kempley and Sibyl his wife def. A messuage, 26 a. of land, 2 a. of meadow, and 2 a. of wood in Kempley. Right of Richard, of which he had 13 a. of land, 1 a. of meadow, 1 a. of wood, and half of the messuage by gift of Thomas and Sibyl. Remise and quitclaim, specifying Sibyl's heirs, to Richard. And grant to him of the reversion of 13 a. of land, 1 a. of meadow, 1 a. of wood, and the other half of the messuage, held by William Jakes and Margaret his wife for term of Margaret's life, of Sibyl's inheritance. (Warranty.) Cons. £20. [*Worn.*]

78/82/115

297. One week [21 June] from Trinity. (Made one week [9 Feb.] from the Purification in the said year.) Agnes Leach (*Lech*) quer.; John Paunton and Joan his wife def. The manor of Lawrence Weston (*Laurence Weston*) and 40s. rent issuing from the manor of Sibland (*Siblond*). Grant and render to Agnes of the manor of Lawrence Weston. To hold during

1394

her life, of John and Joan and Joan's heirs, paying a rose a year at St. John the Baptist and doing service to the chief lords. Reversion to John and Joan and Joan's heirs. And grant and render to Agnes of the rent, to be paid every year by the hand of John and Joan and Joan's heirs during Agnes's life, at the Annunciation and Michaelmas, with right of distraint for non-payment in the manor of Sibland. Cons. £100.

78/82/117

298. Two weeks [28 June] from Trinity. Richard Bushel (*Busshel*) quer.; Henry atte Hall (*Halle*) of Sherborne (*Shirborne*) and Matilda his wife def. Four acres of meadow and pasture for 8 oxen in Sherborne. Right of Richard. Remise and quitclaim, specifying Henry's heirs, to him. (Warranty.) Cons. 10 marks.

78/82/118

[The quindene of Trinity (28 June) 1394 fell in fact in 18 Richard II. In 1393 the quindene was 15 June, which was within 16 Richard II.]

18 Richard II

1394

299. One week [6 Oct.] from Michaelmas. (Made two weeks [8 July] from St. John the Baptist in the said year.) John Young (*Yonge*) chaplain and William Lypiatt (*Lupyate*) the elder quer.; Richard Urdeley (*Urdele*) def. Seven messuages, 2 tofts, 240 a. and 2½ yardlands of land, 40 a. of meadow, and 1 a. of pasture in Little Badminton (*Parva Badmynton*), Hawkesbury (*Haukesbury*), Upper Siddington (*Oversudynton*), and Lower Siddington (*Nethersudynton*), GLOS., and 2 messuages, 2½ yardlands, 10 a. of meadow, and one third of 12 a. of pasture in Shorncote (*Cernecote*) and Somerford Keynes (*Somerford Kaynes*), WILTS. Right of William, as those which he and John had by Richard's gift. For this, grant back and render to Richard. To hold during his life. Remainder to Richard son of William Urdeley and William Lypiatt's daughter Alice and to that Richard's heirs. *Labelled* Glouc', Wiltes'.

290/57/267

[Cf. *Wilts. Fines, 1377–1509*, p. 37, no. 175.]

300. Two weeks [13 Oct.] from Michaelmas. Robert Peek and John Alderley (*Alderlegh*) quer.; Thomas Mill (*Mille*) and Juliana his wife def. The manors of Harescombe (*Harsecombe*) and Duntisbourne Rouse (*Dontesbourne Rous*). Right of Robert, as those which Robert and John had by gift of Thomas and Juliana. For this, grant back and render to Thomas and Juliana. To hold to them and their heirs in tail male. Contingent remainder of the manor of Harescombe to Juliana's heirs. Successive contingent remainders of the manor of Duntisbourne Rouse to the heirs of Thomas and Juliana in tail and to Juliana's heirs.

78/82/121

301. One month [27 Oct.] from Michaelmas. Thomas Fry (*Frye*) and Amice his wife quer.; Ralph Cok and John Acton (*Egton*) the younger def. A messuage, 50 a. of land, 9 a. of meadow, 30 a. of pasture, 1 a. of wood, and 5*s*. rent in Ham (*Hamme*) and Saniger (*Swonhongre*). Right of Ralph, of which he and John had the messuage, 49 a. of land, the meadow, pasture, wood, and rent by gift of Thomas and Amice. For this, grant back and render to Thomas and Amice. To hold to them and their heirs in tail. And grant to them of the reversion of 1 a. of land held by Thomas Burkyng for term of life, of Ralph's

1394

inheritance in the said townships. To hold as above. Successive contingent remainders to Amice's heirs in tail and to Thomas Fry's heirs.

78/82/119

302. One month [27 Oct.] from Michaelmas. John Thornbury (*Thornebury*) parson of the church of Crudwell (*Cruddewell*) and William Chancton (*Changeton*) quer.; John de Alderley (*Alderlegh*) def. A messuage, a toft, 20 a. of land, 10 a. of meadow, 60 a. of pasture, 16 a. of wood, and 12*s*. rent in Hawkesbury (*Haukesbury*), Horton (*Herton*), Wickwar (*Wykewarre*), and Yate (*Yate*). Right of John Thornbury, as those which John and William had by John de Alderley's gift. For this, grant back and render to John de Alderley. To hold during his life. Successive remainders to Elena who was wife of John Collins (*Colyns*) of Alderley and to Thomasia wife of the said John de Alderley, each to hold during her life, and to the heirs of the said John de Alderley.

78/82/120

303. Morrow [12 Nov.] of St. Martin. Roger Pirton (*Pyryton*) quer.; John Roches knight and Wilelma his wife def. A messuage, a mill, and 2 ploughlands in Elmbridge (*Elebrygg*). Right of Roger. Remise and quitclaim, specifying Wilelma's heirs, to him. Cons. 100 marks.

78/82/122

304. Morrow [12 Nov.] of St. Martin. John son of Baldwin de Drayton quer.; Baldwin de Drayton of Cranford (*Craneford*) and Alice his wife def. The manor of Cranford called FitzRanes manor (*Fitz Ranesmanere*), NORTHANTS., and the manor of Dorsington (*Dersyngton*) except for a messuage and 2 ploughlands in the same manor, GLOS. Right of John by gift of Baldwin and Alice. Remise and quitclaim, specifying Alice's heirs, to John. (Warranty.) Cons. £200. *Labelled* Norht', Glouc'.

290/57/270

1395

305. One week [20 Jan.] from Hilary. (Made two weeks from St. Martin in the said year [25 Nov. 1394].) James Cox (*Cokkes*) and Simon Oliver (*Olyver*) quer.; Richard Cook (*Cooke*) and Juliana his wife def. A messuage, 2 dovecots, 160 a. of land, 8 a. of meadow, 40 a. of pasture, and 10 a. of wood in Frenchay (*Fromeshawe*), Hambrook (*Hambrook*), and Harry Stoke (*Stokehenry*). Right of James, as those which James and Simon had by gift of Richard and Juliana. For this, grant back and render to Richard and Juliana. To hold during their lives, of James and Simon and James's heirs, paying a rose a year at St. John the Baptist and doing service to the chief lords. Reversion to James and Simon and James's heirs.

78/82/123

306. One week [20 Jan.] from Hilary. (Made the morrow of St. Martin in the said year [12 Nov. 1394].) John de Stanshawe and Isabel his wife quer.; Edward Dauntsey (*Dauntesey*) parson of the church of Yate (*Yate*) def. A messuage, 2 ploughlands, 24 a. of meadow, and 20 a. of wood in Stanshawe (*Stanshawe*). Right of Edward by gift of John and Isabel. For this, grant back and render to John and Isabel. To hold to them and their heirs in tail. Contingent remainder to Isabel's heirs.

78/82/124

1395

307. Morrow [3 Feb.] of the Purification. John Stoutshill (*Stouteshull*) quer.; John Butler (*Boteler*) of Warminster (*Warministre*) and Juliana his wife def. Two messuages and 7 a. of land in Uley (*Ywele*). Right of John Stoutshill by gift of John Butler and Juliana. Remise and quitclaim, specifying Juliana's heirs, to John Stoutshill. (Warranty.) Cons. 20 marks.

78/82/125

308. Two weeks [25 April] from Easter. Gilbert Denis (*Denys*) 'chivaler' and Margaret his wife quer.; Alan Exhall (*Eckysale*) and Alice his wife def. One third of the manor of Alveston (*Aluostone*). Right of Gilbert. Remise and quitclaim, specifying Alice's heirs, to Gilbert and Margaret and Gilbert's heirs. Cons. 100 marks.

79/83/126

309. One week [13 June] from Trinity. (Made two weeks [25 April] from Easter in the said year.) John Thornbury (*Thornebury*) parson of the church of Crudwell (*Cruddewell*) and Thomas Weston of Cricklade (*Crekkelade*) quer.; Nicholas Chausy the elder and Margaret his wife def. The manor of Alderley (*Alderlegh*) and the advowson of the church of the same manor. Nicholas acknowledged the right of John, as those which John and Thomas had by his gift. For this, John and Thomas granted and rendered the manor and advowson to Nicholas and Margaret. To hold during their lives. Remainder to Robert son of John de Stanshawe and Margaret his wife, daughter of Elizabeth daughter of the said Nicholas, and their heirs in tail. Contingent successive remainders to the heirs of Margaret daughter of Elizabeth in tail, to John de Stanshawe and Isabel his wife, and to that John's heirs.

79/83/127

310. One week [13 June] from Trinity. William Manchester (*Manchestre*) quer.; Thomas Heveningham (*Hevenyngham*) and Margery his wife def. A messuage, 6 shops, and 1 a. of land in Gloucester (*Gloucestre*) and the suburb of the same town. Right of William by gift of Thomas and Margery. Remise and quitclaim, specifying Margery's heirs, to William. Cons. 100 marks.

79/83/128

311. One week [13 June] from Trinity. John Deerhurst (*Derhurst*) and William Clipston (*Clypston*) quer.; Thomas Heveningham (*Hevenyngham*) and Margery his wife def. Two messuages, a toft, and 5 shops in Gloucester (*Gloucestre*) and the suburb of the same town. Grant and render to John and William. To hold to John and William and John's heirs. Cons. 100 marks.

79/83/129

312. One week [13 June] from Trinity. Richard Barrett (*Baret*) quer.; Thomas Heveningham (*Hevenyngham*) and Margery his wife def. A messsuage and a shop in Gloucester (*Gloucestre*). Right of Richard by gift of Thomas and Margery. Remise and quitclaim, specifying Margery's heirs, to Richard. Cons. £20.

79/83/130

19 Richard II

1395

313. One week [1 July] from St. John the Baptist. (Made two weeks from Michaelmas 18 Ric. II [13 Oct. 1394].) John Cassy of Wightfield (*Wyghtfeld*), Richard Wyche parson of the church of Tredington (*Tredyngton*), William Perham parson of the church of Chipping Norton (*Chepyngnorton*), and John de Reed (*Rede*) of Checkendon (*Chakendon*) quer.; William Hampton (*Hompton*) of the county of Hereford (*Hereford'*) def. The manor of Stratton (*Stratton*) by Cirencester (*Circetre*) and the advowson of the church of the same manor, held by Katherine who was wife of John Lucy for term of life, of William Hampton's inheritance. Right of John Cassy. Grant of the reversion to John, Richard, William Perham, and John de Reed and John Cassy's heirs. (Warranty.) Cons. £400.

79/83/131

314. One week [1 July] from St. John the Baptist. (Made one week from St. Martin 18 Ric. II [18 Nov. 1394].) John Cole quer.; Robert Mansell (*Maunsell*) and Joan his wife def. Two messuages in Tewkesbury, held by John le Dyer (*Diare*) of Tewkesbury (*Touk'*) for term of life, of Joan's inheritance. Right of John Cole. Grant of the reversion to him. Cons. £20.

79/83/133

315. One week [6 Oct.] from Michaelmas. (Made two weeks [8 July] from St. John the Baptist in the said year.) Thomas Cole, Thomas Broadwell (*Bradewell*), and John Cole quer.; Ralph Damsel (*Damesele*) and Matilda his wife def. Eight messuages, 2 ploughlands, 3 yardlands, and 24 a. of land, and 15 a. of meadow in Fiddington (*Fydyngton*). Thomas Cole acknowledged the right of Ralph. For this, grant and render by Ralph and Matilda to Thomas, Thomas, and John. To hold to Thomas, Thomas, and John and Thomas Cole's heirs, paying to Ralph and Matilda during their lives 100*s*. a year, at Michaelmas and Easter, with right of distraint if the rent is in arrears. (Warranty.)

79/83/137

316. Two weeks [13 Oct.] from Michaelmas. John Blythe parson of the church of Black Notley (*Blake Nottele*) quer.; Agnes who was wife of Richard de Preston def. Two messuages, a toft, 2 ploughlands, 6 yardlands, and 20 a. of land, and 16 a. of meadow in Stow-on-the-Wold (*Stowe Sancti Edwardi*), Great Rissington (*Brodrisyndon*), and Wick Rissington (*Wykerisyndon*). Right of John. For this, grant and render to Agnes. To hold during her life. Remainder to Agnes daughter of John Saunders (*Saundres*) and her heirs in tail by Alan Spicer. Contingent remainder to the heirs of Agnes who was wife of Richard de Preston.

79/83/138

317. One month [27 Oct.] from Michaelmas. Walter Messenger burgess of the town of Gloucester (*Gloucestre*) quer.; Robert Nibley (*Nubbeley*) and Isabel his wife def. A messuage, 6 a. of land, and 2 a. of meadow in Aylburton (*Ailbryghton*). Right of Walter by gift of Robert and Isabel. Remise and quitclaim, specifying Isabel's heirs, to Walter. (Warranty.) Cons. 10 marks.

79/83/134

1395

318. One month [27 Oct.] from Michaelmas. Reynold Hook (*Hoke*) and George Millward (*Mulleward*) quer.; Walter Bick (*Byke*) of Bromsberrow (*Brommesberwe*) and Sibyl his wife def. Three messuages, 1½ yardlands, 2 a. of meadow, and 13½*d.* rent in Bromsberrow. Right of Reynold, as those which Reynold and George had by gift of Walter and Sibyl. Remise and quitclaim, specifying Sibyl's heirs, to Reynold and George and Reynold's heirs. (Warranty.) Cons. 100 marks.

79/83/136

319. Morrow [12 Nov.] of St. Martin. Thomas Young (*Yonge*) quer.; Richard Prank and Agnes his wife def. Four acres of land in Okle (*Ocle*) within the parish of Newent (*Newent*). Right of Thomas by gift of Richard and Agnes. Remise and quitclaim, specifying Agnes's heirs, to Thomas. (Warranty.) Cons. 100*s.*

79/83/135

320. Morrow [12 Nov.] of St. Martin. The rector of the house or monastery of the order of St. Augustine at Edington (*Edyndon*) in Salisbury (*Sar'*) diocese quer.; John Wass (*Waas*) and Isabel his wife and William Gater and Lucy his wife def. Rent of 40*s.* from 2 messuages and 2 yardlands in Tormarton (*Thormerton*). Right of the rector and his church of All Saints, Edington. Remise and quitclaim, specifying Isabel's heirs, to them. (Warranty.) Cons. 20 marks.

79/83/139

[The rector of Edington presided over a chantry invoking the Blessed Virgin Mary, St. Katharine, and All Saints, whose priests followed a rule based on that of St. Augustine: *The Edington Cartulary*, Wilts. Rec. Soc. xlii, pp. xiii–xiv.]

1396

321. One week [9 Feb.] from the Purification. James Clifford quer.; Andrew Morton (*Moorton*) def. The manor of Hampnett (*Hamptonet*) and the advowson of the church of the same township. Right of James by Andrew's gift. Remise and quitclaim to James. (Warranty.) Cons. £100.

79/83/140

322. One week [4 June] from Trinity. (Made the morrow [12 May] of Ascension in the said year.) James Clifford quer.; Thomas de Twyford of the county of Northampton (*Norht'*) and Eleanor his wife def. The manor of Hampnett (*Hamptonet*) and the advowson of the church of Hampnett. Right of James. Remise and quitclaim, specifying Eleanor's heirs, to him. (Warranty.) Cons. 100 marks.

79/83/132

20 Richard II

1396

323. One week [6 Oct.] from Michaelmas. (Made one week from Trinity 19 Ric. II [4 June 1396].) John Fawler (*Favylour*) quer.; Richard Galpin (*Galpyn*) of Fairford (*Faireford*) and Alice his wife def. A messuage, 2 yardlands, and 6 a. of meadow in Great Rissington (*Magna Rysyndon*), GLOS., and a messuage in Burford (*Boreford*), OXON. Right of John by gift of Richard and Alice. Remise and quitclaim, specifying Alice's heirs, to John. (Warranty.) Cons. £20.

290/57/296

1396

324. Two weeks [13 Oct.] from Michaelmas. Roger de la Hay clerk, Henry Cottesmore (*Cotesmore*) clerk, John Morewall clerk, Walter Whittingslow (*Wyttyggeslowe*) clerk quer.; Richard Chelmick (*Chelmwyk*) and Margaret his wife def. The manor of Staverton (*Staverton*). Right of Walter, as that which Walter, Roger, Henry, and John had by gift of Richard and Margaret. Remise and quitclaim, specifying Margaret's heirs, to Roger, Henry, John, and Walter and Walter's heirs (Warranty.) Cons. 100 marks.

79/83/145

325. One month [27 Oct.] from Michaelmas. John abbot of Biddlesden (*Bitlesden*) quer.; Henry Beamish (*Bemys*) of Limbury (*Lymbergh*) and Alice his wife def. One acre of land in Ebrington (*Ebryghton*) and the advowson of the church of the same township. Right of the abbot and his church of Biddlesden. Remise and quitclaim, specifying Alice's heirs, to them. (Warranty.) Cons. 100 marks.

79/83/144

326. Morrow [12 Nov.] of St. Martin. Walter Sevare the younger quer.; Edmund Draper (*Drapere*) of Tetbury (*Tettebury*) and Edith his wife def. A messuage in Tetbury. Right of Walter. Render to him. (Warranty, specifying Edmund's heirs.) Cons. 10 marks.

79/83/143

1397

327. Two weeks [6 May] from Easter. (Made two weeks [27 Jan.] from Hilary in the said year.) William Wickwick (*Wykwyk*) quer.; Robert Hokenale and Joan his wife def. A messuage, 1 yardland, and 8 a. of meadow in Tockington (*Tokynton*). Right of William by gift of Robert and Joan. For this, grant back and render to Robert and Joan. To hold during their lives. Remainder of half of the holding to Robert's heirs and of the other half to John Smith (*Smyth*) of Wallsend (*Wallende*).

79/83/142

328. Two weeks [6 May] from Easter. (Made two weeks [27 Jan.] from Hilary in the said year.) James Cox (*Cokkes*) burgess of the town of Bristol (*Bristoll'*) quer.; Richard Cook of Winterbourne (*Wynterburne*) and Juliana his wife def. A toft, 50 a. of land, and 8 a. of meadow in Hinton Blewett (*Henton Bluet*), SOM., and 4 a. of land in Frenchay (*Framshawe*), GLOS. Right of James. Render to him. (Warranty, specifying Richard's heirs.) Cons. 100 marks. *Labelled* Somers', Glouc'.

290/58/302

[Cf. *Som. Fines, 1347–99*, p. 211.]

329. One week [24 June] from Trinity. John Cassy of Wightfield (*Wyghtfeld*), Richard Wyche (*Wych*) parson of the church of Tredington (*Tredynton*), William Perham clerk, Henry Rose vicar of the church of Tirley (*Trynley*) quer.; Henry Green (*Grene*) 'chivaler' and Matilda his wife def. Half of the manors of Kilcot (*Kyllecote*) and Little Taynton (*Parva Teynton*). Right of John. Render to John, Richard, William, and Henry Rose. To hold to them and John's heirs. (Warranty, specifying Matilda's heirs.) Cons. 200 marks.

79/83/141

[The fine is dated 20 Ric. II, the regnal year which ran from 22 June 1396 to 21 June 1397, so that 24 June 1397 was after the regnal year had ended. In 1396 one week from Trinity was 4 June, before the beginning of the regnal year 20 Ric. II.]

21 Richard II

1397

330. One week [24 June] from Trinity. (Made one month [20 May] from Easter in the said year.) Philip Bennett (*Benet*) 'mercer' and Juliana his wife and Thomas Cadel (*Cadull*) and Alice his wife quer. by Robert Gilbert; Thomas Heveningham (*Henyngham*) and Margery his wife def. A messuage and 3 shops in Gloucester (*Gloucestre*). Right of Philip. Remise and quitclaim, specifying Margery's heirs, to Philip and Juliana and Thomas Cadel and Alice and Philip's heirs. Cons. 20 marks.

79/83/151

[In the regnal year 21 Ric. II, which ran from 22 June 1397 to 21 June 1398, one week from Trinity fell both on 24 June 1397, as indicated above, and on 9 June 1398, when one month from Easter fell on 5 May.]

331. One week [1 July] from St. John the Baptist. William de Pucklechurch (*Pokelchurche*) and Thomas de Pucklechurch quer.; Thomas FitzNichol (*fitz Nichol*) 'chivaler' def. A messuage, 2 ploughlands, 100 a. of meadow, 20 a. of pasture, 10 a. of wood, and 20*s.* rent in Oldbury upon Severn (*Oldebury*), Morton (*Morton*), Kington (*Kyngton*), and Thornbury (*Thornebury*). Right of William. Render to William and Thomas de Pucklechurch. To hold to them and William's heirs. (Warranty.) Cons. £100.

79/83/146

332. Two weeks [13 Oct.] from Michaelmas. John Holand (*Holond*) earl of Huntingdon (*Huntyngdon*) quer.; Ralph Whitehorse (*Whytehorse*) knight and Elizabeth his wife def. The manor of Tytherington (*Tydryngton*). Right of the earl. Render to him. (Warranty, specifying Elizabeth's heirs.) Cons. 200 marks.

79/83/150

333. Two weeks [13 Oct.] from Michaelmas. Walter Peers parson of the church of St. Aldate, Gloucester (*Gloucestr'*), and John Stabold chaplain quer.; John Saunders (*Saundrys*) and Joan his wife, Peter de Lude (*Loude*) and Agnes his wife, Laurence Messenger (*Messunger*), and Walter Marcle (*Markeleye*) def. Six messuages and 9 shops in Gloucester (*Gloucestre*). Right of Walter Peers. Remise and quitclaim, specifying Walter Marcle's heirs, to Walter Peers and John Stabold and that Walter's heirs. Cons. 100 marks.

79/83/152

334. One month [27 Oct.] from Michaelmas. Thomas Manning (*Mannyng*) and Thomas Crump (*Cromp*) quer.; Richard Marden (*Maurdyn*) and Edith his wife def. The manor of Little Sodbury (*Parva Subbury*) and the advowson of the church of the same manor, GLOS., and the manor of Great Durnford (*Magna Derneford*), WILTS. Right of Thomas Manning, as those which the same Thomas and Thomas Crump had by gift of Richard and Edith. Remise and quitclaim, specifying Edith's heirs, to Thomas and Thomas and Thomas Manning's heirs. (Warranty.) Cons. 200 marks. *Labelled* Glouc', Wiltes'.

290/58/309

[Cf. *Wilts. Fines, 1377–1509*, p. 42, no. 196.]

1398

335. Two weeks [21 April] from Easter. John Banbury (*Bannebury*) of Gloucester (*Gloucestre*) and Joan his wife quer.; John Shipston (*Shippeston*) of Minchinhampton (*Mynchenehampton*) and Agnes his wife def. A messuage in Gloucester. Right of John Banbury, as that which John Banbury and Joan had by gift of John Shipston and Agnes. To hold to John Banbury and Joan and that John's heirs. (Warranty, specifying Agnes's heirs.) Cons. £20.

79/83/147

336. Two weeks [21 April] from Easter. William Warthewyke (*Warthwyke*) quer.; William Briddesmere (*Bryddesmere*) and Alice his wife def. Four messuages, 4 tofts, 1 ploughland and 20 a. of land, 3 a. of meadow, and 10*s*. rent in Great Witcombe (*Magna Wydecombe*), Little Witcombe (*Parva Wydecombe*), Great Bentham (*Magna Bentham*), Little Bentham (*Parva Bentham*), Great Shurdington (*Magna Shrudyngton*), and Badgeworth (*Beggeworth*). Right of William Warthewyke, by gift of William Briddesmere and Alice. Remise and quitclaim, specifying William Briddesmere's heirs, to William Warthewyke. Cons. 100 marks.

79/83/148

337. Three weeks [28 April] from Easter. Ralph Greyndor (*Greyndore*) quer.; Roger Payn and Joan his wife and Margaret Bagot def. Nine messuages, a mill, 3 tofts, 70 a. of land, and 9 a. of meadow in Bulley (*Bulley*), Tibberton (*Tyberton*), and Churcham (*Chyrcheham*). Right of Ralph by gift of Roger, Joan, and Margaret. Remise and quitclaim, specifying Joan's and Margaret's heirs, to Ralph. (Warranty.) Cons. 100 marks.

79/83/149

22 Richard II

1398

338. Two weeks [13 Oct.] from Michaelmas. Robert Janes of Gloucester (*Gloucestr'*) quer.; William Botloe (*Botelowe*) and Margery his wife def. A messuage and a shop in Gloucester. Right of Robert by gift of William and Margery. Remise and quitclaim, specifying Margery's heirs, to Robert. (Warranty.) Cons. 10 marks.

79/83/153

339. Two weeks [13 Oct.] from Michaelmas. Laurence Brown (*Broun*) 'mercer' quer.; Edmund de Ipre [Ypres?] and Elizabeth his wife def. A messuage and 2 shops in Gloucester (*Gloucestre*). Right of Laurence by gift of Edmund and Elizabeth. Remise and quitclaim, specifying Edmund's heirs, to Laurence. (Warranty.) Cons. 20 marks.

79/83/154

1399

340. Morrow [3 Feb.] of the Purification. Richard Parfitt (*Parfeat*) and Richard Spicer (*Spycer*) quer.; John Painter (*Peyntour*) and Agnes his wife def. Eight messuages, a toft, 6 yardlands and 74 a. of land, 17 a. of meadow, and rents of 18*s*. 8*d*. and 1 lb. of pepper in Chedglow (*Chigelewe*), Hankerton (*Hankynton*), Luckington (*Lokyngton*), and Malmesbury (*Malmesbury*), WILTS., and 2 messuages, 60 a. of land, and 10 a. of meadow in Minchinhampton (*Munchenehampton*) and Rodborough (*Rodbergh*), GLOS. Right of

1399

Richard Parfitt, as those which he and Richard Spicer had by gift of John and Agnes. For this, grant back and render to John and Agnes. To hold to them and their heirs in tail. Contingent remainder to John's heirs. *Labelled* Wiltes', Glouc'. [*Worn.*]

290/58/319

[Cf. *Wilts. Fines, 1377–1509*, p. 42, no. 200.]

341. Two weeks [21 April] from Easter. (Made the morrow of St. Martin 20 Ric. II [12 Nov. 1396].) Walter Sevare the younger quer.; Walter Tetbury (*Tettebury*) def. Three messuages in Tetbury, held by Isabel who was wife of Henry le Warner of Charfield (*Charfeld*) for term of life, of Walter Tetbury's inheritance. Right of Walter Sevare. Grant of the reversion to him. Cons. 20 marks. [*Worn.*]

79/83/155

342. One week [1 June] from Trinity. William Cowbridge (*Coubrugge*) quer.; John Martin (*Martyn*) and Margaret his wife def. A messuage, 60 a. of land, and 12 a. of meadow in Widford (*Wydeford*), GLOS., and a toft, 46 a. of land and 3 a. of meadow in Swinbrook (*Swynebrok*) and Fulbrook (*Fulbrok*), OXON. Right of William by gift of John and Margaret. Remise and quitclaim, specifying Margaret's heirs, to William. (Warranty.) Cons. 100 marks. *Labelled* Glouc', Oxon'.

290/58/329

343. One week [1 July] from St. John the Baptist. Robert Henege of Falfield (*Falsefeld*) quer.; Richard Bird (*Bryd*) of Wickwar (*Wykewarre*) and Joan his wife def. A messuage, 29 a. of land, 2 a. of meadow, and 3 a. of wood in Wickwar. Right of Robert by gift of Richard and Joan. Remise and quitclaim, specifying Joan's heirs, to Robert. (Warranty.) Cons. 20 marks.

79/83/156

344. One week [20 Jan.] from Hilary. (Made two weeks from Michaelmas in the said year [13 Oct.1398].) William Greville (*Gryvell*) of Campden (*Caumpeden*) quer.; John Gilbert (*Gilbard*) of Draycott (*Draycote*) def. A messuage and a toft in Campden, held by Geoffrey Good (*Gode*) of Campden 'dyer' for term of life, of John's inheritance. Right of William. Grant to him of the reversion. (Warranty.) Cons. £20.

79/83/157

23 Richard II

1399

345. Saturday after St. John the Baptist. Walter Lambard quer.; William Tocknell (*Tokenyll*) and Agnes his wife def. Six and a half messuages, 6 tofts, 60 a. of land, 10 a. of meadow, and 40s. rent in Fairford (*Faireford*), Milton (*Milton*), and East End (*Estende*). Right of Walter. Render to him. (Warranty, specifying Agnes's heirs.) Cons. £20.

79/83/158

1 Henry IV

1400

346. One month [16 May] from Easter. Richard Heynes of Pucklechurch (*Poculchurche*) and Matilda his wife quer.; John Paunton and Joan his wife def. The manor of Abson (*Abboteston*) and a messuage, 4 yardlands, and 10 a. of meadow in Pucklechurch, Codrington (*Coderyngton*), Churchley (*Churchely*), and Wick (*Wyke*). Grant and render to Richard and Matilda. To hold during their lives, of John and Joan and Joan's heirs, paying £8 a year, at St. John the Baptist, Michaelmas, Christmas, and Easter and doing service to the chief lords, with right of distraint in the said manor and holdings for non-payment. (Warranty.) Reversion to John and Joan and Joan's heirs. Cons. (paid by Richard and Matilda) 100 marks.

79/84/1

347. Morrow [25 June] of St. John the Baptist. Thomas Ridge (*Rigge*) and Katherine his wife quer.; John Devereux 'chivaler' and Joan his wife def. The manors of Charlcombe (*Charlecombe*) and Norton Malreward (*Norton Malreward*), SOM., and the manors of Hanham (*Hanam*), Churchley (*Churcheley*), and Upton Cheyney (*Upton*) except for a toft, half of 1 a. of land, and 8s. 7d. rent in the same manor of Hanham, GLOS. Right of Katherine. Remise and quitclaim, specifying Joan's heirs, to Thomas and Katherine and Katherine's heirs. Cons. 100 marks. *Labelled* Somers', Glouc'.

290/59/10

[Cf. *Som. Fines, 1399–1484*, p. 157.]

348. One week [1 July] from St. John the Baptist. John Devereux knight and Joan his wife quer.; Thomas Ridge (*Rigge*) and Katherine his wife def. The manors of Nass (*Nasse*), Hanham (*Hanam*), Upton Cheyney (*Upton*), and Hurst (*Hurst*) in Lydney (*Lydeney*), GLOS., and the manors of Charlcombe (*Charlecombe*) and Norton Malreward (*Norton Malreward*), SOM. Right of Katherine. For this, Thomas and Katherine granted, for themselves and Katherine's heirs, that they would pay to John and Joan during Joan's life 24 marks a year, at Michaelmas, Christmas, Easter, and St. John the Baptist, with right of distraint in the said manors for non-payment. *Labelled* Glouc', Somers'.

290/59/11

[Cf. *Som. Fines, 1399–1484*, p. 157.]

2 Henry IV

1400

349. Morrow [12 Nov.] of St. Martin. Thomas Cruwe esquire, Nicholas Spenser chaplain, and John Fraysell chaplain quer.; William son and heir of John de Clopton def. The manors of Clopton (*Clopton*) under Meon (*Mune*) and Radbrook (*Rodbroke*). Right of John, as those which John, Thomas, and Nicholas had by William's gift. Remise and quitclaim to Thomas, Nicholas, and John and John's heirs. Cons. 200 marks.

79/84/5

1401

350. Morrow [3 Feb.] of the Purification. Richard Wyche clerk, William Perham clerk, John Reed (*Rede*) of Checkendon (*Chakenden*) and William Cassy quer.; John Gibbs (*Gybbes*) and Katherine his wife def. The manor of Stratton (*Stratton*) by Cirencester (*Cirencestre*) and the advowson of the church of the same manor. Grant to Richard,

1401

William, John Reed, and William, and render to them of whatever John Gibbs and Katherine had in the manor and advowson for term of Katherine's life and one year beyond. To hold to them and the heirs of William Cassy. Cons. 100 marks.

79/84/6

351. Two weeks [17 April] from Easter. Thomas Fladbury parson of the church of St. Michael, Gloucester (*Gloucestr'*), and Robert Turner (*Tournour*) chaplain quer.; John Marcle (*Markeleye*) and Isabel his wife def. A messuage and 4 shops in Gloucester (*Gloucestre*). Right of Thomas. Remise and quitclaim, specifying John's heirs, to Thomas and Robert and Thomas's heirs. (Warranty.) Cons. 20 marks.

79/84/7

352. Three weeks [24 April] from Easter. James Clifford, Anselm de Guise (*Gyse*), Walter Toky, Thomas Mursley (*Murseley*), Robert Gotherington (*Goderyngton*), and Thomas Thorp chaplain quer.; Thomas Dyer (*Dier*) of Bedminster (*Bedmynstre*) and Agnes his wife and Maurice Bryther of Easton in Gordano (*Eston in Gordon*) and Agnes his wife def. Rent of 20*s.* in Elmington (*Aylmyngton*). Right of Robert. Remise and quitclaim, specifying Agnes's and Agnes's heirs, to Robert and the other quer. and Robert's heirs. (Warranty.) Cons. 10 marks.

79/84/4

353. One month [1 May] from Easter. William Brown (*Broun*) of Thornbury (*Thornebury*) clerk quer.; John Paunton of the county of Gloucester (*Glouc'*) esquire and Joan his wife def. The manor of Sibland (*Sybelond*). Grant and render to William. To hold during his life, of John and Joan and Joan's heirs, paying a rose a year at St. John the Baptist and doing service to the chief lords. Reversion to John and Joan and Joan's heirs. Cons. £20.

79/84/2

354. One month [1 May] from Easter. John Barrow (*Barowe*) of Eldersfield (*Heldesfeld*) quer.; George atte Wood (*Wode*) and Margery his wife def. A messuage and 30 a. of land in Corse (*Cors*), and Staunton (*Staunton*). Right of John by gift of George and Margery. Remise and quitclaim, specifying Margery's heirs, to John. (Warranty.) Cons. 20 marks.

79/84/3

[Staunton was until 1931 largely, if not wholly, in Worcs.]

355. One week [5 June] from Trinity. Drew (*Drugo*) Barentyn, John Harrowden (*Harwedon*), William Mackeney, and Richard Kidlington (*Cudlyngton*) clerk quer.; Philip Sinclair (*Seyntclere*) 'chivaler', Ivo FitzWarren (*Fitz Waryn*) 'chivaler' and Matilda his wife, Baldwin St. George (*Seyntgeorge*) 'chivaler', John Hore and Joan his wife, and Thomas Loundres and Joan his wife def. The manor of Measham (*Meysham*), DERB., the manors of Wishaw (*Wyshawe*) and Shotteswell (*Shoteswell*) and the advowson of the church of Wishaw, WARWS., the manors of Steane (*Stene*) and Farthinghoe (*Farvyngho*) and the advowson of the church of Steane, NORTHANTS., the manor of Bickmarsh (*Bykemersshe*), GLOS., the manor of Biscott (*Biscote*), BEDS., the manors of Brightwell Baldwin (*Bryghtwell Huscarlus*) and Newnham Murren (*Newenham*), OXON., and the manor of Long Wittenham (*Wittenham*), BERKS. Right of Richard. Remise and quitclaim,

1401

specifying the heirs of Philip, Matilda, Baldwin, Joan, and Joan, to Drew, John Harrowden, William, and Richard and Richard's heirs. Cons. 1,000 marks. *Labelled* Derb', Warr', Norh't', Glouc', Bed', Oxon', Berk'.

290/59/29

[Cf. *Warws. Fines, 1345–1509*, p. 105, no. 2391. For the identity of Brightwell Baldwin, Newnham Murren, and Long Wittenham, *P.-N. Oxon.* i. 121; *Cal. Inq. p.m.* xvii, p. 312 and below, no. 356; *V.C.H. Berks.* iv. 387. Measham was transferred from Derb. to Leics. in 1897: *P.-N. Derb.* iii. 64 n.]

356. Morrow [25 June] of St. John the Baptist. Baldwin Barford (*Berford*) 'chivaler' and Elizabeth his wife quer.; Drew (*Drugo*) Barentyn, John Harrowden (*Harwedon*), William Mackeney, and Richard Kidlington (*Cudlyngton*) clerk def. The manors of Brightwell Baldwin (*Bryghtwell Huscarlus*), and Newnham Murren (*Newenham*), OXON., the manor of Biscott (*Byscote*), BEDS., the manor of Long Wittenham (*Wyttenham*), BERKS., the manor of Bickmarsh (*Bykemyrssh*), GLOS., the manors of Steane (*Stene*) and Farthinghoe (*Farvyngho*) and the advowson of the church of Steane, NORTHANTS., the manors of Wishaw (*Wysshawe*) and Shotteswell (*Shoteswell*) and the advowson of the church of Wishaw, WARWS., and the manor of Measham (*Meysham*), DERB. Grant and render of the manors of Brightwell Baldwin, Nuneham Courtenay, Biscott, Long Wittenham, Steane, Farthinghoe, Wishaw, Shotteswell, and Measham and the advowsons to Baldwin and Elizabeth. To hold to them and Baldwin's heirs in tail. And grant to them of the reversion of the manor of Bickmarsh (*Bykemerssh*) held by William Greville (*Gryvell*) of Campden (*Caumpden*) for term of life, of Richard's inheritance, to Baldwin and Elizabeth and Baldwin's said heirs. Contingent remainder of half the manors of Brightwell Baldwin, Nuneham, and Biscott to Ivo FitzWarren (*fitz Waryn*) 'chivaler' and Matilda his wife and Matilda's heirs, of the other half of the same manors to Baldwin St. George (*Seyntgeorge*) 'chivaler', of the manors of Steane, Farthinghoe, Shotteswell, and Bickmarsh and the advowson of the church of Steane to Philip Sinclair (*Seintclere*) 'chivaler', of the manors of Wishaw and Long Wittenham (*Wittenham*) and the advowson of [the church of] Wishaw to John Hore and Joan his wife and John's heirs, of the manor of Measham to Thomas Loundres (*Loundrez*) and Joan his wife and Joan's heirs in tail with successive contingent remainders to Thomas's heirs in tail and Joan's heirs. *Labelled* Oxon', Bed', Berk', Glouc', North', Warr', Derb'.

290/59/32

[Cf. *Warws. Fines, 1345–1509*, pp. 105–6, no. 2392; above, no. 355.]

3 Henry IV

1401

357. Two weeks [25 Nov.] from St. Martin. John Glastonbury (*Glastyngbury*) and Isabel his wife quer.; John Paunton and Joan his wife def. The manor of Brinsham (*Brymsham*). Grant and render to John Glastonbury and Isabel. To hold during their lives of the chief lords, paying to John Paunton and Joan and Joan's heirs 100s. a year, at Christmas, Easter, St. John the Baptist, and Michaelmas, with right of distraint in the said manor for non-payment. (Warranty, specifying Joan's heirs.) Cons. £10. [*Stained.*]

79/84/8

[The fine does not state that reversion shall be to John and Joan and Joan's heirs, which may be assumed to be so.]

1402

358. Two weeks [9 April] from Easter. (Made two weeks [27 Jan.] from Hilary in the said year.) John Popham 'chivaler' and Isabel his wife quer.; Walter Romsey (*Romesey*) 'chivaler' def. Twenty acres of meadow and 118*s*. 9*d*. rent in Oxford (*Oxon'*) and the suburbs of the same town, OXON., two thirds of the manor of Winford (*Wynfred*), SOM., a messuage, 1 ploughland, and 10 a. of meadow in Uley (*Uleigh*) and Cam (*Camme*), GLOS., held by Eleanor who was wife of John son of Peter le Veal (*Veel*) knight for term of life. Grant of the reversion, of Walter's inheritance, to John and Isabel and their heirs in tail. To hold of Walter, paying a rose a year at St. John the Baptist and doing service to the chief lords. (Warranty.) Contingent reversion to Walter. Cons. 100 marks. *Labelled* Oxon', Somers', Glouc'.

290/59/44

[Cf. *Som. Fines, 1399–1484*, p. 166.]

359. Three weeks [16 April] from Easter. Joan Scovyle quer.; Henry Veal (*Vyell*) and Alice his wife def. Sixty acres of land in Claverham (*Claverham*), SOM., £4 13*s*. 4*d*. rent in Shenington (*Schenyndon*), GLOS., and 5 marks rent in Coventry (*Covyntre*), WARWS. Right of Henry as to the land and 5 marks rent and of Alice as to the £4 13*s*. 4*d*. rent. For this, grant back and render to Joan. To hold during her life the land and 5 marks rent from Henry and Alice and Henry's heirs and the £4 13*s*. 4*d*. rent from Henry and Alice and Alice's heirs, paying a rose a year and doing service to the chief lords. Reversion to Henry and Alice and their respective heirs. *Labelled* Somers', Glouc', Warr'. [*Worn*.]

290/59/45

[Cf. *Som. Fines, 1399–1484*, p. 166. Omitted from *Warws. Fines, 1345–1509*.]

360. Morrow [5 May] of Ascension. John Oddington (*Odyngton*) quer.; William Dudbridge (*Duddebrugge*) and Cristina his wife def. A messuage, 1 yardland, and 3 a. of meadow in Stonehouse (*Stonehous*). Right of John. For this, grant back and render to William and Cristina. To hold during their lives, of John, paying a rose a year at St. John the Baptist and doing service to the chief lords. Reversion to John.

79/84/9

361. Two weeks [4 June] of Trinity. (Made the morrow [5 May] of Ascension in the said year.) Henry Inkpen (*Ingepenne*), William Tytherley (*Tuderle*), and Philip Shipiere quer.; Amaury de St. Amand (*de Sancto Amando*) 'chivaler' and Eleanor his wife def. The manors of St. Helen (*Seint Eleyne*) by Abingdon (*Abyndon*) and Eaton (*Eton*) by Cumnor (*Comenore*) and a messuage, 1 ploughland, and £10 rent in Chilton (*Chilton*) and Sutton Courtenay (*Sutton*), BERKS., the manors of Pudlicote (*Pudlicote*) and Chilson (*Childeston*), OXON., the manors of Netheravon (*Netheravene*) and Haxton (*Hakleston*), WILTS., the manors of South Cerney (*Southcerney*) and Cerney Wick (*Cerneywyke*), GLOS., and the manor of Catton (*Catton super Trentam*), DERB. Right of Henry, of which Henry, William, and Philip had the manors of St. Helen's, Pudlicote, Chilson, Netheravon, Haxton (*Hacleston*), South Cerney, Cerney Wick (*Cernewyk*), and Catton and the holdings by Amaury's gift. For this, grant and render to Amaury and Eleanor. To hold during their lives. And grant to them of the reversion of the manor of Eaton, held by Margaret who was wife of John Evesham for term of life, of Henry's inheritance. To hold as above. Remainder of all to Thomas Peyure, Geoffrey Ippelpenne, Henry Durnford

1402

(*Durneford*) clerk, and Edmund Danvers (*Daunvers*) and Edmund's heirs. *Labelled* Berk', Oxon', Wiltes', Glouc', Derb'. [*Worn.*]

290/59/50

[Cf. *Wilts. Fines, 1377–1509*, p. 47, no. 217.]

4 Henry IV

1402

362. One week [6 Oct.] from Michaelmas. Stephen Caneday quer.; Walter Caneday and Agnes his wife def. A messuage, 30 a. of land and 10 a. of meadow in Lawrence Weston (*Laueransweston*). Right of Stephen by gift of Walter and Agnes. Remise and quitclaim, specifying Agnes's heirs, to Stephen. (Warranty.) Cons. 20 marks.

79/84/12

363. Morrow [12 Nov.] of St. Martin. Lewis Greville (*Grevell*) quer.; Edward Benstead (*Benstede*) 'chivaler' and Joan his wife def. One third of 23 messuages, 3½ yardlands, and 25*s.* rent in Chipping Campden (*Chepyngcampeden*), Westington (*Westyngton*), Berrington (*Buryton*), Mickleton (*Mukelton*), Pebworth (*Pebbeworth*), and Ullington (*Olynton*), GLOS., and one third of 2 ploughlands in Ilmington (*Ilmyndon*), WARWS. Right of Lewis. Remise and quitclaim, specifying Joan's heirs, to him. Cons. 100 marks. *Labelled* Glouc', Warr'.

290/60/57

[Cf. *Warws. Fines, 1345–1509*, p. 110, no. 2410.]

1403

364. Two weeks [29 April] from Easter. John Bisley (*Byseleye*) and John Wyghale chaplain quer.; Robert Wick (*Wyke*) and Katherine his wife def. A toft, 24 a. of land, and 1 a. of meadow in Wotton (*Wotton*) by Gloucester (*Gloucestr'*). Right of John Bisley, as those which the same John and John Wyghale had by gift of Robert and Katherine. Remise and quitclaim, specifying, Katherine's heirs, to John and John and John Bisley's heirs. (Warranty.) Cons. 20 marks. [*Stained.*]

79/84/13

365. Two weeks [29 April] from Easter. (Made the morrow of All Souls in the said year [3 Nov. 1402].) John Berlegh and Isabel his wife quer.; Edmund Redburgh and Nicholas Hill (*Hull*) def. The manor of Calmsden (*Calmondesden*), GLOS., the manors of Berlegh (*Berlegh*), Cumberwell (*Comerwell*), Compton Bassett (*Compton*) by Calne (*Calne*), and Woodford (*Wodeford*) and 14 messuages, 100 a. of land, 3 a. of meadow, 10 a. of pasture, and rents of 4*d.* and ½ lb. of cumin in Colerne (*Collerne*) and Cumberwell, WILTS., and the manor of Shockerwick (*Shokerwyk*) and 6 messuages, a toft, 1 ploughland and 40 a. of land, 14 a. of meadow 100 a. of pasture, and 6 a. of wood in Hardington (*Hardyngton*) and Middle Chinnock (*Middilchynnok*), SOM. Right of Edmund. For this, grant and render by Edmund and Nicholas to John and Isabel of two thirds of the manors and holdings, and grant of the rents with the homage and all the services of Alice Ashley (*Assheley*) and John her son from the holdings which they held of Edmund and Nicholas in the township of Cumberwell. To hold to John and Isabel and their heirs in tail. And grant to John and Isabel of the reversion of the one third of the manors and holdings held by Alice Berlegh

1403

in dower, of Edmund's inheritance. To hold as above. Contingent remainder to John's heirs. *Labelled* Glouc', Wiltes', Somers'.

290/60/63

[Cf. *Som. Fines, 1399–1484*, p. 167; *Wilts. Fines, 1377–1509*, p. 49, no. 228.]

366. Three weeks [6 May] from Easter. Robert Gilbert (*Gilbard*) quer.; David ap Yeuan of Gloucester (*Gloucestre*) 'chapman' and Margery his wife, Thomas Lydney (*Lydeney*) and Agnes his wife, and Elena Field (*Felde*) of Gloucester def. A messuage in Gloucester. Right of Robert by gift of David and Margery, Thomas and Agnes, and Elena. Remise and quitclaim, specifying Margery's, Agnes's, and Elena's heirs, to Robert. (Warranty.) Cons. 10 marks.

79/84/14

367. One month [13 May] from Easter. Richard Plaistow (*Pleystowe*) quer.; John Skidby (*Skyteby*) and Alice his wife def. A messuage in Tewkesbury (*Teukesbury*). Right of Richard by gift of John and Alice. Remise and quitclaim, specifying Alice's heirs, to Richard. (Warranty.) Cons. 10 marks.

79/84/11

368. Morrow [25 May] of Ascension. Thomas Kemble (*Kemele*) and John Playstead (*Pleystede*) quer.; Thomas Moyne (*Moygne*) and Alice his wife def. The manor of Pirton (*Piryton*) and 3 messuages, 49 a. of land, and 1½ a. of meadow in Brickhampton (*Brighthampton*), Down Hatherley (*Dounhatherley*), Elmbridge (*Elbrugge*), and Quedgeley (*Quedesley*). Right of Thomas Kemble, as those which he and John had by gift of Thomas Moyne and Alice. For this, grant back and render to Thomas Moyne and Alice. To hold to them and Alice's heirs.

79/84/10

5 Henry IV

1403

369. One week [6 Oct.] from Michaelmas. (Made 2 weeks from Trinity 4 Henry IV [24 June 1403].) John Brown (*Broun*) and Geoffrey Wynbold quer.; Richard Urdeley (*Urdele*) and Alice his wife def. A messuage, 1 ploughland, 6 a. of meadow, and 5 a. of wood in Badminton (*Badmynton*) held by William Collins (*Colyns*) and Agnes his wife for term of life. Right of John. Grant of the reversion, of Richard's inheritance, to John and Geoffrey and John's heirs. (Warranty, by Richard and his heirs, without mention of Alice.) Cons. 20 marks. [*Torn.*]

79/84/15

370. Two weeks [13 Oct.] from Michaelmas. (Made one week from Michaelmas 4 Henry IV [6 Oct. 1402].) Reynold de Grey of Ruthin (*Ruthyn*), John Hervy, John Brent, John Merland, Thomas Bolour of the county of Hertford (*Hertf'*), William Otterhampton (*Oterhampton*) parson of the church of Silverton (*Silferton*), John Judde parson of the church of All Saints of Worcester (*Wyrcestre*), John Streech, John Manningford (*Manyngford*), Matthew Coker (*Cokere*), and John Sparrow (*Sparwe*) quer.; Matthew Gurney (*Gournay*) knight and Philippa his wife def. The manor of Shepperton (*Sheperton*) and the advowson of the church of the same manor, MIDDX., half of the

1403

manor of Silverton and the advowson of the church of the same manor, DEVON, the manors of Stoke sub Hamdon (*Stoke Underhamedon*), Curry Mallet (*Corymalet*), Englishcombe (*Inglescombe*), Welton (*Welweton*), Tellisford (*Telisford*), Laverton (*Laverton*), Harptree (*Harpetre*), Farrington Gurney (*Farenton*), Stratton on the Fosse (*Stratton Uppefosse*), Milton Falconbridge (*Milton Fauconberge*), Ryme (*Ryme*), Langton Herring (*Langton et Heryng*), half of the manor of Shepton Mallet (*Shepton Malet*), and the advowsons of the churches of Curry Mallet, Tellisford, Stratton on the Fosse, and Shepton Mallet and of the free chapel of Stoke sub Hamdon, SOM., the manors of Ryme (*Rym*) and Langton Herring (*Langton Heryng*), 8 messuages, 4 ploughlands, and 20 a. of meadow, in Hammoon (*Hamme Mown*), Sturminster Marshall (*Sturmynstre*), *Northalle*, and Baglake (*Babelake*), and the advowsons of the churches of Ryme (*Rym*) and Kington Magna (*Magna Kyngton*), DORSET, half of the manor of Sellinge (*Sellynges*), KENT, half of the manor of Magor (*Magor*) in the lordship of Chepstow (*Chipstowe*) in Wales (*Wall'*), GLOS., and the manor of Maidencourt (*Maydencote*), BUCKS. [*recte* BERKS.] Right of William Otterhampton, as those which he and the other quer. had by gift of Matthew and Philippa. Remise and quitclaim, specifying Matthew's heirs, to the quer. and William's heirs. (Warranty.) Cons. 500 marks. *Labelled* Midd', Devon', Somers', Dors', Kanc', Glouc', Buk'.

290/60/70

[Cf. *Dorset Fines, 1327–1485*, p. 238; *Som. Fines, 1399–1484*, p. 168. The naming of Ryme and Langton Herring as in Somerset in addition to Dorset is evidently erroneous. Magor is in Monmouthshire, places in which were included in final concords as though they were in Glos.]

1404

371. One week [9 Feb.] from the Purification. John atte Wood (*Wode*) and Alice his wife quer. by the same John; Anselm de Guise (*Gyse*) and Anne his wife def. A messuage, 5 ploughlands, 20 a. of meadow, 40 a. of wood, and rent of 1 lb. of cumin in Chedworth (*Cheddeworthe*). Right of John. Remise and quitclaim, specifying Anselm's heirs, to John and Alice and John's heirs. Cons. 20 marks.

79/84/16

372. One month [27 April] from Easter. John Deerhurst (*Derhurst*), Richard Salford (*Salforde*) chaplain, and Adam Apperley (*Appurleye*) quer. by Thomas Galbridge (*Galbrugge*); John Grant (*Graunt*) and Joan his wife def. Two messuages and 2 tofts in Tewkesbury (*Teukesbury*), GLOS., and 8 a. of land and 1 a. of meadow in Conderton (*Conturton*), WORCS. Right of John Deerhurst, as those which he, Richard, and Adam had by gift of John Grant and Joan. Remise and quitclaim, specifying Joan's heirs, to John Deerhurst, Richard, and Adam and that John's heirs. (Warranty.) Cons. 20 marks. *Labelled* Glouc', Wygorn'.

290/60/76

373. Morrow [9 May] of Ascension. John son of Henry Newman (*Neweman*) of Winchcombe (*Wynchecombe*) quer.; Nicholas Atwell (*atte Welle*) 'barbour' and Isabel his wife def. A messuage and 2s. rent in Winchcombe. Right of John. Remise and quitclaim, specifying Isabel's heirs, to him. (Warranty.) Cons. 10 marks.

79/84/17

6 Henry IV

1404

374. One month [27 Oct.] from Michaelmas. Robert Peers (*Piers*) quer.; John Baker (*Bakere*) and Agnes his wife def. Two messuages and 1 a. of land in Thornbury (*Thornbury*). Right of Robert by gift of John and Agnes. Remise and quitclaim, specifying Agnes's heirs, to Robert. (Warranty.) Cons. 20 marks.

79/84/20

375. One month [27 Oct.] from Michaelmas. John Baker (*Bakere*) and Agnes his wife quer.; Robert Joye and Elena his wife def. Two messuages and 1 a. of land in Thornbury (*Thornbury*). Right of Agnes, as those which John and Agnes had by gift of Robert and Elena. Remise and quitclaim, specifying Robert's heirs, to John and Agnes and Agnes's heirs. (Warranty.) Cons. 20 marks.

79/84/21

1405

376. One week [20 Jan.] from Hilary. Thomas de Bridge (*Brugge*) quer.; and Richard Underhill (*Underhull*) and Agnes his wife def. A messuage and 12 a. of land in Lassington (*Lassyndon*). Right of Thomas by gift of Richard and Agnes. Remise and quitclaim, specifying Agnes's heirs, to Thomas. (Warranty.) Cons. 100*s.*

79/84/19

377. Two weeks [3 May] from Easter. (Made two weeks [27 Jan.] from Hilary in the said year.) Edmund Basset and Richard Goodfellow (*Godefelagh*) clerk quer.; William Goodfellow and Joan his wife def. The manors of Sibland (*Sibelond*), Eastleach Turville (*Estlecche*), and Lawrence Weston (*Weston Sancti Laurencii*). Right of Richard, of which Richard and Edmund had the manors of Weston and Eastleach by gift of William and Joan. For this, grant back and render to William and Joan. To hold to them and their heirs in tail. And grant to William and Joan of the reversion of the manor of Sibland held by William Brown (*Broun*) for term of life, of Richard's inheritance. To hold as above. Successive contingent remainders to Joan's heirs in tail and to William Goodfellow's heirs. [*Stained and torn.*]

79/84/18

378. One month [17 May] from Easter. John Fawler (*Faellore*) of Filkins (*Fylkyng*) quer.; William Cowbridge (*Coubruge*) of Beckley (*Bekkeley*) and Agnes his wife def. Four messuages, 2 ploughlands, 24 a. of meadow, 10 a. of pasture, and rents of 16*d.* and a rose in Widford (*Wydeford*), GLOS., and a messuage, 2 tofts, 6½ a. of meadow, 4 a. of pasture, and three quarters of 1 ploughland in Burford (*Boreford*), Fulbrook (*Fulbrok*), and Swinbrook (*Swynebrok*), OXON. Right of John by gift of William and Agnes. Remise and quitclaim, specifying William's heirs, to John. (Warranty.) Cons. 100 marks. *Labelled* Glouc', Oxon'.

290/60/84

7 Henry IV

1405

379. One week [6 Oct.] from Michaelmas. Robert Andrew (*Andrewe*) quer.; John Reppe and Alice his wife def. A messuage, 2 yardlands, and 8 a. of meadow in Kempsford (*Kelmesford*). Right of Robert. Remise and quitclaim, specifying Alice's heirs, to him. (Warranty.) Cons. 20 marks.

79/85/27

380. One month [27 Oct.] from Michaelmas. (Made three weeks from Easter 6 Henry IV [10 May 1405].) John Bullock (*Bullok*) clerk and Roger Yurde clerk quer.; John Ellis (*Elys*) of Fishleigh (*Fisshelegh*) and Margery his wife def. A messuage, 2 tofts, 103 a. of land, 16 a. of meadow, and 6 a. of wood in Tawstock (*Toustoke*) and Atherington (*Atheryngton*), DEVON, and a messuage, 15 a. of land, 4 a. of meadow, and 13*s*. 4¼*d*. rent in Minsterworth (*Mynstreworth*) and Hampton (*Hamptone*), GLOS. John Ellis acknowledged the right of John Bullock, of which John and Roger had the messuages, the tofts, 111 a. of land, the meadow, and the wood by gift of John Ellis. For this, grant and render to John Ellis and Margery of those holdings and the rent with the homage and all the services of John Barrett (*Baret*), Henry Peers (*Piers*), John Huggins (*Huggys*) and Alice his wife, [. . .]field (. . .*ffeld*), Thomas atte Wood (*Wode*), John Rutter (*Rotour*) and Agatha his wife, Richard Lune, and Margery Seabrook (*Sebroke*) from the holdings which they held of John Bullock and Roger in the townships of Minsterworth and Hampton. To hold to John Ellis and Margery and their heirs in tail. And grant to them of the reversion of 8 a. of land in the township of Tawstock held by Walter Sweet (*Swete*) and Joan his wife for term of life and of 4 a. of land in the same township held by Roger Kent for term of life, of John Bullock's inheritance. To hold as above. Successive contingent remainders to Alice daughter of John Ellis and wife of Robert Grigg (*Grigge*) and her heirs in tail and to Thomas Rashleigh (*Raysshelegh*) of Rashleigh. *Labelled* Devon', Glouc'. [*Stained*.]

290/60/94

[Of the first acreage of land, 103 a., only 100 is legible with ultra-violet light but the total is deduced from the acreages given later in the fine.]

381. One month [27 Oct.] from Michaelmas. William Pensford clerk, John Burford clerk, and Henry Haresfield (*Harsfeld*) clerk quer.; John Droys and Margaret his wife def. Twenty-four messuages, 56 shops, 10 tofts, and 10 marks rent in the town of Bristol (*Bristoll'*) and the suburbs of the same, BRISTOL, and 2 messuages, 10 shops, 20 a. of land, and 2 a. of meadow in Belluton (*Belweton*) and Pensford (*Pensford*), SOM. Right of Henry, as those which Henry, William, and John Burford had by gift of John Droys and Margaret. Remise and quitclaim, specifying Margaret's heirs, to William, John Burford, and Henry and Henry's heirs. (Warranty.) Cons. 200 marks. *Labelled* Bristoll', Somers'.

290/60/95

[Cf. *Som. Fines, 1399–1484*, pp. 169–70.]

1406

382. Two weeks [27 Jan.] from Hilary. (Made one week from St. Martin 3 Henry IV [18 Nov. 1401].) Philip atte Nelme chaplain quer.; William Rye and Alice his wife def. The manors of Coates (*Cotes*) and Wiggold (*Wyggewold*) and the advowson of the church of

1406

the said manor of Coates. Right of Philip, of which he had the manor of Coates and the advowson by gift of William and Alice. For this, grant back and render to William and Alice. To hold to them and William's heirs. And grant to them of the reversion of the manor of Wiggold, held by William Tanner (*Tannere*) of Cirencester (*Cirencestre*) and Joan his wife for term of life, of Philip's inheritance. To hold as above. Made in the presence of William Tanner and Joan and with their consent, and they did fealty to William Rye and Alice.

79/84/22

383. Two weeks [25 April] from Easter. (Made the morrow [3 Feb.] of the Purification in the said year.) Richard des Armes clerk and John Woodward (*Wodeward*) of Mitcheldean (*Michelden*) quer.; John Wyther of Cam (*Camme*) and Joan his wife def. Five messuages, 200 a. of land, 20 a. of meadow, and 8 a. of wood in Cam, Coaley (*Coueley*), and North Nibley (*Nibley*). Right of Richard, as those which Richard and John Woodward had by gift of John Wyther and Joan. For this, grant back and render to John Wyther and Joan. To hold to them and their heirs in tail. Contingent remainder to John Wyther's heirs.

79/84/23

384. Two weeks [25 April] from Easter. Thomas Fladbury parson of the church of St. Michael, Gloucester (*Gloucestr'*), and Thomas Gregory chaplain quer.; Robert Gilbert and Joan his wife def. Three messuages and 8 shops in Gloucester (*Gloucestre*). Right of Thomas Fladbury, as those which the same Thomas and Thomas Gregory had by gift of Robert and Joan. Remise and quitclaim, specifying Joan's heirs, to Thomas and Thomas and Thomas Fladbury's heirs. (Warranty.) Cons. £20.

79/84/24

385. Two weeks [25 April] from Easter. Edmund Basset and Richard Goodfellow (*Godefelagh*) clerk quer.; William Goodfellow and Joan his wife def. The manor of Brinsham (*Brimesham*). Right of Richard, as that which the same Richard and Edmund had by gift of William and Joan. For this, grant back and render to William and Joan. To hold to them their heirs in tail. Successive contingent remainders to Joan's heirs in tail and to William's heirs.

79/84/25

386. Three weeks [2 May] from Easter. Thomas Wheatenhurst (*Whytenhurst*) chaplain quer.; Richard atte Water (*Watre*) and Cecily his wife def. (Made one week from St. Martin 22 Ric. II [18 Nov. 1398], when John Cassy knight, Thomas Wheatenhurst chaplain, and John Croys chaplain were quer., of whom John Cassy and John Croys were both dead by the time that the fine was granted and recorded.) A messuage, 60 a. of land, and 3 a. of meadow in Gotherington (*Goderynton*), held by John Chapman (*Chapmon*) of Stoke Orchard (*Stoke*) and Sibyl his wife, late wife of John Sampson, for the term of Sibyl's life. Right of John Cassy. Grant of the reversion, of Cecily's inheritance, to John Cassy, Thomas, and John Croys and John Cassy's heirs. (Warranty.) Cons. £20. [*Torn and stained.*]

79/85/26

8 Henry IV

1406

387. Three weeks [20 Oct.] from Michaelmas. Thomas Compton of Gloucester (*Gloucestre*) quer.; Richard atte Ford (*Forde*) def. A messuage and 2 shops in Gloucester. Right of Thomas by Richard's gift. Remise and quitclaim to Thomas. (Warranty.) Cons. £20.

79/85/28

1407

388. Two weeks [10 April] from Easter. (Made one week [9 Feb.] from the Purification in the said year.) Thomas atte Water (*Watre*) and Joan his wife quer.; Richard Wyatt (*Wyot*) and John Scott (*Scot*) def. Twelve messuages, 6 ploughlands, 20 a. of meadow, 160 a. of wood, and £12 rent in Goring (*Goryng*), South Stoke (*Stoke Abbot*), Gatehampton (*Gathampton*), and Kelmscott (*Kelmescote*) and a fishery in the water of Thames (*Thamisie*) 6 stades long, OXON., the manors called Michael's Court (*Michelscourt*) and Paynel's Court (*Paynelesmaner*), 8 messuages, 110 a. of land, and 26 a. of meadow in Buscot (*Borewardescote*) and Streatley (*Stretele*), a fishery in the water of Thames 6 stades long in the said township of Streatley, and the advowson of the church of the township of Buscot, BERKS., and 6 messuages, a mill, 2 ploughlands, 8 a. of meadow, 60 a. of pasture, 10 a. of wood, and 35*s.* rent in Colesborne (*Collesbourne*), Elkstone (*Elkeston*), Stoke Orchard (*Archerestoke*), and Withington (*Whythyndon*) and half of the manor of Colesborne, GLOS. Thomas acknowledged the right of Richard. For this, grant and render by Richard and John to Thomas and Joan. To hold to Thomas and Joan and their heirs in tail, of Richard and John and Richard's heirs, paying a rose a year at St. John the Baptist and doing service to the chief lords. Contingent reversion to Richard and John and Richard's heirs. *Labelled* Oxon', Berk', Glouc'.

290/61/113

[For South Stoke, *P.-N. Oxon.* i. 156; Michael's Court and Paynel's Court were in Buscot: *V.C.H. Berks.* iv. 413, 515. The reading Michelscourt is uncertain, the middle of the word being lost to the filing hole.]

389. Morrow [25 June] of St. John the Baptist. Thomas Banbury (*Bannebury*) of Gloucester (*Gloucestre*) quer.; Robert Gilbert (*Gilberd*) and Joan his wife def. One third of 6 messuages, 11 shops, 5 cottages, 3 yardlands, 6 a. of meadow, and 30 a. of pasture in Gloucester, Cirencester (*Cirencetre*), Horsemarling (*Horsmarley*), and Longney (*Longeney*). Grant to Thomas, and remise and quitclaim to him of all Joan's right of dower in the premises. Cons. 100 marks.

79/85/29

9 Henry IV

1408

390. Two weeks [29 April] from Easter. (Made one week [20 Jan.] from Hilary in the said year.) Robert Stroud (*Strode*) and Margery his wife quer.; John Burgess (*Burgeys*) clerk and John Granger (*Graunger*) clerk def. A messuage, 1 ploughland, 5 a. of meadow, 3 a. of wood, and 8*s.* rent in Stean Bridge (*Stenesbrugge*). Right of John Burgess, as those which the same John and John Granger had by gift of Robert and Margery. For this, grant back and render to Robert and Margery, with the homage and services of John Mey and Joan his wife for the lands which they formerly held of John Burgess and John Granger in the said township. To hold to Robert and Margery and their heirs in tail. Successive contingent remainders to Henry Fermour son of John Fermour of Paganhill (*Pagenhull*)

1408

in tail, to John son of John atte Quarry (*Qwarer*) in tail, to Roger son of John Reaney (*Reeni*) in tail, and to Margery's heirs.

79/85/33

391. Two weeks [29 April] from Easter. John Swerford, vicar of the church of Hook Norton (*Hoggenorton*) and John Ingram quer.; John Willicote (*Wilcotes*) and Alice his wife def. Four messuages and 1 yardland in Chipping Campden (*Chepyngcampeden*) and Broad Campden (*Brodecampeden*). Right of John Swerford, as those which the same John and John Ingram had by gift of John Willicote and Alice. Remise and quitclaim, specifying Alice's heirs, to John and John and John Swerford's heirs. (Warranty.) Cons. £20.

79/85/32

392. One week [17 June] from Trinity. John Coppe of Gloucester (*Gloucestre*) 'bocher' quer.; John Daunsepront and Katherine his wife def. Rent of 15*s.* from a messuage in Gloucester. Grant to John Coppe of the said rent, which Edward Toky, the tenant of the said holding, used to pay, at Michaelmas and Easter. (Warranty, specifying Katherine's heirs.) Cons. 10 marks.

79/85/30

393. One week [17 June] from Trinity. (Made three weeks from Easter [9?] Hen. IV [6 May 1408?].) Robert [. . .] of Newent (*Newent*) quer.; Guy Whittington (*Whytyngton*) and Cecily his wife def. The manors of Rodborough (*Rodebergh*) and Notgrove (*Nategrave*) and 14 messuages, a toft, [. . .] mills, 3 ploughlands, 12 a. of meadow, and 4 a. of wood in Ebley (*Ebbeley*), Thrupp (*Throp'*), and Harford (*Hertford*). Right of Robert by gift of Guy and Cecily. For this, grant back and render to Guy and Cecily. To hold to them in tail. Contingent remainder of the manor of Rodborough, the messuages, the mills, 1½ ploughlands, 9 a. of meadow, and the wood in Ebley and Thrupp to Cecily's heirs; of the manor of Notgrove, the toft, 1½ ploughland, and 3 a. of meadow in Harford to Robert Whittington during his life, successive remainders to John Browning (*Brounyng*) during his life and to John son of John Browning in tail, with contingent remainder to Cecily's heirs. [*Torn.*]

79/85/31

10 Henry IV

1408

394. Two weeks [13 Oct.] from Michaelmas. Thomas Good (*Gode*) of Chipping Campden (*Chepyngecampeden*) and John Hulot chaplain quer.; John Archer of Ilmington (*Ilmyndon*) and Matilda his wife def. Two messuages and 1 yardland in Mickleton (*Mukelton*). Right of Thomas, as those which Thomas and John Hulot had by gift of John Archer and Matilda. Remise and quitclaim, specifying Matilda's heirs, to Thomas and John Hulot and Thomas's heirs. Cons. 20 marks.

79/85/38

395. Three weeks [20 Oct.] from Michaelmas. Robert Westspreye quer.; John Spendelove and Leticia his wife def. A messuage and ⅛ a. of land in Cirencester (*Cirencestre*). Right of Robert by gift of John and Leticia. Remise and quitclaim, specifying John's heirs, to Robert. (Warranty.) Cons. 10 marks.

79/85/40

1408

396. Morrow [3 Nov.] of All Souls. Hugh Stringer (*Stryngere*) quer.; John son of Thomas Twyning (*Twenynge*) of Tewkesbury (*Teukesbury*) and Isabel his wife def. A toft in Tewkesbury. Right of Hugh by gift of John and Isabel. Remise and quitclaim, specifying Isabel's heirs, to Hugh. (Warranty.) Cons. 100*s*.

79/85/37

397. Morrow [12 Nov.] of St. Martin. John Upford (*Uppeford*) clerk, John Butler (*Boteller*), Richard Maidstone (*Maydeston*), Giles Harleston, and Roger Hunt quer.; William Otterhampton (*Oterhampton*) parson of the church of Silverton (*Silferton*) def. The manor of Shepperton (*Sheperton*) and the advowson of the church of the same manor, MIDDX., the manors of Curry Mallet (*Corymalet*), Englishcombe (*Ingelscombe*), Norton (*Norton*), Welton (*Welweton*), Tellisford (*Telisford*), Laverton (*Laverton*), Harptree (*Harpetre*), Farrington Gurney (*Farenton*), Stratton-on-the-Fosse (*Stratton Uppefosse*), Milton Falconbridge (*Milton Fauconberge*), and Stoke sub Hamdon (*Stoke Underhampdon*) (except for 2 messuages, 40 a. of land, and 4 a. of meadow in the manor of Stoke sub Hamdon), a messuage, 1 ploughland, and 40 a. of meadow in *Northalle*, half of the manor of Shepton Mallet (*Shepton Malet*), and the advowsons of the churches of the manors of Curry Mallet, Tellisford, Stratton on the Fosse, and Shepton Mallet and of the free chapel of the manor of Stoke sub Hamdon, SOM., the manors of Ryme (*Ryme*) and Langton Herring (*Langton Heryng*), 8 messuages, 4 ploughlands, and 60 a. of meadow in Hammoon (*Hammemowne*), Sturminster Marshall (*Sturmynstre*), *Northolt*, and Baglake (*Babbelake*), and the advowsons of the churches of the manor of Ryme and of Kington Magna (*Magna Kyngton*), DORSET, half of the manor of Sellinge (*Sellynges*), KENT, the manor of Maidencourt (*Maydencote*), BERKS., and half of the manor of Magor (*Magor*), GLOS. Right of John Upford. Grant to him and the other quer. and to his heirs of the reversion of the said manors, holdings, halves, and advowsons held by John Tiptoft (*Tiptot*) 'chivaler' and Philippa his wife for term of Philippa's life, of William's inheritance. (Warranty.) Cons. 5,000 marks. *Labelled* Midd', Somers', Dors', Kanc', Berk', Glouc'.

290/61/133

[Cf. *Dorset Fines, 1327–1485*, pp. 240–1; *Som. Fines, 1399–1484*, p. 171; above, no. 370; Magor is in Monmouthshire, places in which were included in final concords as though they were in Glos.]

398. One week [18 Nov.] from St. Martin. Walter Knight (*Knyght*) and Elizabeth his wife and Henry Tailor (*Taillour*) of Cam (*Camme*) quer.; John Rolves def. Twenty-four acres of pasture in Cam called Bowers Lye (*Bourslye*). Grant and render to Walter, Elizabeth, and Henry. To hold to Walter and Elizabeth and Henry and Elizabeth's heirs, paying to John during his life 21*s*. a year, at Christmas, Easter, St. John the Baptist, and Michaelmas, with right of distraint for non-payment, the payment to cease on John's death. Cons. 20 marks.

79/85/39

1409

399. One week [20 Jan.] from Hilary. (Made one week from St. Martin in the said year [18 Nov. 1408].) William Rye and Alice his wife quer.; William Tanner of Cirencester

1409

(*Cirencestre*) and Joan his wife and Geoffrey atte Hyde def. The manor of Wiggold (*Wyggewold*). Right of William Rye as that which that William and Alice had by gift of William Tanner, Joan, and Geoffrey. Quitclaim, specifying Joan's heirs, to William Rye and Alice and William Rye's heirs. Cons. 100 marks.

79/85/35

400. One week [20 Jan.] from Hilary. (Made one week from St. Martin in the said year [18 Nov. 1408].) Henry Tailor (*Taillour*) of Cam (*Camme*) and Joan his wife quer.; Walter Knight (*Knyght*) of Cam and Elizabeth his wife def. A messuage, 72 a. of land, 4 a. of meadow, 13 a. of pasture, and 27*s*. 6*d*. rent in Cam and Coaley (*Coueleye*). Grant and render to Henry and Joan of the holdings and 8*s*. rent. To hold in tail, of Walter and Elizabeth and Elizabeth's heirs, paying 2s. a year, at Easter and Michaelmas, and doing service to the chief lords. And grant of the reversion of 19*s*. 6*d*. rent in Cam held by Thomas de Berkeley (*Berkeley*), lord of Berkeley, for term of life of Elizabeth's inheritance. To hold as above. Contingent reversion to Walter and Elizabeth and Elizabeth's heirs. Cons. 20 marks.

79/85/36

401. One week [9 June] from Trinity. John Leighton (*Leghton*) of Mitcheldean (*Mucheldene*) quer.; John Fletcher (*Fleccher*) of Lea (*Lee*) and Agnes his wife def. A messuage in Mitcheldean. Right of John Leighton by gift of John Fletcher and Agnes. Remise and quitclaim, specifying Agnes's heirs, to John Leighton. (Warranty.) Cons. 10 marks.

79/85/34

11 Henry IV

1409

402. Three weeks [20 Oct.] from Michaelmas. Walter Grove of Hartpury (*Hardepiry*) quer.; Walter Clerk otherwise called Walter Palmer (*Palmere*) of Hartpury and Elena his wife def. A messuage, 8 a. of land, and ½ a. of meadow in Hartpury. Right of Walter Grove. Remise and quitclaim, specifying Elena's heirs, to Walter Grove. (Warranty.) Cons. 10 marks.

79/85/41

403. Three weeks [20 Oct.] from Michaelmas. John Fastolf esquire and Milicent his wife quer.; John Kirtling (*Kirtelyng*) parson of the church of St. Mary, Long Stratton (*Longstratton*), and William Ilketshall (*Ilketishale*) clerk def. The manor of Bentley (*Benteley*) and the advowson of the church of the same manor, YORKS., the manor of Castle Combe (*Castelcombe*) and the advowson of the church of the same manor, WILTS., and the manor of Oxenton (*Oxmanton alias dicto Oxinton*), GLOS. Right of John Kirtling, as those which the same John and William had by gift of John Fastolf and Milicent. For this, grant back and render to John Fastolf and Milicent. To hold to them and to Milicent's heirs in tail by Stephen le Scrope (*Lescrop*) formerly her husband. Contingent remainder to Milicent's heirs. *Labelled* Ebor', Wiltes', Glouc'.

290/61/147

[Cf. *Wilts. Fines, 1377–1509*, pp. 64–5, no. 303.]

1409

404. One month [27 Oct.] from Michaelmas. Robert Stanshawe and Isabel his wife quer.; William Parker and Alice his wife def. A messuage, 9 a. of land, and 5 a. of meadow in Bradley (*Bradeley*), Wotton under Edge (*Wotton*), and Wortley (*Worteley*). Right of Robert, as those which Robert and Isabel had by gift of William and Alice. Remise and quitclaim, specifying Alice's heirs, to Robert and Isabel and Robert's heirs. Cons. 20 marks.

79/85/42

[Cf. *Berkeley Castle Mun.* i, p. 348, A1/52/5 (counterpart).]

1410

405. One week [20 Jan.] from Hilary. (Made the morrow of St. Martin in the said year [12 Nov. 1409].) Richard Walker atte Bridge (*Brugge*) of Newent (*Newent*) and Katherine his wife quer.; John Webber (*Webbe*) of Newent tailor and Margaret his wife def. Seven acres of land in Newent. Right of Richard, as that which Richard and Katherine had by gift of John and Margaret. Remise and quitclaim, specifying Margaret's heirs, to Richard and Katherine and Richard's heirs. Cons. 100*s*.

79/85/43

406. One week [20 Jan.] from Hilary. (Made the morrow of Ascension 10 Hen. IV [17 May 1409].) John Stabold (*Stabald*) chaplain and John Saunders (*Saundris*) burgess of the town of Gloucester (*Gloucestr'*) quer. by Henry Geddington (*Gedyngton*); Richard Brentwood (*Brendewode*) citizen and baker of London (*London*) and Agnes his wife def. A messuage, a garden, 1 a. of land, and 1 a. of meadow in Twigworth (*Twygworthe*) and Wallsworth (*Wallisworthe*). Right of John Stabold, as that which that John and John Saunders had by gift of Richard and Agnes. Remise and quitclaim, specifying Agnes's heirs, to John and John and John Stabold's heirs. (Warranty.) Cons. 100*s*.

79/85/44

407. One week [20 Jan.] from Hilary. (Made one week from St. Martin in the said year [18 Nov. 1409].) Robert Gilbert quer.; Richard Brentwood (*Brendewode*) and Agnes his wife def. Two messuages and a shop in the suburb of Gloucester (*Gloucestr'*). Right of Robert. Render to him of one messuage. And grant to him of the reversion of one messuage and the shop, held by Katherine who was wife of Hugh Parker for term of life, of Agnes's inheritance. (Warranty.) Cons. 20 marks.

79/85/45

12 Henry IV

1410

408. One month [27 Oct.] from Michaelmas. Robert Whittington (*Whytington*) quer.; William Machin (*Machon*) and Denise his wife and John Beale (*Bele*) and Sibyl his wife def. One third of a messuage, a mill, 2 ploughlands, 7 a. of meadow, 12 a. of pasture, 28 a. of wood, and 60*s*. rent in Frampton Mansell (*Frompton Mauncell'*). Right of Robert by gift of William, Denise, John, and Sibyl. Remise and quitclaim, specifying the heirs of Denise and Sibyl, to Robert. (Warranty.) Cons. 100 marks.

79/85/47

1410

409. One week [18 Nov.] from St. Martin. Thomas Berkeley of Berkeley (*Berkeley*) 'chivaler' quer.; Robert Stanshawe and Isabel his wife def. A messuage, 11 a. of land, and 5 a. of meadow in Bradley (*Bradeley*). Right of Thomas by gift of Robert and Isabel. Remise and quitclaim, specifying Isabel's heirs, to him. Cons. 20 marks.

79/85/46

1411

410. One week [20 Jan.] from Hilary. (Made the morrow of St. Martin in the said year [12 Nov. 1410].) Robert Higford (*Huggeford*) and Thomas Gower quer.; Katherine who was wife of John Pecche 'chivaler' and William Montfort (*Mountfort*) of Coleshill (*Colshull*) and Margaret his wife def. The manors of Hampton in Arden (*Hampton in Arderne*), Diddington (*Dydynton*), Honiley (*Honyley*), Blackwell (*Blakwell*), Wormleighton (*Wyrmeleyghton*), Fenny Compton (*Fennycompton*), Avon Dassett (*Avenderset*), Dunchurch (*Dunchirche*), and Toft (*Toft*), rents of 12*s.* and a barbed arrow in Amington (*Amynton*) and Curdworth (*Crudworth*), the homage and service of William Shepey, 2½ knights' fees in Elmdon (*Elmedon*) and Whitacre (*Whitacre*) and in the said townships of Wormleighton and Diddington, and the advowsons of the churches of the said manors of Hampton in Arden, Honiley, and Avon Dassett, WARWS., and the manor of Shenington (*Shenyngton*) and a messuage, 40 a. of land, and 6 a. of meadow in Shenington, GLOS. Right of Robert, as those which Robert and Thomas had by gift of Katherine and William and Margaret. For this, grant back and render to Katherine of the manors of Hampton, Diddington, Honiley, Blackwell, Wormleighton, Fenny Compton, Avon Dassett, and Shenington, the holdings, rents, fees, and advowsons, with the homage and all the services of William Shepey from the holdings which he held of Robert and Thomas in the said townships of Amington and Curdworth. To hold to Katherine during her life. Remainder to William Montfort and Margaret and their heirs in tail. Contingent remainder to Margaret's heirs. And grant back and render to William and Margaret of the manors of Dunchurch and Toft. To hold to them and their heirs in tail. Contingent remainder to Margaret's heirs. *Labelled* Warr', Glouc'.

291/62/159

[Cf. *Warws. Fines, 1345–1509*, p. 122, no. 2462.]

411. One week [20 Jan.] from Hilary. John Giffard and Thomas his brother quer.; John Jeram of Bristol (*Bristoll'*) and Margaret his wife def. Half of a messuage, 2 ploughlands, and 12 a. of meadow in Prestbury (*Prestebury*). Right of John Giffard, as that which that John and Thomas had by gift of John Jeram and Margaret. Remise and quitclaim, specifying Margaret's heirs, to John Giffard and Thomas and John Giffard's heirs. (Warranty.) Cons. 20 marks.

79/85/49

412. One week [9 Feb.] from the Purification. Margaret Seabrook (*Seybroke*) and Lionel Seabrook quer.; Thomas Mursley (*Morslegh*) and Robert Gotherington (*Goderyngton*) def. The manor of Elmington (*Aylmynton*). Right of Thomas, as that which Thomas and Robert had by gift of Margaret and Lionel. For this, grant and render to Margaret. To hold during her life. Reversion to Lionel in tail. Contingent reversion to Margaret's heirs.

79/85/48

1411

413. Two weeks [26 April] from Easter. (Made the morrow [3 Feb.] of the Purification in the said year.) Thomas Capell' clerk and John Wickham (*Wykham*) quer.; John More and Margery his wife def. The manor of Hempton (*Hempton*) and 6 marks rent in Stoke Gifford (*Stoke*) and the Wyck (*Wyke*), held by Alexander Clevedon (*Clyvedon*) and Joan his wife for term of Joan's life. Right of Thomas. Grant to him of the reversion of the manor and rent, of Margery's inheritance. (Warranty.) Cons. 200 marks.

79/85/50

414. One month [10 May] from Easter. Thomas Longley (*Longeley*) bishop of Durham (*Dunelm*), William Thurning (*Thirnyng*) knight, John Henege, Nicholas Motte parson of the church of Swineshead (*Swyneshevede*), Richard Lumbard parson of the church of Haltham (*Holtham*), William Rouceby vicar of the church of Sleaford (*Sleford*), William Auncell, John Overton, and Richard Frith quer.; Thomas la Warre clerk def. The manor of Sixhills (*Sixhill*), LINCS., and the manor of Wickwar (*Wykewarre*) and the advowson of the church of Wickwar, GLOS. Right of William Rouceby, as those which William, the bishop and the other quer. had by Thomas la Warre's gift. For this, grant back and render to Thomas la Warre. To hold to him and his heirs in tail, of the quer. and William Rouceby's heirs, paying a rose a year at St. John the Baptist and doing service to the chief lords. Successive contingent remainders to Thomas West and his heirs in tail and to Thomas West's brother Reynold and his heirs in tail. Contingent reversion to the quer. and William Rouceby's heirs. *Labelled* Lincoln', Glouc'. [*Stained.*]

291/62/162

13 Henry IV

1411

415. One month [27 Oct.] from Michaelmas. William Stephens (*Stevenes*) of Bristol (*Bristoll'*) quer.; Nicholas Mansell (*Maunsel*) otherwise called Nicholas Bailly of Leonard Stanley (*Lethenardestanley*) and Agnes his wife def. Eleven messuages in King's Stanley (*Kyngestanley*). Right of William by gift of Nicholas and Agnes. Remise and quitclaim, specifying Nicholas's heirs, to William. (Warranty.) Cons. 100 marks.

79/85/52

416. Morrow [3 Nov.] of All Souls. John More quer.; Henry Veal (*Vyole*) and Alice his wife def. Two thirds of the manor of Shenington (*Shenyndon*). Right of John by gift of Henry and Alice. Remise and quitclaim, specifying Alice's heirs, to John. Cons. £20.

79/85/51

1412

417. Morrow [3 Feb.] of the Purification. William Wynbold (*Wynbaude*) and Joan his wife and William's son Thomas quer.; Richard Urdeley of Eastcourt (*Escote*) and Alice his wife def. Two tofts, 56 a. of land, 8 a. of meadow, and 12 a. of pasture in Hawkesbury (*Haukesbury*). Right of William. Remise and quitclaim, specifying Richard's heirs, to William, Joan, and Thomas and William's heirs. To hold to William, Joan, and Thomas and William's heirs. (Warranty, by Richard alone.) Cons. 20 marks.

79/85/55

1412

418. One week [9 Feb.] from the Purification. Maurice Russell knight, Thomas Elwelle clerk, and William White clerk quer.; John Drayton knight and Isabel his wife def. The manors of Tormarton (*Tormerton*) and Acton Turville (*Acton Turvyle*). Right of Maurice as those which Maurice, Thomas, and William had by gift of John and Isabel. For this, grant back and render to John and Isabel. To hold during Isabel's life, of Maurice, Thomas, and William and Maurice's heirs, paying one grain of wheat a year at Michaelmas and doing service to the chief lords. Reversion to Maurice, Thomas, and William and Maurice's heirs.

79/85/53

419. One week [9 Feb.] from the Purification. Richard Aylwy quer.; William Cappe and Joan his wife def. A messuage, 1 ploughland, and 8 a. of meadow in Pauntley (*Paunteley*) and Newent (*Newent*). Right of Richard by gift of William and Joan. Remise and quitclaim, specifying Joan's heirs, to Richard. (Warranty.) Cons. 10 marks.

79/85/54

420. One week [9 Feb.] from the Purification. Richard Salford clerk and Walter Gough (*Guygg*) quer.; John Rich (*Riche*) and Alice his wife def. Ten messuages, a toft, 13 a. of land, and 1 a. of meadow in Tewkesbury (*Teukesbury*), GLOS., a messuage and 1 yardland in *Kytebevynton* [Bevington Waste?], WORCS., and a messuage in Bristol (*Bristoll'*), BRISTOL. Right of Walter, as those which Walter and Richard had by gift of John and Alice. Remise and quitclaim, specifying Alice's heirs, to Richard and Walter and Walter's heirs. Cons. 200 marks. *Labelled* Glouc', Wygorn', Bristoll'.

291/62/171

421. Two weeks [17 April] from Easter. (Made two weeks [27 Jan.] from Hilary in the said year.) Nicholas Bernard of Tetbury (*Tettebury*) quer.; Richard Urdeley of Eastcourt (*Escote*) and Alice his wife def. Twenty-five acres of meadow in Hawkesbury (*Haukesbury*). Right of Nicholas. Grant, specifying Richard's heirs, to Nicholas of the reversion of 12½ a. of the said meadow held by William Wynbold (*Wynbaude*) for term of life, and of 12½ a. of the same held by Stephen Chalkley (*Chalkeley*) and Juliana his wife for term of life. (Warranty.) Cons. 20 marks.

79/85/58

422. Two weeks [17 April] from Easter. (Made the morrow [9 Feb.] of the Purification in the said year.) John Obbeton (*Obeton*) and Walter Clerk quer.; William Gore and Joan his wife def. The manor of Abson (*Abboteston*) and a messuage, 4 yardlands and 10 a. of meadow in Pucklechurch (*Pokelchurche*), Codrington (*Coderyngton*), Churchley (*Churchelegh*), and Wick (*Wyke*), held by Matilda who was wife of Richard Heynes of Pucklechurch for term of life. Right of John. Grant to John and Walter of the reversion of the premises, of Joan's inheritance. (Warranty.) Cons. 100 marks.

79/85/59

423. Two weeks [17 April] from Easter. (Made the morrow [9 Feb.] of the Purification in the said year.) John Obbeton and Walter Clerk quer.; William Gore (*Gore*, *Goore*) and Joan his wife def. The manors of Brinsham (*Brymesham*) and Lawrence Weston (*Weston sancti Laurencii*). Right of John, as those which John and Walter had by gift of William

1412

and Joan. For this, grant back and render to William and Joan. To hold to William and Joan and Joan's issue by William Goodfellow (*Goodfelawe*) her late husband. Successive contingent remainders to Joan's issue and to Joan's heirs.

79/85/60

424. Two weeks [17 April] from Easter. (Made the morrow [9 Feb.] of the Purification in the said year.) John Obbeton and Walter Clerk quer.; William Gore and Joan his wife def. The manor of Eastleach Turville (*Estlecche*). Right of John, as that which John and William Clerk had by gift of William Gore and Joan. For this, grant back and render to William and Joan. To hold to them and Joan's issue. Contingent remainder to Joan's heirs.

79/85/61

425. One month [1 May] from Easter. John Thorp and Isabel his wife quer.; Richard Acton (*Ecton*) the elder def. A messuage, 9 a. of land, 3 a. of meadow, 80 a. of pasture, 2 fisheries in the river Severn (*aqua Sabrine*), and 2*s.* rent in Ham (*Hamme*). Right of Isabel, as those which John and Isabel had by Richard's gift. For this, grant back and render to Richard. To hold during his life, of John and Isabel and Isabel's heirs, paying a rose a year at St. John the Baptist and doing service to the chief lords. Remainder to Robert Acton and Richard Acton the younger, sons of Richard Acton the elder, to hold during their lives as above. Reversion to John Thorp and Isabel and Isabel's heirs. (Warranty.) [*Torn and stained.*]

79/85/56

426. One month [1 May] from Easter. Thomas Berkeley of Berkeley (*Berkeley*) 'chivaler' quer.; Robert Stanshawe and Isabel his wife def. A messuage, 20 a. of land, 8 a. of meadow, and 5 a. of wood in Horton (*Horton*) and Yate (*Yate*). Right of Thomas by gift of Robert and Isabel. Remise and quitclaim, specifying Robert's heirs, to Thomas. (Warranty, by Robert alone.) Cons. 20 marks.

79/85/57

427. One month [1 May] from Easter. John Hughes (*Hugges*) quer.; Thomas Sollers (*Solers*) and Alice his wife def. A messuage in Northleach (*Northlecch'*). Right of John. Render to him. (Warranty, specifying Alice's heirs.) Cons. 10 marks.

79/85/62

428. One week [5 June] from Trinity. (Made one month [1 May] from Easter in the said year.) Philip Pole quer.; Thomas Braunston of Tewkesbury (*Teukesbury*) and Joan his wife def. A messuage in Tewkesbury held by Richard Throckmorton (*Throkmerton*) and Alice his wife for term of life. Right of Philip. Grant to Philip of the reversion of the messuage, of Joan's inheritance. (Warranty.) Cons. 20 marks.

79/85/63

14 Henry IV

1413

429. One week [9 Feb.] from the Purification. John Brooke (*Broke*) clerk and William Radford (*Radeford*) clerk quer.; William Palton knight and Elizabeth his wife. The manors of Wick (*Wyke*), *Bourbache* [Burrowbridge?], Hoccombe (*Hockombe*), Brompton Ralph (*Brompton Rauf*), Elworthy (*Elleworthy*), and Withycombe (*Wydecombe*),

1413

30 ploughlands, 100 a. of meadow, 200 a. of pasture, and 200 a. of wood in the same townships, and the advowson of the church of Withycombe, SOM., the manors of Umberleigh (*Womberleye*), Beaford (*Beauford*), Riddlecombe (*Rydelcombe*), Huntshaw (*Hunsshaue*), Stoke Rivers (*Stokeryvers*), Uplowman (*Uplomone*), Gittisham (*Gydesham*), Langley (*Langleye*), and Wonford (*Wamford*), the bailiwick of the hundred of West Budleigh (*Westbuddeleghe*), and the advowsons of the churches of Atherington (*Atheryngton*), High Bickington (*Bykyngton*), Huntshaw, and Uplowman and of the chantries of Umberleigh and Beaford, DEVON, half of the manor of Frampton Cotterell (*Frampton Cottell'*) and one sixth of the manors of Sandhurst (*Sandhurst*) and Ablington (*Ablyngton*) and of 1 ploughland, 10 a. of meadow, and 10 a. of pasture in Moorslade (*Moreslade*), GLOS., the manor of Lanteglos (*Lanteglos*), two thirds of the manors of Trevillis (*Trevilias*) and Fawton (*Fawyton*), and half of the borough of Polruan (*Polruan*), CORNW., and half of the advowson of the chantry of Asserton (*Assarton*), WILTS. Right of John and William Radford as to half of the manor of Frampton Cotterell and of William Radford as to the residue, by gift of William Palton and Elizabeth. For this, grant back and render to William Palton and Elizabeth. To hold to them and their heirs in tail, the manor of Frampton Cotterell of the king and the residue of the chief lords. Successive contingent remainders to Elizabeth's heirs in tail, to William's heirs in tail, to the heirs in tail of that William's brother John Palton, and to Isabel who was wife of William Beaumont (*Beaumond*). Made by the king's order as to Frampton Cotterell. *Labelled* Somers', Devon', Glouc', Cornub', Wiltes'. [*Worn and stained.*]

291/62/184

[Cf. *Cornwall Fines, 1377–1461*, pp. 120–1, no. 193; *Som. Fines, 1399–1484*, p. 174; *Wilts. Fines, 1377–1509*, p. 68, no. 320.]

1 Henry V

1413

430. One week [25 June] from Trinity. (Made one week from the Purification 14 Henry IV [9 Feb. 1413].) William Gore and Joan his wife and Margaret daughter of the same William quer.; John Obbeton (*Obeton*) and Walter Clerk def. The manor of Abson (*Abboteston*) and a messuage, 4 yardlands, and 10 a. of meadow in Pucklechurch (*Pokelchurche*), Codrington (*Coderyngton*), Churchley (*Churchelegh*), and Wick (*Wyke*) held by Matilda who was wife of Richard Heynes of Pucklechurch for term of life. Right of Joan. Grant to William, Joan, Margaret and Joan's heirs of the reversion, of John's inheritance. Cons. 200 marks.

79/86/1

431. One week [25 June] from Trinity. Richard Power esquire and Thomas Holme chaplain quer. Thomas Norton and Cristina his wife def. A mill and 13*s*. 4*d*. rent in Kingston Seymour (*Kyngeston Seymour*), one third of the manor of [. . .] and the advowson of the church of the same manor, SOM., and a messuage in the parish of St. Nicholas, Bristol (*Bristoll'*), called 'le Newe In', BRISTOL. Thomas Norton acknowledged the right of Thomas Holme, as those which the same Thomas and Richard had by Thomas Norton's gift. For this, grant and render to Thomas Norton and Cristina. To hold during their lives. Remainder of the mill, rent, one third, and advowson to Thomas Norton the younger, son of Thomas Norton the elder and Cristina, and his heirs in tail, with successive contingent remainders to the younger Thomas's brother Walter and his heirs in tail, to Walter's sister

1413

Alice and her heirs in tail, and to the heirs of Thomas Norton the elder. Remainder of the messuage to the said Walter and his heirs in tail, with successive contingent remainders to the younger Thomas and his heirs in tail, to the said Alice and her heirs in tail, and to the heirs of Thomas Norton the elder. *Labelled* Somers', Bristoll'. [*Torn, worn, and stained.*]

291/63/4

[Cf. *Som. Fines, 1399–1484*, pp. 174–5. Much of the middle of the document is missing, and the reconstruction of the provisions for the remainders is somewhat speculative.]

432. One week [25 June] from Trinity. Thomas Loud and John Adam quer.; Thomas Brooke (*Brook*) [. . .] and Joan his wife def. The manors of West Bagborough (*Westbaggeburgh*) and Stewley (*Stivelegh*) and the advowson of the church of West Bagborough, SOM., and 14 messuages, 14 [shops?], 4 cellars, 2 a. of land, and 10*s*. 10*d*. rent in Bristol (*Bristoll'*) and the suburbs of the same town, BRISTOL. Right of Thomas Loud, as those which the same Thomas and John had by gift of Thomas Brooke and Joan. For this, grant back and render to Thomas and Joan. To hold to them and their heirs in tail. Contingent remainder to Thomas Brooke's heirs. *Labelled* Somers', Bristoll'. [*Torn.*]

291/63/6

[Cf. *Som. Fines, 1399–1484*, p. 175. The words missing after Thomas Brooke's name evidently indicated his address or calling.]

433. Three weeks [20 Oct.] from Michaelmas. John Limerick (*Lymeryk*) and Thomas Hunt (*Hunte*) chaplain quer.; Richard Lardener of Daglingworth (*Dagelyngworth*) and Agnes his wife def. A messuage and 140 a. of land in Daglingworth. Right of John, as those which John and Thomas had by gift of Richard and Agnes. Remise and quitclaim, specifying Agnes's heirs, to John and Thomas and John's heirs. (Warranty.) Cons. 20 marks.

79/86/3

434. One month [27 Oct.] from Michaelmas. Nicholas Morris (*Morys*) the younger quer.; John Punter and Joan his wife def. A messuage, 1½ yardlands, and 10 a. of meadow in Tockington (*Tokynton*). Right of Nicholas. Remise and quitclaim, specifying Joan's heirs, to Nicholas. (Warranty.) Cons. 20 marks.

79/86/4

435. One month [27 Oct.] from Michaelmas. John Giffard of Leckhampton (*Lechamton*) quer.; John Machin (*Machyn*) of Boughton (*Boghton*) and Agnes his wife def. One quarter of the manor of Up Hatherley (*Uphatherley*). Right of John Giffard by gift of John Machin and Agnes. Remise and quitclaim, specifying Agnes's heirs, to John Giffard. (Warranty.) Cons. 20 marks.

79/86/5

1414

436. One week [20 Jan.] from Hilary. John de Mowbray (*Moubray*) earl marshal and of Nottingham (*Notyngham*) brother and heir of Thomas late earl marshal quer.; John Grey son of Reynold Grey lord of Ruthin (*Ruthyn*) and Constance his wife def. Two thirds of the manors of Epworth (*Eppeworth*) and Wroot (*Wrote*), LINCS., the manors of Aspley (*Aspeley*) and Alspath (*Alspath*), 30 messuages and 30 yardlands in Flecknoe (*Flekkenho*) and Thurlaston (*Thurlaston*), and two thirds of the manor of Caludon (*Caloughdon*), WARWS., two thirds of the manor of Chacombe (*Chacumbe*), NORTHANTS., the manors of

1414

Sileby (*Sylby*) and Mountsorrel (*Mountsorill*), 100 a. of wood and 100 a. of pasture in Cold Overton (*Colde Overton*), and two thirds of the manor of Melton Mowbray (*Melton Moubray*), LEICS., the manors of Dunnington (*Donyngton*) and Thwaite (*Thwayte*) and two thirds of the manors of Thirsk (*Thresk*) and Hovingham (*Hovyngham*), YORKS., the castle of Bedford (*Bedford*) and the manor of Willington (*Wylyngton*), 400 a. of wood, 100 a. of pasture, 40*s*. rent, and one quarter of [. . . in] Haynes (*Hawenes*), Cople (*Coupell*), Cardington (*Kerdyngton*), Barford (*Bereford*), Southill (*Southyevell*), Maulden (*Maldon*), Wootton (*Wotton*), Ickwell (*Yekewell*), Salph End (*Salensho*), and Bedford (*Bedeford*), and the advowson of the the the free chapel of Haynes (*Haw[enes]*) [BEDS.] [the manor of North Piddle] and the advowson of the church of the same manor, WORCS., the manors of Dovercourt (*Dovercourt*) and Upper Hall (*Ladyhalle in Moreton*) [ESSEX, the castle, manor and borough of Bramber (*Br]embre*) and the manors of King's Barns (*Kyngesbarnes*), Beeding (*Bedyng*), Washington (*Wassyngton*), Bewbush (*Beaubussh*), Horsham (*Horsham*), Bosham (*Bosheham*) and Stoughton (*Stokton*), SUSSEX, [the lordships] of Gower (*Gower*) and Kilvey (*Kylveye*) in Wales (*Wall'*), HEREFS., the manor of Tidenham (*Tudenham*) and the castle, manor, [and town of Chepstow] GLOS., a toft and 2 yardlands in Alsthorpe (*Alsthorp juxta Burghley*), RUTLAND, the manor [of Fenstanton and rents] issuing from the same manor, HUNTS., the manors of Hanworth (*Hanworth*), Forncett (*Fornesete*), Lopham (*Loppeham*), Earsham (*Ersham*), Suffield (*South[field]*) NORF.], the manor of Framlingham (*Framelyngham*), SUFF. Right of [the earl. Remise and quitclaim from John and] Constance and Constance's heirs to the earl. Cons. (paid to John Grey and Constance) 5,000 marks. *Labelled* Lincoln', Warr', Norht', Leyc', Ebor', Bed', Wygorn', Essex', Sussex', Hereford', Glouc', Rotele', Hunt', Norff', Suff'. [*Holed and badly stained.*]

291/63/11

[Cf. *Essex Fines, 1327–1422*, p. 261; *Warws. Fines, 1345–1509*, p. 127, no. 2480. The acknowledgement mentions a borough, presumably Bramber; cf. *V.C.H. Sussex*, vi (1), 4, 206. For Chepstow (Mon.), close to the Glos. boundary, *Cal. Inq. p.m.* xviii, p. 81. For Alsthorpe, *V.C.H. Rutland*, ii. 112, 116. For details supplied in square brackets cf. *Cal.Inq. p.m.* (Rec. Com.) iv. 145–52.]

437. Two weeks [27 Jan.] from Hilary. Walter Pole knight and Elizabeth his wife quer.; John Speek and Margaret his wife def. Eight messuages, 100 a. of land, 20 a. of meadow, 20 a. of pasture, 30 a. of wood, and 100*s*. rent in Stinchcombe (*Styntescombe*), Stancombe (*Stancombe*), and Matson (*Metesdone*). Right of Elizabeth, as those which Walter and Elizabeth had by gift of John and Margaret. Remise and quitclaim, specifying Margaret's heirs, to Walter and Elizabeth and Elizabeth's heirs. (Warranty.) Cons. 100 marks.

79/86/2

2 Henry V

1414

438. One week [10 June] from Trinity. (Made one week from the Purification 14 Henry IV [9 Feb. 1413].) Henry Nansumer clerk, Richard Wyche clerk, and John Lanoy quer.; William Clinton (*Clynton*) knight def. The manor of Temple Guiting (*Temple Gutyng*) held by Elizabeth who was wife of John Clinton knight for term of life. Right of Henry, Richard, and John. Grant of the reversion, of William's inheritance, to Henry, Richard, and John and their heirs. (Warranty.) Cons. 100 marks. Made in Elizabeth's presence and

1414

with her consent, and she did fealty to Henry, Richard, and John. Made by the king's order.

79/86/9

[The grant to three men and their heirs is too vague to provide for the succession.]

439. Three weeks [20 Oct.] from Michaelmas. John Woodward (*Wodeward*) and Thomas Marky of Walford (*Walford*) quer.; Joseph Basshe and Margery his wife def. A messuage and 5 a. of land in Mitcheldean (*Mucheldene*). Right of Thomas, as those which Thomas and John had by gift of Joseph and Margery. For this, grant back and render to Joseph and Margery. To hold to them and their heirs in tail. Successive contingent remainder to Agnes daughter of William Basshe and her heirs in tail and to Margery's heirs.

79/86/6

440. One month [27 Oct.] from Michaelmas. John Droys of Bristol (*Bristoll'*) quer.; Richard Webb (*Webbe*) of Hampnett (*Hamptenet*) def. A messuage, 2 tofts, 170 a. of land, and 12 a. of meadow in Hampnett. Right of John. Remise and quitclaim to him. (Warranty.) Cons. 10 marks.

79/86/8

441. Morrow [12 Nov.] of St. Martin. John Fawler (*Faellore*) quer.; Thomas More and Margaret his wife def. A messuage, a mill, 2 yardlands, 7 a. of meadow, and rents of 14*s*. 0½*d*. and 1 lb. of cumin in Widford (*Wydeford*) and the advowson of the church of Widford. Right of John by gift of Thomas and Margaret. Remise and quitclaim, specifying Thomas's heirs, to John. (Warranty.) Cons. 100 marks.

79/86/7

3 Henry V

1415

442. One week [9 June] from Trinity. (Made one month [28 April] from Easter in the said year.) Nicholas Sheepscombe (*Shepyscombe*) quer.; Nicholas Mansell (*Maunsell*) of Leonard Stanley (*Stanley Monachorum*) and Agnes his wife def. A messuage and 20 a. of land in King's Stanley (*Stanley Regis*). Right of Nicholas Sheepscombe by gift of Nicholas Mansell and Agnes. Remise and quitclaim, specifying Nicholas Mansell's heirs, to Nicholas Sheepscombe. (Warranty.) Cons. 20 marks.

79/86/10

443. Morrow [25 June] of St. John the Baptist. Richard [Courtenay] bishop of Norwich (*Norwic'*), Thomas [FitzAlan] earl of Arundel (*Arundell*), Richard [Beauchamp] earl of Warwick (*Warr'*), Henry le Scrope (*Lescrop*) 'chivaler', Thomas de Berkeley, 'chivaler', Edward Charlton (*Charleton*) 'chivaler', Joan who was wife of William Beauchamp of Abergavenny (*Bergevenny*), John Pelham 'chivaler', Robert Corbet 'chivaler', John Greyndor (*Greyndour*) 'chivaler', Walter Lucy, Thomas Chaucer, William Walwyn, Thomas Holgate (*Holgote*), and Richard Wigmore (*Wygmore*) quer.; Edmund [de Mortimer] earl of March (*March*) def. The castles and lordships of Rhayader (*Raydr*), Cefnllys (*Kenlles*), Radnor (*Radenore*), and Knucklas (*Knoclas*) and the town of Radnor, the lordships of Maelienydd (*Melleimyth*), Builth (*Pullith*), Knighton (*Knyghton*), Gwrtheyrnion (*Warthreignon*), Cwmwd Deuddwr (*Comotoidour*), Norton (*Norton*), and

1415

Presteigne (*Presthanid*), the manors of Orleton (*Orleton*), Kingsland (*Kyngeslane*), Pembridge (*Pembrugge*), Mansell Lacy (*Malmeshull Lacy*), Netherwood (*Nethewode*), Marden (*Mawardyn*), and Wolferlow (*Wolferlowe*) and two thirds of the manor of Much Marcle (*Magna Marcle*), HEREFS. and the marches of Wales adjoining thereto, the castle, manor, and town of Ludlow (*Ludlowe*), the manor and lordship of Stanton Lacy (*Staunton Lacy*), and the manors of Cleeton (*Cleeton*) and Farlow (*Farlowe*), SALOP., the manor of Upper Arley (*Arley*), STAFFS., the manors of Bromsgrove (*Brymmesgrove*), King's Norton (*Norton*), and Clifton on Teme (*Clifton*), WORCS., the manors of Whaddon (*Whaddon*) and Steeple Claydon (*Stepulclaydon*), BUCKS., the manors of Ducklington (*Dokelyngton*) and Finmere (*Fynmere*), OXON., the manors of Stratfield Mortimer (*Stratfeld Mortymer*) and Warfield (*Waghfeld*), BERKS., two thirds of the manor of Thaxted (*Thaxstede*), ESSEX, the manor of Martyr Worthy (*Worthy Mortymer*), HANTS., the manors of Cranborne (*Cranburn*), Pimperne (*Pymperne*), Gussage St. Michael (*Gussiche Boun*), Tarrant Gunville (*Tarent Gundevile*), Weymouth (*Weymouth*), Wyke Regis (*Wyke*), Portland (*Portland*), Wareham (*Warham*), Steeple (*Stuple*), and Creech (*Crich*), DORSET, the manors of Swanscombe (*Swannescombe*), Tonge (*Tong*), and Erith (*Erhithe*), KENT, the castle of Bridgwater (*Bruggewater*), the manors of Odcombe (*Odecombe*) and Milverton (*Milverton*), and one third of the lordship of Bridgwater, SOM., and the manors of Bisley (*Byslegh*), Barnsley (*Bardeslegh*), Lechlade (*Lychelade*), Lower Siddington (*Sodyngton*), Miserden (*Mussarder*), Charlton Kings (*Chorlton*), Winstone (*Wynston*), and Brimpsfield (*Brymmesfeld*), GLOS. As to the castles, [the lordships, the towns], and the manors of Orleton, Kingsland, Pembridge, Mansell Lacy, Nethe[rwood, Marden], Wolferlow, Ludlow, Arley, Bromsgrove, Norton, Whaddon, Steeple Claydon, Stratfield Mortimer, W[arfield, Martyr Worthy], Swanscombe, Tonge, Erith, Cranborne, Pimperne, [Gussage, *Bovu*, Tarrant] Gunville, Weymouth, Wyke Regis, Portland, Wareham, Steeple, Creech, Odcombe, Milverton, Bisley, [Barnsley, Lechlade, Siddington, Miserden], Charlton, Winstone, and Brimpsfield and the said [two thirds and one third], the right of the bishop and the other quer. [. . .]. [And as to . . .] the manors of Cleeton, Farlow, [Clifton on Teme, Ducklington, and Finmere], the right of Thomas de Berkeley, as those which he, the bishop, and the other quer. had by gift of the earl of March. (Warranty.) Cons. (given by the bishop, the earl of Arundel, the earl of Warwick, Henry, Thomas, Edward, [. . .], Thomas, William, Thomas, and Richard to the earl of March) £100,000 (*centum millia libras sterlingorum*). Made by the king's order. *Labelled* Hereford', Salop', Staff', Wygorn', Buk', Oxon', Berk', Essex', Sutht', Dors', Kanc', [Somers', Glouc']. [*Stained and holed.*]

291/63/31

[Cf. *Dorset Fines, 1327–1485*, pp. 274–6; *Essex Fines, 1327–1422*, pp. 265–6; *Som. Fines, 1399–1484*, pp. 176–7; *Staffs. Fines, 1327–1547*, p. 225. Much of the foot of fine is illegible, but some of the details of the acknowledgement clauses can be deduced, as indicated above in square brackets, from the *habendum* and warranty clauses.]

1416

444. Two weeks [27 Jan.] from Hilary. William Bagpuize (*Bakepuz*) quer.; Thomas Butler (*Boteler*) of London (*London'*) 'draper' and Alice his wife def. Five messuages, 86 a. of land, and 3 a. of pasture in Winchcombe (*Wynchecombe*), Hawling (*Hallyng*), and Gretton (*Gretton*). Right of William by gift of Thomas and Alice. Remise and quitclaim, specifying Alice's heirs, to William. (Warranty.) Cons. 20 marks.

79/86/11

4 Henry V

1416

445. One week [6 Oct.] from Michaelmas. (Made three weeks from Michaelmas 3 Henry IV [20 Oct. 1415].) John Petty (*Petyt*) and Philippa his wife quer.; William Lisle (*Lysle*) and Amice his wife def. Two messuages, 1½ yardlands, 7½ a. of meadow, and 15*s*. rent in Evenlode (*Evenelode*), WORCS., and 5 messuages, 7½ yardlands, 16 a. of meadow, and 40*s*. rent in Sezincote (*Shesencote*), GLOS. Right of Philippa. For this, grant and render by John and Philippa to William and Amice of 2 messuages, 1½ yardlands, 7½ a. of meadow, and the said rent. To hold to William and Amice during their lives, of John and Philippa and Philippa's heirs, paying after Amice's death if William survives her 3*s*. a year at Michaelmas and doing service to the chief lords. And grant to William and Amice of the reversion of 5 messuages, 7½ yardlands, and 16 a. of meadow held by John Greville (*Grevell*) for term of life, of Philippa's inheritance in the township of Sezincote. To hold as above. Reversion to John and Philippa and Philippa's heirs. *Labelled* Wygorn', Glouc'.

291/63/46

1417

446. Morrow [3 Feb.] of the Purification. Thomas Mortimer (*Mortymer*), John Willicote (*Willicotes*), Robert Andrew (*Andrewe*), Thomas Laurence, and Richard Payn quer.; John Conquest of the county of Bedford (*Bed'*) esquire def. A messuage called Fynegales, 2 ploughlands, 40 a. of meadow, 6 a. of pasture, and 5*s*. rent in Southwick (*Southewyk*) and Gupshill (*Gopushull*). Right of Richard, as those which Richard, Thomas, John Willicote, Robert, and Thomas had by John Conquest's gift. Remise and quitclaim to Thomas, John, Richard, and Thomas and Richard's heirs. (Warranty.) Cons. 50 marks.

79/86/12

5 Henry V

1417

447. Two weeks [25 April] from Easter. (Made one week from the Purification 4 Henry V [9 Feb. 1417].) William Hayward quer.; Walter Knight (*Knyght*) and Elizabeth his wife def. Two messuages, 170 a. of land, 9 a. of meadow, 32 a. of pasture, 51*s*. 4*d*. rent, and half of 1 a. of wood in Cam (*Camme*) and Coaley (*Coueley*). Right of William, of which he had one messuage, 78 a. of land, 5 a. of meadow, 19 a. of pasture, 4*s*. 4*d*. rent, and the half of 1 a. of wood by gift of Walter and Elizabeth. And grant to William of 47*s*. rent with the homage and all the services of Thomas de Berkeley knight lord of Berkeley (*Berkeley*) and Henry Tailor (*Taillour*) of Cam and Joan his wife from all the holdings which they held of Walter and Elizabeth in the said townships. And grant to William of the reversion of a messuage, 92 a. of land, 4 a. of meadow, and 13 a. of pasture held by Henry Tailor of Cam and Joan his wife for term of life, of Elizabeth's inheritance in the said townships. (Warranty.) Cons. 100 marks. [*Worn*.]

79/86/13

448. Morrow [12 Nov.] of St. Martin. William Palecock (*Palcok*) of Tewkesbury (*Teukesbury*) quer.; Giles Large of Bredon (*Breodon*) and Elena his wife def. A messuage in Tewkesbury. Right of William. Remise and quitclaim, specifying Elena's heirs, to William. (Warranty.) Cons. 10 marks.

79/86/14

6 Henry V

1418

449. Two weeks [8 July] from St. John the Baptist. John Richardson (*Rychardyssone*) quer.; John Fletcher (*Fleccher*) and Agnes his wife def. A messuage in Mitcheldean (*Mycheldene*). Right of John Richardson by gift of John Fletcher and Agnes. Remise and quitclaim, specifying Agnes's heirs, to John Richardson. (Warranty.) Cons. 10 marks.

79/86/15

7 Henry V

1419

450. Two weeks [30 April] from Easter. (Made the morrow of Ascension 5 Henry V [21 May 1417].) John Chaddesden (*Chaddusden*) quer.; John Melbourne (*Melburne*) and Elizabeth his wife def. The manor of Munsley (*Mounesley*), HEREFS., and the manor of Bulley (*Bolley*), GLOS. John Melbourne acknowledged the right of John Chaddesden, of which he had the manor of Munsley by John Melbourne's gift. For this, grant and render of that manor to John Melbourne and Elizabeth. To hold to them and their heirs in tail. And grant to them of the reversion of the manor of Bulley held by Richard de la Mare and Isabel his wife for term of Isabel's life, of John Chaddesden's inheritance. To hold as above. Contingent remainder to John Melbourne's heirs. *Labelled* Hereford', Glouc'.

291/64/79

451. One week [18 June] from Trinity. Robert Whittington (*Wityngton*) esquire, William Birdlip (*Bridlep*) burgess of the town of Gloucester (*Gloucestr'*), John Davies (*Davyes*) of Newent (*Newent*) and Joan his wife, and Stephen Mile chaplain quer.; Thomas Freville (*Frevyle*) and Petronilla his wife def. A messuage and half of 1 a. in Gloucester (Gloucestre). Right of John, as those which John and Joan, Robert, William, and Stephen had by gift of Thomas and Petronilla. Remise and quitclaim, specifying Petronilla's heirs, to Robert, William, John and Joan, and Stephen and John's heirs. (Warranty.) Cons. 20 marks.

79/86/17

452. One week [18 June] from Trinity. John Lock (*Lokke*) chaplain, John Lavender chaplain, Richard Darcy clerk, and John Hardwicke (*Herdwyke*) quer.; William Harley (*Harleye*) of Gloucester (*Gloucestre*) and Joan his wife def. A messuage and 4 shops in Gloucester. Right of John Lock, as those which that John, John Lavender, Richard, and John Hardwicke had by gift of William and Joan. Remise and quitclaim, specifying William's heirs, to John, John, Richard, and John and John Lock's heirs. (Warranty.) Cons. 20 marks.

79/86/18

453. One week [6 Oct.] from Michaelmas. (Made one week [1 July] from St. John the Baptist in the said year.) John Bridge (*Brugge*) of Staunton on Wye (*Staundon*), Herefs., esquire, John Russell, and Thomas Heaven (*Hevyn*) quer.; Edith who was wife of Richard Mawardyn esquire def. The manor of Little Sodbury (*Parva Sobbury*) and the advowson of the church of the same manor. Right of John Bridge. Render to that John, John, and Thomas except for 60*s.* rent in the same manor. Grant to John, John, and Thomas of the said rent, with the homage and all the services of John Whiteley, Thomas Palfreyman,

1419

Nicholas atte Hill (*Hulle*), William Cook (*Cooke*), and John Francombe (*Frankhome*) from all the holdings which they held of Edith in the said manor. To hold to John Bridge, John Russell, and John Heaven and John Bridge's heirs. (Warranty.) Cons. 100 marks.

79/86/16

454. One week [6 Oct.] from Michaelmas. (Made one month [14 May] from Easter in the said year.) Lewis Greville (*Grevell*) esquire and Richard Mickleton (*Mikelton*) clerk quer.; John Greville esquire and Sibyl his wife def. The manor of Farmcote (*Farnecote*), GLOS., the manor of Standlake (*Stanlake*), OXON., and the manor of Tubney (*Tubbeney*) and the advowson of the church of the same manor, BERKS., and the manors of Hadley (*Hadley*) and Hatton (*Hatton*), SALOP. Right of Lewis, as those which Lewis and Richard had by gift of John and Sibyl. For this, grant back and render to John and Sibyl. To hold to them and their heirs in tail. Successive contingent remainders to Guy Corbet and his heirs in tail and to Gilbert Corbet and his heirs in tail, then of one quarter to Joan wife of John Winslow (*Wynslowe*) and her heirs in tail, to Margaret wife of Thomas More and her heirs in tail, to Agnes wife of William Rookwood (*Rokewode*) and her heirs in tail, to Elizabeth wife of Thomas Rothwell (*Rothewell*) and her heirs in tail, and to Sibyl's heirs, of the second quarter similarly but in the order Margaret, Joan, Agnes, Elizabeth, of the third quarter similarly but in the order Agnes, Joan, Margaret, Elizabeth, and of the fourth quarter similarly but in the order Elizabeth, Joan, Margaret, Agnes. *Labelled* Glouc', Oxon', Berk', Salop'. [*Worn and stained.*]

291/64/84

[The fine offers an extreme example of verbosity, with the contingent remainders of the four quarters stated in full for each quarter.]

455. Morrow [3 Nov.] of All Souls. Henry Haresfield (*Harsefeld*) chaplain and Thomas Halewey burgess of the town of Bristol (*Bristoll'*) quer.; Henry Gildeny of Bristol and Joan his wife def. A messuage, 200 a. of land, 12 a. of meadow, 200 a. of pasture, and 20 a. of wood in Siston (*Ciston*), GLOS., and 7 messuages and 5 shops (*chopis*) in Bristol and the suburbs of the same, [BRISTOL]. Right of Henry Haresfield, as those which he and Thomas had by gift of Henry Gildeny and Joan. For this, grant back and render to Henry Gildeny and Joan. To hold to them and their heirs in tail. Contingent remainder to Joan's heirs. *Labelled* Glouc', Bristoll'.

291/64/85

8 Henry V

1420

456. One week [9 June] from Trinity. John Weatherhead (*Wethurhird*) and Margaret Weatherhead quer.; John Parkin (*Perkyn*) of Bishop's Cleeve (*Clyve Episcopi*) and Agnes his wife def. A messuage, 30 a. of land, 2 a. of meadow, and 1½d. rent in Bishop's Cleeve, Gotherington (*Goderynton*), and Woodmancote (*Wodmancote*). Right of John Weatherhead, as those which John and Margaret had by gift of John Parkin and Agnes. Remise and quitclaim, specifying Agnes's heirs, to John Weatherhead and Margaret and that John's heirs. (Warranty.) Cons. 20 marks.

79/86/20

1420

457. Morrow [3 Nov.] of All Souls. John prior of Bath (*Bathon'*), Henry Green (*Grene*) parson of the church of Norton, John Horton parson of the church Trowbridge (*Trowebrigge*), Roger Tilly, and John Sumner (*Sompnour*) of Rode (*Rode*) quer.; Robert Long (*Longe*) and Margaret his wife def. Sixteen messuages, 2 ploughlands, 24 a. of meadow, 30 a. of wood, and rents of 19*d.* and a pair of gloves in Coombe (*Combe*) and Wotton under Edge (*Wotton subtus Egge*). Right of John Sumner, as those which that John, John the prior, Henry, John Horton, and Roger had by gift of Roger and Margaret. Remise and quitclaim, specifying Margaret's heirs, to John, Henry, John, Roger, and John and John Sumner's heirs. (Warranty.) Cons. 100 marks.

79/86/19

458. Morrow [3 Nov.] of All Souls. William Palecock (*Palcok*) quer.; Thomas Galbridge (*Galbrigge*) of Tewkesbury (*Teukesbury*) and Mary his wife def. Two messuages, 9 a. of land, and half of 1 a. of meadow in Tewkesbury and Tredington (*Tredyngton*) by Tewkesbury. Right of William by gift of Thomas and Mary. Remise and quitclaim, specifying Mary's heirs, to William. (Warranty.) Cons. 20 marks.

79/86/21

459. One week [18 Nov.] from St. Martin. Robert Russell and Roger Levedon quer.; John Newton (*Nuton*) burgess of the town of Bristol (*Bristoll'*) and Joan his wife def. Eight messuages and 4 gardens in the suburbs of Bristol, [BRISTOL], and 12 messuages, 292 a. of land, 27 a. of meadow, and 6 a. of wood in Hay (*le Haye*) by Filton (*Filton*), Shirehampton (*Shernyhampton*), Westbury on Trym (*Westbury*), Cote (*Cote*), Compton Greenfield (*Compton Grenevyle*), Tockington (*Tokynton*), Wickwar (*Wykewarre*), Wicks Oldbury (*Oldebury*), and Cromhall (*Cromhale*), GLOS. Right of Roger, as those which Roger and Robert had by gift of John and Joan. For this, grant back and render to John and Joan. To hold to them and their heirs in tail. Contingent remainder of half of 2 messuages, 140 a. of land, 17 a. of meadow, and 2 a. of wood in the townships of Shirehampton and Oldbury to John's heirs, of the 18 messuages, the gardens, 152 a. of land, 10 a. of meadow, and 4 a. of wood, and of [the other] half of the 2 messuages, 140 a. of land, 17 a. of meadow, and 2 a. of wood in the said suburbs and the townships of Hay, Shirehampton, Westbury, Cote, Compton Greenfield, Tockington, Wickwar, Oldbury, and Cromhall to Joan's heirs. *Labelled* Bristoll', Glouc'.

291/64/98

9 Henry V

1421

460. Morrow [3 Nov.] of All Souls. Robert Stanshawe, Henry Crook (*Croke*), and Thomas Miles (*Myles*) quer.; Thomas Burton and Agnes his wife and John Rolves def. The manor of Hope (*Hope*) by Thornbury (*Thornbury*) and 2 yardlands in Hope. Right of Robert, as those which Robert, Henry, and Thomas Miles had by gift of Thomas Burton, Agnes, and John. Remise and quitclaim, specifying Agnes's heirs, to Robert, Henry, and Thomas Miles and Robert's heirs. (Warranty.) Cons. 100 marks.

79/86/22

1421

461. Morrow [3 Nov.] of All Souls. Richard Brooke (*Broke*) of Boseley (*Boseley*) quer.; Ralph Huckeley and Isabel his wife def. A messuage and 1½ yardlands in Elton (*Elveton*). Right of Richard by gift of Ralph and Isabel. Remise and quitclaim, specifying Isabel's heirs, to Richard. (Warranty.) Cons. 20 marks.

79/86/23

462. One week [18 Nov.] from St. Martin. John Blunt (*Blount*) of the county of Gloucester (*Glouc'*) esquire quer.; John ap Gwilliam of Monmouth (*Monmoweth*) in Wales (*Wall'*) esquire and Joan his wife def. Half of the manor of Bitton (*Bitton*). Right of John Blunt. Remise and quitclaim, specifying John ap Gwilliam's heirs, to John Blunt. Cons. 100 marks.

79/86/24

[Cf. *Berkeley Castle Mun.* ii, p. 839, E1/1/22 (counterpart).]

463. One week [18 Nov.] from St. Martin. John Blunt (*Blount*) and Willelma his wife quer.; Richard Coles (*Colles*) and Alice his wife def. A messuage and 1 ploughland and 4 a. of land in North Cerney (*Northsarneye*) and Woodmancote (*Wodemancote*). Right of John, as those which John and Willelma had by gift of Richard and Alice. Remise and quitclaim, specifying Alice's heirs, to John and Willelma and John's heirs. (Warranty.) Cons. 20 marks.

79/86/25

1422

464. One week [20 Jan.] from Hilary. (Made one week from the Purification 8 Henry V [9 Feb. 1421].) John Cottesmore (*Cotesmore*), William Falconer (*Fauconer*), David Brecknock (*Brekenok*), William Everdon clerk, Nicholas Clopton, John Herring (*Heryng*) clerk, and David Whitchurch (*Whitchirche*) quer.; Richard Wyatt (*Wyot*) def. Six messuages, a mill, 2 ploughlands, 8 a. of meadow, 60 a. of pasture, 10 a. of wood, and 35*s*. rent in Colesborne (*Collesbourne*), Elkstone (*Elkeston*), Stoke Orchard (*Archerestoke*), and Withington (*Whythyndon*) and half of the manor of Colesborne, all held by William Mullins (*Molyns*) 'chivaler', Thomas Chaucer esquire, William Wyatt esquire, and John Buktoft clerk for term of the life of Joan wife of Simon Rayleigh (*Raylygh*) esquire. Right of David Whitchurch. Grant of the reversion, of Richard's inheritance, to John Cottesmore and the other quer. and David Whitchurch's heirs. (Warranty.) Cons. 100 marks. [*Stained.*]

79/86/26

10 Henry V

1422

465. One week [14 June] from Trinity. (Made one month [10 May] from Easter in the said year.) John Juyn, William [. . .], John Becket (*Beket*) of Farnborough (*Farnebur'*), John Choke (*Chok*), Thomas Daventry (*Daventree*) vicar of the church of West Harptree (*Westharpetre*), John Jeeves (*Jevys*) vicar of the church of Keynsham (*Keynesham*), Som., William Rodberd parson of the church St. Mary in the market of

1422

Bristol (*Bristoll'*), John Cheddar (*Chedder*) parson of the church of Winkfield (*Wynfeld*), Wilts., John Chillington (*Chillyngton*) of the county of Somerset (*Somers'*), William Culver (*Colver*), Thomas Clerk (*Clerke*) of Thornbury (*Thornebury*), Thomas Ruggenale, and Walter Collins (*Colyns*) of the county of Gloucester (*Glouc'*) quer.; John Chesebroke of Oldland (*Oldelonde*) and Joan his wife def. Ten messuages, 200 a. of land, 16 a. of meadow, 18 a. of pasture, 7 a. of wood, and half of 1 a. of land and 1 a. of wood in West Hanham (*Westhanam*), Lower Hanham (*Dounehanam*), Oldland, Bitton (*Button*), and Upton Cheyney (*Upton*). Right of Thomas Clark, as those which Thomas and the other quer. had by gift of John Chesebroke and Joan. Remise and quitclaim, specifying Joan's heirs, to the quer. and Thomas Clark's heirs. (Warranty.) Cons. 200 marks. [*Stained.*]

79/86/27

1 Henry VI

1422

466. Morrow [12 Nov.] of St. Martin. Robert Greyndor (*Greyndore*) quer.; Richard Ordemere and Isabel his wife def. A messuage, 100 a. of land, 6 a. of meadow, and £6 rent in St. Briavels (*Seyntbrevell*), Lydney (*Lydeney*), and Newland (*Neulond*) and the office of chief forester within the forest of Dean (*Dene*) in the county of Gloucester (*Glouc'*). Right of Robert by gift of Richard and Isabel. Remise and quitclaim, specifying Isabel's heirs, to Robert. (Warranty.) Cons. 300 marks.

79/87/1

1423

467. Three weeks [25 April] from Easter. William Butler (*Boteler*) of Gloucester (*Gloucestre*) esquire and Joan his wife quer.; Walter Toky of Wotton (*Wotton*) by Gloucester and Joan his wife def. A messuage, 1 ploughland, 23 a. of meadow, and 3 a. of pasture in Hartpury (*Hardepury*), Hasfield (*Hasfeld*), and Maisemore (*Maysmore*). Right of William, as those which William and Joan had by gift of Walter and Joan. Remise and quitclaim, specifying Walter's heirs, to William and Joan and William's heirs. (Warranty.) Cons. £100.

79/87/2

468. Three weeks [25 April] from Easter. William Burghill (*Burghull*) and Hugh Beinayth quer.; William Butler (*Boteler*) esquire and Joan his wife def. Forty-three messuages and 14*s*. 6*d*. rent in Gloucester (*Gloucestre*). Right of Hugh, as those which Hugh and William Burghill had by gift of William Butler and Joan. Remise and quitclaim, specifying Joan's heirs, to William Burghill and Hugh and Hugh's heirs. (Warranty.) Cons. 200 marks.

79/87/3

2 Henry VI

1424

469. One week [20 Jan.] from Hilary. Thomas Bromwich (*Bromwiche*) son of Walter Bromwich and Joan his wife, John Castle (*Castell*) clerk, George Skidmore (*Skydmore*), Hugh Monnington (*Monyton*), John Shelwick (*Shelwyk*), and John Saunders (*Saundres*) chaplain quer.; Robert Chalons knight and Blanche his wife def. The manor of Bromsberrow (*Bremmesbergh*) and the advowson of the church of the same manor. Right of John Saunders, as those which the same John and the other quer. had by gift of Robert and Blanche. Remise and quitclaim, specifying Blanche's heirs, to Thomas and Joan and the other quer. and the heirs of John Saunders. Cons. 200 marks.

79/87/4

470. Two weeks [7 May] from Easter. (Made the morrow of St. Martin in the said year [12 Nov. 1423].) William Howe (*Houe*) of Hannington (*Hanyndon*) quer.; Thomas George of Rowden (*Roudon*) and Joan his wife def. A messuage, 1 ploughland, and 12 a. of meadow in Down Ampney (*Dounameneye*). Right of William. Render to him. (Warranty, by Thomas alone.) Cons. 20 marks.

79/87/5

471. Two weeks [7 May] from Easter. (Made the morrow of St. Martin in the said year [12 Nov. 1423].) John Blunt (*Blount*) and Willelma his wife quer.; Richard Coles (*Colles*) and Alice his wife def. A messuage, 1 ploughland, and 2 a. of meadow in Woodmancote (*Wodemancote*). Right of John, as those which John and Willelma had by gift of Richard and Alice. Remise and quitclaim, specifying Richard's heirs, to John and Willelma and John's heirs. (Warranty.) Cons. 20 marks.

79/87/6

472. Two weeks [7 May] from Easter. (Made two weeks from St. Martin in the said year [25 Nov. 1423].) Thomas Wick (*Wyke*) quer.; John Chesebroke (*Chesbroke*) and Joan his wife def. Half of the manor of Bitton (*Button*) called Oldland (*Oldeland*) and half of the hundred of Bitton, GLOS.; and 4*s.* 9*d.* rent in Bath (*Bathe*), SOM. Right of Thomas by gift of John and Joan. Remise and quitclaim, specifying Joan's heirs, to Thomas. (Warranty.) Cons. 100 marks. *Labelled* Glouc', Somers'.

291/65/22

[Cf. *Som. Fines, 1399–1484*, p. 184.]

473. One month [21 May] from Easter. Ralph Thorp and Amice his wife quer.; Andrew Pille, Robert Cheyney (*Cheyne*), and Richard Andrew (*Andrewe*) def. The manors of Boscombe (*Borscombe*) and Burdens Ball (*Burdonesball*) and the advowson of the church of Boscombe, WILTS., and the manor of Oldbury-on-Severn (*Oldebury*) and the advowson of the church of Oldbury, GLOS. Right of Andrew, as as those which Andrew, Robert, and Richard had by Ralph's gift. For this, grant and render to Ralph and Amice. To hold to them and their heirs in tail. Contingent remainder to Ralph's heirs. *Labelled* Wiltes', Glouc'.

291/65/24

[Cf. *Wilts. Fines, 1377–1509*, p. 85, no. 394.]

3 Henry VI

1424

474. Three weeks [20 Oct.] from Michaelmas. John Marvan quer.; Petronilla Birdlip (*Bridlip*), John Birdlip citizen and mercer of London (*London'*), Thomas Birdlip citizen and grocer of the same, and Henry Brooke (*Broke*) and Elena his wife def. Eight messuages, 12 a. of land, 8 a. of meadow and 24*s.* rent in Tewkesbury (*Teukesbury*) and Tredington (*Tredynton*). Right of John Marvan by gift of Petronilla, John Birdlip, Thomas, and Henry and Elena. Remise and quitclaim, specifying the heirs of Petronilla, John Birdlip, Thomas, and Elena, to John Marvan. (Warranty.) For this, grant back and render to Petronilla. To hold during her life, of John Marvan, paying a rose a year at St. John the Baptist and doing service to the chief lords. Reversion to John Marvan. [*Worn.*]

79/87/9

1425

475. Two weeks [17 June] from Trinity. John Stears (*Staure*) of Stears quer.; Walter Vaughan (*Boghan*) and Matilda his wife def. A messuage, 102 a. of land, 7 a. of meadow, 2 a. of wood, and 10*d.* rent in Awre (*Aure*). Right of John by gift of Walter and Matilda. (Warranty, specifying Matilda's heirs.) Cons. 100 marks.

79/87/7

476. Two weeks [17 June] from Trinity. Thomas Skin (*Skyn*) quer.; Richard Hollow (*Holowe*) and Alice his wife def. A messuage in Newland (*Neweland*). Right of Thomas by gift of Richard and Alice. Remise and quitclaim, specifying Alice's heirs, to Thomas. (Warranty.) Cons. 10 marks.

79/87/8

4 Henry VI

1425

477. One week [6 Oct.] from Michaelmas. (Made two weeks from St. John the Baptist 3 Henry VI [8 July 1425].) Henry Blakemore clerk, William Payn, John Newburgh (*Neburgh*), John Storke, and John Cheverell quer.; Ralph Bush (*Busshe*) esquire and Eleanor his wife and John Chideock (*Chydyok*) esquire def. The manors of East Chelborough (*Estchelburgh*) and Moor Crichel (*Morekurchull*), DORSET; the manor of Allowenshay (*Alwyneshey*), SOM.; and the manor of Frampton on Severn (*Frampton super Sabrinam*), GLOS. Right of Henry, William, John, John, and John as to the manor of East Chelborough, and right of Henry as to the manors of Moor Crichel, Allowenshay, and Frampton on Severn, by gift of Ralph and Eleanor and John Chideock. For this, grant and render to Ralph and Eleanor. To hold during Eleanor's life, the manor of East Chelborough of the king and the other manors of the chief lords. Remainder to John Chideock. Made as to the manor of East Chelborough by the king's order. *Labelled* Dors', Somers', Glouc'.

291/65/45

[Cf. *Dorset Fines, 1327–1485*, pp. 300–1; *Som. Fines, 1399–1485*, p. 185.]

478. Morrow [3 Nov.] of All Souls. Richard Badcock (*Badecok*) quer.; John Cook (*Coke*) and Joan his wife def. Half of a messuage, 8 a. of land, 2 a. of meadow, 20 a. of

1425

pasture, and 4 a. of wood in Frampton Cotterell (*Frompton Cotell*). Right of Richard by gift of John and Joan. Remise and quitclaim, specifying Joan's heirs, to Richard. Cons. 10 marks.

79/87/10

5 Henry VI

1426

479. Two weeks [13 Oct.] from Michaelmas. John Grove of Gloucester (*Gloucestr'*) 'coteller' quer.; John Nowell of Swindon (*Swyndon*) in the county of Gloucester (*Glouc'*) and Matilda his wife def. A messuage in the suburb of Gloucester (*Gloucestr'*). Right of John Grove by gift of John Nowell and Matilda. Remise and quitclaim, specifying Matilda's heirs, to John Grove. Cons. 10 marks.

79/87/16

1427

480. One week [20 Jan.] from Hilary. (Made one month from Michaelmas in the said year [27 Oct. 1426].) John Stears (*Staure*) of Stears, Robert Awre (*Aure*) of Awre, and Thomas Boxe quer.; John Boxe and Margaret his wife def. A messuage, a dovecot, 2 a. of land, 4 a. of meadow, and 3 a. of wood in Mitcheldean (*Michelden*) and Abenhall (*Abynhale*). Right of Thomas, as those which Thomas, John Stears, and Robert had by gift of John Boxe and Margaret. To hold to Thomas, John Stears, and Robert and Thomas's heirs. (Warranty, specifying Margaret's heirs.) Cons. 20 marks.

79/87/15

481. One week [20 Jan.] from Hilary. (Made the morrow of the Purification 4 Henry VI [3 Feb. 1426].) Thomas Brounflete knight, Hugh Hazleton (*Hasulden*), and Thomas Beaufitz quer.; Edward Brounflete and Joan his wife def. The manors of Charles (*Charles*), West Hagginton (*Westhagynton*), and West Buckland (*Westbokelond*), a messuage, 1 ploughland, and 40 a. of wood in Walson (*Walston*), and half of the manor of Curtisknowle (*Courtesknoll*), DEVON, the manor of Edgeworth (*Eggesworth*) and two thirds of the manor of Lassington (*Lassyngdon*), GLOS., the manor of Claydon (*Cleydon*), OXON., the manor of Farnborough (*Farneburgh*), WARWS., and the manor of Walpan (*Walpenne*) and 2 ploughlands, 100 a. of pasture, and 100 a. of wood in *Wode* and Chillingwood (*Chylyngwode*), HANTS. Right of Thomas Brounflete, of which the same Thomas, Hugh, and Thomas Beaufitz had the manor of Edgeworth (except for 2 messuages, 1 ploughland, and 30 a. of wood in the same manor), two thirds of the manors of Farnborough and Walpan, and the 2 ploughlands, 100 a. of pasture, and 100 a. of wood in the said townships of *Wode* and *Chylyngwode* by gift of Edward and Joan. For this, grant back and render to Edward and Joan. To hold to them and their heirs in tail male. And grant to Edward and Joan and their said heirs of the reversion of the manors of Charles, West Hagginton, and West Buckland, the messuage, 1 ploughland, and 40 a. of wood in the township of *Walston*, and the half of the manor of Curtisknowle held by Thomas Kingsland (*Kyngeslond*) for term of life and of the 2 messuages, 1 ploughland, and 30 a. of wood in the manor of Edgeworth excepted above, the manor of Claydon, the two thirds of the manor of Lassington, and the one third of the manors of

1427

Farnborough and Walpan held by Reynold de Grey the elder 'chivaler' and Joan his wife for term of Joan's life, of the inheritance of Thomas Brounflete. To hold as above. Contingent remainder to the heirs of Joan wife of Edward. *Labelled* Devon', Glouc', Oxon', Warr', Sutht'.

291/65/50

[Cf. *Warws. Fines, 1345–1509*, pp. 144–5, no. 2542.]

482. Two weeks [4 May] from Easter. (Made two weeks [27 Jan.] from Hilary in the said year.) Thomas Poyntz quer.; Robert Strong (*Stronge*) and Margery his wife def. A messuage, a toft, 62 a. of land, 8 a. of meadow, and 4 a. of pasture in Ingst (*Inste*) by Olveston (*Olveston*). Right of Thomas, of which he had the toft, 20 a. of land, 2 a. of meadow, and 1 a. of pasture by gift of Robert and Margery. Remise and quitclaim, specifying Margery's heirs, to Thomas. And grant to him of the reversion of the messuage, 42 a. of land, 6 a. of meadow, and 3 a. of pasture in the said township held by William Waleys (*Walleys*) for term of life, of Margery's inheritance. (Warranty.) Cons. 100 marks.

79/87/13

483. Three weeks [11 May] from Easter. Richard Chapman (*Chapmon*) of Bishop's Cleeve (*Cleve*) in the county of Gloucester (*Gloucestr'*) quer.; Roger Bodenham and Elizabeth his wife def. Six messuages, 2 tofts, 226 a. of land, 10 a. of meadow, and 12 a. of pasture in Southam (*Southam*), Woodmancote (*Wodmecote*), Gotherington (*Godrynton*), Brockhampton (*Brokhampton*), Bishop's Cleeve, and Prestbury (*Prestebury*). Right of Richard by gift of Roger and Elizabeth. Remise and quitclaim, specifying Elizabeth's heirs, to Richard. (Warranty.) Cons. 100 marks.

79/87/14

484. One week [22 June] from Trinity. (Made three weeks [11 May] from Easter in the said year.) Thomas Mill (*Mille*) quer.; Juliana who was wife of Andrew Hurley (*Herle*) knight and William Hurley esquire def. The manors of Harescombe (*Harescombe*) and Duntisbourne Rouse (*Duntesburn Rous*) and the advowson of the church of Harescombe. Right of Thomas by gift of Juliana and William. For this, grant back and render to Juliana. To hold during her life. Remainder to William and his heirs in tail. Successive contingent remainders to Juliana's heirs in tail and to her heirs.

79/87/12

485. One week [22 June] from Trinity. (Made one month [18 May] from Easter in the said year.) John Langley (*Langeley*), Thomas Lygon, Thomas Henster, Geoffrey Hyde, and Thomas Snelle quer.; John Bruce (*Bruyse*) and Elizabeth his wife def. A mill, 5 a. of meadow, and 5 a. of pasture in Cirencester (*Cirencestre*) and Chesterton (*Chesterton*). Right of John Langley, as those which the same John and the other quer. had by gift of John Bruce and Elizabeth. Remise and quitclaim, specifying Elizabeth's heirs, to the quer. and John Langley's heirs. (Warranty.) Cons. 20 marks.

79/87/11

6 Henry VI

1428

486. One month [2 May] from Easter. William Veal (*Vyell*) quer.; Nicholas Stanshawe and Margery his wife def. Twelve messuages, 200 a. of land, 20 a. of meadow, and 40 a. of pasture in Shenington (*Shenendon*). Right of William by gift of Nicholas and Margery. Remise and quitclaim, specifying Margery's heirs, to William. Cons. 100 marks.

79/87/17

487. One week [6 June] from Trinity. (Made two weeks from Easter [18 April] in the said year.) Robert Bennett (*Benet*) chaplain and Thomas Cotes quer.; Robert Liversedge (*Leversegge*) and Agnes his wife def. Eighteen messuages, 2 tofts, 2 mills, 118 a. of land, 28 a. of meadow, 240 a. of pasture, and 40*s*. rent in Frome (*Frome*), Rodden (*Radene*), Marston Bigot (*Mershtonbygod*), and *Oldefeld* [Oldford?], SOM., and a messuage, 2 ploughlands, and 20*s*. rent in Eastleach Turville (*Lacheturvyle*) and Southrop (*Southorp*), GLOS. Robert Liversedge acknowledged the right of Robert Bennett, as those which he and Thomas had by Robert Liversedge's gift. Remise and quitclaim to Robert Bennett and Thomas and that Robert's heirs. For this, grant and render to Robert Liversedge and Agnes. To hold to them and that Robert's heirs. (Warranty.) *Labelled* Somers', Glouc'.

292/66/79

[Cf. *Som. Fines, 1399–1484*, p. 188.]

7 Henry VI

1428

488. One week [6 Oct.] from Michaelmas. (Made one week from St. John the Baptist 6 Henry VI [1 July 1428].) John Mills (*Mulys*), John Cokeworthy, and John d'Abernon (*Dabernoun*) quer.; Robert Grigg (*Grugge*) and Alice his wife def. A messuage, 3 quarter-yardlands (*ferlingis*) and 12 a. of land, and 12 a. of meadow in Tawstock (*Toustoke*) and Umberleigh (*Womberlegh*), DEVON, and a toft and 20 a. of land in Minsterworth (*Mynstreworthy*), GLOS. Right of John d'Abernon, as those which the same John, John Mills, and John Cokeworthy had by gift of Robert and Alice. Remise and quitclaim, specifying Alice's heirs, to John, John, and John and John d'Abernon's heirs. (Warranty.) Cons 100 marks. *Labelled* Devon', Glouc'.

292/66/85

489. One month [27 Oct.] from Michaelmas. John Leach (*Lacche*) quer.; Richard Colas and Agnes his wife def. A messuage in Northleach (*Northelacche*). Right of John by gift of Richard and Agnes. Remise and quitclaim, specifying Richard's heirs, to John. (Warranty.) Cons. 20 marks.

79/87/20

1429

490. One week [20 Jan.] from Hilary. Robert Page and Joan his wife quer.; Thomas Barron (*Baron*) and Margaret his wife def. One third of a messuage in Lechlade (*Lecchelade*). Right of Robert. Remise and quitclaim, specifying Margaret's heirs, to Robert and Joan and Robert's heirs. Cons. 10 marks.

79/87/18

1429

491. Two weeks [10 April] from Easter. John Baker of Northleach (*Northlacche*) quer.; Philip Lacy esquire and Isabel his wife def. A messuage called 'le Georges Inne' in Northleach. Right of John by gift of Philip and Isabel. Remise and quitclaim, specifying Philip's heirs, to John. Cons. 20 marks.

79/87/19

492. One week [29 May] from Trinity. John Davy of *Lee* quer.; Alice Hicks (*Hykkys*) def. A messuage in *Lee*. Right of John by Alice's gift. (Warranty.) Cons. 10 marks.

79/8/21

493. Two weeks [5 June] from Trinity. John Greville (*Grevyll*) esquire and John Shyngey quer.; John Petty (*Petit, Petyt*) and Philippa his wife def. Five messuages, 7½ yardlands, 32 a. of meadow, and 200 a. of pasture in Sezincote (*Shesyncote*) held by Richard Eton and Amisia his wife for term of Amisia's life. Right of John Greville. Grant to John Greville and John Shyngey and John Greville's heirs of the reversion, of Philippa's inheritance. (Warranty.) Cons. 100 marks.

79/87/22

8 Henry VI

1429

494. One week [6 Oct.] from Michaelmas. (Made two weeks from St. John the Baptist 7 Henry VI [8 July 1429].) Roger Linden (*Lyneden*) and Isabel his wife quer.; Edward Bridge (*Brugge*) and Alice his wife def. Six messuages, 2 tofts, 121 a. of land, 18 a. of meadow, 6 a. of heath (*bruere*), 3s. rent, and half of a dovecot and 1 a. of meadow in Olveston (*Olveston*), Tockington (*Tokyngton*), and Hambrook (*Hambroke*). Right of Roger, as those which Roger and Isabel had by gift of Edward and Alice. Remise and quitclaim, specifying Alice's heirs, to Roger and Isabel and Roger's heirs. (Warranty against John [Morwent] abbot of Gloucester (*Glouc'*) and his successors.) Cons. 100 marks.

79/87/24

[The warranty against the abbot of Gloucester is the first instance among the fines relating to Gloucestershire of a warranty against someone named.]

495. Two weeks [13 Oct.] from Michaelmas. Thomas Woodward (*Wodeward*) quer.; William Sherborne (*Shirbourne*) and Elizabeth his wife def. A messuage and ½ a. of land in Mitcheldean (*Magna Dene*). Right of Thomas by gift of William and Elizabeth. (Warranty, specifying Elizabeth's heirs.) Cons. 10 marks.

79/88/26

496. Three weeks [20 Oct.] from Michaelmas. John Spenser and Margaret his wife quer.; Richard Barrett (*Baret*) and Margaret his wife def. Half of a messuage in Tewkesbury (*Teukesbury*). Right of John, as that which John and Margaret had by gift of Richard and Margaret. To hold to John and Margaret and John's heirs. (Warranty, specifying the heirs of Margaret wife of Richard.) Cons. 10 marks.

79/87/25

1429

497. Morrow [3 Nov.] of All Souls. Richard Granger (*Graunger*) clerk, Thomas Franks (*Frankys*) clerk, Thomas Bailly chaplain, and William Stanlowe quer.; William FitzHugh (*Fitz Hugh*) knight and Margery his wife and William Foxholes clerk def. The manor of Quinton (*Quenton*), GLOS., and the manor of Cherry Willingham (*Willyngham*), LINCS. Right of Richard, as those which Richard, Thomas, Thomas, and William Stanlowe had by gift of William FitzHugh and Margery and William Foxholes. Remise and quitclaim, specifying Margery's heirs, to Richard, Thomas, Thomas, and William Stanlowe and Richard's heirs. (Warranty.) Cons. 300 marks. *Labelled* Glouc', Lincoln'.

292/66/89

[For the identity of Quinton, cf. below, no. 499.]

498. One week [18 Nov.] from St. Martin. John Verney clerk, John Hody clerk, Nicholas Morris (*Morys*) clerk, John Vampage, and William Pulesdon (*Pullesdon*) quer.; William Philip knight, Thomas Chaucer (*Chaucers*) esquire, Thomas Dyrham (*Derham*), John Throckmorton (*Throkmarton*), and John Wood (*Wode*) def. Six messuages, 12 tofts, 1 ploughland, 16 a. of meadow, 200 a. of pasture, 10 a. of wood, and 20*s.* rent in Elmestree (*Eylmundestre*) held by Alice who was wife of John Philip knight for term of life. Grant of the reversion, of the inheritance of William Philip (*Phelip*), Thomas, Thomas, John Throckmorton, and John Wood, to John Verney, John Hody, Nicholas, John Vampage, and William Pulesdon and their heirs, to hold of the king, paying a rose a year at St. John the Baptist for all services. Cons. £100. Made by the king's order.

79/87/23

[The statements about inheritance and descent to heirs are unrealistic. The agreement was evidently a prelude to that recorded below, no. 500.]

499. Two weeks [25 Nov.] from St. Martin. Ralph Cromwell knight quer.; Richard Granger (*Graunger*), Thomas Franks (*Frankys*) clerk, Thomas Bailly chaplain, and William Stanlowe def. The manor of Cherry Willingham (*Willyngham*), LINCS., and the manor of Quinton (*Quenton*), GLOS. Grant and render to Ralph. To hold to him and his heirs in tail. Successive contingent remainders to Robert son of William Cromwell knight and his heirs in tail, to Matilda wife of Richard Stanhope knight and sister of the said Ralph and her heirs in tail, and to the heirs of Robert Marmion (*Marmyoun*) knight son of John Marmion knight. *Labelled* Lincoln', Glouc'.

292/66/93

[The reference to the Marmions confirms the identity of Quinton; cf. *P.-N.G.* i. 254.]

1430

500. Two weeks [27 Jan.] from Hilary. John atte Wood (*Wode*) and Alice his wife quer.; John Verney clerk, John Hody clerk, Nicholas Morris (*Morys*) clerk, and John Vampage def. Six messuages, 12 tofts, 1 ploughland, 16 a. of meadow, 200 a. of pasture, 10 a. of wood, and 20*s.* rent in Elmestree (*Eylmundestre*), held by Alice who was wife of John Philip (*Phelip*) knight for term of her life, of the inheritance of John Verney, John Hody, Nicholas, and John Vampage. Grant of the reversion to John atte Wood and Alice and their heirs in tail. To hold of the king, paying a rose a year at St. John the Baptist. Contingent reversion to John atte Wood's heirs. Made by the king's order.

79/88/28

1430

501. One month [14 May] from Easter. John Cadel (*Cadull*) and Matilda his wife quer.; Thomas Ely and Isabel his wife def. A messuage in Lydney (*Lydney*). Right of John, as that which John and Matilda had by gift of Thomas and Isabel. To hold to John and Matilda and John's heirs. (Warranty, specifying Isabel's heirs.) Cons. 10 marks.

79/88/27

502. One week [18 June] from Trinity. (Made one month [14 May] from Easter in the said year.] William Dodesham the younger and Joan his wife quer.; William Gascoigne and William Dodesham the elder def. One quarter of one third of the manor of Oldbury (*Oldebury*) in Stapleton (*Stapulton*) parish and of a messuage, 40 a. of land, and 3 a. of meadow in Clifton (*Clifton*), GLOS.; and one quarter of the manor of Hutton (*Hutton*) and of 2 messuages in Axbridge (*Axebrigge*) and Compton Bishop (*Compton Episcopi*) and the advowson of one quarter of the church of Hutton, SOM. Right of William Dodesham the elder as those which the same William and William Gascoigne had by gift of William Dodesham the younger and Joan. For this, grant back and render to William Dodesham the younger and Joan. To hold to them and their heirs in tail. Contingent remainder to Joan's heirs. *Labelled* Glouc', Somers'.

292/67/102

[Cf. *Som. Fines, 1399–1484*, pp. 189–90.]

9 Henry VI

1430

503. Two weeks [13 Oct.] from Michaelmas. Thomas Smith (*Smyth*) of Gloucester (*Gloucestre*) 'baker' and Clemency his wife quer.; William Colston and Alice his wife def. A messuage in Gloucester. Right of Thomas, as that which Thomas and Clemency had by gift of William and Alice. Remise and quitclaim (specifying Alice's heirs) to Thomas and Clemency and Thomas's heirs. (Warranty.) Cons. 20 marks.

79/88/30

504. Two weeks [13 Oct.] from Michaelmas. Robert Gilbert quer.; William Colston and Alice his wife def. Two messuages in Gloucester (*Gloucestre*). Right of Robert by gift of William and Alice. Remise and quitclaim (specifying Alice's heirs) to Robert. (Warranty.) Cons. 100 marks.

79/88/31

505. One month [27 Oct.] from Michaelmas. Thomas Daventry (*Daventre*) clerk, William Rodberd (*Rodberde*) clerk, and John Huggins (*Huggis*) quer.; William Turner (*Tornour*) of Lower Hanham (*Dounehanam*) and Alice his wife def. A messuage, 50 a. of land, 6 a. of meadow, 1 a. of pasture, and 2 a. of wood in Bitton (*Button*) and Oldland (*Oldelonde*). Right of John, as those which the same John, Thomas, and William Rodberd had by gift of William Turner and Alice. Remise and quitclaim, specifying Alice's heirs, to Thomas, William Rodberd, and John and John's heirs. (Warranty.) Cons. 100 marks.

79/88/29

1430

506. Two weeks [25 Nov.] from St. Martin. John Greville (*Grevell'*) esquire quer.; William Colston of Bristol (*Bristoll'*) and Alice his wife def. Two messuages and 4 gardens in Gloucester (*Gloucestre*). Right of John by gift of William and Alice. Remise and quitclaim (specifying Alice's heirs) to John. (Warranty.) Cons. 100 marks.

79/88/32

10 Henry VI

1431

507. One week [6 Oct.] from Michaelmas. (Made two weeks from St. John the Baptist 9 Henry VI [8 July 1431].) John Vampage the elder quer.; John Cottesmore, William Falconer (*Fawconer*), David Brecknock (*Brekenok*), William Everdon clerk, Nicholas Clopton, John Herring (*Heryng*) clerk, David Whitchurch (*Whitchurche*), and Richard Wyatt (*Wyot*) def. Six messuages, a mill, 2 ploughlands, 8 a. of meadow, 60 a. of pasture, 10 a. of wood, and 35*s*. rent in Colesborne (*Collesburne*), Elkstone (*Elkeston*), Stoke Orchard (*Archerstoke*), and Withington (*Wythyndon*) and half of the manor of Colesborne, held by Thomas Chaucer esquire and John Buktoft for term of the life of Joan wife of Simon Rayleigh (*Rayligh*) esquire, of Richard Wyatt's inheritance. Right of John Vampage. Grant to John Vampage of the reversion. Cons. 200 marks.

79/88/34

508. One week [6 Oct.] from Michaelmas. (Made one week from St. John the Baptist 9 Henry VI [1 July 1431].) Maurice Berkeley of Stoke Gifford (*Gyffardestoke*) knight quer.; Thomas Lynde of Hambrook (*Hambroke*) and Margaret his wife def. Two messuages, 66 a. of land, and 6 a. of meadow in Hambrook and Frenchay (*Framshawe*). Right of Maurice by gift of Thomas and Margaret. Remise and quitclaim (specifying Margaret's heirs) to him. (Warranty.) Cons. £20.

79/88/35

509. One week [18 Nov.] from St. Martin. John Bolnehull and Thomas Waxman quer.; Richard Tasker and Alice his wife def. A messuage in Tewkesbury (*Teukesbury*). Right of John, as that which John and Thomas had by gift of Richard and Alice. Remise and quitclaim (specifying Alice's heirs) to John and Thomas and John's heirs. (Warranty.) Cons. 20 marks.

79/88/37

510. One week [18 Nov.] from St. Martin. John Whittock (*Whyttok*) and Joan his wife quer.; Nicholas Wade and Margaret his wife def. A messuage and a shop in Gloucester (*Gloucestre*). Right of John, as those which John and Joan had by gift of Nicholas and Margaret. Remise and quitclaim (specifying Margaret's heirs) to John and Joan and John's heirs. (Warranty against the abbot of Westminster.) Cons. 20 marks.

79/88/38

1432

511. One week [9 Feb.] from the Purification. Thomas Leny and Eleanor his wife quer.; Guy Whittington (*Whityngton*) and Cecily his wife def. Three messuages, a toft, 3 yardlands, 6 a. of meadow, 30 a. of pasture, and 4 a. of wood in Minchinhampton (*Mynchenhampton*), held by Edmund Rodborough (*Rodebergh*) for term of life, of Cecily's inheritance. Right of Thomas. Grant, specifying Guy's heirs, of the reversion to Thomas and Eleanor and Thomas's heirs. (Warranty, specifying Cecily's heirs, against the abbot of Westminster.) Cons. 100 marks.

79/88/36

[It appears anomalous that the grant specifies Guy's heirs while the warranty specifies Cecily's.]

512. Morrow [30 May] of Ascension. Richard Drayton esquire and William Marmion (*Marmyon*) quer.; Stephen Hatfield (*Haytfeld*) esquire and Isabel his wife def. One acre of land in Tormarton (*Tormerton*) and the advowson of the church or wardenship of Tormarton. Grant and render to Richard and William. To hold to them and Richard's heirs during Isabel's life. Cons. 100 marks.

79/88/33

[For the wardenship, *B. & G. Trans.* lvii. 15–18.]

11 Henry VI

1432

513. Three weeks [20 Oct.] from Michaelmas. Thomas Dyer of Cirencester (*Cirencestre*) quer.; John Winter (*Wynter*) and Joan his wife def. Two messuages in Cirencester. Right of Thomas by gift of John and Joan. Remise and quitclaim (specifying Joan's heirs) to Thomas. (Warranty.) Cons. 20 marks.

79/88/43

514. Three weeks [20 Oct.] from Michaelmas. John Newton (*Neweton*) and Joan his wife quer.; Thomas Baumvyle and Joan his wife def. Twenty acres of pasture in Henbury (*Hembury*). Right of John, as those which John and Joan had by gift of Thomas and Joan. Remise and quitclaim, specifying Joan Baumvyle's heirs, to John and Joan and John Newton's heirs. Cons. 10 marks.

79/88/45

515. One month [27 Oct.] from Michaelmas. John Courtenay, John Bluet (*Blwet*), and Nicholas Ashton (*Ayssheton*) quer.; Edward Greville (*Grevyle*) and Isabel his wife def. The manors of Weston on Avon (*Weston*) and Welford on Avon (*Welford super Avene*). Edward acknowledged the right of John Courtenay, as those which the same John, John Bluet, and Nicholas had by gift of Edward and Isabel. Remise and quitclaim by Edward to John, John, and Nicholas and John Courtenay's heirs. (Warranty by Edward.) For this, grant and render to Edward and Isabel. To hold to them and their heirs in tail. Contingent remainder to Edward's heirs.

79/88/41

1432

516. Morrow [3 Nov.] of All Souls. Geoffrey Holford and John Holford quer.; Richard Gunny and Margaret his wife and Richard Clinton (*Clynton*) and Sibyl his wife def. A messuage, 30 a. of land, and 10 a. of meadow in Tirley (*Trenley*), Hasfield (*Hasfeld*), and Corse (*Cors*). Richard Gunny acknowledged the right of Geoffrey, as those which Geoffrey and John had by gift of Richard Gunny and Margaret and Richard Clinton and Sibyl. For this, grant and render to Richard Gunny and Margaret. To hold during their lives. Remainder to Richard Clinton and Sibyl and their heirs in tail. Successive contingent remainders to Alice daughter of Richard Gunny and her heirs in tail, to Geoffrey Moody (*Mody*) and his heirs in tail, and to Richard Gunny's heirs.

79/88/42

517. Morrow [12 Nov.] of St. Martin. William Cheyney (*Cheyne*) knight, John Cottesmore, William Paston, Robert Bennett (*Benet*) chaplain, and Philip Morgan quer.; Stephen Hatfield (*Haitfeld*) and Isabel his wife and Maurice de la River (*Delarever*) and Margaret his wife def. The manor of Coomb's End (*Combe Cotele*) by Old Sodbury (*Oldsobbury*) and 1 ploughland, 40 a. of meadow, 100 a. of pasture, and 30 a. of wood in Old Sodbury and Coomb's End. Right of William Cheyney as those which the same William, John, William Paston, Robert, and Philip had by gift of Stephen and Isabel and Maurice and Margaret. Remise and quitclaim, specifying Isabel's and Margaret's heirs, to William Cheyney, John, William Paston, Robert, and Philip and William Cheyney's heirs. (Warranty.) Cons. 200 marks.

79/88/44

[John Cottesmore and William Paston were justices of the king's court at the time.]

1433

518. One week [20 Jan.] from Hilary. (Made the morrow of St. Martin 4 Henry VI [12 Nov. 1425].) William Veal (*Vyel*) quer.; John Wickham (*Wykham*) of Westerleigh (*Westerley*) def. Seventeen messuages, 2 mills, 300 a. of land, 20 a. of meadow, 8 a of pasture, 6 a. of wood, and 9*s*. rent in Shenington (*Shenyngdon*), held by Nicholas Stanshawe and Margery his wife for term of Margery's life, of John's inheritance. Right of William. Grant to him of the reversion. Cons. 100 marks.

79/88/47

519. One week [20 Jan.] from Hilary. (Made one week from St. John the Baptist 4 Henry VI [1 July 1426].) William Veal (*Vyell'*) quer.; Thomas Grede of Thorverton (*Thorverton*), Devon, and Agnes his wife def. Seventeen messuages, 2 mills, 300 a. of land, 20 a. of meadow, 8 a of pasture, 6 a. of wood, and 20*s*. rent in Shenington (*Shenyngdon*), held by Nicholas Stanshawe and Margery his wife, late the wife of John More, for term of Margery's life, of Agnes's inheritance. Right of William. Grant to him of the reversion. Cons. 100 marks.

79/88/48

[Cf. no. 518 above, where another share in the what was evidently the same estate had less in rent and Margery's former husband is not mentioned.]

1433

520. Morrow [3 Feb.] of the Purification. John Boure quer.; John Countess (*Countasse*) and Rose his wife def. One quarter of a messuage, 9 a. of land, 1 a. of meadow, and 1 a. of wood in Kilcot (*Kylcote*) by Newent (*Newent*). Right of John Boure by gift of John Countess and Rose. Remise and quitclaim, specifying Rose's heirs, to John Boure. (Warranty against the abbot of Gloucester (*Gloucestr'*).) Cons. 10 marks.

79/88/46

521. Morrow [22 May] of Ascension. Henry Castle (*Castell*) quer.; John Hancocks (*Hancokes*) and Agnes his wife def. Thirty acres of land and 2 a. of meadow in Eccleswall (*Egliswell*) and Upper Lea (*Overlee*), HEREFS., and a messuage and 2d. rent in Upper Lea, GLOS. Right of Henry by gift of John and Agnes. Remise and quitclaim (specifying John's heirs) to Henry. (Warranty.) Cons. 100 marks. *Labelled* Hereford', Glouc'.

292/67/135

522. One week [14 June] from Trinity. (Made two weeks [26 April] from Easter the said year.) William Child (*Chyld*) and Alice his wife quer.; William Gernon of Dowdeswell (*Doudeswell*) and Elizabeth his wife def. The manor of Clanfield (*Clanefeld*), OXON.; and 3 messuages, 92 a. of land, 6 a. of meadow, 10 a. of wood, and 6s. 6d. rent in Pegglesworth (*Pekelesworth*) and Dowdeswell, GLOS. Right of William Child by gift of William Gernon and Elizabeth. Remise and quitclaim, specifying Elizabeth's heirs, to William Child and Alice and William Child's heirs. (Warranty.) For this, grant back and render to William Gernon and Elizabeth. To hold during their lives, paying a rose a year at St. John the Baptist to William Child and Alice and William Child's heirs, and doing service to the chief lords. Reversion to William Child and Alice and William Child's heirs. *Labelled* Oxon', Glouc'. [*Worn.*]

292/67/136

[The foot of another recension of the fine is filed as 292/67/137.]

523. One week [1 July] from St. John the Baptist. John Reeve (*Reve*) of Daglingworth (*Dagelyngworth*) and Joan his wife quer.; Richard Lardener of Daglingworth and Agnes his wife def. A messuage and 140 a. of land in Daglingworth. Right of John, as those which John and Joan had by gift of Richard and Agnes. Remise and quitclaim, specifying Agnes's heirs, to John and Joan and John's heirs. (Warranty.) Cons. 100 marks.

79/88/40

524. Two weeks [8 July] from St. John the Baptist. Thomas Williams and Henry Lye quer.; Thomas Gilmyn (*Gylmyn*) and Henry Cresson and Elizabeth his wife def. Four messuages, a mill, 4 ploughlands, 10 a. of meadow, and 10s. rent in Little Barrington (*Parva Bernyngton*). Right of Thomas Williams, as those which the same Thomas and Henry Lye had by gift of Thomas Gilmyn, Henry Cresson, and Elizabeth. Remise and quitclaim, specifying Elizabeth's heirs, to Thomas Williams and Henry Lye and Thomas Williams's heirs. (Warranty.) Cons. 200 marks.

79/88/39

12 Henry VI

1433

525. One week [6 Oct.] from Michaelmas. Thomas Poyntz and Joan his wife quer.; Robert Poyntz and Katherine his wife def. Rent of £6 in Filton (*Filton*) and half of the manor of Nympsfield (*Nymesfeld*) and the advowson of half of the chantry of Kinley (*Kynley*). Grant and render to Thomas and Joan. To hold to them in tail, the half and the advowson of the king, the rent of the chief lords. Contingent reversion to Thomas's heirs in tail. (Warranty.) Contingent reversion to Robert. Cons. 300 marks. As to the half and the advowson, made by the king's order.

79/89/52

526. One month [27 Oct.] from Michaelmas. John Langley, John Hayward (*Heyward*), John Hamlin (*Hamelyn*), and William Warner quer.; Richard Sage and Joan his wife def. A messuage in Gloucester (*Gloucestr'*). Right of John Hayward, as that which the same John, John Langley, John Hamlin, and William had by gift of Richard and Joan. Remise and quitclaim, specifying Richard's heirs, to John, John, John, and William and John Hayward's heirs. (Warranty.) Cons. 20 marks.

79/89/51

527. Morrow [3 Nov.] of All Souls. John Hody clerk, William Carrant (*Carent*), Thomas Hody, and John Gilbert clerk quer.; Thomas Stawell knight def. Five messuages, a dovecot, 1 ploughland, 20 a. of meadow, 100 a. of pasture, and 30 a. of wood in Earthcott (*Erthecote*). Right of Thomas Hody as those which the same Thomas, John Hody, William, and John Gilbert had by gift of Thomas Stawell. Remise and quitclaim to John, William, Thomas Hody, and John and Thomas Hody's heirs. (Warranty.) Cons. 200 marks.

79/88/49

1434

528. One week [30 May] from Trinity. Alan Rote and Sibyl his wife quer.; Richard Berewell and Robert Berewell def. Two messuages in Tewkesbury (*Tewekesbury*). Right of Alan, as those which Alan and Sibyl had by gift of Richard and Robert. Remise and quitclaim, specifying Richard's heirs, to Alan and Sibyl and Alan's heirs. (Warranty.) Cons. 10 marks.

79/88/50

13 Henry VI

1435

529. Two weeks [1 May] from Easter. (Made three weeks from Michaelmas in the said year [20 Oct. 1434].) William Gernon and Elizabeth his wife quer.; Thomas Seende clerk and John Bisley (*Byseley*) clerk def. The manor of Dowdeswell (*Doudiswell*) and the advowson of the church of the same manor, except 3 messuages, 92 a. of land, 6 a. of meadow, 10 a. of wood, and 6s. 6d. rent in the same manor, GLOS.; and the manor of Leckhampstead (*Lekhamstede*) and the advowson of the church of the same manor, BUCKS. Right of Thomas, as those which Thomas and John had by gift of William and Elizabeth. For this, grant back and render to William and Elizabeth. To hold to them and their heirs in tail. Contingent remainder to Elizabeth's heirs. *Labelled* Glouc', Buk'.

292/68/160

1435

530. Two weeks [1 May] from Easter. (Made the morrow of All Souls in the said year [3 Nov. 1434].) Roger Jones, the warden, and the vicars of the college of vicars in the choir of the cathedral church of Hereford (*Hereford*) quer.; William de Aune and Margaret his wife def. Six acres of land in Westbury on Severn (*Wesbury*) and the advowson of the church of Westbury. Right of the warden and vicars. Remise and quitclaim, specifying Margaret's heirs, to them. (Warranty.) Cons. a young sparrowhawk. Made by the king's order.

79/89/53

531. Two weeks [1 May] from Easter. (Made one week [20 Jan.] from Hilary in the said year.) Maurice Berkeley of Uley (*Uley*) knight, John Kemes clerk, Maurice Kemes, Nicholas Alderley (*Aderlegh*), and John Codrington (*Codryngton*) quer.; John Kemes esquire and Margaret his wife and Stephen Hatfield (*Haitfeld*) and Isabel his wife def. The advowson of the church of Dyrham (*Derham*), half of the manor of Aust (*Auste*), one third of 6 ploughlands in Dyrham, and the manor of Dyrham except 1 a. of land in the same manor, GLOS., half of the manor of Litton Cheney (*Lytton*) and the advowson of the church of the same manor, one third of the manor of Kingston Russell (*Kyngeston Russell*) and the advowson of the free chapel of the same manor, DORSET, and 3 tofts, 2 ploughlands and 2 a. of land, 12 a. of meadow, 60 a. of pasture, and 3 a. of wood in Horsington (*Horsyngton*) and North Cheriton (*Northcheryton*) and the advowsons of the church of Horsington and of the free chapel of South Cheriton (*Southcheryton*) and one third of the manor of Horsington, SOM. As to the manor [sc. of Dyrham], the 2 a. of land, the one third of 6 ploughlands, the one third of the manor of Kingston Russell, the one third of the manor of Horsington, and the advowsons of Kingston Russell and Horsington, the right of John Kemes clerk, Maurice, Nicholas and John Codrington; as to the holdings [in Horsington and North Cheriton], the half of the manor of Aust, the half of the manor of Litton, and the advowson of Litton, the right of John Kemes clerk; of which Maurice, John Kemes clerk, Maurice, Nicholas, and John Codrington had the manor [of Dyrham], the 2 a. of land, two thirds of the halves of the manors of Aust and Litton and of the other holdings, and the advowsons of Dyrham, Litton, Horsington, and South Cheriton by gift of John Kemes esquire and Margaret and Stephen and Isabel. To hold the manor [of Dyrham], the 2 a. of land, the advowsons of Dyrham, Horsington, and South Cheriton to Maurice, John Kemes clerk, Maurice, Nicholas, and John Codrington and their heirs, of the king; and to hold two thirds of the halves of the manors of Aust and Litton and the two thirds of the said holdings to Maurice, John Kemes clerk, Maurice, Nicholas, and John Codrington and the heirs of Maurice Kemes clerk, of the chief lords. And grant to the quer. of the reversion of the other one third of the halves of the manors of Aust and Litton, of the 6 ploughlands, and of the manors of Horsington and Kingston Russell and the advowson of Kingston Russell, held by John Stradelyng knight and Joan his wife in dower for the term of Joan's life, of the inheritance of Margaret and Isabel. To hold with the manor [of Dyrham] etc. as above. (Warranty.) Cons. 300 marks. Made, as to the said manor, the land, the one third part of the manors of Horsington and Kingston Russell, and the one third part of the 6 ploughlands and the advowsons of Dyrham, Horsington, South Cheriton, and Kingston Russell, by the king's order. *Labelled* Glouc', Dors', Somers'.

292/68/161

[Cf. *Dorset Fines, 1327–1485*, pp. 310–12; *Som. Fines, 1399–1484*, p. 192.]

1435

532. One month [15 May] from Easter. Ralph Seymour of Winchcombe (*Wynchecombe*) quer.; Joan Thorp (*Throope*) def. A messuage and 4½ a. of land in Winchcombe and Gretton (*Gretton*). Right of Ralph by Joan's gift. Remise and quitclaim to Ralph. (Warranty.) Cons. 10 marks.

79/89/55

533. Morrow [27 May] of Ascension. Henry Clifford (*Clyfford*) quer.; Hugh Twysull and Joan his wife def. Three messuages, 80 a. of land, 6 a. of meadow, 8 a. of pasture, and 2 a. of wood in Haresfield (*Haresfelde*), Standish (*Standyssh*), and Moreton Valence (*Moreton*). Right of Henry by gift of Hugh and Joan. Remise and quitclaim, specifying Joan's heirs, to Henry. (Warranty.) For this, grant back and render to Hugh and Joan. To hold to them and Hugh's heirs.

79/89/54

534. One week [19 June] from Trinity. Robert Stanshawe quer.; John Stonehouse (*Stonhous*) def. Two messuages, 1 ploughland, 20 a. of meadow, and 20 a. of pasture in Stonehouse and King's Stanley (*Stanley Regis*). Right of Robert by John's gift. Remise and quitclaim to Robert. (Warranty.) Cons. 100 marks.

79/89/56

14 Henry VI

1435

535. Morrow [3 Nov.] of All Souls. William Smith (*Smyth*) of Lower Hanham (*Dounhanham*), John Turner (*Tournour*) of Lower Staunton (*Netherstaunton*), Herefs., and Robert Turner of Shobdon (*Shobdon*), Herefs., quer.; William Turner of Lower Hanham, Glos., and Alice his wife def. The manor of Brokenborough (*Brokynborowe*). Right of William Smith, as that which the same William, John, and Robert had by gift of William Turner and Alice. Remise and quitclaim, specifying Alice's heirs, to William Smith, John, and Robert and William Smith's heirs. (Warranty.) Cons. 100 marks.

79/89/58

536. Morrow [12 Nov.] of St. Martin. John Vampage quer.; Thomas Mill (*Mulle*), Robert Bushel (*Busshell*), John West, and Richard Urdeley and Isabel his wife def. The manor of Colesborne (*Collesburn'*), 8 messuages, a mill, 1 ploughland and 8 yardlands, 10 a. of meadow, 140 a. of pasture, 60 a. of wood, 60s. rent and rent of 1 lb. of pepper in Great Colesborne (*Magna Collesburn'*), Little Colesborne (*Parva Collesburn'*), Withington (*Wythyndon*), Chedworth (*Chedworth*), and Stoke Orchard (*Archerstoke*). Right of John Vampage, of which he had 4 messuages, 4 yardlands, 5 a. of meadow, 70 a. of pasture, 30 a. of wood, 30s. rent, the said rent [of pepper], and half of the manor, the mill, and 1 yardland by gift of Thomas, Robert, John West, Richard, and Isabel. Remise and quitclaim [of the whole], specifying Isabel's heirs, to John Vampage. (Warranty.) Cons. 300 marks.

79/89/59

1436

537. One week [20 Jan.] from Hilary. John Grey of Ruthin (*Ruthyn*) 'chivaler' and Nicholas Thorley 'chivaler' quer.; Humphrey [of Lancaster] duke of Gloucester and Eleanor his wife def. The castle and town of Hadleigh (*Haddeley*) and the castle of Colchester (*Colchestre*) and the fee farm of the town of Colchester and the hundred of Tendring (*Tendryng*), ESSEX; the isle and lordship of Wight (*Wyght*) and the castle and lordship of Carisbrooke (*Carsbroke*), HANTS.; the manor or barton of Bristol (*Bristoll'*) and the hundred of Barton Regis (*Berton Bristoll'*), GLOS.; the castle and lordship of Pembroke (*Pembrok'*), the castle and lordship of Tenby (*Tembeigh*), the castle and lordship of Cilgerran (*Kilgaren'*), the castle and lordship of Llanstephan (*Lanstephan'*), and the commotes of *Oestrelawe*, *Treyne*, and St. Clears (*Seyntclere*) in the marches of Wales, adjoining HEREFS.; the manor of Milton Regis (*Middelton*) by Sittingbourne and the hundreds of Milton and Marden (*Merden*), KENT; the manors of Cookham (*Cokham*) and Bray (*Bray*), BERKS.; and the manor and forest of Feckenham (*Fekenham*), WORCS. Right of John and Nicholas by gift of the duke and Eleanor. To hold to John and Nicholas and their heirs, of the king. (Warranty, by the duke alone.) For this, grant back and render to the duke and Eleanor. To hold to them and the duke's heirs in tail male as to the castle of Colchester, the Isle of Wight, the castle and lordship of Carisbrooke, the manor of Bristol, and the hundreds of Tendring and Barton Regis; to them and the duke's heirs in tail as to the castle and town of Hadleigh, the castles and lordships of Pembroke, Tenby, Cilgerran, and Llanstephan, the commotes, the manors of Cookham, Bray, Feckenham, and Milton, the forest of Feckenham, and the hundreds of Milton and Marden. Contingent remainder to the king. Made by the king's order. *Labelled* Essex', Sutht', Glouc', Hereford', Kanc', Berk', Wygorn'.

292/68/180

[Cf. *Essex Fines, 1423–1547*, p. 23.]

538. Morrow [18 May] of Ascension. John Buckland (*Boklond*) quer.; Richard Walpole (*Wawepole*) of Pendock (*Pendok'*) def. Two messuages, 30 a. of land, and 4 a. of meadow in Newent (*Newent*). Right of John by Richard's gift. Remise and quitclaim to John. (Warranty.) For this, John granted that he would pay to Richard during Richard's life 13*s.* 9*d.* a year, at Michaelmas and Easter, with right of distraint in the said holding for non-payment.

79/89/57

539. Morrow [18 May] of Ascension. William Alnwick (*Alnewyk*) bishop of Norwich (*Norwicen'*), Richard [Beauchamp] earl of Warwick (*Warr'*), Walter Hungerford (*Hungreford*) knight, John Beaumont (*Beaumond*) knight, John Tyrrel (*Tirell*) knight, Ralph Butler (*Boteler*) knight, John Marbury (*Merbury*) esquire, Richard Dixton esquire, and William Wolston esquire quer.; Richard [Plantagenet] duke of York (*Ebor'*), Walter Lucy 'chivaler', and Richard Wigmore (*Wyggemore*) esquire def. The castles and lordships of Rhayader (*Raydre*), Cefnllys (*Kenlles*), Radnor (*Radenore*), and Knucklas (*Knoklas*), the town of Radnor, the lordships of Maelienydd (*Mellenyth*), Builth (*Pullyth*), Knighton (*Knyghton*), Gwrtheyrnion (*Warthreignon*), Cwmwd Deuddwr (*Comotoydour*), Norton (*Norton*), and Presteigne (*Prestheind*) in the marches of Wales adjoining HEREFS., the manors of Orleton (*Orleton*), Kingsland (*Kyngeslane*), Pembridge (*Pembrugge*), Mansell Lacy (*Malmeshullasy*), Netherwood *(Nethewode)*, Marden (*Mawardyn*), and Wolferlow (*Wolforlowe*) and two thirds of the manor of Much Marcle (*Magna*

1436

Marcle), HEREFS., the castle, manor, and town of Ludlow (*Ludelowe*) and the manors and lordships of Stanton Lacy (*Staunton Lacy*), Cleeton (*Cleoton*), and Farlow (*Farlowe*), SALOP., the manors of Bromsgrove (*Brymesgrove*) and King's Norton (*Norton*), WORCS., the manors of Whaddon (*Whaddon*) and Steeple Claydon (*Stepulclaydon*), BUCKS., the manors of Stratfield Mortimer (*Stratfeld Mortemer*) and Warfield (*Waghfeld*), BERKS., two thirds of the manor of Thaxted (*Thaxstede*), ESSEX, the manor of Martyr Worthy (*Worthy Mortemer*), HANTS., the manors of Swanscombe (*Swannescombe*) and Erith (*Erhyth*), KENT, the manors of Cranborne (*Cranburum*), Pimperne (*Pymperne*), Tarrant Gunville (*Tarent Gundevile*), Weymouth (*Weymouth*), Wyke Regis (*Wyke*), Portland (*Portland*), Wareham (*Warham*), Steeple (*Stuple*), and Creech (*Crich*), DORSET, the castle of Bridgwater (*Bruggewater*), the manors of Odcombe (*Odycombe*) and Milverton (*Milverton*), and two thirds of the lordship of Bridgwater, SOM., and the manors of Charlton Kings (*Charleton*), Winstone (*Wynston*), and Brimpsfield (*Brymmesfeld*), GLOS. Right of the bishop and the other quer. by gift of the duke, Walter Lucy, and Richard Wigmore. To hold to the bishop and the other quer., of the king. (Warranty.) Cons. £1,000. *Labelled* Hereford', Salop', Wygorn', Buk', Berk', Essex', Suth't', Kanc', Dors', Somers', Glouc'.

292/68/186

[Cf. *Dorset Fines, 1327–1485*, pp. 312–13; *Essex Fines, 1423–1547*, pp. 23–4; *Som. Fines, 1399–1484*, p. 193. It is surprising that there is no statement that the fine was made by the king's order; cf. above, no. 443, which includes ten additional manors and an additional lordship.]

540. One week [10 June] from Trinity. (Made the morrow [18 May] of Ascension in the said year.) John Jervis (*Gerveys*) and Alice his wife quer.; Richard Morris (*Morys*) of Cirencester (*Cirencestre*) 'smyth' def. A messuage, 3 a. of meadow, and half of 1 yardland in Daglingworth (*Daglyngworth*), held by Robert Woodward (*Wodeward*) and Agnes his wife for term of Agnes's life of Richard's inheritance. Right of John. Grant of the reversion to John and Alice. To hold to them and John's heirs. (Warranty.) Cons. 10 marks.

79/89/61

541. One week [10 June] from Trinity. Thomas Natton quer.; William Comber and Alice his wife def. Two messuages in Tewkesbury (*Tewekesbury*). Right of Thomas by gift of William and Alice. Remise and quitclaim, specifying Alice's heirs, to Thomas. (Warranty.) For this, grant and render to William and Alice. To hold to them during their lives, of Thomas, during Alice's life paying a rose a year at St. John the Baptist, and after Alice's death, if William survives, 20*s.* a year, at Michaelmas and Easter, and doing service to the chief lords. Remainder to Thomas Bray and Alice his wife and their heirs in tail. To hold of Thomas Natton, paying a rose a year at St. John the Baptist and doing service to the chief lords. Contingent reversion to Thomas Natton.

79/89/62

542. One week [1 July] from St. John the Baptist. Joan le White quer.; Henry Northcote and Alice his wife def. Seven and a half acres in Chesterton (*Chesterton*). Grant and render to Joan. To hold to her and her heirs in tail. Contingent remainder to John Langley (*Langeley*). (Warranty, specifying Alice's heirs.) Cons. 40*s.*

79/89/60

15 Henry VI

1436

543. Morrow [3 Nov.] of All Souls. Thomas Parkhouse (*Parkhous*), Alan Withyford (*Wythyford*), and John Withyford quer.; Geoffrey John draper and Margaret his wife def. A messuage, 40 a. of land, 10 a. of meadow, and 10 a. of pasture in Tickenham (*Tykkenham*), SOM.; and 7 messuages, 15 shops, 2 cellars, and 16 gardens in the town of Bristol (*Bristoll'*) and the suburbs of the same town. Right of Thomas, as those which Thomas, Alan, and John had by gift of Geoffrey and Margaret. Remise and quitclaim, specifying Margaret's heirs, to Thomas, Alan, and John and Thomas's heirs. (Warranty.) Cons. 100 marks. *Labelled* Somers', Villa Bristoll'.

292/68/194

1437

544. One week [25 June] from St. John the Baptist. Thomas Hussey (*Husee*), Nicholas Cifrewast, John Bedlowe, James Burston, and William Combe quer.; John Chideock (*Chidiok*) knight and Katherine his wife def. The manor of Frampton on Severn (*Frampton super Sabrinam*). Right of Thomas, as that which the same Thomas, Nicholas, John Bedlowe, James, and William had by gift of John Chideock and Katherine. Remise and quitclaim, specifying John Chideock's heirs, to Thomas, Nicholas, John Bedlowe, James, and William. (Warranty, specifying Katherine's heirs.) For this, grant and render to John Chideock. To hold to him for term of the life of Ralph Bush (*Busshe*) esquire. Remainder to William Stafford esquire son of Humphrey Stafford knight and Katherine his [William's] wife, one of the daughters and heirs of the said John Chideock, and their heirs in tail. Contingent remainder to John Chideock and his heirs.

79/89/63

[It appears anomalous that the remise and quitclaim specifies John Chideock's heirs while the warranty specifies Katherine's.]

16 Henry VI

1437

545. One week [18 Nov.] from St. Martin. Richard Stake quer.; Henry Aylworth (*Ayleworth*) and Emma his wife def. Two messuages, a dovecot, 2 yardlands and 8 a. of land, and 2 a. of meadow in Berry Wormington (*Parva Wormynton*). Right of Richard by gift of Henry and Emma. Remise and quitclaim, specifying Emma's heirs, to Richard. (Warranty.) Cons. 100 marks.

79/89/65

546. One week [18 Nov.] from St. Martin. Geoffrey Holford and John Jervis (*Gerveys*) quer.; Guy Whittington (*Whytyngton*) esquire and Cecily his wife def. The manor of Leigh (*Leygh*) by Deerhurst (*Derhurst*). Right of Geoffrey, as that which Geoffrey and John had by gift of Guy and Cecily. Remise and quitclaim, specifying Cecily's heirs, to Geoffrey and John and Geoffrey's heirs. (Warranty.) For this, grant back and render to Guy and Cecily. To hold without impeachment of waste during their lives. Remainder to Richard their son and his heirs in tail. Successive contingent remainders to Richard's brother William and his heirs in tail, to William's brother Giles and his heirs in tail, to Giles's brother Thomas and his heirs in tail, to Thomas's sister Margery and her heirs in tail, to Margery's sister Elizabeth and her heirs in tail, and to Cecily's brother William Browning (*Brownyng'*).

79/89/70

1438

547. Morrow [3 Feb.] of the Purification. William Wyther clerk and Henry Dean (*Dene*) quer.; Robert Webb (*Webbe*) and Elizabeth his wife and Joan who was wife of William Marsh (*Maryse*) def. A messuage, 20 a. of land, 3 a. of meadow, 2 a. of pasture, and 2*s*. 6*d*. rent in Upper Ley (*Overlee*). Right of William Wyther, as those which the same William and Henry had by gift of Robert, Elizabeth, and Joan. Remise and quitclaim, specifying Elizabeth's and Joan's heirs, to William Wyther and Henry and William Wyther's. (Warranty). Cons. 20 marks.

79/89/64

548. One month [11 May] from Easter. Thomas Holloway (*Holewey*) quer.; Geoffrey Holford and Alice his wife def. A toft, 20 a. of land, and 6 a. of meadow in Earthcott (*Erdcote*) and Lee (*Lee in Salso Marisco*). Right of Thomas. Remise and quitclaim, specifying Alice's heirs, to him. (Warranty.) Cons. 20 marks.

79/89/68

549. Morrow [23 May] of Ascension. John Vampage, John Langley, John Edwards (*Edward*), Thomas Bisley (*Byseley*), and Thomas Lane clerk quer.; Richard Sage citizen and goldsmith of London (*London'*) and Joan his wife, John Chesham, John Chester (*Chestre*), and John Brillyng def. A messuage and 3*s*. 1½*d*. rent in Gloucester (*Gloucestre*). Right of John Langley, as those which the same John and the other quer. had by gift of Richard and Joan and the other def. Remise and quitclaim, specifying Richard's heirs, to the quer. and John Langley's heirs. (Warranty.) Cons. £20.

79/89/66

550. Morrow [23 May] of Ascension. John Cadel (*Cadull*), William Naylor (*Nayler*), and John Verney quer.; Robert Hicks (*Hicches*) of Lydney (*Lydeney*) and Alice his wife def. A messuage, a garden, and 1½ a. of land in Lydney. Right of John Cadel, as those which the same John, William, and John Verney had by gift of Robert and Alice. Remise and quitclaim, specifying Alice's heirs, to John Cadel, William, and John Verney and John Cadel's heirs. (Warranty.) Cons. 20 marks.

79/89/69

551. One week [15 June] from Trinity. (Made one week [9 Feb.] from the Purification in the said year.) John Arnold the elder clerk and Philip Hook (*Hoke*) quer.; John Edwards (*Edwardes*) of Gloucester (*Gloucestre*) and John Arnold the younger def. Twenty messuages, 7 shops, 60 a. of land, 6 a. of meadow, and 20 a. of wood in Gloucester and Paganhill (*Pagenhull*). Right of Philip. Grant to John Arnold the elder and Philip of the reversion of 18 messuages in the said towns, held by Alice who was wife of Robert Gilbert for term of 12 years, and of 2 messuages and the said shops, land, meadow, and wood, held by the said Alice for term of life and which will remain to John son of Robert Gilbert for term of life if he should survive Alice, of John Edwards's inheritance. To hold to John Arnold the elder and Philip and Philip's heirs. Cons. 300 marks.

79/89/67

17 Henry VI

1438

552. Two weeks [13 Oct.] from Michaelmas. William Prelatte quer.; Richard Janyver and Agnes his wife def. Two messuages, a garden, a dovecot, 13½ a. of land, and 2 a. of meadow in Lechlade (*Lechelade*). Right of William by gift of Richard and Agnes. Remise and quitclaim, specifying Agnes's heirs, to William. (Warranty.) Cons. 20 marks.

79/89/72

553. Three weeks [20 Oct.] from Michaelmas. Thomas Poyntz esquire quer.; Clement Williams (*William*) and Joan his wife def. A messuage, 2 tofts, 70 a. of land, 4 a. of meadow, 6 a. of pasture, and 1 a. of wood in Tytherington (*Tedryngton*). Right of Thomas by gift of Clement and Joan. Remise and quitclaim, specifying Joan's heirs, to Thomas. (Warranty.) Cons £40.

79/89/71

554. Three weeks [20 Oct.] from Michaelmas. Thomas Doughton (*Doweghton*) clerk and Robert Barber (*Barbour*) quer.; Thomas Veyre def. Four messuages, 30 a. of land, 20 a. of meadow, and 30 a. of pasture in Old Sodbury (*Oldesobbury*) and Chipping Sodbury (*Chepyngsobbury*). Right of Thomas Doughton as those which the same Thomas and Robert had by Thomas Veyre's gift. Remise and quitclaim to Thomas Doughton and Robert and the same Thomas's heirs. (Warranty.) Cons. 100 marks.

79/89/73

1439

555. One week [20 Jan.] from Hilary. (Made the morrow of St. Martin 15 Henry VI [12 Nov. 1436].) Richard Venables quer.; Thomas Gossington (*Gosyngton*) and Joan his wife def. Two messuages, 116 a. of land, 22 a. of meadow, 14 a. of pasture, 8 a. of wood, and 4*s.* rent in Gossington, Slimbridge (*Slymbrugge*), Hurst (*Hurst*), and Ham (*Hamme*). Right of Richard. Grant to Richard of the rent with the homage and all the services of John Smith (*Smyth*) and his heirs from all the holdings which John held of Thomas and Joan in Hurst. And grant to Richard, specifying Joan's heirs, of the reversion of a messuage, 66 a. of land, 20 a. of meadow, 12 a. of pasture, and the said wood in Gossington, Slimbridge, and Hurst, held by Richard Hitchcocks (*Hischecokkes*) for term of life, of 16 a. of land in Gossington, held by Walter Baker for term of life, of 14 a. of land in Gossington, held by Robert Oak (*Oake*) for term of life, of 9 a. of land and 2 a. of meadow in Hurst and Ham, held by Thomas Frigg (*Frigge*) for term of life, of 2 a. of pasture in Gossington and Hurst, held by Robert Gilmyn for term of life, of 5 a. of land in Gossington, held by Walter Heynes (*Hanyes*) for term of life, of 1 a. of land in Slimbridge, held by John Tailor (*Taillour*) for term of life, and of a messuage and 5 a. of land, held by Hugh Glastonbury (*Glastyngbury*) for term of life, of Thomas Gossington's inheritance, in Gossington. (Warranty, specifying Joan's heirs.) Cons. 100 marks. [*Worn.*]

79/90/78

[It appears anomalous that the grant and the warranty specify Joan's heirs while the holdings granted in reversion are said to be of Thomas Gossington's inheritance.]

1439

556. Two weeks [19 April] from Easter. Henry Clifford quer.; Hugh Twysull and Joan his wife def. Three messuages, 80 a. of land, 6 a. of meadow, 8 a. of pasture, and 2 a. of wood in Haresfield (*Haresfeld*), Standish (*Standyssh*), and Moreton Valence (*Moreton*). Right of Henry by gift of Hugh and Joan. Remise and quitclaim, specifying Joan's heirs, to Henry. (Warranty.) For this, grant back and render to Hugh and Joan. To hold to them and Joan's heirs in tail. Successive contingent remainders to Hugh's brother John Twysull and his heirs in tail and to Joan's heirs.

79/89/74

557. Two weeks [19 April] from Easter. Ralph Butler (*Boteler*) knight, Thomas Wickham (*Wykeham*) knight, John Beauchamp knight, William Lucy esquire, John Norris (*Norys*) esquire, Thomas Harwell esquire, and Thomas Palmer esquire quer.; William Bishopton (*Bysshopeston*) knight def. The manor of Lark Stoke (*Larkestoke*), GLOS., the manors of Bishopton, Thornton (*Thorndon*), Lapworth (*Lapworth*), and Wilnecote (*Wilmecote*), and 33 messuages, 2 ploughlands and 18 yardlands, 30 a. of meadow, 20 a. of pasture, 40 a. of wood, and 72*s*. rent in Lapworth, Rowington (*Rowynton*), Bushwood (*Bysshewode*), Lyndon End (*Lynden*), Shottery (*Shotrith*), Drayton (*Drayton*) and Clopton (*Clopton*), Upper Ettington (*Overetyndon*), Stratford-upon-Avon (*Stratford super Aven*), Wellesbourne Mountford (*Wellesburgh Mountford*), Moreton Morrell (*Moreton*), and Sheldon (*Sheldon*), WARWS.; and 25 messuages, 14 yardlands, 20 a. of meadow, 30 a. of pasture, 4 a. of wood, and 11*s*. rent in Pepwell (*Pyppewell*), Waresley (*Waresley*), Hill (*Hulle*), Moor (*More*), and *Brymerton*, WORCS. Grant and render to Ralph, Thomas, John, William Lucy, John, Thomas, and Thomas. To hold during the life of Thomas Chapman of Drayton. Remainder to Thomas Messenger (*Messanger*) parson of the church of Preston (*Preston*), Richard Compton clerk, Thomas Palmer of Holt (*Holt*), and Robert Osgodesby. To hold during the life of William Bourdon parson of the church of Rockingham (*Rokyngham*). Remainder to Thomas Green (*Grene*) esquire, Thomas Palmer esquire, Thomas East (*Est*) of Warwick (*Warwyk*), John Palmer, and John Clerk during the life of of Robert Wyville esquire. Remainder to John Northwood (*Northwode*), Philip Leweston, and Thomas Palmer of Keythorpe (*Keythorp*). To hold during the life of John Whiteside (*Whitside*). Remainder to the heirs in tail of William Bishopton and Philippa late his wife. Contingent remainder to William Bishopton's heirs. Cons. (paid by Ralph and the other quer. to William Bishopton), 300 marks. *Labelled* Glouc', Warr', Wygorn'. [*Worn*.]

292/69/221

[Cf. *Warws. Fines, 1345–1509*, pp. 159–60, no. 2600.]

558. One month [3 May] from Easter. Thomas Adnet parson of the church of Hampnett (*Hamptonet*) quer.; Thomas Molder of Shipton Oliffe (*Shipton Olyfe*) and Alice his wife def. Two messuages, 4 yardlands and 24 a. of land, 2 a. of meadow, and 2 a. of pasture in Shipton Solers (*Overshipton*) and Hampen (*Hannepenne*). Right of Thomas Adnet by gift of Thomas Molder and Alice. Remise and quitclaim, specifying Alice's heirs, to Thomas Adnet. (Warranty.) Cons. £40.

79/90/76

1439

559. One month [3 May] from Easter. William Browning (*Brounyng*) esquire quer.; John Brown (*Broun'*) and Joan his wife def. Eight messuages, 10 yardlands, 20 a. of meadow, and 10*s*. rent in Bourton on the Water (*Burton*), Nethercote (*Nethercote*), and Aylworth (*Ayleworthe*). Right of William by gift of John and Joan. Remise and quitclaim, specifying Joan's heirs, to William. (Warranty.) Cons. 100 marks.

79/90/77

560. One month [3 May] from Easter. Richard Bradford (*Bradeford*) quer.; Robert Witcombe (*Wydecombe*) and Emma his wife def. Two yardlands, 2 a. of land, half of 1 yardland, and 8 a. of meadow in Tewkesbury (*Tewkesbury*), Mitton (*Mitton*), and Corse (*Cors*), GLOS., and 3 messuages, 1½ yardlands, and 8 a. of meadow in Staunton (*Staunton*) by Corse, WORCS. Right of Richard, of which he had the messuages, 1 yardland, 2 a. of land, ½ yardland, and 8 a. of meadow by gift of Robert and Emma. Remise and quitclaim, specifying Emma's heirs, to Richard. And grant to Richard of the reversion of 2½ yardlands and 8 a. of meadow in Tewkesbury and Mitton, held by Helen who was wife of Richard Wyche for term of life, of Emma's inheritance. (Warranty.) Cons. 100 marks.

292/69/223

[Mitton was largely, if not wholly, in Worcs.; Corse was largely in Glos.]

561. Morrow [15 May] of Ascension. William Wall (*Walle*) quer.; John Harris (*Harreys*) and Joan his wife def. Three messuages, 6 gardens, 16½ a. of land, 3 a. of meadow, 1½ a. of pasture, half of a messuage, and one third of 4 messuages, 2 tofts, 62 a. of land, 5 a. of meadow, and 3 a. of pasture in Arlingham (*Erlyngham*). Right of William by gift of John and Joan. Remise and quitclaim, specifying Joan's heirs, to William. (Warranty.) Cons. £40.

79/89/75

18 Henry VI

1439

562. One week [6 Oct.] from Michaelmas. (Made one week from St. John the Baptist 17 Henry VI [1 July 1439].) Thomas Brooke (*Brook*) knight, John Hody, John Batcombe (*Battescombe*), John Corbridge (*Cobrygge*) clerk, and William Taverner quer.; John Chideock (*Chidyok*) knight and Katherine his wife def. The manor of Clifton (*Clyfton*) and a messuage, 60 a. of land, and 20 a. of meadow in Clifton. Right of Thomas, as those which the same Thomas and the other quer. had by gift of John Chideock and Katherine. Remise and quitclaim, specifying Katherine's heirs, to the quer. and Thomas's heirs. (Warranty against the abbot of Cerne.) For this, grant back and render to John Chideock and Katherine. To hold to John Chideock of Thomas and the quer. during the life of Ralph Bush (*Bussh*), paying a rose a year at St. John the Baptist and doing service to the chief lords. Reversion to the quer. and Thomas's heirs.

79/90/79

1439

563. One week [6 Oct.] from Michaelmas. (Made one week from Trinity 17 Henry VI [7 June 1439].) William [Henley] abbot of the church of St. Mary of Hailes (*Hayles*) quer.; Richard Urdeley and Isabel his wife def. Five messuages, 5 tofts, 3 ploughlands and 5 yardlands, 15 a. of meadow, 20 a. of pasture, 15 a. of wood, and 30*s.* rent in Newington Bagpath (*Newenton Bampton*). Right of the abbot. Remise and quitclaim, specifying Isabel's heirs, to the abbot. (Warranty.) The abbot received Richard and Isabel and Isabel's heirs into all prayers henceforth.

79/90/80

564. Two weeks [13 Oct.] from Michaelmas. Ralph Butler (*Buteler*) knight, John Beauchamp knight, William Montfort knight, William Thomas knight, John Throckmorton (*Throkmarton*), John Norris (*Norys*), John Nanfan, William Menston, and John Say clerk quer.; Isabel countess of Warwick (*Warr'*) who was wife of Richard de Beauchamp (*de Bello Campo*) late earl of Warwick def. The manors of Fairford (*Faireford*) and Chipping Sodbury (*Sobbury*), GLOS., the manor of Shipton-under-Wychwood (*Shipton*) and the hundred of Chadlington (*Chadlyngton*), OXON., the manor of Sherston (*Sherston*), WILTS., the manor of Stanford in the Vale (*Stanford*), BERKS., the manor of Marlow (*Merlowe*), BUCKS., and the manor of Thorley and Wellow (*Thorley Wolowe*), HANTS. Right of John Say, as those which he and the other quer. had by the countess's gift. Remise and quitclaim to the quer. (Warranty.) Cons. £1,000. *Labelled* Glouc', Oxon', Wiltes', Berk', Buk', Sutht'.

292/69/233

[Cf. *Wilts. Fines, 1377–1509*, p. 113, no. 526. For the identity of Stanford in the Vale, *V.C.H. Berks.* iv. 480.]

565. Morrow [12 Nov.] of St. Martin. John Limerick (*Lymeryk*) and Roger Capes quer.; Thomas Mascall and Agnes his wife def. Five messuages, a toft, 3 dovecots, 2½ yardlands, 8 a. of meadow, 2 a. of pasture, and half of 1 a. of wood in Stratton (*Stratton*) by Cirencester (*Cirencestre*). Right of John as those which John and Roger had by gift of Thomas and Agnes. Remise and quitclaim, specifying Agnes's heirs, to John and Roger and John's heirs. (Warranty.) Cons. 100 marks.

79/90/85

566. One week [18 Nov.] from St. Martin. John Reed (*Rede*) burgess of the town of Gloucester (*Gloucestr'*) quer.; Thomas Ball (*Balle*) burgess of the town of Bristol (*Bristoll*) and Alice his wife def. Sixteen messuages in Gloucester and King's Barton (*Berton Regis*) by Gloucester. Right of John by gift of Thomas and Alice. Remise and quitclaim, specifying Alice's heirs, to John. Cons. 100 marks.

79/90/83

1440

567. One week [20 Jan.] from Hilary. (Made two weeks from St. Martin in the said year [23 Nov. 1439].) Ralph Butler (*Boteller*) knight, John Beauchamp knight, William Montfort (*Mountfort*) knight, William Thomas knight, John Throckmorton (*Throkmarton*), John Norris (*Noreys*), John Nanfan, and William Menston quer.; Isabel countess of Warwick (*Warr'*) def. The manors of Tewkesbury (*Tewekesbury*) and

1440

Whittington (*Whityngton*), GLOS., the manors of Hanley Castle (*Hanley super Severne*), Bushley (*Busheley*), and Redmarley d'Abitot (*Ridmerley*), WORCS., the manors of Caversham (*Caversham*) and Burford (*Burford*), OXON., the manors of Rotherfield (*Retherfeld*) and Mereworth (*Mereworth*), KENT, the manor of Winterton (*Wynterton*), WARWS., and the manors of Winterslow (*Wynterslowe*), Ashley (*Assheley*), and Broad Town (*Brodtoune*), WILTS. Right of Ralph and the other quer. by the countess's gift. (Warranty.) To hold of the king, in order to execute the countess's will. Cons. 1,000 marks. Made by the king's order. *Labelled* Glouc', Wygorn', Oxon', Kanc', Warr', Wiltes'.

292/69/238

[Cf. *Warws. Fines, 1345–1509*, p. 161, no. 2605; *Wilts. Fines, 1377–1509*, p. 114, no. 529.]

568. One month [24 April] from Easter. John Forthey of Cirencester (*Cirencestre*) and Edith his wife quer.; Alice Laurence of Cookham (*Cokham*), Berks., def. A messuage in Cirencester. Right of John, as that which John and Edith had by Alice's gift. Remise and quitclaim to John and Edith and John's heirs. (Warranty.) Cons. 20 marks.

79/90/81

569. Morrow [6 May] of Ascension. William Golding (*Goldyng*) and Joan his wife quer.; William Howe (*Houe*) late of Hannington (*Hanyngton*) and Isabel his wife. A messuage, 1 ploughland, and 12 a. of meadow in Down Ampney (*Dounameney*). Right of William Golding, as those which the same William and Joan had by gift of William Howe and Isabel. Remise and quitclaim, specifying William Howe's heirs, to William Golding and Joan and William Golding's heirs. (Warranty.) Cons. £40.

79/90/84

570. Morrow [25 June] of St. John the Baptist. Giles Bridge (*Brugge*), Robert Matson (*Mattesdon*), John Holford, and Laurence Clerk quer.; Geoffrey Holford and Alice his wife def. Six messuages, 4 yardlands, 12 a. of meadow, 40 a. of pasture, and £4 rent in Frampton on Severn (*Frampton super Sabrinam*), Fretherne (*Frethorne*), Saul (*Salle*), Eastington (*Estyngton*), and Dymock (*Dymmok*). Right of Giles, as those which Giles, Robert, John, and Laurence had by gift of Geoffrey and Alice. Remise and quitclaim, specifying Alice's heirs, to Giles, Robert, John, and Laurence. (Warranty.) For this, grant back and render to Geoffrey and Alice. To hold to them without impeachment of waste during their lives. Remainder to Alice's heirs.

79/90/82

19 Henry VI

1440

571. One week [18 Nov.] from St. Martin. Nicholas Poyntz esquire and Elizabeth his wife quer.; James Berkeley knight and Isabel his wife def. The manor of Brokenborough (*Brokenburgh*) with appurtenances in Almondsbury (*Almondesbury*), Tockington (*Tokynton*), Hempton (*Hempton*), Patchway (*Petishawe*), Upper Woodland (*Overwodeland*), and Winterbourne (*Wynterbourn*), the manor of Daglingworth (*Daggelyngworth*) and a messuage, 2 ploughlands, 12 a. of meadow, 100 a. of wood, and half of a mill in Daglingworth and Cirencester (*Cirencestre*), and the advowson of the chantry of St. Mary of Almondsbury. Right of Nicholas, as those which Nicholas and Elizabeth had by gift of James and Isabel. Remise and quitclaim, specifying James's

1440

heirs, to Nicholas and Elizabeth and Nicholas's heirs. (Warranty, specifying Isabel's heirs, against Reynold [Boulers] abbot of St. Peter's, Gloucester (*Glouc'*), and his successors.) Cons. 300 marks.

79/90/87

[It appears anomalous that the remise and quitclaim specifies James's heirs while the warranty specifies Isabel's.]

1441

572. One week [20 Jan.] from Hilary. Nicholas Poyntz and Elizabeth his wife quer.; James Berkeley knight and Isabel his wife def. The manor of Little Marshfield (*Parva Mersshefeld*) and 200 a. of land, 60 a. of meadow, 12 a. of pasture, 3 a. of wood, and 100*s.* rent in Little Marshfield. Right of Nicholas and Elizabeth by gift of James and Isabel. Remise and quitclaim, specifying Isabel's heirs, to Nicholas and Elizabeth and Nicholas's heirs. (Warranty against Reynold [Boulers] abbot of St. Peter's, Gloucester (*Glouc'*), and his successors.) Cons. 200 marks.

79/90/88

573. One week [20 Jan.] from Hilary. (Made one week from the Purification 17 Henry VI [9 Feb. 1439].) Ralph Butler (*Boteler*) knight and John Edwards (*Edward*) quer.; William FitzWarren (*Fitz Waryn*) def. The manor of Rodmarton (*Rodmerton*), the advowson of the church of Rodmarton, and 8 messuages, 200 a. and 3 yardlands and 1 ploughland, 60 a. of meadow, 200 a. of pasture, 4 a. of wood, and £6 11*s.* 8*d.* rent in Rodmarton, Tarlton (*Torleton*), Cherington (*Cheryngton*), Henbury (*Hembury*), Lawrence Weston (*Weston Laurencii*), and King's Weston (*Weston Regis*) and half of the manor of Lawrence Weston, GLOS., and a toft, 2 yardlands, and 10 a. of meadow in Somerford Keynes (*Somerford Kaynes*), WILTS., all held by Roger Capes and Margaret his wife who was wife of Robert Gurdon for term of Margaret's life, of William's inheritance. Right of John. Grant of the reversion to Ralph and John and John's heirs. (Warranty.) Cons. £300. *Labelled* Glouc', Wiltes'.

292/69/246

[Cf. *Wilts. Fines, 1377–1509*, p. 115, no. 537.]

574. Morrow [3 Feb.] of the Purification. John Langley (*Langeley*) quer.; William Bond (*Bonde*) and Margaret his wife, one of the daughters and heirs of Thomas Cockerell (*Cokerell*), def. Five messuages, 10 tofts, 160 a. of land, and 30 a. of meadow in Fairford (*Fayreford*). Right of John, of which he had half of one third of the premises by gift of William and Margaret. Remise and quitclaim of the whole, specifying Margaret's heirs, to John. (Warranty.) Cons. 100 marks.

79/90/89

575. One month [14 May] from Easter. Thomas Heath (*Hethe*) quer.; Clement Bagot of Bristol (*Bristoll'*) 'marchaunt' and Alice his wife and Robert son of Clement and Margaret his wife def. The manor called 'Hall' in Biddestone (*Bydston*), WILTS., and 16 messuages in Bristol and the suburbs of the same town, all held by Elizabeth Russell for term of life, of Thomas's inheritance. Right of Thomas. For this, grant of the reversion of the manor and 9 messuages to Robert and Margaret and their heirs in tail. Successive

1441

contingent remainders to Alice and the heirs of Clement and Alice in tail and to Alice's heirs. And grant of the reversion of 7 messuages to Alice. To hold during her life. Remainder to Robert and Margaret and their heirs in tail. Contingent remainder to Alice's heirs. *Labelled* Wiltes', Bristoll'.

292/69/250

[Cf. *Wilts. Fines, 1377–1509*, p. 116, no. 541.]

576. One week [18 June] from Trinity. (Made the morrow [26 May] of Ascension in the said year.) John Throckmorton (*Throkmarton*) and John Rouse (*Rous*) quer.; John Giffard (*Gyfford*) the elder esquire and Matilda his wife, Robert Giffard and Joan his wife, and Alice who was wife of William Tracy def. The manors of Weston Subedge (*Weston Underegge*) and Norton Subedge (*Norton Underegge*) and the advowson of the church of Weston. John Giffard and Matilda and Robert acknowledged the manors and the advowson to be the right of John Throckmorton, as those which the same John and John Rouse had by gift of John Giffard and Matilda and Robert. Remise and quitclaim, specifying John Giffard's heirs, to John Throckmorton and John Rouse and John Throckmorton's heirs. (Warranty by John Giffard and Matilda, specifying Matilda's heirs.) For this, grant and render to Robert and Joan of the manor of Weston and the advowson. To hold to Robert and Joan and their heirs in tail. Successive contingent remainders to John Giffard and Matilda and John's heirs in tail male and to John's heirs. And grant and render to Alice of the manor of Norton. To hold during her life. Remainder to John Giffard during his life and to Robert and Joan and their heirs in tail. Successive contingent remainders to John Giffard's heirs in tail male and to John Giffard's heirs.

79/90/86

20 Henry VI

1442

577. One week [20 Jan.] from Hilary. (Made the morrow of All Souls in the said year [3 Nov. 1441].) John Kendal (*Kendale*) quer.; William Nottingham (*Notyngham*) and Elizabeth his wife def. Thirteen messuages, 4 tofts, a mill, 2 ploughlands and 6½ yardlands and 29 a. of land, 60 a. of meadow, 200 a. of pasture, 60 a. of wood, and 40*s.* rent in Great Taynton (*Magna Teynton*), Leigh (*Lee*), Evington (*Yevynton*), Hayden (*Heydon*), Deerhurst Walton (*Walton juxta Durherst*), Uckington (*Okynton*), Bagendon (*Bagynden*), Baunton (*Baudynton*), Daglingworth (*Daglyngworth*), Stroud (*Strode*), Stratton (*Stratton*), and South Cerney (*Southcerney*), GLOS., a toft and 40 a. of pasture in Great Chelworth (*Magna Chelworth*), WILTS., and a messuage, a dovecot, 20 a. of meadow, and 100 a. of pasture in Botley (*Botley*), BERKS. Right of John, of which he had 13 messuages, the tofts, mill, and dovecot, 2 ploughlands and 6½ yardlands, the meadow, pasture, wood, and rent in all the said places [*all named except Evington*] by gift of William and Elizabeth. Remise and quitclaim, specifying Elizabeth's heirs, to John. (Warranty.) For this, grant back and render to William and Elizabeth. To hold to them and Elizabeth's heirs. And grant to them of the reversion of a messuage and 30 a. of land in Evington, held by Simon Hale for term of life, of John's inheritance. To hold as above. *Labelled* Glouc', Wiltes', Berk'.

293/70/256

[Cf. *Wilts. Fines, 1377–1509*, p. 117, no. 547. The discrepancy between the 29 a. of land in the initial statement of the property and the 30 a. specified as held by Simon is unexplained.]

1442

578. One week [9 Feb.] from the Purification. Thomas Jones quer.; John Batchcott (*Bacchecote*) and Isabel his wife def. A messuage, 4 a. of land, and 4 a. of meadow in Tetbury (*Tettebury*) Right of Thomas by gift of John and Isabel. Remise and quitclaim, specifying Isabel's heirs, to Thomas. (Warranty.) Cons. £20.

79/90/90

579. One week [3 June] from Trinity. (Made the morrow [11 May] of Ascension in the said year.) Richard Talbot archbishop of Dublin (*Dublin'*) quer.; John Talbot knight and Margaret his wife def. The manors of Blake Mere (*Blakemere*), Whitchurch (*Whytchirche*), and Dodington (*Dodyngton*) and the advowson of the church of the manor of Whitchurch, SALOP., and the manor of Painswick (*Payneswyke*), GLOS. Right of the archbishop, of which he had the manors of Blake Mere, Whitchurch, and Dodington and the advowson by gift of John and Margaret and the manor of Painswick by John's gift. Remise and quitclaim, specifying John's heirs, to the archbishop and his heirs. For this, grant back and render to John and Margaret. To hold to them and their heirs in tail. Contingent remainder to John's heirs. (Warranty.) *Labelled* Salop', Glouc'.

293/70/262

21 Henry VI

1442

580. One week [6 Oct.] from Michaelmas. Nicholas Daunt quer.; Robert Frampton (*Frompton*) and Joan his wife. Three messuages, a toft, 12 a. of land, 3 a. of meadow, 2 a. of pasture, and 1 a. of wood in Wotton-under-Edge (*Wotton*) borough, Wotton foreign, and Bradley (*Bradeley*). Right of Nicholas by gift of Robert and Joan. Remise and quitclaim, specifying Joan's heirs, to Nicholas. (Warranty.) Cons. £20.

79/90/91

581. Morrow [3 Nov.] of All Souls. John Shingay (*Shyngey*) quer.; John Greville (*Grevyll'*) the elder and Leonard Stapleton (*Stepulton*) and Mary his wife def. The manors of Weston-on-Avon (*Weston super Aven*), Welford-on-Avon (*Welneford alias Welford*), and Meon (*Moene*). Right of John Shingay by gift of John Greville and Leonard and Mary. For this, grant and render to John Greville. To hold to John Greville and his heirs in tail male. Successive contingent remainders to the heirs in tail male of Lewis Greville (*Grevill'*), to Mary and her heirs in tail male, and to the heirs of William Greville the elder, father of the said John Greville and Mary. (Warranty against Edmund [Kirton] abbot of Westminster (*Westm'*) and his successors.) [*Worn.*]

79/90/92

1443

582. Two weeks [5 May] from Easter. Nicholas Ashton (*Ayssheton*), Robert Joce, William Hyndeston, and John Wydeslade quer.; William Bourgchier and Thomasia his wife def. The manors of Tawstock (*Toustoke*), Nymet Tracey (*Nymettracy*), Bampton (*Baunton*), Uffculme (*Ufcolmp*), Holne (*Holne*), and Little Totnes (*Parva Tottenes*), the hundred and borough of Bampton, the advowsons of the churches of Tawstock and Nymet Tracey and of the chantry of Bampton, 2 messuages, a toft, and 1 ploughland in Exeter (*Exon'*), Shillingford (*Shillyngford*), and Crediton (*Criditon*), and half of the manor of Milton Damerel (*Milton Daumarll*) and of 4 messuages, 300 a. of land, and 20 a. of meadow in

1443

Exeter, Milton Damerel, Waite (*Wayte*), Braundsworthy (*Brendesworthy*), and Stadson (*Stoddesdon*), DEVON, the manors of Huntspill (*Honyspyll*), Wigborough (*Wyggebeare*), and Huntstile (*Hunstyle*), the advowson of the church of Huntspill, and half of a messuage, 300 a. of land, 20 a. of meadow, and 20 a. of wood in Quarme (*Quarm*), SOM., half of the manors of Crofton (*Crofton*) and Stanton (*Staunton*) and the advowson of the church of Stanton, WILTS., the manor of Bentham (*Bentham*) called Hunt Court (*Huntecourt*), GLOS., one third of the manor Dilwyn (*Dyllowe*), HEREFS., the castle and manor of Whittington (*Whytyngton*), the advowsons of the churches of Whittington and Selattyn (*Sullaton*), and one third of the manors of Edgmond (*Egmondon*) and Redcastle (*Rubii Castri*), SALOP. and the march of Wales adjoining, the manor Wantage (*Wantynge*) and the hundred of Wantage, BERKS., the manor Edlington (*Edlyngton*), YORKS., and one third of the manors of Tunstall (*Tunstall*), Horton (*Horton*), Betley (*Betley*), and Heighley (*Heley*) and of 30*s*. rent in Over Longsdon (*Overlangesdon*), STAFFS. Right of Robert, as those which Robert, Nicholas, William Hyndeston, and John had by gift of William Bourgchier and Thomasia. For this, grant back and render to William Bourgchier and Thomasia. To hold to them and their heirs in tail. Contingent remainder to Thomasia's heirs. *Labelled* Devon', Somers', Wiltes', Glouc', Hereford', Salop', Berk', Ebor', Stafford'. [*Worn.*]

293/70/272

[Cf. *Som. Fines, 1399–1484*, pp. 196–7; *Wilts. Fines, 1377–1509*, pp. 119–20, no. 558.]

22 Henry VI

1443

583. Two weeks [13 Oct.] from Michaelmas. John Langley (*Langeley*) quer.; John Hodgkin (*Hogekyn*) and Amice his wife, elder daughter and one of the heirs of Thomas Cockerell (*Cokerell*), def. Five messuages, 10 tofts, 160 a. of land, and 30 a. of meadow in Fairford (*Faireford*). Right of John Langley, of which he had half of one third of the premises by gift of John Hodgkin and Amice; remise and quitclaim, specifying Amice's heirs, of the whole to him. (Warranty.) Cons. 100 marks.

79/90/93

[Cf. above, no. 573.]

584. Morrow [12 Nov.] of St. Martin. Nicholas Poyntz esquire and Elizabeth his wife quer.; Roger Bodenham esquire def. A messuage, 26*s*. rent, rent of 1 lb. pepper and a sparrowhawk, and half of 1 yardland in Colesborne (*Collesborn*). Right of Nicholas, as those which Nicholas and Elizabeth had by Roger's gift. Remise and quitclaim to Nicholas and Elizabeth and Nicholas's heirs. (Warranty). Cons. £20.

79/90/94

1444

585. One week [20 Jan.] from Hilary. Matilda [Muston] abbess of the monastery of St. Saviour and of St. Mary the Virgin and St. Bridget (*Brigitte*) of Syon (*Syon*) of the order of St. Augustine called St. Saviour quer.; Edmund [Lacey] bishop of Exeter (*Exon'*) late bishop of Hereford (*Hereford'*) def. The townships of Brede (*Brede*) and Steyning (*Stenynges*), the manors of Brede, Steyning, Charlton (*Cherlton*), Warminghurst (*Wormynghurst*), Wiggenholt (*Wygenholt*), Ecclesden (*Ecclesdon*), Basset's Fee (*Bassettesfee*), Angmering (*Angmeryng*), Sompting (*Soumtynge*), Langhurst (*Langenhurst*),

1444

Barphamwick (*Barpham Wyke*), and Billingshurst (*Billynghurst*), and the advowsons of the churches of Steyning, Angmering, and Ashurst (*Asshurst*), SUSSEX, and the manors of Cheltenham (*Cheltenham*), Salmonsbury (*Salmondesbury*), and Lower Slaughter (*Sloughtre*) and the hundreds of Cheltenham, Salmonsbury, and Slaughter (*Sloughtre*), GLOS., held by John Cornwall (*Cornewaill*) knight for term of life. Right of the abbess and her monastery. Grant to them of the reversion. To hold in free alms. Cons. a young sparrowhawk. Made by the king's order. *Labelled* Sussex', Glouc'.

293/70/284

[Cf. *Sussex Fines, 1307–1509*, pp. 257–8, no. 3070. Syon abbey belonged to the order of St. Saviour and followed the Augustinian rule: *V.C.H. Middx.* i. 182.]

586. Morrow [3 Feb.] of the Purification. John Greville (*Grevill*) the elder esquire and John Shingay (*Shyngey*) quer.; Henry Hussey (*Husee*) of Harting (*Hertyng*) the elder, knight, and Constance his wife def. The manor of Great Rissington (*Magna Resyngdon*) and 10 messuages, 10 yardlands, 30 a. of meadow, 200 a. of pasture, and 100*s.* rent in Great Rissington. Right of John Greville, as those which the same John and John Shingay had by gift of Henry and Constance. Remise and quitclaim, specifying Constance's heirs, to John Greville and John Shingay and John Greville's heirs. (Warranty.) Cons. 500 marks. Made by the king's order.

79/90/95

587. Morrow [3 Feb.] of the Purification. John Stafford archbishop of Canterbury (*Cantuarien'*) quer.; Robert Stanshawe the elder and Isabel his wife def. The manor of Stanshawe (*Stanshawe*). Right of the archbishop by gift of Robert and Isabel. For this, grant and render to Robert and Isabel. To hold, without impeachment of waste, during Robert's life. Remainder to Robert de Stanshawe, son of the same Robert, and his wife Joan and their heirs in tail. Contingent remainder to the heirs of Robert the father.

79/90/96

588. Two weeks [26 April] from Easter. William Walwyn (*Walwayn*) quer.; Richard Staunton and Alice his wife def. Two messuages, 3 tofts, 200 a. of land, 20 a. of meadow, and 2*s.* 2*d.* rent in English Bicknor (*Bykemore*). Right of William by gift of Richard and Alice. Remise and quitclaim, specifying Alice's heirs, to William. (Warranty.) Cons. £40.

79/90/99

589. Three weeks [3 May] from Easter. Walter Birch (*Byrche*) quer.; John Kiddle (*Kydell*) and Joan his wife def. A messuage, a toft, and 2 a. of meadow in Newland (*Newelond*). Right of Walter by gift of John and Joan. Remise and quitclaim, specifying Joan's heirs, to Walter. (Warranty.) Cons. 20 marks.

79/90/98

590. One month [10 May] from Easter. John Carpenter quer.; John ap Jevan ap Guyllim ap Adam of Monmouth (*Monemouth*) and Joan his wife def. Two messuages, 21 a. of land, and 1 a. of meadow in Coleford (*Colford*) in the parish of Newland (*Newelonde*). Right of John Carpenter by gift of John ap Jevan and Joan. Remise and quitclaim, specifying Joan's heirs, to John Carpenter. (Warranty.) Cons. 20 marks.

79/90/97

23 Henry VI

1445

591. Two weeks [27 Jan.] from Hilary. Richard Winter (*Wynter*) parson of the church of Coates (*Cotes*) quer.; William Paunton and Joan daughter of William Golding (*Goldyng*) def. Twenty-six messuages, 4 tofts, 6 ploughlands and 12 yardlands, 64 a. of meadow, 300 a. of pasture, 80 a. of wood, 13*s*. 6*d*. rent, and rent of 4 cocks and 12 hens in Eastleach Turville (*Estlecche Turvill*), Abson (*Abbotteston*), and Pucklechurch (*Poklechyrche*). William acknowledged the right of Richard by William's gift. Remise and quitclaim by William to Richard. (Warranty.) For this, grant and render to William and Joan. To hold to them and William's heirs in tail. Contingent remainder to William's heirs.

79/91/101

592. Two weeks [27 Jan.] from Hilary. Richard Winter (*Wynter*) parson of the church of Coates (*Cotes*) quer.; William Golding (*Goldyng*) and Joan his wife def. Four messuages, 1 ploughland and 2½ yardlands and 2 a. of land, and 30 a. of meadow in Down Ampney (*Dounameney*), Bidfield (*Bydefeld*), Leckhampton (*Lekehampton*), and Coates, GLOS., and 3 messuages, 2 ploughlands, and 10 a. of meadow in Poole Keynes (*Pole*) and Shorncote (*Shernecote*), WILTS. William acknowledged the right of Richard by William's gift. Remise and quitclaim to Richard. (Warranty.) For this, grant and render to William and Joan. To hold to them during their lives without impeachment of waste. Remainder to William Paunton and William Golding's daughter Joan and that Joan's heirs in tail. Contingent remainder to William Golding's heirs. *Labelled* Glouc', Wiltes'.

293/70/295

[Cf. *Wilts. Fines, 1377–1509*, p. 122, no. 568.]

593. Two weeks [11 April] from Easter. (Made one week [9 Feb.] from the Purification in the said year.) John Troutbeck (*Troutbek*) esquire and Margery his wife quer.; John Vampage and Richard Townley (*Tounlay*) def. Half of the manors of Ford (*Fordesham*) and Newport (*Neuport*) and one third of the manor of Edgmond (*Egemundon*), SALOP., one third of the manors of Monnington on Wye (*Monyton super Wayam*), and Dilwyn (*Dillewe*), HEREFS., half of one half of the manors of Broughton Gifford (*Broughton*) and Ashton Giffard (*Asshton Gyffard*) and the advowson of half of the church of Codford (*Codeford*), WILTS., the manor of Oxhey (*Oxey Richard*), HERTS., half of the manors of West Raddon (*Westraddon*), George Nympton (*Nymet Sancti Georgii*), and Newton Tracey (*Neweton Tracy*) by Barnstaple (*Bernestaple*), 6*s*. rent in East Anstey (*Estansty*) and West Anstey (*Westansty*), one quarter of the manor of Kilmington (*Kylmynton*), and the advowson of half of the church of Newton Tracey, DEVON, and half of one half of the manor of Badgeworth (*Beggeworth*), GLOS. As to the half of the manors of Ford and Newport and the one third of the manor of Edgmond, right of John Vampage and Richard, and as to the manor, the halves of the manors of Broughton Gifford, Ashton Giffard, West Raddon, George Nympton, Newton Tracey, and Badgeworth, the rent, the thirds of the manors of Monnington on Wye and Dilwyn, the quarter, and the advowsons, right of Richard, as those which Richard and John Vampage had by gift of John Troutbeck and Margery. For this, grant back and render to John Troutbeck and Margery. To hold to them and their heirs in tail, the half of the manors of Ford and Newport and the one third of the manor of Edgmond of the king and the residue of the chief lords. Contingent remainder to Margery's heirs. Made, as to Ford,

1445

Newport, and Edgmond, by the king's order. *Labelled* Salop', Hereford', Wiltes', Hertf', Devon', Glouc'.

293/70/298

[Omitted from *Wilts. Fines, 1377–1509.* Cf. above, no. 278, which relates to only one half of the quarter of the manor of Kilmington and one half of the rent in East and West Anstey.]

594. One week [30 May] from Trinity. (Made one month from Michaelmas in the said year [27 Oct. 1444].) Richard Sheweley of Cromhall (*Cromhall*) and John Dorney and Joan his wife quer.; William Henege def. Three messuages, a toft, 44 a. of land, 8 a. of meadow, 59 a. of pasture, and 10 a. of wood in Falfield (*Falfeld*), Tortworth (*Torteworth*), Wickwar (*Wykewarre*), and Morton (*Morton*). Right of Joan, as those which John and Joan and Richard had by William's gift. Remise and quitclaim to Richard and John and Joan and Joan's heirs. (Warranty.) Cons. 100 marks.

79/90/100

24 Henry VI

1445

595. One week [6 Oct.] from Michaelmas. William Beef (*Beof*) and Henry Fillongley (*Fylengley*) quer.; James Ormond knight son of James earl of Ormond (*Ormond*) and Avice his wife def. The manors of Borley (*Borle*) and Foxearth (*Foxherde*), ESSEX, the manors of Torbryan (*Torbrian*), Slapton (*Slapton*), Northam (*Northam*), Dartmouth (*Dertemouth*), Clifton (*Clifton*), and *Hardenesshe*, the isle of Lundy (*Lunday*) and the advowsons of the church of Torbryan and the chantry of St. Mary of Slapton, DEVON, the manors of Oxenhall (*Oxenhale*) and Okle Grandison (*Ocle Graunson*), GLOS., the manors of Chelsfield (*Chellesfeld*), *Esthall*, Ash (*Asshe*), and Fawkham (*Favkeham*) and the advowsons of the churches of Chelsfield and Fawkham, KENT, the manors of Wraxall (*Wroxhale*), Woodsford (*Werdeford Bolet*), Rampisham (*Rammesham*), Chilfrome (*Childefrome*), Toller Porcorum (*Swyntoller*), Mapperton (*Maperton*), Puncknowle (*Pomknolle*), and Lower Kingcombe (*Netherkentcombe*), the bailiwick of guarding the banks of the waters of Frome (*Frome*) and Stour (*Stoure*), and the advowsons of the churches of Rampisham, Wraxall, and Puncknowle, DORSET, the manors of Shockerwick (*Shokerwyke*), Batheaston (*Batheneston*), Kingsdon (*Kyngesdon*), Somerton Erleigh (*Somerton Erle*), Somerton Randolph (*Somerton Randolf*), and Downhead (*Dounheved*), 9 messuages, 368 a. of land, 92 a. of meadow, 40 a. of pasture, 80 a. of wood, and 8*s.* rent in Batheaston, Kingsdon, Somerton Erleigh, and Somerton Randolph, and the advowson of the church of Kingsdon, SOM., and the manors of Over Hall (*Overhalle*) and Nether Hall (*Netherhalle*) in Bures (*Bures Beate Marie*), Great Waldingfield (*Magna Waldyngfeld*), Acton (*Aketon*), Raydon (*Reydon*), and Wherstead (*Werstede*), 28 messuages, 5 mills and a quarter of a mill, 390 a. of land, 133 a. of meadow, 8 a. of pasture, 107 a. of wood, 50 a. of marsh (*alucti* [recte *alluvii*?]), 60 a. of heath (*bruere*), and 23*s.* rent in Bures (*Magna Bures*), Wissington (*Whiston*), Assington (*Asyngton*), Little Cornard (*Parva Cornard*), Milden (*Meldyng*), Monks Eleigh (*Illegh Monachorum*), Lavenham (*Lavenham*), Cockfield (*Cowfeld*), Preston (*Preston*), Thorpe Morieux (*Thorp Moreux*), Raydon (*Reydon*), Great Wenham (*Brendwenham*), Hadleigh (*Hadlegh*), Layham (*Leyham*), Higham (*Hegham*), Holton St. Mary (*Holoughton*), Capel St. Mary (*Chapels*), Stratford St. Mary (*Stretford*), Little Wenham (*Parva Wenham*), Wherstead (*Worstede*), Freston (*Freston*), and Westerfield (*Westerfeld*), and the advowsons of the

1445

churches of Raydon and Wherstead, SUFFOLK. Right of William, as those which William and Henry had by gift of James and Avice. (Warranty, specifying Avice's and William's heirs.) For this, grant back and render to James and Avice. To hold to them and their heirs in tail. Successive contingent remainders to Avice's heirs in tail and to James's heirs. *Labelled* Essex', Devon', Glouc', Kanc', Dors', Somers', Suff'. [*Stained.*]

293/71/302

[Cf. *Dorset Fines, 1327–1485*, pp. 322–3; *Essex Fines, 1423–1547*, pp. 37–8; *Som. Fines, 1399–1484*, p. 198.]

596. Three weeks [20 Oct.] from Michaelmas. Joan Greyndor (*Greyndoure*), Robert Warren (*Wareyn*) chaplain, and Nicholas Waterfall quer.; Reynold West (*Weste*) knight and Elizabeth his wife def. A messuage, a toft, a dovecot, 110 a. of land, 28 a. of meadow, and 3 a. of wood in Newland (*Neulond*) and Staunton (*Staunton*). Right of Joan as those which Joan, Robert, and Nicholas had by gift of Reynold and Elizabeth. Remise and quitclaim, specifying Elizabeth's heirs, to Joan, Robert, and Nicholas and Joan's heirs. (Warranty.) Cons £40.

79/91/103

597. Three weeks [20 Oct.] from Michaelmas. Robert Stanshawe the elder quer.; Maurice de la River (*Delarever*) esquire and Isabel his wife def. The manor of Tormarton (*Tormerton*) and the advowson of the church of the same manor. Maurice acknowledged the right of Robert by Maurice's gift. For this, grant and render to Maurice and Isabel. To hold to them and Maurice's heirs in tail, of Robert, paying a rose a year at St. John the Baptist and doing service to the chief lords. Contingent reversion to Robert. [*Worn.*]

79/91/104

598. One month [27 Oct.] from Michaelmas. Thomas Poyntz esquire quer.; Robert Tanner and Margaret his wife def. Two messuages, 70 a. of land, 16 a. of meadow, and 20 a. of pasture in Bevington (*Bevynton*) and Oldbury-on-Severn (*Oldebury*). Right of Thomas by gift of Robert and Margaret. Remise and quitclaim, specifying Margaret's heirs, to Thomas. (Warranty.) Cons. 40 marks.

79/91/105

1446

599. Morrow [3 Feb.] of the Purification. Robert Long (*Longe*) and John Giles (*Gilys*) quer.; Walter Hungerford knight, Robert Hungerford the elder, knight, and Margaret his wife, and Edmund Hungerford knight def. The manors of Down Ampney (*Downeamney*) and the Wick (*Wyke*). Right of John, as those which the same John and Robert Long had by gift of Walter, Robert Hungerford and Margaret, and Edmund. Remise and quitclaim, specifying Margaret's heirs, to Robert Long and John and John's heirs. (Warranty against John [Taunton] abbot of Cirencester (*Cirencestr'*) and his successors.) For this, grant and render to Walter. To hold during his life. Remainder to the said Edmund, Walter Rodney (*Rodeney*) knight, Edward Hill (*Hull*) knight, and John St. Lo (*Seintlo*) esquire, and Edmund's heirs in tail male. Successive contingent remainders to Walter Hungerford's heirs in tail male, to Walter Hungerford's heirs in tail, and to Walter Hungerford's heirs.

79/91/102

25 Henry VI

1446

600. Two weeks [13 Oct.] from Michaelmas. John Kemes (*Kemmyes*) esquire and Roger Kemes quer.; John Avery (*Averey*) and Katherine his wife def. A messuage, a mill, 6 a. of land, 4 a. of meadow, 6 a. of pasture, and 4 a. of wood in Stapleton (*Stapulton*). Right of John Kemes, as those which the same John and Roger had by gift of John Avery and Katherine. Remise and quitclaim, specifying Katherine's heirs, to John Kemes and Roger and John Kemes's heirs. (Warranty.) Cons. 100 marks.

79/91/108

1447

601. Two weeks [23 April] from Easter. William Child quer.; Walter Barron (*Baron*) and Joan his wife def. A messuage, 3 tofts, 3 yardlands, 20 a. of meadow, and 4*d*. rent in Withington (*Wythyngdon*) and Foxcote (*Foxcote*). Right of William by gift of Walter and Joan. Remise and quitclaim, specifying Joan's heirs, to William. (Warranty.) Cons. 100 marks.

79/91/106

602. Two weeks [23 April] from Easter. (Made one month from Michaelmas in the said year [27 Oct. 1446].) John St. Lo (*Sayntlo*) esquire quer.; John Kemes (*Kemys*) esquire and Margaret his wife def. The manor of Siston (*Syston*) and the advowson of the church of the same manor. Right of John St. Lo by gift of John Kemes and Margaret. Remise and quitclaim, specifying Margaret's heirs, to John St. Lo. For this, grant back and render to John Kemes and Margaret. To hold to them and Margaret's heirs in tail. Contingent remainder to the heirs of Gilbert Denis (*Denys*) knight.

79/91/107

603. One week [11 June] from Trinity. (Made two weeks [23 April] from Easter in the said year.) John Carkyk clerk and William King (*Kyng*) quer.; Thomas Whittington (*Whityngton*) and Alice his wife def. Eight messuages, 200 a. of land, 40 a. of meadow, 60 a. of pasture, and 12 a. of wood in Flax Bourton (*Borton*), Failand (*Feylond*), Wraxall (*Wroxhale*), Tickenham (*Tykenham*), *Raggel*, and Long Ashton (*Assheton*), SOM., and a messuage in Bristol (*Bristoll'*), county of BRISTOL. Right of John, as those which John and William had by gift of Thomas and Alice. Remise and quitclaim, specifying Alice's heirs, to John and William and John's heirs. (Warranty.) For this, grant back and render to Thomas and Alice. To hold during their lives without impeachment of waste. Remainder to John Whittington, son of Thomas and Alice. *Labelled* Somers', Bristoll'.

293/71/318

[Cf. *Som. Fines, 1399–1484*, p. 199.]

26 Henry VI

1447

604. Morrow [3 Nov.] of All Souls. John Baker, Thomas Forthey, Richard Webb (*Webbe*), and John Holder quer.; John Goules and Margaret his wife def. A messuage and 1 a. of land in Northleach (*Northlecch*). Right of John Holder, as those which the same John, John Baker, Thomas, and Richard had by gift of John Goules and Margaret. Remise and quitclaim, specifying Margaret's heirs, to John Baker, Thomas, Richard, and John Holder and John Holder's heirs. (Warranty.) Cons. £20.

79/91/112

1447

605. Two weeks [25 Nov.] from St. Martin. Eleanor who was wife of John Throckmorton (*Throkmarton*) and Thomas Throckmorton quer.; John Throckmorton esquire and Isabel his wife def. The manors of Priors Court (*Pryourscourt*) and Moor Place (*Moreplace*) and 41 messuages, 340 a. of land, 80 a. of meadow, 60 a. of pasture, 30 a. of wood, 11 leaden vessels (*plumbariis*) for salt water, and 6 marks rent in Pendock (*Pendok*), Berrow (*Berugh*), Birtsmorton (*Moreton Brutte*), Longdon (*Longdon*), Eldersfield (*Eldersfeld*), and Droitwich (*Dyrtwyche*), WORCS., and 34 messuages, a toft, 200½ a. of land, 80 a. of meadow, 30 a. of pasture, 20 a. of wood, and half of 1 yardland in Cheltenham (*Cheltenham*), Charlton Kings (*Charleton*), Kingsholm (*Kyngeshome*), Alveston (*Alveston*), Hasfield (*Hasfeld*), and Tirley (*Trynle*), GLOS. Right of Thomas, as those which Thomas and Eleanor had by gift of John and Isabel. Remise and quitclaim, specifying Isabel's heirs, to Thomas and Eleanor and Thomas's heirs. (Warranty.) Cons. 300 marks. *Labelled* Wygorn', Glouc'.

293/71/326

1448

606. Two weeks [7 April] from Easter. Edmund Inglethorpe (*Inglysthorp*) knight quer.; John Owlpen (*Oulepen*) and Joan his wife def. The manor of Melksham (*Mylkesham*). Right of Edmund. Remise and quitclaim, specifying Joan's heirs, to Edmund. (Warranty against Walter [Newbury] abbot of St. Augustine's, Bristol (*Bristoll*), and his successors.) Cons. 100 marks.

79/91/109

607. Two weeks [7 April] from Easter. John [Stafford] archbishop of Canterbury (*Cantuar'*), William [de la Pole] marquess of Suffolk (*Suff'*), Marmaduke [Lumley] bishop of Carlisle (*Karl'*), Adam [Moleyns] bishop of Chichester (*Cicestr'*), Ralph Cromwell knight, John Dudley (*Duddeley*) knight, John Vampage the elder, William Sydney (*Sydeney*) the elder, Thomas Barrett (*Baret*), and William Ernle (*Ernele*) quer.; William [FitzAlan] earl of Arundel (*Arundell*) def. The castle, township, manor, and lordship of Clun (*Clon*), the castle, township, manor, and lordship of Oswestry (*Oswaldestre*), the castle and manor of Shrawardine (*Shrewardyn*), the manors of Ryton (*Ruyton*), Bucknell (*Bukkenell*), Clunbury (*Clombury*), Dodington (*Dodyngton*), Hints (*Hyntes*), Church Stretton (*Stretton*), Lydley Heys (*Lyddeley*), Cound (*Conde*), Acton Round (*Acton Ronde*), Wroxeter (*Wroxcestre*), Upton (*Upton*), Dawley (*Dalleley*), Westhope (*Westehop*), Heath (*Heythe*), High Ercall (*Ercall*), Tibberton (*Tyberton*), and Clunton (*Clompton*), and the hundred of Purslow (*Posselowe*), SALOP., the manors of Bignor (*Bygenere*), Lyminster (*Leuemynstre*), Cocking (*Cokkyng*), Wepham (*Wappeham*), Offham (*Offeham*), Storrington (*Storgheton*), Preston (*Preston*), Stansted (*Stansted*), East Hampnett (*Esthamptonet*), Westhampnett (*Westhamptonet*), Woolbeding (*Wolbodyng*), Pinkhurst (*Pynkeherst*), Wonworth (*Wonwroth*), Old Shoreham (*Oldshorham*), Stopham (*Stopham*), Cudlow (*Cudlawe*), Barecourt (*Barrecourt*), Wildbridge (*Wylbrugge*), Almodington (*Almodyngton*), Linch (*Lynche*), Orfold (*Overfeld*), Legh (*Legh*), Clayland (*Cleyland*), *Rotteslond* [Redlands, in North Chapel?], Poling (*Polyng*), Up Marden (*Upmerden*), and Woolavington (*Wollavyngton*), two thirds of the sheriff's tourn with reasonable aid of the same in the rapes (*le ropes*) of Arundel and Chichester (*Chichestre*), and the advowsons of the college of Holy Trinity in Arundel and of the hospital of

1448

Arundel, SUSSEX, the manors of Limington (*Lymyngton*), Stoke Trister (*Stoketrystre*), Cucklington (*Coklyngton*), Bayford (*Bayford*), Leigh (*Legh*), Spargrove (*Spertegrove*), and Great Somerford (*Somerford Mautravers*) and the office of custody of the forest of Selwood (*Selwod*), SOM., the manors of *Lordes*, Bingham's Melcombe (*Byngeham*), Langton Matravers (*Langton*), Woolcombe (*Wollecombe*), Hampreston (*Hamme Preston*), Philipston (*Phipiston*), Wimborne St. Giles (*Upwymburne*), Frome Whitfield (*Frome Whitteffeld*), *Longton*, *Lordes* [again], Wootton (*Wodton*), Lytchett Matravers (*Lichet Mautravers*), East Morden (*Estmordon*), Worth Matravers (*Wroth*), Wootton Fitzpaine (*Wotton Fitzpayn*), Ramsbury (*Remmesbury*), *Lodery*, Woolcombe [again] (*Wollecombe Mautravers*), and Stapleford (*Stapulford*), DORSET, the manors of Woodchester (*Wodchestre*), King's Stanley (*Kyngestanley*), Stonehouse (*Stonehous*), Shurdington (*Shirdyngton*), and Achards (*Archades*), GLOS., the manors of Buckland (*Bukkelond*) and Colley (*Colley*), SURREY, the castle, township, and manor of Castle Acre (*Castellacre*), the manors of Mileham (*Mylleham*), Beeston (*Buston*) by Mileham, and Flockthorpe (*Flokkethorp*), and the advowsons of the priory of Castle Acre and of the church of Beeston Regis (*Buston juxta mare*), NORFOLK, the manors of Knighton (*Knyghton*), Keevil (*Kyvele*), Winterbourne Stoke (*Wynterburnestoke*), Boyton (*Boyton*), and Hill Deverill (*Hyldeverell*) and half of the manor of Bulkington (*Bulkyndon*) by Keevil, WILTS., the manor of Aynho (*Eyneho*) and the advowson of the hospital of St. James and St. John of Aynho, NORTHANTS., the manor of Great Gransden (*Grandesden*), HUNTS., the manor of Croxton (*Crokesden*), CAMBS., and the manor of Postling (*Postelyng*), KENT. Right of the archbishop and the other quer. by the earl's gift. Grant and render to the quer. To hold to them and their heirs, of the king. (Warranty.). Cons. £1,000. Made by the king's order. *Labelled* Salop', Sussex', Somers', Dors', Glouc', Surr', Norff', Wiltes', Norht', Hunt', Cantebr', Kanc'. [*Worn and stained.*]

293/71/330

[Cf. *Dorset Fines, 1327–1485*, p. 327; *Som. Fines, 1399–1484*, p. 200; *Sussex Fines, 1307–1509*, pp. 261–2, no. 3091; *Wilts. Fines, 1377–1509*, pp. 126–7, no. 586. Great Somerford is in Wilts., not Som.]

608. Three weeks [14 April] from Easter. John Jervis (*Gerveys*), Thomas Chedworth, and William Frost quer.; Isabel who was wife of John Dudbridge (*Dudbrigge*) def. Two tofts, 1 yardland, and 4 a. of meadow in Clissold (*Clyffeshale*) and Througham (*Thoroweham*). Right of John, as those which John, Thomas, and William had by Isabel's gift. Remise and quitclaim to John, Thomas, and William and John's heirs. (Warranty.) Cons. 100*s*.

79/91/110

609. Three weeks [14 April] from Easter. John Cox (*Cokkes*) and Alice his wife quer.; John Bussage (*Bysterigge*) and Denise his wife def. A messuage and a shop in Cirencester (*Cirencestr'*) opposite 'Kilbullesynne'. Right of John Cox, as those which the same John and Alice had by gift of John Bussage and Denise. Remise and quitclaim, specifying Denise's heirs, to John Cox and Alice and John Cox's heirs. (Warranty.) Cons. £20.

79/91/111

610. One month [21 April] from Easter. Richard Choke (*Chok*) quer.; John Vampage the elder and Elizabeth his wife, daughter of Richard Vernon (*Vernoun*) knight def. The manors of Pebworth (*Pebworth*) and Broad Marston (*Merston*) and 2 ploughlands, 10 a.

1448

of meadow, 10 a. of pasture, and 100*s*. rent in Pebworth and Broad Marston, GLOS., and the manor of Wick (*Wyke*) by Pershore (*Pershore*) and 3 ploughlands, 3 yardlands, and 50 a. of land, 20 a. of meadow, 20 a. of pasture, and £3 rent in Wick, Pinvin (*Pyndefen*), Wyre Piddle (*Pedull*), and Peopleton (*Pepulton*), WORCS. John acknowledged the right of Richard by John's gift. For this, grant and render to John and Elizabeth. To hold to them and their heirs in tail male. Contingent remainder to John's heirs. *Labelled* Glouc', Wygorn'.

293/71/333

27 Henry VI

1448

611. Morrow [12 Nov.] of St. Martin. John Codrington (*Codryngton*) and Alice his wife quer.; Maurice Berkeley of Uley (*Eweley*) knight, Nicholas Alderley, and Thomas Parkhouse (*Parkhous*) def. The manor of Chalkley (*Chalkley*). Grant and render to John and Alice. To hold during their lives. Remainder to Alice Codrington, daughter of Geoffrey Codrington, and her heirs in tail. Successive contingent remainders to the heirs in tail of John and Alice and to the heirs of Alice daughter of Geoffrey.

79/91/114

612. One week [18 Nov.] from St. Martin. Richard Teysant quer.; John Skey son and heir of Thomas Skey of North Nibley (*Nybeley*) and Joan his wife def. The manor of Pitt Court (*Pytcote*) and 12 messuages, 100 a. of land, 20 a. of meadow, 20 a. of pasture, 108 a. of wood, and half of the manor of Rangeworthy (*Ryngeworth*) with appurtenances in North Nibley (*Nybley*), Symond's Hall (*Symondsale*), Swinhay (*Swynhey*), and Stancombe (*Stancombe*), GLOS., and half of the manor of Surrendell (*Surynden*), WILTS. Right of Richard by gift of John and Joan. Remise and quitclaim, specifying John's heirs, to Richard. For this, grant back and render to John and Joan. To hold to them and their heirs in tail. Contingent remainder to John's heirs. *Labelled* Glouc', Wiltes'.

293/71/341

[Cf. *Wilts. Fines, 1377–1509*, p. 127, no. 589.]

1449

613. One week [15 June] from Trinity. Walter Devereux knight and Elizabeth his wife quer.; Nicholas Poyntz (*Poynes*) esquire def. The manor of Dymock (*Dymmok*). Grant and render to Walter and Elizabeth. To hold to them and their heirs in tail. Contingent remainder to the heirs of John Marbury (*Merbury*) esquire, Elizabeth's father. (Warranty against Walter [Newbury] abbot of St. Augustine, Bristol (*Bristoll*), and his successors.) Cons. £100.

79/91/113

28 Henry VI

1449

614. One week [6 Oct.] from Michaelmas. (Made two weeks from St. John the Baptist 27 Henry VI [8 July 1449].) William Alnwick (*Alnewyk*) bishop of Lincoln (*Lincoln'*), John [Beaumont] viscount of Beaumont (*Beamont*), Ralph Butler (*Boteler*) knight, Walter Hungerford knight, Ralph Cromwell knight, John Fastolf knight, William Oldhall knight, William Tresham esquire, William Burley esquire, Thomas Young (*Yonge*), and Thomas

1449

Willoughby quer.; Richard [Plantagenet] duke of York (*Ebor'*) and Cecily his wife def. The manor of Odcombe (*Odecombe*), SOM., the manor of Marshwood (*Mershewode*), the isle of Portland (*Portelonde*), and the hundred of Whitchurch (*Whitchirch*), DORSET, and the manors of Charlton Kings (*Charleton*) and Winstone (*Wynston*), GLOS. Right of the bishop and the other quer. by gift of the duke and Cecily. To hold to the quer. and their heirs, of the king. (Warranty, specifying Cecily's heirs.) Cons. 1,000 marks. Made by the king's order. *Labelled* Somers', Dors', Glouc'.

293/71/347

[Cf. *Dorset Fines, 1327–1485*, p. 328; *Som. Fines, 1399–1484*, p. 201.]

1450

615. One week [20 Jan.] from Hilary. Robert Lathbury esquire and Peter Clayton quer.; Henry Hussey (*Husee*) knight and Constance his wife def. Half of the manor of Sapperton (*Saperton*). Right of Robert, as that which Robert and Peter had by gift of Henry and Constance. Remise and quitclaim, specifying Henry's heirs, to Robert and Peter and Robert's heirs. (Warranty.) For this, grant back and render to Henry and Constance. To hold to them and their heirs in tail. Contingent remainder to Nicholas Hussey, Henry's son, during his life and to Henry's heirs.

79/91/116

616. Morrow [3 Feb.] of the Purification. William Cannings (*Canynges*) citizen and burgess of the town of Bristol (*Bristoll'*), William Pavy citizen and burgess of the town of Bristol, William More citizen and burgess of the town of Bristol, Thomas Hawkins (*Hawekyns*) citizen and grocer of London (*London'*), Richard Lee citizen and grocer of London, John Beke citizen and grocer of London, and Thomas Young (*Yonge*) quer.; John Newton (*Neuton*) son and heir of John Newton late merchant of the town of Bristol def. Three messuages, a toft, 120 a. of land, 40 a. of meadow, 100 a. of pasture, and 60 a. of wood in Wickwar (*Wykewarre*), Wicks Oldbury (*Oldebury*), and Cromhall (*Cromehale*). Right of Richard, as those which Richard and the other quer. had by gift of John Newton [the son]. Remise and quitclaim to the quer. and Richard's heirs. (Warranty.) Cons. £100.

79/91/115

[In the lower right-hand corner, 'Exemplificatur', i.e. 'It is to be exemplified'.]

617. Morrow [3 Feb.] of the Purification. William Cannings (*Canynges*) citizen and burgess of the town of Bristol (*Bristoll'*), William Pavy citizen and burgess of the town of Bristol, William More citizen and burgess of the town of Bristol, and Thomas Young (*Yonge*) quer.; John Newton (*Neuton*) son and heir of John Newton late merchant of the town of Bristol def. Eleven messuages and 6 gardens in Bristol and 12 messuages, 292 a. of land, 27 a. of meadow, and 6 a. of wood in Hay (*le Hay*) by Filton (*Filton*), Shirehampton (*Shiruyhampton*), Westbury-on-Trym (*Westbury*), Cote (*Cote*), Compton Greenfield (*Compton Grenevyle*), Tockington (*Tokyngton*), and Wickwar (*Wykewarre*), GLOS. Right of William More, as those which William More, William Cannings, William Pavy, and Thomas had by John's gift. Remise and quitclaim to William, William, William, and Thomas and William More's heirs. (Warranty.) *Labelled* Bristoll', Glouc'.

293/72/352

[In the lower right-hand corner, 'Exemplificatur', i.e. 'It is to be exemplified'.]

1450

618. One week [7 June] from Trinity. (Made one week [20 Jan.] from Hilary in the said year.) Edward Brounflete esquire quer.; William Raleigh (*Ralegh*) esquire and Elizabeth his wife and John Onley and Idonia his wife def. The manor of Farnborough (*Farneburgh*) and 6 messuages and 4 yardlands in Farnborough, WARWS., the manors of Claydon (*Cleydon*) and Lawn (*Laundse*) and 300 a. of land and 40 a. of meadow in Claydon and Lawn, OXON., the manor of Edgeworth (*Eggesworth*), two thirds of the manor of Lassington (*Lassyngdon*), and the advowsons of the churches of Edgeworth and Lassington, GLOS., and the manors of Charles (*Charles*), West Hagginton (*Westhagynton*), and West Buckland (*Westbokelonde*), the advowsons of the churches of Charles and West Buckland, a messuage, 1 ploughland, 10 a. of meadow, and 100 a. of wood in Woolstone (*Walston*), and half of the manor of Curtisknowle (*Courtesknoll*), DEVON. Grant and render to Edward. To hold during his life without impeachment of waste, of William, paying a rose a year at St. John the Baptist and doing service to the chief lords. (Warranty, specifying Elizabeth's and Idonia's heirs.) Reversion to William. Cons. 1,000 marks. *Labelled* Warr', Oxon', Glouc', Devon'.

293/72/355

[Cf. *Warws. Fines, 1345–1509*, p. 171, no. 2643.]

29 Henry VI

1451

619. One week [20 Jan.] from Hilary. (Made two weeks from St. Martin in the said year [25 Nov. 1450].) Robert Hungerford the elder knight and Thomas Tropenell quer.; Thomas Burton and William Burton his son def. The manor of Luckington (*Lokyngton*), the advowson of the church of the same manor, and 3 tofts, 60 a. of land, 2 a. of meadow, and 4 a. of pasture in Luckington and Alderton (*Aldryngton*), WILTS., and the manor of Horton (*Horton*) and 3 messuages, 2 tofts, 200 a. of land, 60 a. of meadow, 100 a. of pasture, and 4 a. of wood in Horton, GLOS. Right of Robert, as those which Robert and Thomas Tropenell had by gift of Thomas Burton and William. To hold to Robert and Thomas Tropenell and Robert's heirs. (Warranty, specifying Thomas Burton's heirs.) For this, grant and render to Thomas Burton. To hold to him and his heirs in tail, of Robert and Thomas Tropenell and Robert's heirs, paying a rose a year at St. John the Baptist and doing service to the chief lords. Contingent remainder to William and his heirs in tail. Contingent reversion to Robert and Thomas Tropenell and Robert's heirs. *Labelled* Wiltes', Glouc'. [*Worn*.]

293/72/359

[Cf. *Wilts. Fines, 1377–1509*, pp. 128–9, no. 594.]

620. Two weeks [9 May] from Easter. (Made one week [9 Feb.] from the Purification in the said year.) Henry Clifford (*Clyfford*) esquire and John Hayward quer.; William Pitt (*Putte*) and Isabel his wife def. A messuage, 56 a. of land, 5 a. of meadow, and 4 a. of pasture in Preston (*Preston*). Right of John, as those which John and Henry had by gift of William and Isabel. Remise and quitclaim, specifying Isabel's heirs, to Henry and John and John's heirs. (Warranty.) Cons. £20.

79/91/117

30 Henry VI

1451

621. Morrow [12 Nov.] of St. Martin. John Cassy quer.; John Sneyd (*Snede*) and Joan his wife def. Twenty-four messuages, 300 a. of land, 20 a. of meadow, and 6 a. of wood in Newent (*Newent*), Little Taynton (*Lyttyl Teynton*), Boulsdon (*Bullesdon*), Kilcot (*Kylcote*), and Oxenhall (*Oxenhale*). Right of John Cassy by gift of John Sneyd and Joan. Remise and quitclaim, specifying Joan's heirs, to John Cassy. (Warranty.) Cons. £100.

79/91/118

31 Henry VI

1452

622. Morrow [3 Nov.] of All Souls. John Barre knight and Joan his wife quer.; Hugh Shelwick (*Shelwyk*), Henry Quarrell, and John Gronowe def. The manors of East Hanham (*Esthanam*) and Upton Cheyney (*Upton Chanu*) and 4 messuages and 7 ploughlands in Bitton (*Button*), East Hanham, Oldland (*Oldelond*), West Hanham (*Westhanam*), Upton Cheyney, Siston (*Syston*), Pucklechurch (*Pokylchirch*), and Churchley (*Churcheley*). Right of Hugh, as those which Hugh, Henry, and John Gronowe had by gift of John Barre and Joan. Remise and quitclaim, specifying Joan's heirs, to Hugh, Henry, and John Gronowe and Hugh's heirs. (Warranty.) For this, grant back and render to John Barre. To hold without impeachment of waste during his life. Remainder to Joan and her heirs.

79/91/119

1453

623. Morrow [25 June] of St. John the Baptist. Walter Devereux knight quer.; William Neville (*Nevyle*) lord of Fauconberg (*Faucomberge*) knight and Joan his wife def. One seventh of the manor of Dymock (*Dymmok*). Right of Walter by gift of William and Joan. Remise and quitclaim, specifying Joan's heirs, to Walter. (Warranty.) Cons. £40.

79/91/122

624. One week [1 July] from St. John the Baptist. John Edwards (*Edward*) quer.; Henry Hussey (*Husee*), Richard Bitterley (*Bytterley*) esquire, and John Hole citizen and tailor of London (*London'*) def. The manor of Sapperton (*Saperton*) and 10 messuages, 1,000 a. of land, 20 a. of meadow, 1,000 a. of pasture, and 40 a. of wood in Sapperton, Bisley (*Bysle*), and Frampton Mansell (*Framtonmaunsell*). Right of John Edward by gift of Henry, Richard, and John Hole. Remise and quitclaim, specifying Henry's heirs, to John Edward. (Warranty.) Cons. £100.

79/91/120

625. One week [1 July] from St. John the Baptist. John Edwards (*Edward*) quer.; William Walker and Joan his wife def. Six messuages, a dovecot, 50 a. of land, 12 a. of meadow, 60 a. of pasture, 2 a. of wood, and 10*s*. rent in Evington (*Evyngton*), Leigh (*Lye*), Staverton (*Staverton*), and Down Hatherley (*Dounehatherley*). Right of John by gift of William and Joan. Remise and quitclaim, specifying Joan's heirs, to John. (Warranty.) Cons. £40.

79/91/121

32 Henry VI

1453

626. Three weeks [20 Oct.] from Michaelmas. Richard Rowe clerk and Roger Russell quer.; Thomas Harris (*Harrys*) and Margery his wife def. Six messuages, 2 dovecots, 15 yardlands, 34 a. of meadow, and 15*d*. rent in Hampnett (*Hampnet*), Harnhill (*Harnhill*), Northleach (*Northleche*), and Cirencester (*Cirencestre*). Right of Richard, as those which Richard and Roger had by gift of Thomas and Margery. For this, grant back and render to Thomas and Margery. To hold to them and Margery's heirs.

79/91/124

627. One week [18 Nov.] from St. Martin. (Made two weeks from St. John the Baptist 31 Henry VI [8 July 1453].) Thomas Smith (*Smyth*) parson of the church of Dodington (*Dodyngton*) quer.; Isabel who was wife of Roger Lyveden, Agnes who was wife of John Withyford (*Wythiford*), Joan who was wife of Richard Wimbish (*Wymbysshe*), and John Cole and Agnes his wife def. Twelve messuages, 300 a. of land, 40 a. of meadow, 100 a. of pasture, 20 a. of wood, and 20*s*. rent in Hambrook (*Hambroke*), Olveston (*Olveston*), and Tockington (*Tokyngton*). Right of Thomas by gift of Isabel, Agnes, Joan, and John and Agnes. Remise and quitclaim, specifying the heirs of Agnes wife of John Cole, to Thomas. (Warranty by John Cole and Agnes his wife against Edmund [Kirton] abbot of St. Peter's, Westminster (*Westm'*), and his successors.) For this, grant and render to Isabel. To hold during her life. Remainder to Agnes who was wife of John Withyford and her heirs by the said John. Successive contingent remainders to the same Agnes's heirs in tail, to Joan and her heirs in tail, to John Cole and Agnes his wife and Agnes's heirs in tail, and to Roger Lyveden's heirs. [*Worn.*]

79/91/123

628. One week [18 Nov.] from St. Martin. Thomas Porter quer.; William Skoryer and Elizabeth his wife def. A messuage, 80 a. of land, and 7 a. of meadow in Wotton (*Wotton*) by Gloucester (*Gloucestr'*). Right of Thomas by gift of John and Elizabeth. Remise and quitclaim, specifying Elizabeth's heirs, to Thomas. (Warranty.) Cons. 40 marks.

79/92/126

1454

629. Two weeks [27 Jan.] from Hilary. Nicholas Morris (*Morys*) clerk, Robert Pullen (*Poleyn*), and John Chamber (*Chambre*) and Agnes his wife quer.; John Sollers (*Solers*) and Elizabeth his wife def. Sixteen messuages, 6 tofts, 200 a. of land, 60 a. of meadow, 24 a. of pasture, 10 a. of wood, 14*s*. rent, and rent of 3 cocks, 6 hens, and 1 lb. of cumin in Deerhurst Walton (*Walton*), Tredington (*Tredyngton*), Tirley (*Trenley*), the Haw (*Hawe*), Wightfield (*Wyghtfeld*), Apperley (*Appurley*), Cobney (*Cobney*), and Evington (*Yevynton*). Right of Robert as those which Nicholas, Robert, and John Chamber and Agnes had by gift of John Sollers and Elizabeth. Remise and quitclaim, specifying Elizabeth's heirs, to Nicholas, Robert, and John Chamber and Agnes and Agnes's heirs. (Warranty against John [Hartlebury] prior of St. Mary's, Worcester (*Wygorn'*), and his successors.) Cons. 200 marks.

79/91/125

[By 1454 Prior John Hartlebury had been dead for eight years, and the prior 1445–69 was Thomas Musard: *V.C.H. Worcs.* ii. 110.]

1454

630. One month [19 May] from Easter. Nicholas Cowley (*Coweley*) quer.; Thomas Freeman (*Freman*) and Joan his wife def. Three messuages, a toft, 7½ yardlands, 12 a. of meadow, and 20 a. of pasture in Aston Subedge (*Aston under Egge*), GLOS., and a messuage, 1 yardland, and 6 a. of meadow in Aston Magna (*Hangyng Aston*), WORCS. Right of Nicholas by gift of Thomas and Joan. Remise and quitclaim, specifying Thomas's heirs, to Nicholas. (Warranty.) Cons. £100. *Labelled* Glouc', Wygorn'.

293/72/385

631. Two weeks [30 June] from Trinity. William Brown (*Broun*) and Richard Bedford quer.; William Wickham (*Wykeham*) and Joan his wife def. The manors of Headington (*Hedyngdon*), Woodperry (*Wodpury*), Tackley (*Takley*), Chastleton (*Chastelton*), Salford (*Salford*), North Leigh (*Northlye*), Wilcote (*Wyvelcote*), and Epwell (*Ipwell*), 10 messuages, 6 ploughlands, 13 yardlands, 1 bovate, and 69 a. of land, and 60 a. of meadow, the hundreds of Bullingdon (*Bolyngden*) and Northgate (*Northyate*) outside the north gate of Oxford (*Oxon'*), and the view of frankpledge of the said manors of Headington and Woodperry and of the said hundreds, and £9 0s. 2d. rent in Whitehill (*Wyghthyll*), Foukenend, Over Norton (*Overnorton*), Cornwell (*Cornwell*), Tilgarsley, and Stanton St. John (*Staunton Seynt John*) and in the said townships of Woodperrry, Tackley, Chastleton, Salford, North Leigh, Wilcote, and Epwell, the advowsons of the churches of the said townships of Tackley and Salford, and half of 1 yardland in Wilcote, OXON., the manor of Seacourt (*Sewkeworth*), BERKS., the manor of Hill Croome (*Hill Crombe*), WORCS., and the manor of Willicote (*Willecote*) and a messuage, 2 ploughlands, and 6 a. of meadow in Alscot (*Alvescote*), GLOS. Right of William Brown, as those which William Brown and Richard had by gift of William Wickham and Joan. Remise and quitclaim, specifying Joan's heirs, to William Brown and Richard and William Brown's heirs. (Warranty.) Cons. £300. *Labelled* Oxon', Berk', Wygorn', Glouc'.

293/72/386

[The location of the 10 messuages etc. in Oxon. is not made clear.]

33 Henry VI

1454

632. One month [27 Oct.] from Michaelmas. Elizabeth Russell, John Cassy, William Tracy, and Robert Clinton (*Clynton*) quer.; Richard Tailor (*Taillour*) clerk and John Cox (*Cokkys*) and Alice his wife def. A messuage, 60 a. of land, 20 a. of meadow, 10 a. of pasture, and 8 a. of wood in Wightfield (*Wyghtfeld*), Deerhurst (*Durehurst*), Deerhurst Walton (*Walton*), Apperley (*Appurley*), and Evington (*Yevynton*). Right of John Cassy, as those which the same John, Elizabeth, William, and Robert had by gift of Richard and John Cox and Alice. Remise and quitclaim, specifying John Cox's heirs, to Elizabeth, John Cassy, William, and Robert and John Cassy's heirs. (Warranty, specifying Alice's heirs.) Cons. £40.

79/92/129

[It appears anomalous that the remise and quitclaim specifies John Cox's heirs while the warranty specifies Alice's.]

1454

633. Morrow [12 Nov.] of St. Martin. Robert Rodway (*Rodwey*) quer.; Edith who was wife of Roger Rodway def. Six messuages, 100 a. of land, 4 a. of meadow, 60 a. of pasture, 2 a. of wood, and 2*s*. rent in Cherington (*Chyrynton*), Avening (*Avennyng*), Aston (*Aston*), Minchinhampton (*Mynchynhampton*), Tetbury (*Tedbury*), Bisley (*Bysley*), Stroud (*Strode*), Woodchester (*Wuchestr'*), Lypiatt (*Lepyat*), and Rodmarton (*Rodmarton*). Right of Edith by Robert's gift. Remise and quitclaim to her. For this, grant back and render to Robert. To hold to him and his legitimate heirs in tail. Successive contingent remainders to William Rodway, Robert's brother, and his legitimate heirs in tail, to Thomas Rodway, Robert's and William's brother, and his legitimate heirs in tail, to Joan Rodway, Robert's, William's, and Thomas's sister, and her legitimate heirs in tail, and to Edith's heirs. (Warranty.) [*Worn.*]

79/92/127

[The qualification of the various heirs in tail as 'legitimate' is unusual.]

1455

634. One month [4 May] from Easter. John Butler (*Boteler*) esquire, Laurence Forster, Robert Rome, and Richard Parker quer.; Thomas Webb (*Webbe*) and Cristina his wife def. Five messuages in Marshfield (*Mershefeld*). Right of Robert, as those which Robert, John, Laurence, and Richard had by gift of Thomas and Cristina. Remise and quitclaim, specifying Cristina's heirs, to John, Laurence, Robert, and Richard and Robert's heirs. (Warranty.) Cons. £40.

79/92/128

635. One month [4 May] from Easter. Thomas [Bourgchier] archbishop of Canterbury (*Cantuarien'*), Richard [Beauchamp] bishop of Salisbury (*Sar'*), Edmund de Grey knight, Ralph Butler (*Boteller*) knight, John Fortescue (*Fortescu*) knight the king's chief justice for pleas coram rege, Richard Bingham (*Byngham*) one of the king's justices for pleas coram rege, Edmund Hampden knight, Henry Norbury knight, Thomas Eborall clerk, John Dyve, William Cumberford, and Richard Burton quer.; Elizabeth who was wife of William Ferrers knight def. One third of the manor of Bugbrooke (*Bukbrook*), NORTHANTS., 7 messuages, 200 a. of land 12 a. of meadow, 10 a. of pasture, 100 a. of wood, and rents of 14*s*., 1 lb. of pepper, and 4 capons in Chinnor (*Chynnore*), Oakley (*Okeley*), and Sydenham (*Sidenham*), and one third of the manor of Chinnor, OXON., 4 messuages, 4 tofts, 100 a. of land, 20 a. of meadow, 100 a. of pasture, 50 a. of wood, and rents of 20*s*., 1 capon, 2 hens (*gallinarum*), 1 lb. of pepper, 1 lb. of cumin, a pair of spurs, and a pair of white gloves (*unius paris calcarium alborum et unius paris cirotecarum* [sic]) in Little Paxton (*Parva Paxton*), Eynesbury (*Eynesbury*), Meagre (*Maugreth*), and Southoe (*Southo*), HUNTS., the manor of Castle Bromwich (*Castelbromwych*), 30 a. of pasture in Bordesley (*Bordesley*), half of the manor of Nether Whitacre (*Nethirwhitacre*), and one quarter of the manors of Glascote (*Glascote*) and Perry Croft (*Purycroft*), WARWS., the manors of Charlton Musgrove (*Chorleton Musegrose*) and Norton Ferris (*Norton Bovewode*) and the hundred of Norton (*Norton*), SOM., half of the manor of Dorton (*Dourton*), BUCKS., 8 messuages, 6 tofts, 100 a. of land, 20 a. of meadow, 300 a. of pasture, 100 a. of wood, 40*s*. rent, and one third of a messuage in Chartley (*Charteley*), Grindley (*Greneley*), Drointon (*Drengton*), Moreton (*Moreton*), and Rugeley (*Riggeley*), half of the manor of Great Barr (*Barre*), and one third of the manor of Chartley, STAFFS., the manor of English Bicknor (*Bykenore Englyssh*) and one third of the manor of Great Taynton (*Magna Teynton*), GLOS.

1455

Grant and render to the archbishop and the other quer. of the said manors, hundred, holdings, rents, halves, thirds of the manors of Bugbrooke, Chinnor, and Chartley, and quarter. To hold the manors of English Bicknor and Norton Ferris, the hundred, the one third of the manor of Great Taynton, and the 50 a. of wood in Southoe of the king and the manors of Castle Bromwich, Charlton Musgrove, the holdings, rents, halves, thirds of the manors of Bugbrooke, Chinnor, and Chartley, and the quarter of the chief lords, during Elizabeth's life. And grant to the archbishop and the other quer. of the reversion of one third of the manor of Great Taynton held by Martin Ferrers esquire for term of sixty years, of which Elizabeth has the reversion during her life. To hold as above. (Warranty.) Cons. £1,000. Made as to the manors of English Bicknor and Norton Ferris, the hundred, the third part of the manor of Great Taynton, and the 50 a. of wood in Southoe by the king's order. *Labelled* Norht', Oxon', Hunt', Warr', Somers', Buk', Staff', Glouc'. [*Worn.*]

293/72/394

[Cf. Cf. *Som. Fines, 1399–1484*, pp. 201–2; *Staffs. Fines, 1327–1547*, pp. 248–9; *Warws. Fines, 1345–1509*, pp. 175–6, no. 2657.]

636. Morrow [25 June] of St. John the Baptist. William Stafford and Thomas Bodyn quer.; William Heron of London (*London'*) 'haberdassher' and Joan his wife def. Four messuages in Salisbury (*Nova Sar'*), WILTS., and 4 messuages, 20 a. of land, 12 a. of meadow, and 8 a. of wood in Thornbury (*Thornebury*), GLOS. Right of Thomas, as those which Thomas and William Stafford had by gift of William Heron and Joan. Remise and quitclaim, specifying Joan's heirs, to William Stafford and Thomas and Thomas's heirs. (Warranty.) For this, grant and render to William Heron. To hold to him and his heirs. *Labelled* Wiltes', Glouc'.

293/72/396

[Cf. *Wilts. Fines, 1377–1509*, p. 133, no. 614. The fine evidently transfers the succession from the wife's inheritance to the husband's.]

34 Henry VI

1455

637. One week [6 Oct.] from Michaelmas. (Made one week from the Purification 28 Henry VI [9 Feb. 1450].) John Kemes (*Kemys*) and Roger Kemes quer.; William Dodesham and Joan his wife def. One third of the manor of Oldbury (*Oldebury*) in the hundred of Barton Regis (*Bertona juxta Bristoll'*). Right of Roger, as that which Roger and John had by gift of William and Joan. Remise and quitclaim, specifying Joan's heirs, to John and Roger and Roger's heirs. (Warranty.) Cons. 40 marks.

79/92/132

638. One month [27 Oct.] from Michaelmas. Maurice Berkeley esquire and Walter Hearne (*Herne*) quer.; Robert West of Brokenborough (*Brokynbourgh*) and Thomas Hazard (*Hasard*) of Leigh (*la Lee*) and Alice his wife def. A messuage, a garden, and 1 a. of meadow in Tetbury (*Tettebury*). Right of Walter, as those which Walter and Maurice had by gift of Robert and Thomas and Alice. Remise and quitclaim, specifying Alice's heirs, to Maurice and Walter and Walter's heirs. (Warranty, by Robert alone.) Cons. 40 marks.

79/92/134

[It appears anomalous that the remise and quitclaim specifies Alice's heirs while the warranty is by Robert alone, for himself and his heirs.]

1455

639. Morrow [3 Nov.] of All Souls. John Thorp and Margaret his wife quer.; John Boulsdon (*Bullesdon*) and Alice his wife def. A messuage, 1 ploughland, 15 a. of meadow, 8 a. of wood, and 7*s*. 8*d*. rent in Wick (*Wyke*), Lorridge (*Lodwynche*), Walgaston (*Walmegarston*), Berkeley (*Berkeley*), Ham (*Hamme*), Alkington (*Alkynton*), and Halmore (*Halmare*). Right of John Thorp, as to the holdings, as those which John Thorp and Margaret had by gift of John Boulsdon and Alice. Remise and quitclaim, specifying Alice's heirs, to John Thorp and Margaret and that John's heirs. And grant to John Thorp and Margaret of the rent together with the homage and all the services of Thomas Sargent (*Serjeaunt*) of Monmouth (*Monmoth*), John Russell, and John Horsley of Newport (*Newport*) chaplain from all the holdings which they held of John Boulsdon and Alice in the said townships. (Warranty, specifying Alice's heirs, of the rent.) To hold to John Thorp and Margaret and that John's heirs. Cons. £30.

79/92/130

640. Morrow [3 Nov.] of All Souls. James Hyatt (*Hyot*) quer.; Thomas Almally and Cecily his wife def. A messuage, 6 tofts, 80 a. of land, 6 a. of meadow, 20 a. of pasture, and 10 a. of wood in Staunton (*Staunton*) and Newland (*Neweland*) in the forest of Dean (*Dean*). Right of James by gift of Thomas and Cecily. Remise and quitclaim, specifying Cecily's heirs, to James. (Warranty.) For this, grant back and render to Thomas and Cecily. To hold the tofts, land, meadow, and 5 a. of the pasture during their lives and the messuage, wood, and 15 a. of the pasture during Cecily's life, of James, paying a rose a year at St. John the Baptist and doing service to the chief lords. Reversion to James.

79/92/131

1456

641. One week [9 Feb.] from the Purification. William Brown and Richard Bedford quer.; William Fenys knight and Margaret his wife def. The manors of Headington (*Hedyngdon*), Woodperry (*Wodpury*), Tackley (*Takley*), Chastleton (*Chastelton*), Salford (*Salford*), North Leigh (*Northly*), Wilcote (*Wyvelcote*), Walcot (*Walcote*), and Epwell (*Ipwell*), 10 messuages, 6 ploughlands, 13 yardlands, 1 bovate, and 69 a. of land, 60 a. of meadow, the hundreds of Bullingdon (*Bolyngden*) and Northgate (*Northyate*) outside the north gate of Oxford (*Oxon'*), the view of frankpledge of the said manors of Headington and Woodperry and the said hundreds of Bullingdon and Northgate, £9 0*s*. 2*d*. rent in Whitehill (*Wyghthill*), *Foukenend*, Over Norton (*Overnorton*), Cornwell (*Cornwell*), *Tilgarsley*, and Stanton St. John (*Staunton Seynt John*) and in the said townships of Woodperry, Tackley, Chastleton, North Leigh, Wilcote, and Epwell, the advowsons of the churches of the said townships of Tackley and Salford, and half of 1 yardland in Wilcote, OXON., the manor of Seacourt (*Sewekeworth*), BERKS., the manor of Hill Croome (*Hill Crombe*), WORCS., and the manor of Willicote (*Wyllecote*) and a messuage, 2 ploughlands, and 6 a. of meadow in Alscot (*Alvescote*), GLOS. Right of William Brown, as those which the same William and Richard had by gift of William Fenys and Margaret. Remise and quitclaim, specifying William Fenys's heirs, to William Brown and Richard and William Brown's heirs. (Warranty.) Cons. £300. *Labelled* Oxon', Berk', Wygorn', Glouc'.

293/73/406

[The location of the 10 messuages, 6 ploughlands, etc. is not stated.]

1456

642. One week [30 May] from Trinity. (Made the morrow [7 May] of Ascension in the said year.) Maurice Berkeley esquire and Walter Hearne (*Herne*) quer.; Wibert Charlton (*Charleton*) son and heir of Walter Charlton def. A messuage, a garden, and 1 a. of meadow in Tetbury (*Tettebury*). Right of Walter, as those which Walter and Maurice had by Wibert's gift. Remise and quitclaim to Walter and Maurice and Walter's heirs. (Warranty.) Cons. 40 marks.

79/92/133

35 Henry VI

1456

643. One month [27 Oct.] from Michaelmas. Maurice Denis (*Denys*) esquire and John Poyntz esquire and Alice his wife quer.; Nicholas Poyntz esquire def. The manor of Elkstone (*Elkeston*) and the advowson of the church of the same manor. Right of John, as those which John and Alice and Maurice had by Nicholas's gift. For this, grant back and render to Nicholas. To hold during his life without impeachment of waste, of Maurice and John and Alice and John's heirs, paying a rose a year at St. John the Baptist and doing service to the chief lords. Remainder to Humphrey Poyntz esquire and his heirs in tail male. (Warranty, specifying Alice's heirs.) Contingent reversion to Maurice and John and Alice and John's heirs.

79/92/135

[It appears anomalous that, while the tenure is to be of John's heirs and the contingent remainder is to his heirs, the warranty specifies Alice's heirs.]

1457

644. One month [15 May] from Easter. Hugh Snailham (*Snaylham*) and Joan his wife quer.; Robert Woolridge (*Wolrych*) and Katherine his wife def. Three messuages, 3 yardlands, 10 a. of meadow, and 20 a. of pasture in Nympsfield (*Nymdesfeld*) and Owlpen (*Oulepen*). Right of Joan, as those which Hugh and Joan had by gift of Robert and Katherine. Remise and quitclaim, specifying Robert's heirs, to Hugh and Joan and Joan's heirs. (Warranty.) Cons. 40 marks.

79/92/138

645. Morrow [27 May] of Ascension. Philip Lewes and Robert Bell quer.; Richard atte Well (*Welle*) and Elizabeth his wife daughter and heir of Thomas Franklin (*Frankeleyn*) late of Fairford (*Fayreford*) def. Seven messuages, 2 tofts, and 6 a. of land in Fairford. Right of Philip, as those which Philip and Robert had by gift of Richard and Elizabeth. Remise and quitclaim, specifying Elizabeth's heirs, to Philip and Robert and Philip's heirs. Cons. £40.

79/92/137

646. Two weeks [26 June] from Trinity. Nicholas Poyntz esquire and John Poyntz esquire and Alice his wife quer.; Thomas Poyntz esquire def. Half of the manor of Nympsfield (*Nymesfeld*). Right of Nicholas, as that which Nicholas and John and Alice had by Thomas's gift. To hold to Nicholas and John and Alice and Nicholas's heirs, of the king. For this, grant back and render to Thomas. To hold to him and his legitimate heirs in tail. (Warranty, by Alice and her heirs alone, against Edmund [Kirton] abbot of

1457

Westminster (*Westm'*) and his successors.) Contingent reversion to Nicholas's heirs. Made by the king's order.

79/92/136

[The provision for the contingent reversion to Nicholas's heirs assumes that Nicholas himself would not outlive Thomas. It also appears anomalous that the warranty was by Alice and her heirs, not Nicholas and his heirs. The qualification of Thomas's heirs in tail as 'legitimate' is unusual.]

36 Henry VI

1457

647. One week [6 Oct.] from Michaelmas. Walter Hearne (*Herne*) quer.; John Poler and Alice his wife daughter and heir of Walter Hudde def. A messuage and a garden in Tetbury (*Tettebury*). Right of Walter by gift of John and Alice. Remise and quitclaim, specifying Alice's heirs, to Walter. (Warranty.) Cons. £20.

79/92/144

648. Two weeks [13 Oct.] from Michaelmas. William Nottingham (*Notyngham*), Thomas Bisley (*Bysley*), Walter Brockhampton (*Brokhampton*), and John Dodding (*Dodyng*) quer.; Thomas Allen (*Aleyn*) and Alice his wife def. The manor of Elmbridge (*Elbrugge*) and 14 messuages, 300 a. of land, 30 a. of meadow, 100 a. of pasture, and 20*s*. rent in Elmbridge, Down Hatherley (*Dounhatherley*), Churchdown (*Chirchedon*), the Noake (*Noke*), Hucclecote (*Hukilcote*), and Wood Hucclecote (*Wodehokilcote*) in the county of Gloucester (*Glouc'*). Right of John, as those which John, William, Thomas Bisley (*Bisley*), and Walter had by gift of Thomas Allen and Alice. Remise and quitclaim, specifying Alice's heirs, to William, Thomas Bisley, Walter, and John and John's heirs. (Warranty.) Cons. 200 marks.

79/92/142

649. Two weeks [13 Oct.] from Michaelmas. John Fortescue (*Fortescu*) knight, Thomas Young (*Yonge*) son and heir of Thomas Young late of Bristol (*Bristoll'*) merchant, and William le Venour esquire quer.; Maurice de la River (*Delaryver*) esquire and Joan his wife def. The manors of Tormarton (*Tormarton*), Littleton-upon-Severn (*Lytelton*), West Littleton (*Westlytelton*), and Acton Turville (*Acton Turvyle*), the advowsons of the churches of Tormarton, Littleton-upon-Severn, West Littleton, and Acton Turville, and 100 messuages, 30 tofts, 20 ploughlands, 200 a. of meadow, 500 a. of pasture, 500 a. of wood, and £5 rent in Tormarton, Littleton-upon-Severn, West Littleton, and Acton Turville. Right of Thomas Young the son, as those which the same Thomas, John, and William had by gift of Maurice and Joan. Remise and quitclaim, specifying Maurice's heirs, to John, Thomas Young the son, and William and the heirs of Thomas Young the son. (Warranty against Thomas [Seabrook] abbot of St. Peter's, Gloucester (*Gloucestr'*), and his successors.) Cons. £400.

79/92/143

650. Three weeks [20 Oct.] from Michaelmas. Thomas Poyntz esquire, John Vale clerk, Nicholas Hall (*Halle*), John Champneys (*Champeneys*), William Chandler (*Chaundeler*) clerk, and Nicholas Whete chaplain quer.; John Boulsdon (*Bollesdon*) and Alice his wife def. The manors of Shirehampton (*Hempton*), Sturden (*Stourdon*), and Hinton (*Henton*) and 12 messuages, a mill, 10 yardlands and 180 a. of land, 104 a. of meadow, 126 a. of

1457

pasture, and 6 a. of wood in Barton Regis (*Berton Regis*) by Bristol (*Bristoll'*), Old Sodbury (*Oldesobbury*), Chipping Sodbury (*Chepyngsobbury*), and Hambrook (*Hambroke*). Right of Thomas, as those which Thomas and the other quer. had by gift of John Boulsdon and Alice. Remise and quitclaim, specifying Alice's heirs, to Thomas and the other quer. and Thomas's heirs. (Warranty.) For this, grant and render of the manors of Sturden and Hinton to John Boulsdon. To hold during his life without impeachment of waste, the manor of Sturden of the king, the manor of Hinton of the quer. and Thomas's heirs, paying a rose a year at St. John the Baptist and doing service to the chief lords. Reversion to the quer. and Thomas's heirs. Made as to the manor of Sturden by the king's order.

79/92/141

651. Three weeks [20 Oct.] from Michaelmas. Thomas Poyntz esquire quer.; John ap Tomlin (*Tomlyn*) otherwise called John Huntley (*Hunteley*) and Joan his wife def. Half of the manor of Redwick (*Radewyke*) and Northwick (*Northwyke*). Right of Thomas by gift of John and Joan. Remise and quitclaim, specifying Joan's heirs, to Thomas. (Warranty.) Cons. £100.

79/92/145

652. One month [27 Oct.] from Michaelmas. William Whittington (*Whytyngton*) esquire, Thomas Barton, and John Bridge (*Brugge*) quer.; Joan Henbarowe and Thomas Bridge and Matilda his wife def. Fifteen messuages, 460 a. of land, 24 a. of meadow, 100 a. of pasture, 4 a. of wood, and 18*s*. rent in Winchcombe (*Wynchecombe*), Gretton (*Gretton*), Swindon (*Swyndon*), Greet (*Grete*), Stallion (*Stallynge*) in the parish of Newent (*Newent*), and Ketford (*Ketford*) in the parish of Dymock (*Dymmock*), and one third of 5 messuages, 400 a. of land, 16 a. of meadow, and 40 a. of pasture in Hampnett (*Hampenet*), Dowdeswell (*Doudeswell*), and Quedgeley (*Quaddesley*), GLOS., and one third of 4 messuages, 34 a. of land, 4 a. of meadow, 16 a. of pasture, and 6*s*. 1*d*. rent in Clifton (*Clifton*) in the parish of Severn Stoke (*Severnestoke*), WORCS. Right of John, as those which John, William, and Thomas Barton had by gift of Joan and Thomas Bridge and Matilda. Remise and quitclaim, specifying Joan's and Matilda's heirs, to William, Thomas Barton, and John and John's heirs. (Warranty.) Cons. 200 marks. *Labelled* Glouc', Wygorn'.

293/73/423

653. Morrow [3 Nov.] of All Souls. John Hayward quer.; William May and Agnes his wife def. Half of two messuages, 28 a. of land, 6 a. of meadow, 8 a. of pasture, 2 a. of wood, and 6*d*. rent in Oxenhall (*Oxenhale*). Right of John by gift of William and Agnes. Remise and quitclaim, specifying Agnes's heirs, to John. (Warranty, against Thomas [Seabrook] abbot of St. Peter's, Gloucester (*Gloucestr'*), and his successors.) Cons. 40 marks.

79/92/139

1458

654. Morrow [3 Feb.] of the Purification. John Fortescue (*Fortescu*) knight, John Cheyney (*Cheyny*) of *Pynne* esquire, John Gough (*Gogh*), Thomas Nicholl (*Nicoll*), John

1458

Nicholl, and Thomas Povey (*Povy*) quer.; Robert Corbet knight def. The manor of Ebrington (*Ebrughton* otherwise called *Ebrighton*) held by Joyce who was wife of John Greville (*Grevyle*) late esquire for term of life. Right of John Fortescue. Grant of the reversion to him and the other quer. and John Fortescue's heirs. (Warranty.) Cons. £400.

79/92/140

655. Morrow [3 Feb.] of the Purification. Thomas Charlton (*Charleton*) knight, Thomas Wytham, and John Say quer.; Richard [Neville] earl of Salisbury (*Sar'*) and Alesia his wife and John Neville knight their son and Isabel his wife def. The manor of Shenley (*Shenley*) except 200 a. of wood there, HERTS., the manors of Eastney (*Estney*) and Efford (*Efford*), HANTS., the manor of Oakford (*Okeford*), DEVON, the manors of Knowle (*Knoll*) and Goathurst (*Gotehull*) except the advowsons of Knowle and Goathurst, SOM., the manor of Row Earthcott (*Rougherdcote*), GLOS., and 2 messuages, 1 toft, 90 a. of land, 20 a. of meadow, and 2 a. of pasture in Featherstone (*Federstan*), YORKS. Right of Thomas Wytham, as those which the same Thomas, Thomas Charlton, and John Say had by gift of the earl and Alesia and John Neville and Isabel. For this, grant and render to John Neville and Isabel. To hold to them and their heirs in tail. Successive contingent remainders of the manors of Shenley, Efford, Oakford, Knowle, Goathurst, and Row Earthcott to the earl and Alesia and Alesia's heirs in tail and to Alesia's heirs; of the manor of Eastney and the holding in Featherstone to the earl and his heirs in tail and to his heirs. *Labelled* Hertf', Sutht', Devon', Somers', Glouc', Ebor'.

293/73/426

[Cf. *Som. Fines, 1399–1484*, p. 205.]

37 Henry VI

1458

656. One week [18 Nov.] from St. Martin. John Trussell and Margaret his wife quer.; Thomas Porter of Newent (*Newent*) def. Fifty-two acres of land, 20 a. of meadow, 22 a. of pasture, and half of a messuage in Over (*Over*), Minsterworth (*Mynstreworthe*), Highnam (*Hyneham*), and Maisemore (*Maysmore*). Right of Margaret, as those which John and Margaret had by Thomas's gift. Remise and quitclaim to John and Margaret and Margaret's heirs. For this, grant back and render to Thomas. To hold to him and his heirs in tail, of John and Margaret and Margaret's heirs, paying a rose a year at St. John the Baptist and doing service to the chief lords. (Warranty, against Edmund [Kirton] abbot of Westminster (*Westm'*) and his successors.) Contingent reversion to John and Margaret and Margaret's heirs.

79/92/146

1459

657. Two weeks [3 June] from Trinity. William Brome and William Cobcote quer.; Thomas Conyers esquire def. The manors of Headington (*Hedyngdon*), Walcot (*Walcote*), and Epwell (*Ipwell*), the hundreds of Headington, Bullingdon (*Bolyngden*), and Northgate (*Northyate*) outside the north gate of Oxford (*Oxon'*), and the view of frankpledge of the said manor of Headington and the said hundreds of Headington, Bullingdon, and Northgate, OXON., and the manor of Alscot (*Alvescote*), GLOS. Right of William Brome. Grant to the same William and William Cobcote and William Brome's

1459

heirs of the reversion of the premises, held by Elizabeth who was wife of Thomas Blunt (*Blount*) for term of life, of the inheritance of Thomas Conyers. (Warranty.) Cons. £200. *Labelled* Oxon', Glouc'.

293/73/441

38 Henry VI

1459

658. Morrow [3 Nov.] of All Souls. John Fortescue (*Fortescu*) knight, William Venour esquire, and Thomas Young (*Yonge*) son and heir of Thomas Young late merchant of the town of Bristol (*Bristoll'*) quer.; John Stourton of Stourton (*Stourton*) knight, William Carrant (*Carent*) esquire, Robert Liversedge (*Leversegge*) and Agnes his wife daughter of William Westbury (*Westebury*) late one of the justices of King's Bench, Philip Morgan, John Chaffin (*Chafyn*), and John Newburgh (*Neuburgh*) esquire and Alice his wife def. The manor of Coomb's End (*Cotellescombe* otherwise called *Combe Cotell*) and 6 messuages, 2 ploughlands, 80 a. of meadow, 120 a. of pasture, and 50 a. of wood in Old Sodbury (*Oldesobbury*) and Coomb's End. Right of Thomas Young the son, as those which the same Thomas, John Fortescue, and William Venour had by gift of the def. Remise and quitclaim, specifying Agnes's heirs, to John Fortescue, William Venour, and Thomas Young the son and that Thomas's heirs. (Warranty, by Robert and Agnes, specifying Agnes's heirs, against John [Selwood] abbot of St. Mary's, Glastonbury (*Glaston'*), and his successors.) For this, grant and render to John Newburgh and Alice. To hold during Alice's life without impeachment of waste, of John Fortescue, William Venour, and Thomas Young the son and the same Thomas's heirs, paying a rose a year at St. John the Baptist and doing service to the chief lords. Reversion to John Fortescue, William Venour, and Thomas Young the son and the same Thomas's heirs.

79/92/147

[In the lower right-hand corner, 'Exemplificatur', i.e. 'It is to be exemplified'.]

1460

659. Morrow [3 Feb.] of the Purification. Richard Choke (*Chokke*) and Margaret his wife quer.; Nicholas Giffard (*Gifford*) esquire and Margery his wife def. The manors of Cromhall (*Cromhale*), *Byddeleston* [Bibstone?], Matson (*Madesdon*), and Leckhampton (*Lekhampton*), the advowsons of the churches of the same manors of Cromhall and Leckhampton, and 10 messuages, 300 a. of land, 40 a. of meadow, 300 a. of pasture, and 100 a. of wood in Cromhall, Leckhampton, and Matson. Right of Nicholas, as those which Nicholas and Margery had by gift of Richard and Margaret. Remise and quitclaim, specifying Margaret's heirs, to Nicholas and Margery and Nicholas's heirs. For this, grant back and render to Richard and Margaret of the manors of Cromhall and *Byddeleston* and of 6 messuages, 200 a. of land, 20 a. of meadow, 100 a. of pasture, and 50 a. of wood of the said holdings in the township of Cromhall and of the advowson of Cromhall. To hold without impeachment of waste during their lives, of Nicholas and Margery and Nicholas's heirs, paying a rose a year at St. John the Baptist and doing service to the chief lords. Reversion to Nicholas. And grant back and render to Richard and Margaret of the manors of Matson and Leckhampton and of 4 messuages, 100 a. of land, 20 a. of meadow, 200 a. of pasture, and 50 a. of wood of the said holdings in the townships of Matson and Leckhampton and of the advowson of Leckhampton. To hold without

1460

impeachment of waste during Margaret's life, of Nicholas, paying 10 marks a year, at Whitsun and All Saints, and doing service to the chief lords, with right of distraint for non-payment. (Warranty, specifying Margery's [*reading uncertain*] heirs, against John [*recte* Richard Hauley] abbot of Gloucester (*Glouc'*) and his successors.) Reversion to Nicholas. [*Badly worn.*]

79/92/148

[It appears anomalous that, while the acknowledgement, remise and quitclaim, and *habendum* specify Nicholas and his heirs, the warranty seems, under ultra-violet light, to specify Margery's heirs.]

1 Edward IV

1461

660. One week [18 Nov.] from St. Martin. John Hodgkin (*Hoigekyns*) quer.; William Smith (*Smyth*) and Elizabeth his wife def. A messuage, 2 tofts, 16 a. of land, 5 a. of meadow, 7 a. of pasture, and 3*d.* rent in Tirley (*Trilley*). Right of John by gift of William and Elizabeth. Remise and quitclaim, specifying Elizabeth's heirs, to John. (Warranty against Richard [Hauley] abbot of St. Peter's, Gloucester (*Glouc'*), and his successors). Cons. £40.

79/93/3

1462

661. Morrow [3 Feb.] of the Purification. John Thorp and Margaret his wife quer.; Isabel Darling (*Derlyng*) daughter of William Scott (*Scot*) def. Four messuages, 20 a. of land, 8 a. of meadow, and 6 a. of pasture in Berkeley (*Berkeley*), Avery's (*Avereys*), and Ham (*Hamme*). Right of Margaret as those which John and Margaret had by Isabel's gift. Remise and quitclaim to John and Margaret and Margaret's heirs. (Warranty against William [Farley] abbot of St. Peter's, Gloucester (*Glouc'*), and his successors.) Cons. 40 marks.

79/93/1

662. Morrow [3 Feb.] of the Purification. John Child (*Chylde*) and Agnes his wife quer.; John Butlin (*Butvelyn*) and Alice his wife def. The manor of Batsford (*Bacchesoure*). Right of Agnes, as that which John Child and Agnes had by gift of John Butlin and Alice. Remise and quitclaim, specifying Alice's heirs, to John Child and Agnes and Agnes's heirs. (Warranty). For this, John Child and Agnes granted that they would pay to John Butlin and Alice 4 marks a year, at the Annunciation and Michaelmas, during Alice's life only, with right of distraint for non-payment.

79/93/2

2 Edward IV

1463

663. One week [20 Jan.] from Hilary. Thomas Bridge (*Brugge*) and Matilda his wife and John Bridge quer.; John Garun and Elizabeth his wife def. Sixteen messuages, 580 a. of land, 45 a. of meadow, 120 a. of pasture, 64 a. of wood, 29*s.* rent, and one third of 5 messuages, 400 a. of land, 16 a. of meadow, and 40 a. of pasture in Dymock (*Dymmok*), Winchcombe (*Wynchecombe*), Gretton (*Gretton*), Swindon (*Swyndon*), Greet (*Grete*),

1463

Hampnett (*Hampnet*), Dowdeswell (*Dowedeswell*), and Quedgeley (*Queddesley*), GLOS.,and one third of 4 messuages, 34 a. of land, 4 a. of meadow, 16 a. of pasture, and 6*s*. 1*d*. rent in Clifton (*Clifton*) in the parish of Severn Stoke (*Severenstok*), WORCS. Right of John Bridge, as those which he and Thomas and Matilda had by gift of John Garun and Elizabeth. Remise and quitclaim, specifying Elizabeth's heirs, to Thomas and Matilda and John Bridge and that John's heirs. (Warranty.) Cons £200. *Labelled* Glouc', Wygorn'.

294/74/9

3 Edward IV

1463

664. One month [8 May] from Easter. William Francombe (*Francom*) of Gloucester (*Gloucestr*') quer.; William Hill of Worcester (*Wygorn*') and Elena his wife def. A messuage in Gloucester. Right of William Francombe by gift of William Hill and Elena. Remise and quitclaim, specifying Elena's heirs, to William Francombe. (Warranty.) Cons. £20.

79/93/4

665. One week [12 June] from Trinity. William Nottingham (*Notyngham*), Walter Brockhampton (*Brokhampton*) esquire, John Dodding (*Dodyng*), Richard Batchelor (*Bacheler*) chaplain, and Thomas Dunstable (*Dunstaple*) chaplain quer.; John Lisle (*Lysle*) and Margaret his wife def. Half of the manor of Sapperton (*Saperton*) and the advowson of the church of Sapperton. Right of Willam, as those which William, Walter, John Dodding, Richard, and Thomas had by gift of John Lisle and Margaret. Remise and quitclaim, specifying John Lisle's heirs, to William, Walter, John Dodding, Richard, and Thomas and William's heirs. (Warranty, specifying Margaret's heirs.) Cons. £100.

79/93/5

[It appears anomalous that the remise and quitclaim specifies John Lisle's heirs while the warranty specifies Margaret's.]

4 Edward IV

1464

666. Two weeks [15 April] from Easter. (Made one week from the Purification 3 Edward IV [9 Feb. 1464].) John Lyneham (*Leynham*), Richard Danvers, and William Danvers quer.; Robert Corbet knight and Elizabeth his wife, Robert Corbet son of the said Robert, John Corbet, and John Dorwyn def. The manor of Farmcote (*Farnecote*). Right of John Lyneham, as that which the same John, Richard, and William had by gift of Robert Corbet and Elizabeth, Robert Corbet the son, John Corbet, and John Dorwyn. Remise and quitclaim, specifying Elizabeth's heirs, to John Lyneham, Richard, and William and John Lyneham's heirs. (Warranty.) Cons. £200.

79/93/6

667. Morrow [3 Nov.] of All Souls. Thomas Young (*Yong*) serjeant at law quer.; Thomas Vachell and Agnes his wife daughter of Maurice de la River (*Delaryver*) esquire def. The manor of Coomb's End (*Cotellescombe* otherwise called *Combe Cotell*) and 6 messuages, 2 ploughlands, 80 a. of meadow, 120 a. of pasture, and 50 a. of wood in Old Sodbury

1464

(*Oldesobbury*) and Coomb's End. Right of Thomas Young by gift of Thomas Vachell and Agnes. Remise and quitclaim, specifying Agnes's heirs, to Thomas Young. (Warranty, specifying Thomas Vachell's heirs against George [Norwich] abbot of the house and church of St. Peter, Westminster (*Westm'*) in Middlesex, and his successors.) Cons. £200.

79/93/7

[It appears anomalous that the remise and quitclaim specifies Agnes's heirs while the warranty specifies Thomas Vachell's.]

668. Morrow [3 Nov.] of All Souls. Thomas Young (*Yong*) serjeant at law, John Young citizen and grocer of London (*London'*), Philip Mead (*Mede*) merchant of the town of Bristol (*Bristoll'*), and Thomas Hore of Bristol merchant quer.; Thomas Vachell and Agnes his wife daughter of Maurice de la River (*Delaryver*) esquire def. The manors of Tormarton (*Tormarton*), Littleton-upon-Severn (*Lytelton*), West Littleton (*Westlytelton*), and Acton Turville (*Acton Turvyle*), the advowsons of the churches of Tormarton, Littleton-upon-Severn, West Littleton, and Acton Turville, and 100 messuages, 30 tofts, 20 ploughlands, 200 a. of meadow, 500 a. of pasture, 500 a. of wood, and £5 rent in Tormarton, Littleton-upon-Severn, West Littleton, and Acton Turville. Right of Philip as those which Philip, Thomas Young, John, and Thomas Hore had by gift of Thomas Vachell and Agnes. Remise and quitclaim, specifying Agnes's heirs, to Thomas Young, John, Philip, and Thomas Hore and Philip's heirs. (Warranty, specifying Thomas Vachell's heirs, against George [Norwich], abbot of the house and church of St. Peter, Westminster (*Westm'*) in Middlesex, and his successors.) Cons. £400.

79/93/8

[Cf. note to no. 667, above.]

669. Morrow [3 Nov.] of All Souls. John Moody (*Mody*) esquire quer.; John Fry (*Frye*) son and heir of John Fry def. Ten messuages, a dovecot, 250 a. of land, 20 a. of meadow, and 9 a. of pasture in Chedglow (*Chegelewe*), Malmesbury (*Malmesbury*), Bulidge (*Bulleywyke*), Burton (*Burton*), Charlton (*Charleton*), Little Somerford (*Parva Somerford*), Great Somerford (*Magna Somerford*), and Thornhill (*Thornehill*), WILTS., and 2 messuages, 60 a. of land, 10 a. of meadow, 10 a. of pasture, and 20 a. of wood in Minchinhampton (*Mynchynhampton*) and Rodborough (*Radborowe*), GLOS. Right of John Moody, of which he had 2 messuages, 60 a. of land, 10 a. of pasture, and 20 a. of wood in Minchinhampton and Rodborough by gift of John Fry. Remise and quitclaim to John Moody. And grant to him of the reversion of 10 messuages, 250 a. of land, 30 a. of meadow, 9 a. of pasture, and the dovecot in Chedglow, Malmesbury, Bulidge, Burton, Charlton, Little Somerford, Great Somerford, and Thornhill, held by Henry Gregory and Joan his wife for term of Joan's life, of John Fry's inheritance. (Warranty.) Cons. 100 marks. *Labelled* Wiltes', Glouc'.

294/74/23

[Cf. *Wilts. Fines, 1377–1509*, p. 143, no. 651. The 10 a. of meadow initially listed as in Glos. townships are silently assumed in the acknowledgement and the grant of the reversion to be in the Wilts. townships.]

1464

670. Two weeks [25 Nov.] from St. Martin. John Peers (*Peres*) clerk, Gregory Westby, and John Mervyn quer.; Thomas Burgh knight and Margaret his wife late wife of William Botreaux of Botreaux knight def. The manors of Flexland (*Flexlond*), Pennington (*Penyton*), and Bedenham (*Bedynham*), HANTS., 2 messuages and 110 a. of land in Maddington (*Maydynwynterborne*), and pasture for 4 oxen or cows, for 4 beasts, and for 40 sheep in Maddington, WILTS., 5s. rent in Bristol (*Bristoll'*), 2 messuages, 80 a. of land, and 2 a. of meadow in Maiden Newton (*Maydyn Newton*), DORSET, 2 messuages, 70 a. of land, and 2 a. of meadow in Upton (*Upton Moylys*), BERKS., the manors of Cheddar (*Chedder*) and Walton (*Walton*), SOM., and the manors of Cadbury (*Catbery Castell*), Stockleigh English (*Stokley Englich*), and Langford (*Langford*), DEVON. Right of John Mervyn, as those which the same John, John Peers, and Gregory had by gift of Thomas and Margaret. Remise and quitclaim, specifying Margaret's heirs, to John, Gregory, and John and John Mervyn's heirs. Cons. £1,000. *Labelled* Sutht'. Wiltes', Bristoll', Dors', Berk', Somers', Devon'.

294/74/25

[Cf. *Dorset Fines, 1327–1485*, 391; *Som. Fines, 1399–1484*, p. 207; *Wilts. Fines, 1377–1509*, pp.143–4, no. 654.]

5 Edward IV

1465

671. Three weeks [5 May] from Easter. Robert Woolworth (*Wollesworth*) of Dursley (*Durseley*) and Matilda his wife quer.; Richard Henmarsh (*Henmershe*) formerly of Bristol (*Bristoll'*) and Edith his wife def. Two messuages, 2 gardens, and half of a messuage in Wickwar (*Wykwarre*). Right of Robert, as those which Robert and Matilda had by gift of Richard and Edith. Remise and quitclaim, specifying Edith's heirs, to Robert and Matilda and Robert's heirs. (Warranty.) Cons. £20.

79/93/11

672. Morrow [25 June] of St. John the Baptist. James Woolworth (*Wollesworth*) quer.; John Stafford of Wotton-under-Edge (*Wotton under Egge*) and Alice his wife and Cecily King (*Kynge*) of Wotton-under-Edge, widow, def. Two thirds of half of a messuage and two thirds of a garden in Wotton-under-Edge. Right of James by gift of John and Alice and Cecily. Remise and quitclaim (specifying Alice's and Cecily's heirs) to James. (Warranty.) Cons. £10.

79/93/10

673. Morrow [3 Nov.] of All Souls. John Marshal (*Marchall*) 'mercer', John Stockton (*Stokton*), John Dunne the elder, William Redknap, John Aldburgh (*Alburgh*), and Richard Hart (*Hert*) quer.; William Milner (*Mylnar*) and Margery his wife def. Two messuages, a dovecot, and 1 a. of land in Stratford-upon-Avon (*Straford super Avenne*), WARWS., and 3 messuages in Campden (*Campeden*), GLOS. Right of John Marshal, as those which the same John, John Stockton, John Dunne, William Redknap, John Aldburgh, and Richard had by gift of William Milner and Margery. Remise and quitclaim, specifying Margery's heirs, to John, John, John, William Redknap, John, and Richard and John Marshall's heirs. (Warranty.) Cons. 40 marks. *Labelled* Warr', Glouc'.

294/74/30

[Cf. *Warws. Fines, 1345–1509*, p. 182, no. 2678.]

1466

674. Morrow [3 Feb.] of the Purification. Roger Kemes (*Kemys*) and Alice his wife quer.; John Poyntz (*Poyntys*) esquire and Alice his wife def. One third of the manor of Oldbury (*Oldbery*). Right of Roger, as that which Roger and Alice had by gift of John and Alice. Remise and quitclaim, specifying the heirs of Alice wife of John, to Roger and Alice and Roger's heirs. (Warranty against Walter [Newbury] abbot of St. Augustine's, Bristol (*Bristoll'*), and his successors.) Cons. 40 marks.

79/93/9

6 Edward IV

1466

675. One month [4 May] from Easter. John Shipward of Bristol (*Bristoll'*) the elder, merchant, quer.; Walter Rodney (*Rodeney*) knight, Thomas Rodney esquire son of the said Walter, and John Rodney esquire brother of the said Walter def. Eleven messuages and a garden in Bristol and 7 a. of meadow in Redcliffe field (*Redclyffeld*) in the parish of Bedminster (*Bedmystre*), SOM. Right of John Shipward by gift of Walter, Thomas, and John Rodney. Remise and quitclaim, specifying Walter's heirs, to John Shipward. (Warranty.) Cons. 400 marks. *Labelled* Bristoll', Somers'.

294/74/36

[Cf. *Som. Fines, 1399–1484*, p. 208.]

676. One week [6 Oct.] from Michaelmas. (Made two weeks from Trinity 28 Henry VI [14 June1450].) Thomas Colt and Henry Sotehill quer; Richard Neville earl of Warwick (*Warr'*) and Anne his wife def. The castle and manor of Warwick (*Warrewyk*), the manors of Sutton under Brailes (*Sutton*), Brailes (*Brayles*), Claverdon (*Claverdon*), Tanworth (*Tonworth*), Berkswell (*Berkeswell*), Lighthorne (*Lyghthorn*), and Barford (*Bereford*) and 14 messuages, 2 ploughlands and 200 a. of land, 20 a. of meadow, 100 a. of pasture, 10 a. of wood, and £20 rent in Warwick, Myton (*Myton*), Whitley (*Whitloge*), Guy's Cliffe (*Gybbeclyffe*), Berkswell, and Stratford-upon-Avon (*Stretford super Aven*), WARWS., one quarter of the manors of Hanslope (*Hampslap*), Quarrendon (*Querndon*), and Olney (*Olney*) and £6 rent in Milton Keynes (*Multon*) issuing from a chantry in the church of Castle Thorpe (*Castelthorpe*), BUCKS.; the manors of Walsall (*Walshale*) and Pattingham (*Patyngham*), 15 messuages, 3 tofts, 100 a. of land, 20 a. of meadow, 10 a. of pasture, 20 a. of wood, and 10s. rent in in Walsall and Pattingham, and one quarter of the manor of Perry Barr (*Pury Barre*) and of 5 messuages and 1 toft in Walsall and Pattingham, STAFFS., the manor of Kirtling (*Kyrtelyng*) and 30 messuages, 7 tofts, 3 ploughlands and 200 a. of land, 20 a. of meadow, 100 a. of pasture, 100 a. of wood, and £10 rent in Kirtling and Longstanton (*Longa Staunton*), CAMBS., one quarter of a knight's fee in Westbarrow Hall (*Barowe*) and the advowson of one quarter of the churches of Great Stambridge (*Stanbrigge*) and North Fambridge (*Fanbrigge*), ESSEX, one quarter of the manor of Flamstead (*Flamstede*) and the advowson of one quarter of the church of the said township, HERTS., the advowson of the chantry called 'Beauchamp chaunterie' in the church of St. Paul, LONDON, the castles, lordships, and manors of Painscastle (*Maudescastell*), Elfael (*Elvell*), Snodhill (*Snodhull*), Aberedw (*Abredough*), and Kilvey (*Kylvey*) and 4,000 a. of land and 1,000 a. of wood in Elfael, Snodhill, Aberedw, and Kilvey, in the march of Wales adjacent to HEREFS., one quarter of the manors of Yardley (*Yerdeley*), Abberley (*Abbotesley*), Syntley (*Syntley*), Shrawley (*Shraveley*), Elmley

1466

Lovett (*Elmeley Lovet*), Flyford Flavell (*Fleford*), Hadzor (*Haddesore*), Perry (*Pury juxta Wigorn'*), Wick Piddle (*Wykepedill*), Wyre Piddle (*Wyrepedull*), and Earl's Croome (*Simondescrombe*) and one quarter of half of the manor of Fickenappletree (*Thickenappiltre*), WORCS., one quarter of 2 messuages and the office of weigher in the town of Southampton (*Suthampton*), [HANTS.], the keeping of the forest of Westbury (*Westbere*), the advowson of the church of Woodborough (*Wodebergh*) and half a knight's fee in Woodborough, and one quarter of the manors of Cherhill (*Chyriell*) and Hinton (*Henton*), WILTS., 6 messuages, 20 a. of land, and 12 a. of meadow in Preston (*Preston*) and Uppingham (*Uppingham*), 26s. rent in Uppingham, and one quarter of the manors of Preston and Uppingham, RUTLAND, the hundred of South Tawton (*Southtauton*), the manor of South Tawton, and the borough or manor of Zeal (*Seele*), DEVON, the manors of Penzance (*Penzans*), Carnanton (*Carnaunton*), Balston (*Blyston*), and Helston (*Helston Tony*) and 20 messuages, 2 tofts, a mill, 60 ferlings of land, 12 a. of meadow, 300 a. of pasture, and 100 a. of wood in Treleigh Wells (*Treleigh Welles*), and Treleigh Worthy (*Treleigh Worthy*), Redruth (*Redrewithe*), and Lanjeth (*Langweyth*), CORNW., the islands or lordships of Jersey (*Jernesey*), and Guernsey (*Guernesey*) and the castles and manors of Gorey (*Gurrey*), Castle Cornet (*Cornet*), Sark (*Serk*), Herm (*Erme*), and Alderney (*Aurney*) in the said islands, DORSET, the manors of Potterspury (*Potterspury*), Cosgrove (*Covesgrave*), and Puxley (*Pokeslee*), the advowson of the church of Potterspury, 5 knights' fees in Potterspury, Cosgrove, and Puxley, 10 messuages, 100 a. of land, 20 a. of meadow, 100 a. of pasture, and 40 a. of wood in Potterspury, Cosgrove, and Puxley, and one quarter of the manors of Long Buckby (*Bukby*) and Moulton (*Multon*), NORTHANTS., and the castle of St. Briavels (*Seintbrevell*), the manors of St. Briavels (*Seyntbrevell*), Kemerton (*Kenmerton*), and Barton Regis (*Berton*) by Bristol (*Bristoll'*), 20,000 a. of land, 100 a. of meadow, 100 a. of pasture, and 400 a. of wood in St. Briavels (*Seint Brevell*), Barton Regis, Chedworth (*Chedworth*), and Lydney (*Lyddeney*), one quarter of the manors of Chedworth and Lydney, and the advowson of one quarter of the church of Notgrove (*Natgrave*), GLOS. Right of Thomas, of which Thomas and Henry had the islands, castles, and lordships and the manors of Warwick, Sutton, Brailes, Claverdon, Tanworth, Berkswell, Lighthorne, Barford, Walsall, Pattingham, Kirtling, Painscastle, Elfael, Snodhill, Aberedw, Kilvey, Gorey, Cornet, Sark, Herm, Alderney, Potterspury, Cosgrove, Puxley, St. Briavels, and Barton Regis [i.e. the manors in Warws., Staffs., Cambs., Wales, the Channel Islands, Northants., and, except for Kemerton, Glos.] and 5½ knights' fees, the keeping of the forest, 68 messuages, 10 tofts, 24,005 ploughlands and 594 a. of land, 179½ a. of meadow, 410 a. of pasture, 1,170 a. of wood, and 30 and 10s. rent [*sic*] and the said knights' fees and holdings in Potterspury, Cosgrove, Puxley, Warwick, Myton, Whitley, Guy's Cliffe, Berkswell, Stratford-upon-Avon, St. Briavels, Barton Regis, Kirtling, Longstanton, Elfael, Snodhill, Aberedw, Kilvey, Walsall, and Pattingham and the advowsons of Woodborough and Potterspury by gift of the earl and Anne. For this, grant back and render to them. To hold to them and their heirs in tail. And grant to them of the reversion of the hundred, borough, and manors of Penzance, Carnanton, Balston, Helston, South Tawton, Zeal, Kemerton, and 26 messuages, 2 tofts, the mill, 60 ferlings and 20 a. of land, 24 a. of meadow, 300 a. of pasture, 500 a. of wood, and £7 6s. rent in Milton Keynes, Treleigh, Redruth, Lanjeth, Preston, Uppingham, Chedworth, and Lydney, the quarters and the advowson of the Beauchamp chantry and the advowsons of the quarters of the churches of Flamstead, Stambridge, Fambridge,

1466

and Notgrove held by John [Tiptoft] earl of Worcester (*Wygorn'*) and Cecily his wife, who was wife of Henry [Beauchamp] duke of Warwick, in Cecily's dower, and of one quarter of a messuage in the said town of Warwick held by Nicholas Rody, one quarter of a messuage in the same town held by John Brewster, one quarter of a messuage and 24 a. of land and 2 a. of meadow in the same town held by John Prince (*Prynce*), one quarter of a messuage in the same town held by Simon Grove, and one quarter of the manors of Perry Barr, Wick Piddle, Wyre Piddle, and Earl's Croome held by Isabel who was wife of Richard Curson esquire, each for term of life, of Thomas's inheritance. To hold as above. Contingent remainders of all to Anne's heirs in tail. Successive contingent remainders of the castle of Warwick, the manors of Warwick, Sutton, and Brailes, and 7 messuages, 1 ploughland and 100 a. of land, 10 a. of meadow, 50 a. of pasture, 5 a. of wood, and £10 rent in Warwick to Margaret daughter of Richard Beauchamp late earl of Warwick who was wife of John [Talbot] earl of Shrewsbury (*Salop'*) and her heirs in tail male, to her heirs in tail, to the heirs in tail of Richard late earl of Warwick, and to his heirs. Successive contingent remainders of all the residue to the heirs in tail of Richard late earl of Warwick and to his heirs. *Labelled* Warr', Buk', Staff', Cantebr', Essex', Hertf', London', Hereford', Wygorn', Villa Sutht', Wiltes', Rotel', Devon', Cornub', Dors', Norht', Gloc'.

294/74/41

[Cf. *Dorset Fines, 1327–1485*, pp. 393–4; *Essex Fines, 1423–1547*, pp. 62–3; *Staffs. Fines, 1327–1547*, pp. 249–50; *Warws. Fines, 1345–1509*, pp. 183–6, no. 2683; *Wilts. Fines, 1377–1509*, pp. 145–7, no. 660.]

677. Morrow [25 June] of St. John the Baptist. John Monmouth quer.; Richard Payn (*Payne*) and Isabel his wife def. Four messuages and 20 a. of land in Cirencester (*Cirencestr'*), Stratton (*Stratton*), and Baunton (*Baudynton*). Right of John by gift of Richard and Isabel. Remise and quitclaim, specifying Isabel's heirs, to John. (Warranty.) Cons. £20.

79/93/14

678. One week [1 July] from St. John the Baptist. Walter Denis (*Denys*) esquire and Agnes his wife quer.; Maurice Denis esquire and Richard Denis clerk def. The manor of Dyrham (*Derham*). Right of Maurice, as that which Maurice and Richard had by Walter's gift. For this, grant and render to Walter and Agnes. To hold to Walter and Agnes and their heirs in tail, of Maurice and Richard and Maurice's heirs, paying a rose a year at St. John the Baptist and doing service to the chief lords. (Warranty.) Contingent remainder to Maurice and Richard and Maurice's heirs.

79/93/15

679. One week [6 Oct.] from Michaelmas. (Made two weeks [8 July] from St. John the Baptist in the said year.) William Vance clerk, Thomas Hawkins (*Haukyns*) clerk, John Salway (*Salwey*) esquire, and Edmund Hecker quer.; Margaret Hungerford widow, daughter and heir of William late Lord Botreaux and Moleyns (*Mulys*), and Thomas Hungerford knight, son of Robert late Lord Hungerford and Moleyns (*Moleyns*) son of the said Margaret, and Anne his wife def. Four messuages, 4 tofts, 100 a. of land, 30 a. of meadow, 100 a. of pasture, and 10 a. of wood in Redwick (*Radewyke*). Right of Edmund as those which Edmund, William, Thomas Hawkins, and John had by gift of Margaret,

1466

Thomas Hungerford, and Anne. Remise and quitclaim, specifying Anne's heirs, to William, Thomas Hawkins, John, and Edmund and Edmund's heirs. (Warranty.) Cons. 100 marks.

79/93/16

680. Morrow [3 Nov.] of All Souls. Thomas Morgan quer.; John Barre knight and Joan his wife def. Two messuages, 120 a. of land, 4 a. of meadow, 20 a. of pasture, and 12 a. of wood in Lydney (*Lyddeney*). Right of Thomas by gift of John and Joan. Remise and quitclaim, specifying Joan's heirs, to Thomas. (Warranty.) Cons. £100.

79/93/12

681. Morrow [3 Nov.] of All Souls. Humphrey Poyntz and Thomas Limerick (*Lymeryk*) quer.; Maurice Denis (*Denys*) esquire and Alice his wife def. The manors of Alveston (*Alleweston*) and Earthcott (*Erthecote*) and the hundreds of Langley (*Langeley*) and Alveston. Right of Humphrey and Thomas by gift of Maurice and Alice. To hold of the king. (Warranty, specifying Alice's heirs.) For this, grant back and render to Maurice and Alice. To hold during their lives, without impeachment of waste, of the king. Remainder to Maurice's heirs in tail. Contingent remainder to Maurice's heirs. Made by the king's order.

79/93/17

1467

682. Two weeks [27 Jan.] from Hilary. William Nottingham (*Notyngham*) quer.; William Grey and Margaret his wife def. The manor of Elmbridge (*Elbrigge*) and 10 messuages, 200 a. of land, 20 a. of meadow, 40 a. of pasture, 10 a. of wood, and 11*s.* rent in Elmbridge, Churchdown (*Churchedon*), the Noake (*Noke*), and Earthcott (*Erdecote*). Right of William Nottingham by gift of William Grey and Margaret. Remise and quitclaim, specifying Margaret's heirs, to William Nottingham. (Warranty.) Cons. 200 marks.

79/93/13

7 Edward IV

1467

683. One month [26 April] from Easter. William Vance clerk, Thomas Hawkins (*Hawkyns*) clerk, Thomas Everdon, John Salway (*Salwey*), Richard Jowett (*Jouettes*), Edmund Hecker (*Hekker*), and Henry Jowett quer.; William Jowett and Isabel his wife def. The manor of Foxcote (*Foxcote*) and 3 messuages, 5 ploughlands, 50 a. of meadow, and 100 a. of wood in Foxcote and Withington (*Wythyndon*), GLOS., and 2 messuages, 200 a. of land, and 17 a. of meadow in Little Comberton (*Parva Cumberton*) and Pensham (*Pendesham*), WORCS. Right of William Vance, as those which the same William and the other quer. had by gift of William Jowett and Isabel. Remise and quitclaim, specifying Isabel's heirs, to the quer. and William Vance's heirs. (Warranty.) Cons. 400 marks. *Labelled* Glouc', Wygorn'.

294/74/48

1467

684. Two weeks [13 Oct.] from Michaelmas. William Nottingham (*Notyngham*) quer.; William Llywelyn (*Lewelyn*) and Joan his wife def. Three messuages, a toft, 5 yardlands, 20 a. of meadow, 20 a. of pasture, and 3 a. of wood in Down Ampney (*Dounamney*) and Coates (*Cotes*), GLOS., and 2 messuages, 1 yardland, 6 a. of meadow, and 12 a. of pasture in Shorncote (*Shernecote*), WILTS. Right of William Nottingham by gift of William Llywelyn and Joan. Remise and quitclaim, specifying Joan's heirs, to William Nottingham. (Warranty.) Cons. £100. *Labelled* Glouc', Wiltes'.

294/74/49

[Cf. *Wilts. Fines, 1377–1509*, p. 148, no. 664.]

8 Edward IV

1468

685. One month [15 May] from Easter. John Greville (*Grevyle*) knight and Joan his wife quer.; John Rouse (*Rous*) esquire and Margaret his wife def. Sixteen messuages, 500 a. of land, 40 a. of meadow, 100 a. of pasture, and 20 a. of furze in Weston on Avon (*Weston Maudyt*). Right of John Greville, as that which John Greville and Joan had by gift of John Rouse and Margaret. Remise and quitclaim, specifying Margaret's heirs, to John and Greville and Joan and John Greville's heirs. (Warranty.) Cons. £100.

79/93/19

686. Three weeks [20 Oct.] from Michaelmas. William [Herbert] earl of Pembroke (*Pembroch*) quer.; John [de Mowbray] duke of Norfolk (*Norff'*) and Elizabeth his wife def. The castle, manor, lordship, and borough of Chepstow (*Chepstowe*), the manor of Barton (*Berton*), and the manor and lordship of Tidenham (*Tudenham*) with members and appurtenances in the marches of Wales adjacent to the county of Gloucester (*Glouc'*). Right of the earl by gift of the duke and Elizabeth. Remise and quitclaim, specifying the duke's heirs, to the earl. (Warranty, specifying Elizabeth's heirs.) Cons. £1,000.

79/93/18

[It appears anomalous that the remise and quitclaim specifies the duke's heirs while the warranty specifies Elizabeth's.]

1469

687. One week [20 Jan.] from Hilary. (Made one month from Michaelmas in the said year [15 May 1468].) Henry Zeme of Ruardean (*Ruwarden*) quer.; John Malpas of Goodrich Castle (*Goderichcastell*) 'taillour' and Agnes his wife def. A messuage, a garden, and 2 a. of land in Ruardean. Right of Henry by gift of John and Agnes. Remise and quitclaim, specifying Agnes's heirs, to Henry. (Warranty.) Cons. £20.

79/93/20

688. One week [20 Jan.] from Hilary. Thomas Hoo esquire, Richard Lewknor (*Leukenore*) esquire, Bartholomew Bolney, Henry Kyghley esquire, Roger Philpot, Henry Ashburn (*Assheburn*), William Lemyng, John Sherman, and Thomas Boket quer.; John [de Mowbray] duke of Norfolk (*Norff'*) and Elizabeth his wife and Henry Bradfield (*Bradfeld*) clerk def. The manor of Upton St. Leonards (*Upton Seynt Leonardes*) and 12 a. of land, 4 a. of meadow, 20 a. of pasture, and 15*s*. 6*d*. rent in Upton St. Leonards, GLOS., the manor of Moreton (*Moreton*) by Thame (*Thame*) and 500 a. of land, 20 a. of meadow, and 4 marks rent in Chinnor (*Chynnore*), Henton (*Heynton*), and

1469

Moreton, OXON., the manor of Ryarsh (*Ryerssh*), KENT, the manors of Brooms (*Bromes*) in Chilgrove (*Chilgrove*), Shopwyke (*Shapwyke*), Egley (*Egle*), Compton (*Compton*), West Marden (*Westmerdon*), and Littleworth (*Litilworth*) and 1,600 a. of land, 100 a. of meadow, 740 a. of wood, 40 a. of heath, and £13 18s. rent in Chilgrove, Barcombe (*Bercompe*), Compton, West Marden, Worth (*Worthe*), Horsham (*Horsham*), West Dean (*Westden*), Boxgrove (*Boxgrave*), Ilsham (*Ilesham*), and Treyford (*Treford*), SUSSEX, the manors of Hooley (*Houghley*), Gatton (*Gatton*), Groves (*Groveshed*), and Bradley (*Bradley*) and 1,500 a. of land, 50 a. of meadow, 400 a. of pasture, 200 a. of wood, and 60s. rent in Reigate (*Reygate*), Gatton, Merstham (*Mestham*), Leigh (*Lye*), Charlwood (*Charlewode*), Horley (*Horle*), Newdigate (*Neudegate*), Betchworth (*Estbechesworth*), and Dorking (*Dorkyng*), SURREY, the manor of Weston (*Weston*) by Cherington (*Cheriton*), WARWS., the manors of Medmenham (*Medmenham*), Southcott (*Southcote*) and Linslade (*Lynchelade*) and 300 a. of land, 120 a. of meadow, 148 a. of pasture, 200 a. of wood, and £4 rent in Medmenham, BUCKS., the manor of West Hatch (*Westhacche*), WILTS., a messuage and 2 yardlands in Alsthorpe (*Alesthorpe*) by Burley (*Burley*), RUTLAND, the manor of Whetstone (*Wheston*) and 16 messuages and 9 yardlands in Whetstone, LEICS., the manor of Barton Seagrave (*Barton Segrave*) and 24s. rent in Northampton (*Norhampton*), NORTHANTS., the manor of Berwick (*Berewyk*) by Barkway (*Berkewey*), HERTS., the manor of Boarhunt (*Boroughunt*) and 200 a. of land, 20 a. of meadow, and 40 a. of pasture in Boarhunt, HANTS., the manor of Wellington Hay (*Welyngton Hay*) and 100 a. of land, 500 a. of wood, and 200 a. of heath in Wellington (*Welyngton*), SALOP., half of the manors of Woolston Hall (*Wolhampton*), High Roding (*Alta Rothyng*), Housham Hall (*Oveshamhall*), Margaretting (*Gyng Margarete*), and Langthorns (*Langetons*) in Little Canfield (*Parva Canefeld*), half of 1,080 a. of land, 100 a. of meadow, 450 a. of pasture, and £20 rent in Chigwell (*Chikewelle*), High Roding, Margaretting, and Little Canfield, and half of the advowson of the church of High Roding, ESSEX, and the manor of Ickleton (*Iklyngton*) and 26s. 8d. rent in Ickleton, CAMBS. Right of Thomas Boket, as that which the same Thomas and the other quer. had by gift of the duke and Elizabeth and Henry Bradfield. Remise and quitclaim, specifying Elizabeth's heirs, to the quer. and Thomas Boket's heirs. (Warranty.) Cons. £10,000. *Labelled* Glouc', Oxon', Kanc', Sussex', Surr', Warr', Buk', Wiltes', Rotel', Leyc', Norht', Hertf', Sutht', Salop', Essex', Cant'.

294/74/64

[Cf. *Warws. Fines, 1345–1509*, pp. 187–8; *Wilts. Fines, 1377–1509*, pp. 149–50, no. 671.]

9 Edward IV

1469

689. Two weeks [16 April] from Easter. (Made one week from the Purification 8 Edward IV [9 Feb. 1469].) William Vance clerk, Thomas Hawkins (*Haukyns*) clerk, and John Salway (*Sallewey*) esquire quer.; William Heynes (*Heyne*) and Agnes his wife def. The manor of Berry Wormington (*Parva Wormyngton*), the advowson of the church of the same manor, and 6 messuages, 200 a. of land, 40 a. of meadow, 300 a. of pasture, and 20s. rent in Berry Wormington. Right of Thomas, as those which Thomas, William Vance, and John had by gift of William Heynes and Agnes. Remise and quitclaim, specifying Agnes's heirs, to William Vance, Thomas, and John and Thomas's heirs. (Warranty.) Cons. £100.

79/93/21

1469

690. One month [30 April] from Easter. Walter Goodrich (*Goderige*) son of Thomas Goodrich and of Katherine his wife quer.; Thomas Goodrich and Katherine his wife def. The manor of Pirton (*Pyryton*) and 5 messuages, 5 tofts, 200 a. of land, 6 a. of meadow, 60 a. of pasture, 6 a. of wood, and 18*d.* rent in Pirton, Parton (*Parton*), Brickhampton (*Brighthampton*), Down Hatherley (*Dounhatherley*), and Quedgeley (*Quedesley*). Right of Walter by gift of Thomas and Katherine. Remise and quitclaim, specifying Katherine's heirs, to Walter. (Warranty.) Cons. £200.

79/93/22

691. One month [30 April] from Easter. John Tame of Fairford (*Fayreford*), John de la Mare (*Delamare*) esquire, and William Whitchurch (*Whitechurche*) clerk quer.; Richard Tame and Margaret his wife def. Six messuages, 4 tofts, 4½ yardlands and 100 a. of land, and 16 a. of meadow in Idbury (*Iddebury*), Foscot (*Foxcote*), Churchill (*Chyrchehill*), and Burford (*Burford super le Wold*), OXON., and 3 tofts, a dovecot, 1 ploughland, 2 yardlands, and 2 a. of land, and 6 a. of meadow in Notgrove (*Nattegrave*), GLOS. Right of John Tame, as those which the same John, John de la Mare, and William had by gift of Richard and Margaret. Remise and quitclaim, specifying Margaret's heirs, to John, John, and William and John Tame's heirs. (Warranty against John [Sodbury] abbot of Cirencester (*Cirencestr'*) and his successors.) Cons. £200. *Labelled* Oxon', Glouc'.

294/74/67

692. One week [1 July] from St. John the Baptist. Richard [Woodville] earl de Rivers (*Ryvers*), William [Herbert] earl of Pembroke (*Pembroch*), Anthony Woodville (*Wydevyle*) de Scales (*Scales*) knight, William Hastings (*Hastynges*) of Hastings knight, Thomas Bonefaunt clerk, Thomas Vaughan esquire, and Richard Fowler (*Foweler*) quer.; Ralph Butler (*Boteler*) of Sudeley (*Sudeley*) knight and Alesia his wife def. The castle and manor of Sudeley, 20 messuages, 400 a. of land, 80 a. of meadow, 200 a. of pasture, 100 a. of wood, and £20 rent in Sudeley, Toddington (*Todyngton*), Stanley Pontlarge (*Stanley*), Greet (*Grette*), Gretton (*Gretton*), Catesthrop (*Catesthorp*), and Naunton (*Newenton*), and the advowson of the church or chapel of Sudeley. Right of Thomas Bonefaunt as those which the same Thomas and the other quer. had by gift of Ralph and Alesia. Remise and quitclaim, specifying Ralph's heirs, to the quer. and Thomas Bonefaunt's heirs. (Warranty, against George [Norwich] abbot of Westminster (*Westm'*) and his successors.) Cons. £1,000.

79/93/24

693. Three weeks [20 Oct.] from Michaelmas. Walter Hearne (*Herne*), John Twynyho, Thomas Arnold, and John Twysull (*Twesyll*) quer.; John Way (*Wey*) and Alice his wife, daughter and heir of Stephen Fisher (*Fyssher*) late of Tetbury (*Tetbury*), def. Two messuages, 12 a. of land, and 1 a. of pasture in Tetbury in the street called Church Street (*Churchestrete*) and Charlton (*Charlton*) by Tetbury. Right of Walter as those which Walter, John Twynyho, Thomas, and John Twissell had by gift of John Way and Alice. Remise and quitclaim, specifying Alice's heirs, to Walter, John Twynyho, Thomas, and John Twissell and Walter's heirs. (Warranty, against Richard [Hauley] abbot of Gloucester (*Glouc'*) and his successors.) Cons. 100 marks.

79/93/25

1469

694. One month [27 Oct.] from Michaelmas. Richard Harcourt (*Harecourt*) knight and Henry Spelman quer.; Thomas Conyers esquire and Isabel his wife def. One quarter of the manors of Tackley (*Takeley*), Whitehill (*Wyghthyll*), Salford (*Salford*), and Chastleton (*Chastelton*), one quarter of 60 messuages, 20 ploughlands, 100 a. of meadow, 300 a. of pasture, and 40 a. of wood in Tackley, Whitehill, Salford, Chastleton, and Woodperry (*Wodepery*), and the advowsons of the churches of Tackley, Salford, and Chastleton, OXON., one quarter of the manor of Seacourt (*Sekworth*) and one quarter of 100 a. of land, 30 a. of meadow, 100 a. of pasture and 6 a. of wood in Seacourt, BERKS., and one quarter of 4 messuages and 100 a. of land in Willicote (*Willicote*), GLOS. Right of Richard, as those which the same Richard and Henry had by gift of Thomas and Isabel. Remise and quitclaim, specifying Isabel's heirs, to Richard and Henry and Richard's heirs. (Warranty.) Cons. £300. *Labelled* Oxon', Berk', Glouc'.

294/74/71

695. Morrow [12 Nov.] of St. Martin. Walter Hearne (*Hurne*) quer.; John Butler (*Boteler*) and Juliana his wife def. A messuage, 100 a. of land, 20 a. of meadow, 40 a. of pasture, 5 a. of wood, and 4*s.* 2*d.* rent in Bagpath (*Bagpath*) and Wanswell (*Wanneswell*). Right of Walter by gift of John and Juliana. Remise and quitclaim, specifying Juliana's heirs, to Walter. (Warranty.) Cons. 100 marks.

79/94/27

1470

696. One week [20 Jan.] from Hilary. (Made two weeks from St. John the Baptist 8 Edward IV [8 July 1468].) Walter Osborne (*Oseborne*) clerk, George Houghton (*Houton*), Edward Basing (*Basyng*), George Ireland (*Irlond*), Richard Lee the younger, and John Mitchell (*Michell*) citizen and grocer of London (*London'*) quer.; Edmund Hungerford knight and Margery his wife def. The manors of Down Ampney (*Dounamney*) and the Wick (*Wyke*) and 24 messuages, 500 a. of land, 400 a. of meadow, 500 a. of pasture, and 100*s.* rent in Down Ampney and the Wick. Right of Richard, as those which Richard and the other quer. had by gift of Edmund and Margery. Remise and quitclaim, specifying Margery's heirs, to the quer. and Richard's heirs. (Warranty.) Cons. £600.

79/94/26

697. Morrow [3 Feb.] of the Purification. John Routhale and Nicholas Purpeys quer.; Thomas Limerick (*Lymeryk*) and Elizabeth his wife def. The manors of Stowell (*Stowell*) and Hampnett (*Hamptonet*) and the advowsons of the churches of Stowell and Hampnett. Right of Nicholas, as those which Nicholas and John had by gift of Thomas and Elizabeth. Remise and quitclaim, specifying Elizabeth's heirs, to John and Nicholas and Nicholas's heirs. (Warranty.) For this, grant and render to Thomas of the manor and advowson of Stowell. To hold during his life. Remainder to Elizabeth and her issue by Edmund Catesby her late husband. Contingent remainder to Nicholas's heirs. And grant and render to Thomas and Elizabeth of the manor and advowson of Hampnett. To hold to them and their heirs in tail. Successive contingent remainders to Elizabeth's heirs by Edmund Catesby, to her heirs in tail, and to Nicholas's heirs.

79/93/23

1470

698. One week [9 Feb.] from the Purification. John Markham knight, Robert Danby knight, Richard Bingham (*Byngham*) knight, and John Needham (*Nedeham*) knight quer.; John [Talbot] earl of Shrewsbury (*Salop'*) and Thomas [Talbot] Viscount Lisle (*Lisle*) def. The manors of Whitchurch (*Whytchurch*), Black Mere (*Blakemere*), Dodington (*Donyngton*), Wrockwardine (*Wrokwardyn*), Cheswardine (*Cheswardyn*), Sutton Maddock (*Suttonmadok*), Tasley (*Tasseley*), Alberbury (*Alburbury*), and Bitterley (*Bytterley*), SALOP., and the manors of Painswick (*Payneswyk*), Moreton Valence (*Moreton*), and Whaddon (*Whaddon*), GLOS. Right of Richard, as those which Richard, John Markham, Robert, and John Needham had by gift of the earl and the viscount. Remise and quitclaim, specifying the earl's heirs, to John Markham, Robert, Richard, and John Needham and Richard's heirs. Cons. £4,000. *Labelled* Salop', Glouc'.

294/74/74

[Robert Danby, Richard Bingham, and John Needham were all judges.]

49 Henry VI

1470

699. Morrow [3 Nov.] of All Souls. (Made 2 weeks from St. John the Baptist 10 Edward IV [8 July 1470].) William Bolaker and Philip Parker quer.; John Codrington (*Codrynton*) esquire and Alice his wife def. Ten messuages, 4 tofts, a dovecot, 5 gardens, 400 a. of land, 100 a. of meadow, and 120 a. of pasture in Codrington, Tormarton (*Tormerton*), Leighterton (*Leyghterton*), Hawkesbury (*Haukesbury*), Hawkesbury Upton (*Upton*), Hennel (*Hamell*), Old Sodbury (*Oldesodbury*), Lyegrove (*Lygrove*), Chipping Sodbury (*Chepyngsodbury*), and Dodington (*Dodyngton*), GLOS., and 3 messuages and a garden in Bristol (*Bristoll'*). Right of William, as those which William and Philip had by gift of John and Alice. Remise and quitclaim, specifying John's heirs, to William and Philip and William's heirs. (Warranty.) For this, grant back and render to John and Alice. To hold without impeachment of waste during their lives. Remainder as to 2 messuages, a toft, 240 a. of land, 30 a. of meadow, and 40 a. of pasture in Codrington and Tormarton to Humphrey Codrington esquire son of John and Alice and his heirs in tail, with successive contingent remainders to Humphrey's brother John Codrington and his heirs in tail, to John's brother Thomas Codrington and his heirs in tail, to the heirs in tail of John and Alice Codrington, to Margery Besilles (*Besiles*) late wife of Peter Besilles knight and her heirs in tail, and to Alice's heirs. Remainder as to 5 messuages, a toft, 5 gardens, 60 a. of land, 40 a. of meadow, and 40 a. of pasture in Old Sodbury, Chipping Sodbury, Lyegrove, and Dodington to the said John Codrington son of John and Alice and his heirs in tail, with successive contingent remainders to the younger John's brother Thomas and his heirs in tail, to Thomas's brother Humphrey and his heirs in tail, to the heirs in tail of John and Alice, to Margery Besilles and her heirs in tail, and to Alice's heirs. Remainder as to 6 messuages, 2 tofts, a garden, a dovecot, 100 a. of land, 30 a. of meadow, and 40 a. of pasture in Bristol, Leighterton, Hawkesbury, Upton, and Hennel to Thomas Codrington, with successive contingent remainders to Thomas's brother John and his heirs in tail, to John's brother Humphrey and his heirs in tail, to the heirs in tail of John and Alice Codrington, to Margery Besilles and her heirs in tail, and to Alice's heirs. *Labelled* Glouc', Bristoll'.

294/75/1

[The list of places in the remainder of the third part of the estate has 'and' before *Upton* rather than before *Hamell*, evidently in error.]

1470

700. Morrow [12 Nov.] of St. Martin. Robert Poyntz esquire quer.; William Stock (*Stokke*) and Isabel his wife def. A fishery called Chestle Pill (*Chesylpyll*) and 1 a. of meadow and 12 a. of pasture in Redwick (*Radewyke*) and Northwick (*Northwyke*) in the parish of Henbury (*Hembury in Salso Marisco*). Right of Robert by gift of William and Isabel. Remise and quitclaim, specifying William's heirs, to Robert. (Warranty.) Cons. 40 marks. *Labelled* Glouc'.

294/75/11

12 Edward IV

1472

701. One week [31 May] from Trinity. (Made three weeks [19 April] from Easter in the said year.) John Spore clerk and John Staunton quer.; David Lewes and Alice his wife def. Half of 6 messuages, 80 a. of land, 20 a. of meadow, 20 a. of pasture, and 4 a. of wood in Portbury (*Portbury*), Clapton in Gordano (*Clopton*), and Clevedon (*Clyvedon*), SOM., and half of 4 messuages and 5 gardens in Bristol (*Bristoll'*). Right of John Spore, as those which the same John and John Staunton had by gift of David and Alice. Remise and quitclaim, specifying Alice's heirs, to John and John. (Warranty.) Cons. £40. *Labelled* Somers', Bristoll'.

294/76/83

[Cf. *Som. Fines, 1399–1484*, p. 210.]

702. Morrow [3 Nov.] of All Souls. John Twynyho, Thomas Arnold, and Walter Hearne (*Herne*) quer.; John Charlton (*Charleton*) esquire and Joan his wife def. Three messuages, 1 a. of land called 'Hedacre', and 2 a. of pasture in Tetbury (*Tetbury*). Right of Walter, as those which Walter, John Twynyho, and Thomas had by gift of John Charlton and Joan. Remise and quitclaim, specifying Joan's heirs, to John Twynyho, Thomas, and Walter and Walter's heirs. (Warranty.) Cons. £40.

79/94/29

703. One week [18 Nov.] from St. Martin. Walter Hicks (*Hykkys*) quer.; Robert Topping (*Topyn*) and Alice his wife def. A messuage, a toft, and 5½ a. of land in Sudeley (*Seudeley*) and Greet (*Grete*). Right of Walter by gift of Robert and Alice. Remise and quitclaim, specifying Alice's heirs, to Walter. (Warranty.) Cons. 20 marks.

79/94/28

13 Edward IV

1473

704. One week [6 July] from St. John the Baptist. John Forster of Bristol (*Bristoll'*) merchant quer.; Richard Bull (*Bole*) and Margaret his wife, daughter and heir of Richard Cadel (*Cadull*), def. Twenty-four acres of land and 4 a. of meadow in Arlingham (*Erlyngham*). Right of John by gift of Richard and Margaret. Remise and quitclaim, specifying Margaret's heirs, to John. (Warranty against William [Farley] abbot of Gloucester and his successors.) Cons. £20.

79/94/30

1473

705. One week [6 July] from St. John the Baptist. William Stowford (*Stoweford*) quer.; Roger Kemes (*Kemys*) and Agnes his wife def. Eight messuages, 120 a. of land, 20 a. of meadow, 120 a. of pasture, and 20 a. of wood in Tadwick (*Tatewike*) and half of the manor of Tadwick, GLOS., and a messuage, 30 a. of land, 6 a. of meadow, 4 a. of pasture, and 5 a. of wood in Tadwick (*Atewike*) in the parish of Swainswick (*Swayneswike*), SOM. Right of William by gift of Roger and Agnes. Remise and quitclaim, specifying Agnes's heirs, to William. (Warranty against Thomas [Milling] abbot of Westminster (*Westm'*) and his successors.) Cons. 200 marks. *Labelled* Glouc', Somers'.

294/76/92

[Cf. *Som. Fines, 1399–1484*, p. 210. Tadwick was largely if not entirely in Swainswick parish and Somerset.]

1474

706. Morrow [3 Feb.] of the Purification. William Nottingham (*Notyngham*) quer.; Thomas Saunders (*Saundres*) and Joan his wife def. The manor of Trewsbury (*Trusebury*) and 100 a. of land, 40 a. of meadow, and 200 a. of pasture in Trewsbury. Right of William by gift of Thomas and Joan. Remise and quitclaim, specifying Joan's heirs, to William. (Warranty.) Cons. £60.

79/94/31

14 Edward IV

1474

707. Morrow [25 June] of St. John the Baptist. William [Waynflete] bishop of Winchester (*Wynton'*), John Denham (*Dynham*) knight, Thomas Billing (*Billynge*) knight, Thomas Tyrrel (*Tyrell*) knight, Richard Harcourt (*Harecourte*) knight, Robert Wingfield (*Wyngfeld*) knight, Thomas Stonor (*Stonore*) esquire, Richard Fowler (*Fouler*) esquire, Thomas Frowick (*Frowyk*) esquire, Thomas Danvers esquire, John Lenton (*Leynton*) esquire, William Huddefelde esquire, John Waleys esquire, and Benedict Fortescue (*Fortescu*) esquire quer.; Robert Corbet esquire and Leticia his wife def. The manor of Ebrington (*Eberton*). Right of Benedict, as that which Benedict and the other quer. had by gift of Robert and Leticia. Remise and quitclaim, specifying Leticia's heirs, to the quer. and Benedict's heirs. (Warranty.) Cons. £400.

79/94/32

708. One week [1 July] from St. John the Baptist. John Wicks (*Wykes*) esquire quer.; Edmund Berkeley son and heir of John Berkeley otherwise called John Planche def. The manors of Dursley (*Durseley*), Newington (*Newenton*), Bagpath (*Bagpath*), Dodington (*Dodyngton*), and Stanley. Right of John. Remise and quitclaim to him. (Warranty.) Cons. £100.

79/94/34

[Newington and Bagpath appear to be named as separate manors.]

1475

709. One week [20 Jan.] from Hilary. (Made one week from St. Martin in the said year [18 Nov. 1474].) John Farley quer.; Edward Grey de Lisle (*Lysle*) knight and Elizabeth

1475

his wife def. A messuage in the town of Gloucester (*Gloucestr'*). Right of John. Remise and quitclaim, specifying Elizabeth's heirs, to John. (Warranty.) Cons. £60.

79/94/35

710. One week [9 Feb.] from the Purification. Walter Hearne (*Herne*), John Twynyho (*Twyneho*), Thomas Arnold, and Henry Hammond (*Hamond*) quer.; William Batchcott (*Bachecote*) and Agnes his wife def. Eight messuages, 200 a. of land, 20 a. of meadow, and 30 a. of pasture in Charlton (*Charleton*) by Tetbury (*Tettebury*) and Tetbury. Right of Walter as those which Walter, John, Thomas, and Henry had by gift of William and Agnes. Remise and quitclaim, specifying Agnes's heirs, to Walter [etc.]. (Warranty against John [Sodbury] abbot of Cirencester (*Cirencestr'*) and his successors.) Cons. £100.

79/94/33

15 Edward IV

1475

711. One month [23 April] from Easter. Richard Swannington (*Swanynton*) chaplain quer.; Edward Grey knight and Elizabeth his wife, sister and heir of Thomas Talbot knight late Viscount Lisle (*Lysle*), def. The manors of Moreton Valence (*Mortonvalence*) and Whaddon (*Whaddon*). Right of Richard by gift of Edward and Elizabeth. Remise and quitclaim, specifying Elizabeth's heirs, to Richard. (Warranty against John [Eastney] abbot of Westminster (*Westm'*) and his successors.) Cons. £300.

79/94/37

712. Morrow [5 May] of Ascension. Humphrey Talbot knight quer.; Edward Grey knight and Elizabeth his wife def. The manor of Langdon (*Langdon*), DEVON, a messuage in Iron Acton (*Irunacton*), GLOS., and £5 6*s*. 8*d*. rent in Haygrove (*Heygrove*), Milverton (*Milverton*), and Bridgwater (*Bruggewater*), SOM. Grant and render to Humphrey. To hold to him and his heirs in tail male, of Edward and Elizabeth and Elizabeth's heirs, paying a rose a year at St. John the Baptist and doing service to the chief lords. (Warranty.) Contingent reversion to Edward and Elizabeth and Elizabeth's heirs. *Labelled* Devon', Glouc', Somers'.

294/76/100

[Cf. *Som. Fines, 1399–1484*, pp. 210–11.]

713. Two weeks [4 June] from Trinity. The king quer.; Richard Martin (*Martyn*) clerk def. The castles, towns, lordships, and manors of Monmouth (*Monemouthe*), Caldicot (*Caldecote*), White Castle (*White Castell*), Skenfrith (*Skenfryth*), Grosmont (*Grossemont*), Hadenock (*Hodenak*), Ebwy (*Ebbothe*), Ogmore (*Oggemore*), Glyncorrwg (*Glynngoure*), Kidwelly (*Kedwelly*), Iscoed (*Iscoidmorice*), *Quartercadogan*, Penrhyn (*Penryn*), Llanelli (*Llanelthe*), Is Cennen (*Iskennen*), *Mairdreff,* and Carnwyllion (*Carnwallan*), in Wales (*Wall'*) and in the marches of Wales adjacent to GLOS., 100 messuages, 2,000 a. of land, 500 a. of meadow, 2,000 a. of pasture, 600 a. of wood, and £200 rent in Monmouth, Caldicot, White Castle, Skenfrith, Grosmont, Hadenock, Ebwy, Ogmore, Glyncorrwg, Kidwelly, Iscoed*, Quartercadogan*, Penrhyn, Llanelli, Is Cennen, *Mairdreff,* and Carnwyllion, and the constitution and grant of the office of north and south bailiff of Ogmore and of Welsh bailiff of Ogmore, in the said marches in [*sic*] GLOS., the manors of

1475

Westcott (*Wescote*), Datchet (*Dachet*), and Thames Ditton (*Ditton*), 10 messuages, 200 a. of land, 40 a. of meadow, 100 a. of pasture, 40 a. of wood, and £10 rent in Westcott, Datchet, and Ditton, and the constitution and grant of the office of feodary and bailiff of the liberty of the duchy of Lancaster (*Lancastr'*), BUCKS., the constitution and grant of the office of feodary and bailiff of the liberty of the duchy of Lancaster, BEDS., the manors of Kirtlington (*Kyrtlyngton*), Deddington (*Dadyngton*), and Ascott-under-Wychwood (*Ascote*), 20 messuages, 300 a. of land, 40 a. of meadow, 200 a. of pasture, 100 a. of wood, and £10 rent in Kirtlington, Deddington, and Ascott, and the constitution and grant of the office of feodary and bailiff of the liberty of the duchy of Lancaster, OXON., the manor of Yarkhill (*Yerkhull*), 6 messuages, 100 a. of land, 20 a. of meadow, 20 a. of pasture, 10 a. of wood, and £4 rent in Yarkhill, and the constitution and grant of the office of feodary and bailiff of the liberty of the duchy of Lancaster, HEREFS., the manors of Wheatenhurst (*Whetenhurst*), Southam (*Southam*), Minsterworth (*Mynstreworth*), Tibberton (*Tyberton*), Rodley (*Rodley*), *Rye*, Etloe (*Ettelowe*), *Asporton* [Purton?], and Stratton (*Stratton*), and the constitution and grant of the office of feodary and bailiff of the liberty of the duchy of Lancaster, GLOS., the manor of Savoy (*Savoy*) and 6 messuages and 100*s.* rent in Savoy and the constitution and grant of the office of feodary and bailiff of the liberty of the duchy of Lancaster, MIDDX., the constitution and grant of the office of feodary and bailiff of the liberty of the duchy of Lancaster, KENT, and the constitution and grant of the office of feodary and bailiff of the liberty of the duchy of Lancaster, DEVON. Right of the king by Richard's gift. For this, grant back and render to Richard. To hold by the services and customs thence due for one month then next following. Remainder to Elizabeth the queen, Thomas [Bourgchier] cardinal priest of St. Ciriac, archbishop of Canterbury (*Cantuar'*), and primate of England (*Angl'*), William [Grey] bishop of Ely (*Elien'*), Richard [Beauchamp] bishop of Salisbury (*Sar'*), Robert [Stillington] bishop of Bath [and Wells] (*Bathon'*), Thomas [Rotherham] bishop of Lincoln (*Lincoln'*), John [Alcock] bishop of Rochester (*Roffen'*), Henry [Bourgchier] earl of Essex (*Essex'*), Anthony [Woodville] Earl Rivers (*Ryvers*), William Hastings (*Hastynges*) of Hastings knight, John Russell clerk, William Dudley clerk, John Gunthorp clerk, Thomas Burgh knight, Thomas Montgomery (*Mongomery*) knight, Thomas Vaughan knight, Richard Fowler knight, William Hussey (*Husee*), and their heirs. Made by the king's order. *Labelled* Glouc', Buk', Bed', Oxon', Hereford', Glouc' [*again*], Midd', Kanc', Devon'.

294/76/103

714. One week [6 Oct.] from Michaelmas. (Made two weeks [8 July] from St. John the Baptist the same year.) John More quer.; John Norton and Elena his wife def. Six acres of meadow and 4*s.* 8*d.* rent in Newland (*Newelond*). Right of John More by gift of John Norton and Elena. Remise and quitclaim, specifying Elena's heirs, to John More. (Warranty.) Cons. 20 marks.

79/94/36

715. Three weeks [20 Oct.] from Michaelmas. John Cantrell (*Chaunterell*) quer.; Robert Trevarrick (*Trevaroke*) and Joan his wife def. A messuage and a garden in Gloucester (*Gloucestria*). Right of John by gift of Robert and Joan. Remise and quitclaim, specifying Joan's heirs, to John. (Warranty.) Cons. 40 marks.

79/94/38

16 Edward IV

1476

716. Two weeks [28 April] from Easter. (Made one week from the Purification 15 Edward IV [9 Feb. 1476].) William Hastings (*Hastynges*) of Hastings knight, John Morton clerk, Thomas Urswick (*Urswyk*) knight, chief baron of the Exchequer, John Catesby king's serjeant at law, John Baker clerk, Humphrey Starky, Thomas Frowick (*Frowyk*), Thomas Davers, William Davers, and Richard Burton quer.; Matilda who was wife of Gervase Clifton (*Clyfton*) knight, cousin and one of the heirs of Ralph Cromwell late of Cromwell (*Cromwell*) knight, and Robert Radcliffe (*Radclyff*) esquire and Joan his wife, cousin and the other of the heirs of the said Ralph, def. The manor of Quinton (*Queynton*). Right of Thomas Frowick. Remise and quitclaim, specifying Matilda's and Joan's heirs, to the quer. and Thomas Frowick's heirs. (Warranty against John [Eastney] abbot of St. Peter's, Westminster (*Westm'*) and his successors.) Cons. £300.

79/94/39

717. One month [12 May] from Easter. Richard Croft knight quer.; Ralph Seymour (*Seymore*) esquire and Isabel his wife def. The manors of Marsh Court (*le Marshe*), Hill Court (*Hulcourt*), and Muchgros (*Muchegros*) and 20 messuages, 2 tofts, 315 a. of land, 76 a. of meadow, 10 a. of pasture, 4 a. of wood, and 53*s.* 10*d.* rent in Eldersfield (*Eldisfeld*), Redmarley d'Abitot (*Ridmarley*), Grimes (*Grymers*), Longdon (*Longdon*), and Chaddesley Corbett (*Chaddesley*), WORCS.; and 3 messuages, 2 ploughlands, 24 a. of meadow, 10 a. of pasture, and 1 a. of wood in Tredington (*Tredynton*) and Tirley (*Trynley*), GLOS. Right of Richard by gift of Ralph and Isabel. Remise and quitclaim, specifying Isabel's heirs, to Richard. (Warranty.) Cons. 500 marks. *Labelled* Wygorn', Glouc'.

294/76/109

718. Two weeks [23 June] from Trinity. (Made the morrow of St. John the Baptist 15 Edward IV [25 June 1475].) Robert Keen (*Kynne*) quer.; Maurice Leny def. Three messuages, a dovecot, 200 a. of land, 20 a. of meadow, 100 a. of pasture, and 10 a. of wood in St. Chloe (*Seyntclere*) in the parish of Minchinhampton (*Mynchynhampton*) held by James Prower and Eleanor his wife, who was wife of Thomas Leny, for term of Eleanor's life. Right of Robert. Grant to him of the reversion. (Warranty against John [Eastney] abbot of Westminster (*Westm'*) and his successors.) Cons. £100.

79/94/40

17 Edward IV

1477

719. One week [1 July] from St. John the Baptist. William Nottingham (*Notyngham*) quer.; Alexander Stanter esquire and Margaret his wife def. A messuage, a dovecot, 3 ploughlands, and 10 a. of meadow in Coates (*Cotes*), Cirencester (*Cirencestr'*), and South Cerney (*South Serney*). Right of William by gift of Alexander and Margaret. Remise and quitclaim, specifying Margaret's heirs, to William. (Warranty.) Cons. 100 marks.

79/94/42

1477

720. One week [18 Nov.] from St. Martin. Thomas Norton, John Arfos clerk, and Thomas Hexton quer.; William Banner (*Bannar*) and Joan his wife def. Half of 4 messuages, 60 a. of land, 40 a. of meadow, 20 a. of pasture, and 4 a. of wood in Portbury (*Portbury*), Clapton in Gordano (*Clopton*), and Clevedon (*Clyvedon*), SOM., and 3 messuages, a toft, 2 gardens, and half of 4 messuages and 5 gardens in Bristol (*Bristoll'*). Right of John, as those which John, Thomas, and Thomas had by gift of William and Joan. Remise and quitclaim, specifying Joan's heirs, to Thomas, John, and Thomas and John's heirs. (Warranty.) Cons. £100. *Labelled* Somers', Bristoll'.

294/76/119

[Cf. *Som. Fines, 1399–1484*, p. 212.]

1478

721. Morrow [3 Feb.] of the Purification. Robert Coffey (*Coffe*) quer.; John Deerhurst (*Derehurst*) def. A messuage in Gloucester (*Gloucestr'*). Right of Robert by John's gift. Remise and quitclaim to Robert. (Warranty against John [Eastney] abbot of St. Peter's, Westminster (*Westm'*), and his successors.) Cons. £20.

79/94/41

18 Edward IV

1478

722. One month [19 April] from Easter. Robert Strange (*Straunge*) merchant of the town of Bristol (*Bristoll'*) and Richard Forster esquire quer.; Elizabeth Cannings (*Canynges*) widow and Thomas Cannings esquire def. The manor of Moundscourt (*Monescourte*) and a messuage, 200 a. of land, 24 a. of meadow, 200 a. of pasture, and 8 a. of wood in Siston (*Syston*). Right of Robert, as those which Robert and Richard had by gift of Elizabeth and Thomas. Remise and quitclaim, specifying Elizabeth's heirs, to Robert and Richard and Robert's heirs. (Warranty.) Cons. £100.

79/94/44

723. Morrow [3 Nov.] of All Souls. Henry Vaughan (*Vaghan*), John Bailly (*Baylly*), John Bridgeman (*Briggeman*) clerk, William Bridgeman clerk, and Roger Sutton clerk quer.; Thomas Cannings (*Canynges*) esquire, son and heir of William Cannings late of Bristol (*Bristoll'*) 'gentilman' and of Elizabeth his wife, def. Two messuages, 2 gardens, 20 a. of land, and 2½ a. of meadow in Barton Regis (*Bartona domini regis*) by Bristol. Right of Henry, as those which Henry, John Bailly, John Bridgeman, William, and Roger had by gift of Thomas. Remise and quitclaim to Henry, John, John, William, and Roger and Henry's heirs. (Warranty.) Cons. £40.

79/94/43

724. Morrow [3 Nov.] of All Souls. Walter Hicks (*Hykkys*) quer.; Nicholas Baker otherwise called Nicholas Barber (*Barbour*) of Winchcombe (*Wynchecombe*) and Elena his wife def. A toft, 40 a. of land, 1 a. of meadow, and 6 a. of wood in Gretton (*Gretton*). Right of Walter by gift of Nicholas and Elena. Remise and quitclaim, specifying Elena's heirs, to Walter. Cons. 40 marks.

79/94/46

1478

725. Morrow [12 Nov.] of St. Martin. Thomas Berkeley esquire, Maurice King (*Kynge*), and John atte Wood (*Wode*) quer.; Walter Skey (*Skaye*) esquire def. The manor of Pitt Court (*Pytcourt*) and half of the manor of Rangeworthy (*Ryngeworth*) held by Christopher Comberford and Joan his wife for term of Joan's life. Right of Maurice. Grant of the reversion, of Walter's inheritance, to Thomas, Maurice, and John and Maurice's heirs. (Warranty.) Cons. £200.

79/94/45

19 Edward IV

1479

726. Morrow [12 Nov.] of St. Martin. Richard Gale quer.; Margaret Whitehorn widow def. Half of a messuage in Northleach (*Northlatche*). Right of Richard by Margaret's gift. Remise and quitclaim to Richard. (Warranty.) Cons. 20 marks.

79/94/47

20 Edward IV

1480

727. One month [30 April] from Easter. John Reynold (*Raynold*) of Purton (*Peryton*) and John Tailor (*Taillour*) of Lydney (*Lyddeney*) quer.; John Barre knight and Joan his wife def. Five messuages, 2 tofts, a water-mill, 80 a. of land, 1 a. of meadow, and 4*d.* rent in Lydney, Purton, and Blakeney (*Blakeney*). Right of John Reynold, as those which the same John and John Tailor had by gift of John Barre and Joan. Remise and quitclaim, specifying Joan's heirs, to John Reynold and John Tailor and John Reynold's heirs. (Warranty against William [Farley] abbot of St. Peter's, Gloucester (*Gloucestr'*), and his successors.) For this, John Reynold and John Tailor granted that they would pay to John and Joan during Joan's life 37*s.* 8*d.* a year, at Michaelmas and the Annunciation, with right of distraint for non-payment.

79/94/52

728. One month [30 April] from Easter. Thomas Newman (*Neweman*) of Lydney (*Lyddeney*) 'bocher' and John Hitchens (*Hychons*) quer.; John Barre knight and Joan his wife def. Two messuages, 3 tofts, 7 a. of land, and 1 a. of meadow in Lydney and Nass (*Nasse*). Right of Thomas, as those which Thomas and John Hitchens had by gift of John Barre and Joan. Remise and quitclaim, specifying Joan's heirs, to Thomas and John Hitchens and Thomas's heirs. (Warranty against William [Farley] abbot of St. Peter's, Gloucester (*Gloucestr'*), and his successors.) For this, Thomas and John Hitchens granted that they would pay to John and Joan during Joan's life 12*s.* 5*d.* a year, at Michaelmas and the Annunciation, with right of distraint for non-payment.

79/94/53

729. One week [1 July] from St. John the Baptist. William Nottingham (*Notyngham*) knight quer.; Thomas Whittington (*Whityngton*) and Margaret his wife def. Half of the manor of Sapperton (*Saperton*) and also 17 messuages, 17 yardlands and 4½ a. of land, 20 a. of meadow, 60 a. of pasture, and 500 a. of wood in Sapperton and Hailey (*Hayle*). Right of William by gift of Thomas and Margaret. Remise and quitclaim, specifying Margaret's heirs. to William. (Warranty against William [Farley] abbot of St. Peter's, Gloucester (*Gloucestr'*), and his successors.) Cons. 200 marks.

79/94/54

1480

730. One month [27 Oct.] from Michaelmas. William Lander (*Launder*) and Alice his wife quer.; Richard Morley (*Moreley*) and Joan his wife def. A messuage in Tewkesbury (*Teukesbury*). Right of William, as that which William and Alice had by gift of Richard and Joan. Remise and quitclaim, specifying Joan's heirs, to William and Alice and William's heirs. (Warranty.) Cons. £20.

79/94/56

1481

731. Morrow [3 Feb.] of the Purification. Thomas Wall (*Walle*) quer.; John Barre knight and Joan his wife def. A messuage and 100 a. of land in Yorkley (*Yarkeley*) in the parish of Newland (*Newelond*). Right of Thomas by gift of John and Joan. Remise and quitclaim, specifying Joan's heirs, to Thomas. (Warranty against William [Farley] abbot of St. Peter's, Gloucester (*Gloucestr'*), and his successors.) For this, Thomas granted that he would pay to John and Joan during Joan's life 10s. a year, at the Annunciation and Michaelmas, with right of distraint for non-payment.

79/94/48

732. Morrow [3 Feb.] of the Purification. Thomas Keigwin (*Kegewyn*) quer.; John Barre knight and Joan his wife def. A messuage, 4 tofts, and 201 a. of land in Lydney (*Lyddeney*) and in Gorstyfield (*Gorstfeld*) and Badhamsfield (*Badamesfeld*) in the parish of Newland (*Newelond*). Right of Thomas by gift of John and Joan. Remise and quitclaim, specifying Joan's heirs, to Thomas. (Warranty against William [Farley] abbot of St. Peter's, Gloucester (*Gloucestr'*), and his successors.) For this, Thomas granted that he would pay to John and Joan during Joan's life 35s. 4d. a year, at the Annunciation and Michaelmas, with right of distraint for non-payment.

79/94/49

733. Morrow [3 Feb.] of the Purification. Thomas Buck (*Bukke*) quer.; John Barre knight and Joan his wife def. A messuage, a toft, a garden, 16½ a. of land, and 18s. 5d. rent in Lydney (*Lyddeney*) and Aylburton (*Ayleberton*). Right of Thomas by gift of John and Joan. Remise and quitclaim, specifying Joan's heirs, to Thomas. (Warranty against William [Farley] abbot of St. Peter's, Gloucester (*Gloucestr'*), and his successors. For this, Thomas granted that he would pay to John and Joan during Joan's life 33s. 3d. a year, at the Annunciation and Michaelmas, with right of distraint for non-payment.

79/94/50

734. Morrow [3 Feb.] of the Purification. William Naylor (*Nayler*) chaplain, Richard Hammond (*Hamond*), and William Downing (*Dounyng*) quer.; John Barre knight and Joan his wife def. A messuage, a garden, a water-mill, and 83 a. of pasture in Lydney (*Lyddeney*) and Newerne (*Newarne*) and in Whitecroft (*Whetecrofte*) in the parish of Newland (*Newelond*). Right of William Naylor, as those which the same William, Richard, and William Downing had by gift of John and Joan. Remise and quitclaim, specifying Joan's heirs, to William, Richard, and William and William Naylor's heirs. (Warranty against William [Farley] abbot of St. Peter's, Gloucester (*Gloucestr'*), and his successors.) For this, William Naylor, Richard, and William Downing granted that they

1481

would pay to John and Joan during Joan's life 37*s.* 6*d.* a year at the Annunciation and Michaelmas, with right of distraint for non-payment.

79/94/51

735. One week [9 Feb.] from the Purification. Thomas Limerick (*Lymeryk*), Richard Greville (*Grevyle*), John de Arle (*Alre*), and William Greville quer.; Ralph Wolsley and Margaret his wife def. The manor of Upper Lemington (*Lemynton*) and 2 messuages, 6 yardlands, 6 a. of meadow, 200 a. of pasture, and 100 a. of heath in Lemington. Right of Richard, as those which Richard, Thomas, John, and William had by gift of Ralph and Margaret. Remise and quitclaim, specifying Margaret's heirs, to Thomas, Richard, John, and William and Richard's heirs. (Warranty.) Cons. 100 marks.

79/94/55

21 Edward IV

1481

736. Three weeks [20 Oct.] from Michaelmas. William Nottingham (*Notyngham*) knight and Henry Tracy esquire quer.; John Lisle (*Lysle*) esqire and Margery his wife def. The manor of Great Rissington (*Broderysyngdon*), the advowson of the church of Great Rissington, and 6 messuages, 4 ploughlands, 40 a. of meadow, 100 a. of pasture, and 40*s.* rent in Great Rissington and Notgrove (*Nuttegrove*). Right of William, as those which William and Henry had by gift of John and Margery. Remise and quitclaim, specifying John's heirs, to William and Henry and William's heirs. (Warranty.) Cons. 300 marks.

79/94/59

737. One month [27 Oct.] from Michaelmas. John Longford (*Langforde*) and Nicholas Saint (*Saunt*) quer.; John Bodefaunt esquire and Joan his wife def. The manor of Stanshawe (*Stanshawe*). Right of John Longford. Remise and quitclaim, specifying Joan's heirs, to John Longford, Nicholas Saint, and John Longford's heirs. (Warranty.) Cons. £40.

79/94/57

738. Morrow [3 Nov.] of All Souls. Richard Beale (*Bele*) quer.; John Purlewent and Anne his wife def. A messuage, 3 yardlands, 10 a. of meadow, and 20 a. of pasture in Guiting Power (*Nethergytyng*). Right of Richard by gift of John and Anne. Remise and quitclaim, specifying Anne's heirs, to Richard. (Warranty.) Cons. £20.

79/94/60

739. Morrow [12 Nov.] of St. Martin. John Twynyho and John Walsh (*Walshe*) quer.; Thomas Withyford (*Withiford*) and Margaret his wife def. Twelve messuages, 300 a. of land, 40 a. of meadow, 100 a. of pasture, 20 a. of wood, and 20*s.* rent in Hambrook (*Hambroke*), Olveston (*Olveston*), and Tockington (*Tokyngton*). Right of John Walsh, as those which the same John and John Twynyho had by gift of Thomas and Margaret. Remise and quitclaim, specifying Margaret's heirs, to John Twynyho and John Walsh and John Walsh's heirs. (Warranty against John [Eastney] abbot of St. Peter's, Westminster (*Westm'*), and his successors.) Cons. 200 marks.

79/94/58

1482

740. Two weeks [27 Jan.] from Hilary. Christopher Twynyho clerk, John Twynyho of Cirencester (*Cirencestr'*) esquire, William Twynyho of Shipton Solers (*Shipton Solers*) esquire, John Tame of Fairford (*Fayreford*) esquire, Edmund Langley (*Langeley*) of Upper Siddington (*Sudyngton Langeley*) esquire, Thomas Delalynde of *Clencheston* [Aston Clinton *or* Aston on Clun?] esquire, John Walsh (*Walshe*) of Olveston (*Olveston*) esquire, William Lovel (*Lovell*) of *Raffeston* [Ravenstone?], and Thomas Warner of Cirencester esquire quer.; Walter Denis (*Denys*) esquire and Agnes his wife def. The manor of North Cheriton (*Northcheryton*) and the advowson of the free chapel of South Cheriton (*Southcheryton*), SOM., the manor of Siston (*Siston*) and the advowson of the church of Siston, GLOS., and half of the manor of Litton Cheney (*Lytton*) and the advowson of the church of Litton, DORSET. Right of John Twynyho, as those which the same John and the other quer. had by gift of Walter and Agnes. Remise and quitclaim, specifying Agnes's heirs, to the quer. and John Twynyho's heirs. (Warranty against Richard [Clive] abbot of the monastery of St. Mary, Cirencester (*Cirencestr'*), and his successors.) Cons. £600. *Labelled* Somers', Glouc', Dors'.

294/77/137

[Cf. *Dorset Fines, 1327–1485*, pp. 399–400; *Som. Fines, 1399–1484*, pp. 212–13.]

1 Edward V

1483

741. Two weeks [8 June] from Trinity. William Cole quer.; Thomas Bisley (*Bysseley*) 'gentilman', John Winstone (*Wynston*) the younger and Margery his wife, and Thomas Payn (*Payne*) and Margaret his wife def. Five messuages and 5 gardens in Gloucester (*Gloucestr'*). Right of William by gift of Thomas, John and Margery, and Thomas and Margaret. Remise and quitclaim, specifying Margery's and Margaret's heirs, to William. (Warranty.) Cons. 40 marks. *Labelled* Glouc'.

294/78/3

1 Richard III

1483

742. Two weeks [13 Oct.] from Michaelmas. John Elliotts (*Eliottis*) quer.; Thomas Payn (*Payne*) and Margaret his wife and John Winstone (*Wynston*) and Margery his wife def. A messuage and a garden in Gloucester (*Gloucestr'*). Right of John Elliotts by gift of Thomas and Margaret and John Winstone and Margery. Remise and quitclaim, specifying Margaret's and Margery's heirs, to John Elliotts. (Warranty.) Cons. £20.

79/95/2

1484

743. Morrow [28 May] of Ascension. William Midwinter (*Midwynter*) quer.; John Purlewent (*Purlewyn*) and Anne his wife, daughter and heir of John Dodding (*Dodyng*), def. Two messuages and 2 gardens in Northleach (*Northlacche*). Right of William by gift of John and Anne. Remise and quitclaim, specifying Anne's heirs, to William. (Warranty.) Cons. £20.

79/95/3

1484

744. One week [20 June] from Trinity. (Made the morrow [3 Feb.] of the Purification in the said year.) John Twynyho (*Twynyhoo*) and John Underhill (*Underhull*) quer.; John Clinton (*Clynton*) Lord Clinton and Say, John Smith (*Smyth*) clerk, and William Warbleton (*Warbilton*) def. A toft, 1 yardland and 10 a. of land, 2 a. of pasture, and 11*s*. 11*d*. rent in Naunton (*Newenton*), and Temple Guiting (*Overgytyng*). Right of John Underhill. Remise and quitclaim, specifying John Clinton's heirs, to John Twynyho and John Underhill and John Underhill's heirs. (Warranty.) Cons. £40.

79/95/1

2 Richard III

1485

745. Three weeks [24 April] from Easter. Agnes Bridges (*Brugges*) widow, Walter Brockhampton (*Brokhampton*), Richard Russell, John Hartland (*Hertlond*) the elder, William Cole, and John Cole quer.; Walter Berrow (*Berwe*) and Elizabeth his wife def. A messuage, 3 shops, a dovecot, and a garden in Gloucester (*Gloucestr'*). Right of Agnes, as those which Agnes and the other quer. had by gift of Walter Berrow and Elizabeth. Remise and quitclaim, specifying Elizabeth's heirs, to the quer. and Agnes's heirs. (Warranty against William [Farley] abbot of St. Peter's, Gloucester, and his successors.) Cons. £40. *Labelled* Villa Glouc'.

79/95/4

1 Henry VII

1486

746. One week [9 Feb.] from the Purification. John Mason (*Mayson*) quer.; Robert Hill and Mary his wife def. A messuage, a toft, 40 a. of land, 8 a. of meadow, 10 a. of pasture, and 1 a. of wood in Painswick (*Payneswike*), Bisley (*Bysseley*), and Stroud (*Strode*). Right of John by gift of Robert and Mary. Remise and quitclaim, specifying Mary's heirs, to John. (Warranty.) Cons. £30.

79/96/1

747. Two weeks [9 April] from Easter. Henry Weston the elder quer.; John Dibden (*Dipdene*) and Elizabeth his wife who was wife of William Cannings (*Canynges*) esquire def. A garden and annual rent of 13*s*. 4*d*. in Bristol (*Bristoll'*). Right of Henry. Remise and quitclaim, specifying Elizabeth's heirs, to him. (Warranty.) Cons. 20 marks. *Labelled* Bristoll'.

294/82/1

748. Three weeks [16 April] from Easter. John Walsh (*Walshe*) esquire quer.; Richard Forster esquire and Thomas Morton and Dorothy his wife def. The manor of Little Sodbury (*Parva Sobbury*), the advowson of the church of St. Aldhelm of Little Sodbury, and 600 a. of land, 100 a. of meadow, 500 a. of pasture, and 200 a. of wood in Little Sodbury, Old Sodbury (*Vetus Sobbury*), Chipping Sodbury (*Chepyng Sobbury*), Serridge (*Shirigge*), Hamfield (*Hamefeld*), Pucklechurch (*Pokilchirche*), and Dursley (*Durisley*). Right of John by gift of Richard and Thomas and Dorothy. Remise and quitclaim, specifying Richard's and Dorothy's heirs, to John. (Warranty, specifying Dorothy's but not Richard's heirs, against John [Eastney] abbot of St. Peter's, Westminster (*Westm'*) and his successors.) Cons. 200 marks.

79/96/2

2 Henry VII

1487

749. Two weeks [13 Oct.] from Michaelmas. Thomas Hexton quer.; John Dibden (*Dipdene*) and Elizabeth his wife who was wife of William Cannings (*Canynges*) esquire def. A garden and 1 a. of land in Bristol (*Bristoll'*). Right of Thomas. Remise and quitclaim, specifying Elizabeth's heirs, to him. (Warranty.) Cons. £10. *Labelled* Bristoll'.

294/82/2

3 Henry VII

1488

750. Two weeks [27 Jan.] from Hilary. The king quer.; Anne [Neville] countess of Warwick (*Warr'*) def. The castle and manor of Warwick (*Warrewyk*), the manors of Sutton under Brailes (*Sutton*), Brailes (*Brayles*), Claverdon (*Claverdon*), Tanworth (*Tonworth*), Berkswell (*Berkeswell*), Lighthorne (*Lyghthorn*), Barford (*Bereford*), and Ladbrook (*Ludbrokes*) in Tanworth, and 14 messuages, 2 ploughlands and 200 a. of land, 20 a. of meadow, 100 a. of pasture, 10 a. of wood, and £20 rent in Warwick, Myton (*Mytton*), Whitley (*Whitloge*), Guy's Cliffe (*Gybbeclyffe*), Berkswell, and Stratford-upon-Avon (*Stretford super Aven*), WARWS., the manors of Hanslope (*Hampslap*), Quarrendon (*Querndon*), Olney (*Olney*), and Marlow (*Marlawe*), the hundred of Ashridge (*Assherigge*), £6 rent in Milton Keynes (*Multon*), a chantry in the church of Castle Thorpe (*Castelthorp*), and the office of chamberlain and usher in the king's Exchequer, BUCKS., the manors of Walsall (*Walshale*), Pattingham (*Patyngham*), Perry Barr (*Purybarre*), and Drayton Bassett (*Drayton Basset*) and 15 messuages, 3 tofts, 100 a. of land, 20 a. of meadow, 10 a. of pasture, 20 a. of wood, and 10*s*. rent in Walsall and Pattingham, STAFFS., the manor of Kirtling (*Kirtelyng*) and 30 messuages, 7 tofts, 3 ploughlands and 200 a. of land, 20 a. of meadow, 100 a. of pasture, 100 a. of wood, and £10 rent in Kirtling and Longstanton (*Longe Staunton*), CAMBS., the manors of Walthamstow Tony (*Waltamstowe Tony*) and Walthamstow Francis (*Fraunceys*), one quarter of a knight's fee in Westbarrow Hall (*Barowe*), and the advowson of one quarter of the churches of Great Stambridge (*Stanbrigge*) and North Fambridge (*Flanbrigge*), ESSEX, the manor of Flamstead (*Flamsted*) and the advowson of the church of Flamstead, HERTS., the advowson of the chantry called 'Beauchamp chaunterie' in St. Paul's church in the city of London (*London'*), the castles, lordships, and manors of Painscastle (*Maudescastell*), Elfael (*Elvell*), Snodhill (*Snodhull*), Aberedw (*Abredough*), Kilvey (*Kylvey*), and Fownhope (*Fawnhope*) in the marches of Wales adjoining Herefs. and 4,000 a. of land and 1,000 a. of wood in Elfael, Snodhill, Aberedw, Kilvey, and Fownhope, HEREFS., the manors of Sherston (*Sherston*), Broad Town (*Brodton*), Cherhill (*Chiriell*), and Hinton (*Henton*), the keepership of the the forest of Woodborough (*Wodebere*), the advowson of the church of Woodborough (*Wodebergh*), and half a knight's fee in Woodborough, WILTS., the office of weighing and one quarter of 2 messuages in the town of Southampton (*Suthampton*), [HANTS.], the manors of Barrowden (*Beroughdon*) and Greetham (*Gretham*), the hundred of Wrandike (*Wrangdyk*), 6 messuages, 20 a. of land, 12 a. of meadow, and 26s. rent in Preston (*Preston*) and Uppingham (*Uppyngham*), and one quarter of the manors of Preston and Uppingham, RUTLAND, the hundred of South Tawton (*Southtauton*), the manor of South Tawton, and the borough or manor of Zeal (*Sele*), DEVON, the manors of Penzance

1488

(*Pensans*), Carnanton (*Carnaunton*), Balston (*Blyston*), and Helston (*Helston Tony*) and 20 messuages, 2 tofts, a mill, 60 ferlings of land, 12 a. of meadow, 300 a. of pasture, and 100 a. of wood in Treleigh Wells (*Treleigh Woles*), Treleigh Worthy (*Treleigh Wartha*), Redruth (*Redrewith*), and Lanjeth (*Langwyth*), CORNW., the islands or lordships of Jersey (*Jernesey*) and Guernsey (*Guernesey*) and the castles and manors of Gorey (*Gurrey*), Cornet (*Cornet*), Sark (*Serk*), Herm (*Erme*), and Alderney (*Aureney*) in the said islands, DORSET, the manors of Moulton (*Multon*), Long Buckby (*Bukby*), Potterspury (*Potterspury*), Cosgrove (*Covesgrave*), and Puxley (*Pokesle*), the advowson of the church of Potterspury, and 5 knights' fees and 10 messuages, 100 a. of land, 20 a. of meadow, 100 a. of pasture, and 40 a. of wood in Potterspury, Cosgrove, and Puxley, NORTHANTS., the lordships and manors of Tewkesbury (*Teukesbury*), Tredington (*Tredyngton*), Pamington (*Pamyngton*), Fiddington (*Fydyngton*), Northway (*Northey*), Mythe (*Muth*), Stoke Orchard (*Stokearcher*), Chipping Sodbury (*Sobbury*), Fairford (*Fayreford*) and Wickwar (*Wykewarre*), the castle of St. Briavels (*Seyntbravell*), the manors of St. Briavels (*Seyntbrevell*), Kemerton (*Kenmerton*), and Barton Regis (*Barton*) by Bristol (*Bristoll'*), 20,000 a. of land, 100 a. of meadow, 100 a. of pasture, and 400 a. of wood in St. Briavels, Barton Regis, Chedworth (*Chedworth*), and Lydney (*Lydney*), one quarter of the manors of Chedworth and Lydney, and the advowson of one quarter of the church of Notgrove (*Natgrave*), GLOS., the manors of Shipton-under-Wychwood (*Shipton*), Burford (*Burford*), and Langley (*Langeley*) and the hundred of Chadlington (*Chadlyngton*), OXON.; the manor of Caversham (*Taversham*), BERKS.; the manors of Saham Toney (*Saham*), Necton (*Nekton*), and Little Cressingham (*Parva Crassyngtham*) and the hundreds of Wayland (*Wayland*) and Grimshaw (*Grymmeshogh*), NORF., the castle and shrievalty of Worcester (*Wygorn'*) with its hundreds and members, the castle of Elmley Castle (*Elmeley Castell*), the lordships and manors of Kersoe (*Crideshoo*), Wadborough (*Wadbarough*), Stoulton (*Stoulton*), Abberley (*Abbottesley*), Syntley (*Cynteley*), Shrawley (*Shraveley*), Elmley Lovett (*Elmeleylovet*), Grafton Flyford (*Grafton Flevord*), Beoley (*Beoley*), Salwarpe (*Salwarp*), Hill Court (*Hullesplace*), Droitwich (*Wyth*), Hadzor (*Haddesore*), Perry (*Pury*) by Worcester, Wick Piddle (*Wykepedull*), Wyre Piddle (*Wyrepedull*), and Earl's Croome (*Symondescrombe*), 35 messuages, 14 saltwater pans (*salinis aque salse*), 37 lead vats (*plumbar' buller'*) of salt water, a leaden brine pit (*puteo plumbar'*), and vats (*buller'*) of salt water called 'Sherevesputte', a mill called 'Frogmulle' by Worcester castle, 1 ploughland called Hill Court (*Hullaplace*), and £23 6s. 8d. rent in Droitwich (*Wyche*), Upwich (*Upwyche*), Worcester, Whittington (*Whityngton*), and Grafton Flyford, half of the manors of Fickenappletree (*Thikenappultre*) and Perry (*Pyrye*) by Worcester, half of a knight's fee in Redmarley d'Abitot (*Rodmerlay*), and the advowsons of the churches of Abberley, Shrawley, Ribbesford (*Rybbesford*), Grafton Flyford, Elmley Lovett, and Salwarpe, WORCS. Grant and render to the king. To hold to him and his heirs in tail male. (Warranty against John [Eastney] abbot of St. Peter's, Westminster (*Westm'*), and his successors.) Contingent reversion to the countess. *Labelled* Warr', Buk;, Staff', Cantebr', Essex', Hertf', London', Heref', Wiltes', Sutht', Rotel', Devon', Cornub', Dors', Norht', Glouc', Oxon', Berk', Norff', Wygorn'. [*Worn and stained.*]

294/79/7

[Cf. *Warws. Fines, 1345–1509*, pp. 200–2, no. 2729; *Wilts. Fines, 1377–1509*, pp. 161–2, no. 716. Cf. also above, no. 676.]

1488

751. Morrow [3 Feb.] of the Purification. William [de Berkeley] earl marshal and earl of Nottingham (*Notyngham*) quer.; John Fisher (*Fyssher*) serjeant at law, Edward Willoughby esquire, and Robert Logge clerk def. The castle and manor of Berkeley (*Berkeley*) and the manors of Ham (*Hamme*) and Appleridge (*Appulrigge*). Right of John, as those which John, Edward, and Robert had by the earl's gift. For this, grant back and render to the earl. To hold to him and his heirs in tail. Successive contingent remainders to the king and his heirs in tail male and to the earl's heirs.

79/96/3

752. Morrow [3 Feb.] of the Purification. William [de Berkeley] earl marshal and earl of Nottingham (*Notyngham*) quer.; Edward Willoughby (*Wylloughby*) esquire and Robert Logge clerk def. The manor of Coaley (*Coweley*). Right of Edward, as that which Edward and Robert had by the earl's gift. For this, grant back and render to the earl. To hold to him and his heirs in tail. Successive contingent remainders to the king and his heirs in tail male and to the earl's heirs.

79/96/4

753. Morrow [3 Feb.] of the Purification. William [de Berkeley] earl marshal and earl of Nottingham (*Notyngham*), James [Goldwell] bishop of Norwich (*Norwicen'*), Christopher Willoughby knight, Robert Willoughby knight, Edward Willoughby esquire, Richard Willoughby esquire quer.; John Fisher (*Fyssher*) serjeant at law and Robert Logge clerk def. The manors of Slimbridge (*Slymbrigge*) and Hurst (*Hurst*). Right of John, as those which John and Robert Logge had by gift of the earl and the other quer. For this, grant back and render to the quer. To hold to them and the earl's heirs in tail. Successive contingent remainders to the king and his heirs in tail male and to the earl's heirs. [*Stained.*]

79/96/5

754. Morrow [3 Feb.] of the Purification. William [de Berkeley] earl marshal and earl of Nottingham (*Notyngham*) and Anne his wife, Thomas [Rotherham] archbishop of York (*Ebor'*), George FitzHugh dean of the cathedral church of Lincoln (*Lincoln'*), and Thomas Fenys esquire quer.; John Fisher (*Fyssher*) serjeant at law, Edward Willoughby esquire, and Robert Logge clerk def. The manors of Alkington (*Alkyngton*), Cam (*Camme*), and Hinton (*Hynton*), GLOS., and the manor of Portbury (*Portbury*), SOM. Right of John, as those which John, Edward, and Robert had by gift of the earl and Anne, the archbishop, George, and Thomas. For this, grant back and render to the earl and Anne, the archbishop, George, and Thomas and the earl's heirs in tail. Successive contingent remainders to the king and his heirs in tail male and to the earl's heirs. *Labelled* Glouc', Somers'.

294/79/9

755. One week [9 Feb.] from the Purification. Richard Merrick (*a Meryk*) quer.; John Dibden (*Depden*) and Elizabeth his wife late wife of William Cannings (*Canynges*) esquire def. Thirty messuages, 3 a. of land, and 19 gardens in Bristol (*Bristoll'*) and the suburbs of the same town. Right of Richard by gift of John and Elizabeth. Remise and quitclaim, specifying Elizabeth's heirs, to Richard. (Warranty against John [Eastney] abbot of St. Peter's, Westminster (*Westm'*), and his successors.) Cons. 200 marks. *Labelled* Bristoll'.

294/82/5

1488

756. One week [1 July] from St. John the Baptist. Edward Willoughby esquire and Robert Logge quer.; William [de Berkeley] earl marshal and earl of Nottingham (*Notyngham*) def. The manors of Wotton-under-Edge (*Wotton under Egge*), Symond's Hall (*Symondeshale*), and Arlingham (*Erlyngham*), the advowson of the church of Wotton-under-Edge and the advowsons of the chantries of St. John of Wortley (*Wortele*) and St. Giles of Hillesley (*Hildesley*), and 20 messuages, 246 a. of land, 86 a. of meadow, 412 a. of pasture, and £12 2s. 4d. rent in Slimbridge (*Slymbrigge*), Kingscote (*Kyngescote*), Horwood (*Horwode*), Horton (*Horton*), North Nibley (*Nibley*), Sharncliffe (*Sarnclyffe*), Arlingham, Iron Acton (*Iren Acton*), and Acton Ilger (*Acton Ilger*). Right of Robert, as those which Robert and Edward had by the earl's gift. Remise and quitclaim to Edward and Robert and Robert's heirs. (Warranty.) For this, grant back and render to the earl of the manors of Wotton-under-Edge and Symond's Hall, 19 messuages, 244 a. of land, 86 a. of meadow, 412 a. of pasture, and £5 15s. rent of the said holdings in the townships of Slimbridge, Kingscote, Horton, Horwood, North Nibley, Sharncliffe, Iron Acton, and Acton Ilger, and the said advowsons. To hold to the earl without impeachment of waste during his life. Remainder to the earl's wife Anne during her life and then to the earl's heirs in tail. Successive contingent remainders to the king and his heirs in tail male and to the earl's heirs. And grant and render to the earl of the manor of Arlingham and a messuage, 2 a. of land, and £6 6s. 8d. rent in Arlingham, the residue of the holdings, to hold for term of one month, with remainder at the end of the month to John Beauchamp knight and Anne his wife, Edward's sister, to hold during their lives, and then to the earl's heirs in tail with successive contingent remainders as above.

79/96/6

[The rent of £5 15s. should be £5 15s. 8d., which when added to £6 6s. 8d. makes the total of £12 2s. 4d.]

4 Henry VII

1488

757. One month [27 Oct.] from Michaelmas. Thomas Young (*Yong*) quer.; John St. Lo (*Seyntelowe*) knight and Isabel his wife def. The manor of Coomb's End (*Cotellescombe*) and 5 messuages, 40 a. of land, 60 a. of meadow, and 10 a. of wood in Coomb's End. Right of Thomas by gift of John and Isabel. Remise and quitclaim, specifying Isabel's heirs, to Thomas. (Warranty.) Cons. £200.

79/96/7

758. Two weeks [25 Nov.] from St. Martin. Henry Haydon (*Heydon*) knight and Robert Throckmorton (*Throkmarton*) esquire quer.; Edward Berkeley knight and Alice his wife def. The manor of Syde (*Syde*) and 2 messuages, 2 ploughlands and 100 a. of land, and 60 a. of meadow in Falfield (*Falevelde*), Leckhampton (*Lekehampton*), and Charfield (*Charfylde*), GLOS. and 2 messuages and 3 ploughlands in Cheddar (*Cheddre*), SOM. Right of Henry, as those which Henry and Robert had by gift of Edward and Alice. Remise and quitclaim, specifying Alice's heirs to Henry and Robert and Henry's heirs. (Warranty against John [Eastney] abbot of St. Peter's, Westminster (*Westm'*), and his successors.) Cons. £500. *Labelled* Glouc', Somers'.

294/79/14

1489

759. One week [1 July] from St. John the Baptist. John Hawkins (*Hawekys*) quer.; William Joyce and Alice his wife def. Four messuages and a garden in Bristol (*Bristoll'*). Right of John. Remise and quitclaim, specifying Alice's heirs, to him. (Warranty.) Cons. £30. *Labelled* Bristoll'.

294/82/7

5 Henry VII

1490

760. One week [20 Jan.] from Hilary. (Made two weeks from St. Martin in the said year [25 Nov. 1489].) Robert Constable quer.; John Wroughton (*Wroghton*) esquire and John Thornbury (*Thornburgh*) def. The manor of West Alvington (*Alvyngton*) and 24 messuages, 20 gardens, 600 a. of land, 100 a. of meadow, 400 a. of pasture, 40 a. of wood, 50 a. of heath [*see note below*], 50 a. of moor, and 40*s*. rent in Woodhouse (*Wodehous*) and the borough of Alvington, DEVON, and the manor of Didmarton (*Dudemerton*), 12 messuages, 12 tofts, 100 a. of land, 40 a. of meadow, 100 a. of pasture, 40 a. of wood, and 40*s*. rent in Didmarton, and the advowson of the church of Didmarton, GLOS. Right of Robert by gift of John and John. Remise and quitclaim, specifying John Wroughton's heirs, to Robert. (Warranty against John [Eastney] abbot of St. Peter's, Westminster (*Westm'*) and his successors.) For this, grant and render to John Thornbury. To hold for term of one month next following. Remainder to John Wroughton and Margaret his wife. To hold without impeachment of waste during their lives. Remainder of the manor of Alvington and the holdings in Woodhouse and the borough of Alvington to Thomas Wroughton son of John and Margaret and his heirs in tail male, with successive contingent remainders to Thomas's brother Alexander and his heirs in tail male, to Alexander's brother John and his heirs in tail male, and to the heirs of John Wroughton the father. Remainder of the manor of Didmarton, the holdings there, and the advowson to the same Alexander and his heirs in tail male, with successive contingent remainders to Alexander's brother John and his heirs in tail male, to the same Thomas and his heirs in tail male, and to the heirs of John Wroughton the father. *Labelled* Devon', Glouc'.

294/79/18

[What is described in the recitation of the subject of the fine as 50 a. of heath is mentioned in the clause about the remainder as 100 a. of furze and heath.]

761. One week [13 June] from Trinity. (Made the morrow [21 May] of Ascension in the said year.) Richard Spenser and Joan his wife quer.; William Hardygyst and Margery his wife def. Two messuages and a garden in the suburb of the town of Gloucester (*Glouc'*). Right of Richard, as those which Richard and Joan had by gift of William and Margery. Remise and quitclaim, specifying Margery's heirs, to Richard and Joan and Richard's heirs. (Warranty.) Cons. £10. *Labelled* Villa Glouc'.

294/82/10

6 Henry VII

1491

762. Two weeks [17 April] from Easter. (Made the morrow of Ascension 5 Henry VII [21 May 1490].) John Walsh (*Walshe*) quer.; Richard Forster esquire def. The manor of Little Sodbury (*Parva Sobbury*), 600 a. of land, 100 a. of meadow, 500 a. of pasture, and 200 a. of wood in Little Sodbury, Old Sodbury (*Vetus Sobbury*), Chipping Sodbury (*Chepyng Sobbury*), Serridge (*Shirigge*), Henfield (*Hamefeld*), Pucklechurch (*Poculchurch*), and Dursley (*Durysley*), and the advowson of the church of St. Aldhelm of Little Sodbury, GLOS., and 50 messuages, 380 a. of land, 60 a. of meadow, 200 a. of pasture, 80 a. of wood, in *Buttescombe* [Batcombe, Bittiscombe, or Butcombe?], Portishead (*Porteshed*), *Capenor*, Compton Dando (*Comptondando*), Lamyatt (*Lamyet*), Milton Clevedon (*Milton Clivedon*), Littleton (*Littilton*), Bedminster (*Bedmester*), and *Bysshopstoke*, SOM. Right of John by Richard's gift. Remise and quitclaim to John. (Warranty.) For this, grant back and render to Richard. To hold without impeachment of waste during his life, of John, paying a rose a year at St. John the Baptist and doing service to the chief lords. Reversion to John. *Labelled* Glouc', Somers'. *Endorsed with note of proclamations.*

294/79/25

[*Bysshopstoke* was apparently not Stoke Bishop, which was in Glos., in Westbury-on-Trym. It may have been linked with Rodney Stoke, since the bishop of Bath and Wells had manorial rights in Draycott (immediately north of Rodney Stoke) and Stoke in 1535: *Valor Eccl.* i. 123.]

763. One week [1 July] from St. John the Baptist. Robert Ricardes (*Rycard*) quer.; William Joyce and Alice his wife def. Six messuages in Bristol (*Bristoll'*). Right of Robert by gift of William and Alice. Remise and quitclaim, specifying William's heirs, to Robert. (Warranty, specifying Alice's heirs.) Cons. £40. *Labelled* Villa Bristoll'. *Endorsed with note of proclamations.*

294/82/11

[It appears anomalous that the remise and quitclaim specifies William's heirs while the warranty specifies Alice's.]

7 Henry VII

1491

764. Two weeks [8 Oct.] from Michaelmas. Robert Kenn (*Kyn*) quer.; William Elland the elder and Joan his wife def. A messuage, a mill, a garden, 20 a. of land, 8 a. of meadow, 8 a. of pasture, and 1 a. of wood in Ebley (*Ebbeley*) and Stonehouse (*Stonehouse*). Right of Robert by gift of William and Joan. Remise and quitclaim, specifying Joan's heirs, to Robert. (Warranty against William [Farley] abbot of St. Peter's, Gloucester (*Glouc'*), and his successors.) Cons. £40. *Endorsed with note of proclamations.*

79/96/8

1492

765. Morrow [1 June] of Ascension. William Elland the younger quer.; William Elland the elder and Joan his wife def. A messuage, a garden, 16 a. of land, 2 a. of meadow, and 2 a. of wood in Rodborough (*Roddeburgh*) and Rooksmoor (*Rokesmore*) within the lordship of Minchinhampton (*Mynchenhampton*). Right of William the younger by gift of William the elder and Joan. Remise and quitclaim, specifying Joan's heirs, to William the younger. (Warranty.) For this, grant back and render to William the elder and Joan. To

1492

hold during their lives, of William the younger, paying a rose a year at St. John the Baptist and doing service to the chief lords. Reversion to William the younger.

79/96/9

8 Henry VII

1492

766. Morrow [3 Nov.] of All Souls. Thomas Molyneux esquire, James Molyneux clerk, Robert Sheffield (*Sheffeld*), Richard Churchyard (*Chyrchyerd*), Ralph Josselyn, and Richard Goodwin (*Goodwyn*) quer.; John Josselyn and Cecily his wife def. The manor of Chipping Campden (*Campden*) and the advowson of the free chapel of St. Katherine in Campden, GLOS., the manor of Perry Hall (*Pyryhall*) and 6 messuages, 100 a. of land, 40 a. of meadow, 100 a. of pasture, 40 a. of wood, and £4 rent in Perry (*Pery*), Perry Barr (*Parva Barre*), Hamstead (*Hampsted*), and Handsworth (*Hounesworth*), STAFFS. Right of Ralph, as those which the quer. had by gift of John and Cecily. Remise and quitclaim, specifying Cecily's heirs, to the quer. and Ralph's heirs. (Warranty against John [Eastney] abbot of St. Peter's, Westminster (*Westm'*), and his successors.) For this, grant back and render to John and Cecily. To hold without impeachment of waste during their lives. Remainder to Richard Bolkey and Thomas Hoste for term of seven years then following and to Cecily's heirs. *Labelled* Glouc', Staff'.

294/79/32

[Cf. *Staffs. Fines, 1485–1558*, p. 177.]

767. Morrow [12 Nov.] of St. Martin. Robert Throckmorton (*Throkmarton*) esquire quer.; Thomas Thomasson and Margaret his wife def. Six messuages, a toft, a garden, 40 a. of land, and 12 a. of meadow in Stratford-upon-Avon (*Stratford super Aven*), Alveston (*Alston*), and Tiddington (*Tydyngton*), WARWS., and 3 messuages, 300 a. of land, 100 a. of pasture, and 20 a. of meadow in Westington (*Westondon*), GLOS. Right of Robert by gift of Thomas and Margaret. Remise and quitclaim, specifying Margaret's heirs, to Robert. (Warranty.) Cons. £100. *Labelled* Warr', Glouc'. *Endorsed with note of proclamations.*

294/79/33

[Cf. *Warws. Fines, 1345–1509*, p. 205, no. 2739. The description of the meadow and pasture in Westington does not follow the usual order.]

1493

768. One week [20 Jan.] from Hilary. John Woolworth (*Wolworth*) and Elena his wife quer.; Joan Skey widow def. Two messuages in Wotton-under-Edge (*Wotton Underegge*). Right of John, as those which John and Elena had by Joan's gift. Remise and quitclaim to John and Elena and John's heirs. (Warranty.) Cons. £20. *Endorsed with note of proclamations.*

79/96/10

769. Three weeks [28 April] from Easter. William Baynham (*Baynam*) 'gentilman' and William Garon quer.; Thomas Rawlings (*Raulyns*) and Joan his wife def. Six messuages, 20 a. of land, 12 a. of meadow, 20 a. of pasture, and 3 a. of wood in Huntley (*Huntley*). Right of William Baynham, as those which the same William and William Garon had by gift of Thomas and Joan. Remise and quitclaim, specifying Joan's heirs, to William and William and William Baynham's heirs. (Warranty.) Con. £30. *Endorsed with note of proclamations.*

79/96/11

1493

770. One month [5 May] from Easter. William Greville (*Grevyle*), Robert Greville, Thomas Lye clerk, and Richard Palmer quer.; Richard Greville def. The manor of Upper Lemington (*Overlemynton*) and 2 messuages, 5 tofts, 12 yardlands, 12 yards (*virgatis*) of meadow, 200 a. of pasture, and 100 a. of moor in Upper Lemington. (Plea of warranty of charter.) Right of William, as those which William, Robert, Thomas, and Richard Palmer had by gift of Richard Greville. Remise and quitclaim to William, Robert, Thomas, and Richard Palmer and William's heirs. (Warranty.) Cons. 500 marks. *Endorsed with note of proclamations.*

79/96/12

[The fine is the earliest instance among the Gloucestershire fines of the revival of the use of a plea of warranty of charter to initiate an agreement. Cf. above, p. xii.]

771. One month [5 May] from Easter. William Easterby (*Esteby*) 'marchaunt' quer.; Elena Dove widow def. A messuage in Bristol (*Bristoll'*). Right of William by Elena's gift. Remise and quitclaim to William. (Warranty.) Cons. £20. *Labelled* Bristoll'. *Endorsed with note of proclamations.*

294/82/17

772. One week [1 July] from St. John the Baptist. John Jay, John Walsh (*Walshe*), George Moneux, and Richard Vaughan quer.; John Fulbrook (*Fulbroke*) and Isabel his wife defendants. Five messuages in Bristol (*Bristoll'*). Right of John Jay, as those which the same John, John Walsh, George, and Richard had by gift of John Fulbrook and Isabel. Remise and quitclaim, specifying Isabel's heirs, to John Jay, John Walsh, George, and Richard and John Jay's heirs. (Warranty.) Cons. £200. *Labelled* Villa Bristoll'. *Endorsed with note of proclamations.*

294/82/18

9 Henry VII

1493

773. One week [18 Nov.] from St. Martin. John Easterfield (*Esterfeld*), John Walsh (*Walshe*), John Heming (*Hemmyng*), Robert Bolton, and Thomas Brown (*Broun*) pet.; Thomas Baker def. Ten messuages, 2 dovecots, 180 a. of land, 20 a. of meadow, 14 a. of pasture, 4 a. of wood, and £4 13s. 4d. rent in Gossington (*Gosyngton*), Slimbridge (*Slymbrige*), and Arlingham (*Erlyngham*). (Plea of warranty of charter.) Right of John Easterfield, as those which the pet. had by Thomas Baker's gift. Remise and quitclaim to the pet. and John Easterfield's heirs. (Warranty.) Cons. £100. *Endorsed with note of proclamations.*

79/96/13

774. One week [18 Nov.] from St. Martin. John Mitchell (*Michell*), John Goldney (*Goldenay*), John Jay, and John Popelay quer.; John Bagot (*Bagod*) esquire and Elizabeth his wife def. Four messuages in Bristol (*Bristoll'*). Right of John Mitchell, as those which the same John, John Goldney, John Jay, and John Popelay had by gift of John Bagot and Elizabeth. Remise and quitclaim, specifying John Bagot's heirs, to John Mitchell, John Goldney, John Jay, and John Popelay and John Mitchell's heirs. (Warranty.) Cons. £100. *Labelled* Villa Bristoll'. *Endorsed with note of proclamations.*

294/82/19

1494

775. One month [27 April] from Easter. John Cheyney (*Cheyne*) knight and Robert Sheffield (*Sheffeld*) pet.; William Pawne and Anne his wife defendants. The manor of Paganhill (*Pagenhull*) and 12 messuages, 6 gardens, 10 yardlands, 100 a. of meadow, 200 a. of pasture, 30 a. of wood, and 20*s.* rent in Paganhill, Randwick (*Ronewyke*), Stonehouse (*Stonehouse*), Bisley (*Bysseley*), Ebley (*Ebbeley*), Stroud (*Strode*), Painswick (*Paneswyke*), King's Stanley (*Kyngestanley*), and Cirencester (*Circetur*). (Plea of warranty of charter.) Right of John, as those which John and Robert had by gift of William and Anne. Remise and quitclaim, specifying Anne's heirs, to John and Robert and John's heirs. (Warranty.) For this, grant back and render to William and Anne. To hold to them and their heirs in tail. Successive contingent remainders to Robert Bigg (*Bygge*) and his heirs in tail and to William's heirs. *Endorsed with note of proclamations.*

79/96/14

776. Morrow [25 June] of St. John the Baptist. William Greville (*Gryvell*) and William Baynham (*Baynam*) quer.; Thomas Rawlings (*Raulyns*) and Joan his wife def. Two messuages, 20 a. of land, 12 a. of meadow, 20 a. of pasture, and 5 a. of wood in Prestbury (*Prestbury*), Oxenton (*Oxynton*), Charlton (*Charlton*), and Cheltenham (*Cheltenham*). Right of William Baynham, as those which the same William and William Greville (*Grevell*) had by gift of Thomas and Joan. Remise and quitclaim, specifying Joan's heirs, to William and William and William Baynham's heirs. (Warranty.) Cons. £40. *Endorsed with note of proclamations.*

79/96/15

777. One week [1 July] from St. John the Baptist. Richard Dryland (*Driland*) quer.; Richard Wincot (*Wyncote*), Robert Sherborne (*Shirborn*), and Humphrey Coningsby (*Conyngesby*) def. The manor of Wincot and 1,600 a. of land, 80 a. of meadow, and 20 a. of furze and heath in Wincot. Right of Richard Dryland by gift of Richard Wincot, Robert, and Humphrey. Remise and quitclaim, specifying Richard Wincot's heirs, to Richard Dryland. (Warranty, by Richard Wincot alone.) For this, grant back and render to Richard Wincot, Robert, and Humphrey. To hold to them during Richard Wincot's life. Remainder to Richard Wincot's son John Wincot and his heirs in tail. Contingent remainder to Richard Wincot's heirs. *Endorsed* with *note of proclamations.*

79/96/16

778. One week [1 July] from St. John the Baptist. John Smith (*Smyth*) of London (*London'*) quer.; Richard Dalby and Mary his wife def. Two tofts and 4 a. of land in Moreton-in-Marsh (*Morton Henmershe*). Right of John by gift of Richard and Mary. Remise and quitclaim, specifying Mary's heirs, to John. (Warranty.) Cons. £10.

79/96/17

10 Henry VII

1494

779. Morrow [12 Nov.] of St. Martin. William Baynham (*Beynam*) and Richard a Merrick (*a Meryk*) of Bristol (*Bristoll'*) quer.; William Baker and Elizabeth his wife def. A messuage, 16 a. of land, 8 a. of pasture, and 13 a. of wood in Lindors (*Lynhurst*) in the parish of St. Briavels (*de Sancto Briavello*). Right of Richard, as those which Richard and

1494

William Baynham had by gift of William Baker and Elizabeth. Remise and quitclaim, specifying Elizabeth's heirs, to William Baynham and Richard and Richard's heirs. (Warranty.) Cons. £20. *Endorsed with note of proclamations.*

79/96/18

1495

780. Three weeks [10 May] from Easter. John Daa and Richard Brooke (*Broke*) chaplain quer.; Henry Homerston and Alice his wife def. A messuage and a garden in Minchinhampton (*Mynchyn Hampton*). Right of Richard, as those which Richard and John had by gift of Henry and Alice. Remise and quitclaim, specifying Alice's heirs, to John and Richard and Richard's heirs. (Warranty.) Cons. £20. *Endorsed with note of proclamations.*

79/96/19

781. One month [17 May] from Easter. Alexander Baynham (*Beynam*) knight, William Baynham, Reynold Hody, and John Brooke (*Broke*) pet.; John Berrow (*Berewe*) tenant; Fifteen messuages, 66½ a. of land, 43½ a. of meadow [43½ a. of meadow *repeated*], 69 a. of pasture, 60 a. of wood, a several piece of water in the Severn (*Sabrina*), and 27s. 7d. rent in the townships and in the parishes of Awre (*Aure*), Gatcombe (*Gatcome*), Etloe (*Etlowe*), Blakeney (*Blakeney*), and St. Briavels (*Seynt Brevellis*). (Plea of warranty of charter.) Right of William, as those which William, Alexander, Reynold, and John Brooke had by John Berrow's gift. Remise and quitclaim to Alexander, William, Reynold, and John Brooke and William's heirs. (Warranty against John [Eastney] abbot of St. Peter's, Westminster (*Westm'*), and his successors.) Cons. £100. *Endorsed with note of proclamations.*

79/96/20

11 Henry VII

1495

782. Three weeks [20 Oct.] from Michaelmas. John Tyler (*Tiler*, *Tyler*), Philip Merrick (*Merik*), Richard Rolf, John Cantelow (*Cantelowe*, *Cantlowe*), John Camp (*Campe*), and Peter White quer.; John Fulbrook (*Fulbroke*) and Isabel his wife def. A messuage and 2s. rent in Bristol (*Bristoll'*). Right of Richard, as those which the quer. had by gift of John Fulbrook and Isabel. Remise and quitclaim, specifying Isabel's heirs, to the quer. and Richard's heirs. (Warranty.) Cons. £30. *Labelled* Bristoll'.

294/82/23

783. One week [18 Nov.] from St. Martin. Thomas Davies (*Davyes*) quer.; John Daa and Alice his wife def. Two messuages, 2 gardens, a fulling mill (*molendino fullonico*), and 3 a. of land in Brimscombe (*Brymescombe*) and Swells (*Swelys*) in the parish of Minchinhampton (*Mynchen Hampton*). Right of Thomas by gift of John and Alice. Remise and quitclaim, specifying Alice's heirs, to Thomas. (Warranty.) Cons. £30.

79/96/21

[*Swelys* is identified as Swellshill in *P.-N.G.* i. 104, but there is no evidence that the suffix –hill had been added by 1495.]

1496

784. Morrow [3 Feb.] of the Purification. Maurice Berkeley the elder and Isabel his wife pet.; William Betson tenant. The manor of Upton St. Leonards (*Upton Sancti Leonardi*). (Plea of warranty of charter.) Grant and render to Maurice and Isabel. To hold to them and Maurice's heirs in tail male. Contingent remainder to Maurice's heirs. Cons. £100. *Labelled* Villa Glouc'. *Endorsed with note of proclamations.*

294/82/24

785. One month [1 May] from Easter. John Walsh (*Walssh*) esquire, Arthur Kemes (*Kemys*) esquire, William Fream (*Freme*) esquire, and William Smith (*Smyth*) pet.; William Berkeley knight and Anne his wife tenants. The manor of Elberton (*Ailberton*) and 24 messuages, 24 gardens, a mill, 700 a. of land, 272 a. of meadow, 208 a. of pasture, 54 a. of wood, and rents of 2*d.*, 2 red roses, 1 lb. of cumin, and a clove in Elberton, Ingst (*Inste*), Cote (*Cotes*), and Olveston (*Wolston*). (Plea of warranty of charter.) Right of John. Remise and quitclaim, specifying Anne's heirs, to John, Arthur, William Fream, and William Smith and John's heirs. (Warranty.) Cons. £600. *Endorsed with note of proclamations.*

79/86/22

786. One week [5 June] from Trinity. (Made the morrow [13 May] of Ascension in the said year.) Hugh Denis (*Denys*) esquire, John Walsh (*Walshe*) esquire, and William Huntley 'gentilman' pet.; John Paunton imp. The manor of Abson (*Abboston*) and 100 a. of land, 40 a. of meadow, 20 a. of pasture, 100 a. of wood, and 20*s.* rent in Abson, Churchley (*Chercheley*), and Wick (*Wyke*). (Plea of warranty of charter.) Right of Hugh. Remise and quitclaim to Hugh, John Walsh, and William and Hugh's heirs. (Warranty.) Cons. £100. *Endorsed with note of proclamations.*

79/96/23

787. Two weeks [12 June] from Trinity. William Berkeley knight, Richard Berkeley esquire, Matthew Bamfield (*Bamfeld*), William Large, Thomas Snigg (*Snygge*), and John Cater pet.; John Walsh esquire and Elizabeth his wife imp. The manor of Berwick (*Berwik*) and 13 messuages, 200 a. of land, 100 a. of meadow, 80 a. of pasture, 100 a. of wood, and 40*s.* rent in Berwick and Crooks Marsh (*Crokismersshe*). (Plea of warranty of charter.) Right of William Berkeley, as those which the pet. had by gift of John Walsh and Elizabeth. Remise and quitclaim, specifying Elizabeth's heirs, to the pet. and William Berkeley's heirs. (Warranty.) Cons. 500 marks. *Endorsed with note of proclamations.*

79/96/24

788. One week [1 July] from St. John the Baptist. William Dorset (*Derset*) and Edmund Bushel (*Busshell*) quer.; William Dalby and Mary his wife def. Nine messuages, 418 a. of land, 39 a. of meadow, and 10*s.* rent in Preston on Stour (*Preston super Stoure*), Alscot (*Alscote*), Lower Quinton (*Netherquynton*), Upper Quinton (*Overquynton*), Foxcote (*Foxcote*), and Mickleton (*Mikylton*). Right of William Dorset (*Darset*), as those which the same William and Edmund had by gift of William Dalby and Mary. Remise and quitclaim, specifying Mary's heirs, to William Dorset and Edmund and that William's heirs. (Warranty.) Cons. £100. *Endorsed with note of proclamations.*

79/96/25

12 Henry VII

1496

789. One week [18 Nov.] from St. Martin. Roger Porter and John Seabourne (*Seburn*) quer.; Edward Wyman and Margaret his wife def. Three messuages, 2 yardlands, 10 a. of meadow, and 20 a. of pasture in Guiting Power (*Nether Gytyng*). Right of John, as those which John and Roger had by gift of Edward and Margaret. Remise and quitclaim, specifying Margaret's heirs, to Roger and John and John's heirs. (Warranty.) Cons. £40. *Endorsed with note of proclamations.*

79/96/26

790. One week [18 Nov.] from St. Martin. John Seabourne (*Seburn*) and Roger Porter quer.; Richard de Beauchamp (*de Bello Campo*) knight lord of Beauchamp (*Beauchamp*) def. A messuage, a dovecot, 30½ a. of land, and 7 a. of meadow in Uckington (*Okyngton*) and Hardwicke (*Hardewyke*). Right of John, as those which John and Roger had by Richard's gift. Remise and quitclaim to John and Roger and John's heirs. (Warranty.) Cons. £40. *Endorsed with note of proclamations.*

79/96/27

1497

791. Morrow [3 Feb.] of the Purification. William Fream (*Freme*), William Smith (*Smyth*), and Thomas Tyler pet.; John Stanshawe esquire and Humphrey Stanshawe his brother defendants. The manor of Kingrove (*Kyngrave*) and 30 messuages, 1,000 a. of land, 200 a. of meadow, 600 a. of pasture, 40 a. of wood, and 40*s*. rent in Kingrove, Old Sodbury (*Oldsobbury*), Chipping Sodbury (*Chepyngsobbury*), Dodington (*Dodyngton*), Doynton (*Donyngton*), Codrington (*Coderyngton*), Wapley (*Wappeley*), Yate (*Yate*), Stonehouse (*Stonehouse*), North Nibley (*North Nybley*), Wotton-under-Edge borough (*Wotton Borough*), Wotton-under-Edge foreign (*Wotton Foreyn*), Charfield (*Charrefeld*), Hawkesbury (*Hawekesbury*), Tresham (*Tresham*), Thornbury (*Thornbury*), and Norton (*Norton*). (Plea of warranty of charter.) Right of William Fream, as those which the same William, William Smith, and Thomas had by gift of John and Humphrey. Remise and quitclaim, specifying Humphrey's heirs, to William, William, and Thomas and William Fream's heirs. (Warranty.) For this, grant and render to John. To hold during his life, without impeachment of waste, of William, William, and Thomas and William Fream's heirs, paying a rose a year at St. John the Baptist and doing service to the chief lords. Reversion to William, William, and Thomas and William Fream's heirs. *Endorsed with note of proclamations.*

79/96/28

792. Morrow [3 Feb.] of the Purification. William Smith (*Smyth*) quer.; Thomas Mimms (*Mymmes*) def. A messuage, 4 tofts, 200 a. of land, 20 a. of meadow, 100 a. of pasture, and 10 a. of wood in Chedworth (*Chedworth*). Right of William by Thomas's gift. Remise and quitclaim to William. (Warranty.) Cons. 100 marks. *Endorsed with note of proclamations.*

79/96/29

1497

793. Morrow [3 Feb.] of the Purification. John Walsh (*Walshe*) and William Fream (*Freme*) quer.; John Parmenter def. A messuage, 20 a. of land, 10 a. of meadow, and 20 a. of pasture in Tockington (*Tokynton*) in the parish of Olveston (*Olveston*). Right of John Walsh, as those which the same John and William had by John Parmenter's gift. For this, grant back and render to John Parmenter. *In the left-hand margin* Exp[ens]a. *Endorsed with note of proclamations.*

79/96/30

794. Two weeks [9 April] from Easter. Thomas Baker quer.; William Baker and Elizabeth his wife def. Three messuages, 2 tofts, 3 gardens, 120 a. of land, 10 a. of meadow, 12 a. of pasture, 20 a. of heath, 30 a. of marsh, and 20*s.* rent in the parish of St. Briavels (*Sancti Bryavelli*). Right of Thomas by gift of William and Elizabeth. Remise and quitclaim, specifying Elizabeth's heirs, to Thomas. (Warranty.) Cons. 100 marks. *Endorsed with note of proclamations.*

79/96/31

795. Two weeks [9 April] from Easter. (Made one week [9 Feb.] from the Purification in the said year.) Edmund Greville (*Grevyle*), Thomas Lee clerk, Thomas Kinnersley (*Keynersley*), and Matthew Morton quer.; John Agard esquire and Thomas Agard esquire and Margaret his wife daughter and heir of Geoffrey St. German (*Seynt Jermyn*) def. The manors of Ditchford Frary (*Dycheford Frary*) and Sugarswell (*Shakerswell*) and 6 messuages, a garden, 420 a. of land, 66 a. of meadow, 960 a. of pasture, and 20 a. of wood in Sugarswell, Tysoe (*Tysho*), Sibford (*Sybford*), Stretton-on-Fosse (*Stretton super Fosse*), and Barton-on-the-Heath (*Barton Henmersh*), WARWS., 9 messuages, 9 gardens, 240 a. of land, 40 a. of meadow, and 100 a. of pasture in Bodicote (*Bodicote*) and Bicester (*Bysseter*), OXON., half of the manor of Sugarswell in Sugarswell and Tysoe, GLOS., and the manor of Broughton (*Broughton Seynt Jermyn*) and half of a messuage, 100 a. of land, 10 a. of meadow, and 20 a. of pasture in Barnwell (*Barnewell*), NORTHANTS. (Plea of warranty of charter.) Right of Thomas Kinnersley, as those which the same Thomas, Edmund, Thomas Lee, and Matthew had by gift of John and Thomas Agard and Margaret. Remise and quitclaim, specifying Margaret's heirs, to Edmund, Thomas, Thomas, and Matthew and Thomas Kinnerlsey's heirs. (Warranty.) Cons. £1,000. *Labelled* Warr', Oxon', Glouc', North'. *Endorsed with note of proclamations.*

294/80/63

[Cf. *Warws. Fines, 1345–1509*, p. 210, no. 2758. Sugarswell is in Shenington parish, a detached part of Glos. transferred to Oxon. in 1845 and bordering Tysoe (Warws.)]

796. One month [23 April] from Easter. Andrew Windsor (*Wyndesore*), William Burgoyne (*Burgoyn*), George Puttenham (*Puttynham*), William Lytton (*Litton*), Guy Pannes, John FitzJames the younger, John Marshall, John Portman, and Constantine Rowe quer.; William Juyn and Joan his wife def. The manors of Battleborough (*Batilburgh*) and Long Ashton (*Asshton*), 70 messuages, a toft, 1,300 a. of land, 240 a. of meadow, 240 a. of pasture, 160 a. of wood, 80 a. of heath, 80 a. of moor, and rents of £7, a red rose, and 1 lb. of pepper in Pensford (*Pennesford*), Belluton (*Belweton*), Bishopsworth (*Bysshopworth*), Bedminster (*Bedmynster*), Felton (*Felton*), Knowle (*Knolle*) by Bristol (*Brystoll'*), Batheaston (*Batheneston*), Nailsea (*Naylesy*), Worthyston, Battleborough, Edingworth (*Edenworth*), and Long Ashton (*Long Asshton*), and half of the manor of Batheaston, SOM.,

1497

20 messuages, 300½ a. of land, 30 a. of meadow, 40 a. of pasture, 11 a. of wood, 40 a. of heath, 40 a. of moor, and 10*s.* rent in West Hanham (*Westhannam*), Lower Hanham (*Dounehannam*), Hanham (*Hannam*), Oldland (*Oldlond*), Bitton (*Button*), and Upton Cheyney (*Upton*), GLOS., and 8 messuages and 10 a. of meadow in the town of Bristol and the suburb of the same. Right of William Lytton (*Lytton*). Remise and quitclaim, specifying Joan's heirs, to the quer. and William Lytton's heirs. (Warranty.) Cons. £600. *Labelled* Somers', Glouc', Bristoll'. *Endorsed with note of proclamations.*

294/80/67

797. One week [28 May] from Trinity. John Walsh (*Walish*) esquire, William Fream (*Freme*), and Thomas Tyler pet.; Richard Forster esquire def. Half of the manor of Stock (*Stokke*) by Calne (*Calne*) and half of 2 messuages, 2 ploughlands, 20 a. of meadow, 100 a. of pasture, 16 a. of wood, and rents of 50*s.*, 5 lb. of pepper, and 1 lb. of cumin in Stock, Studley (*Stodeley*), Stockley (*Stokley*), Quemerford (*Comerford*), and Blackland (*Blakland*), WILTS., and half of the manors of Nympsfield (*Nymesfeld*), Gosling (*Gosselyns*), and Hill (*Hull*), half of the advowson of the chantry in the free chapel of Kinley (*Kynley*), half of 30 messuages, 600 a. of land, 200 a. of meadow, 500 a. of pasture, 100 a. of wood, and 40*s.* rent in Frampton Cotterell (*Frampton Cotell*), Nympsfield, Hill, Winterbourne (*Wynterbourn*), Hambrook (*Hambroke*), Tytherington (*Tyderyngton*), Thornbury (*Thornbury*), Oldbury-on-Severn (*Oldbury*), Bevington (*Bevyngton*), *Frampton Episcopi*, Winstone (*Wynston*), Woodfield (*Waldfeld*), Stoke (*Stoke*), Alveston (*Alveston*), Stidcot (*Scudycote*), Ingst (*Inste*), Olveston (*Olveston*), Wick (*Wyke*), Charlton (*Charleton*), Stone (*Stone*), Falfield (*Falefeld*), and Ham (*Hamme*) by Berkeley (*Berkelay*), GLOS. (Plea of warranty of charter.) Right of John, as those which John, William, and Thomas had by Richard's gift. Remise and quitclaim to John, William, and Thomas and John's heirs. (Warranty.) Cons. £500. *Labelled* Wiltes', Glouc'. *Endorsed with note of proclamations.*

294/80/70

[Cf. *Wilts. Fines, 1377–1509*, p. 168, no. 743.]

13 Henry VII

1497

798. One week [18 Nov.] from St. Martin. John Tame and Edmund Tame quer.; Thomas Mimms (*Mymmes*) def. Five messuages, 60 a. of land, 40 a. of pasture, and 4 a. of wood in Fairford (*Fareforde*), Williamstrip (*Williamsthorp*), and Hatherop (*Hatherop*). Right of Edmund, as those which Edmund and John had by Thomas's gift. Remise and quitclaim to John and Edmund and Edmund's heirs. (Warranty.) Cons. 100 marks.

79/96/32

1498

799. One week [9 Feb.] from the Purification. John Walsh (*Walshe*) esquire, Arthur Kemes (*Kemys*) esquire, William Fream (*Freme*) esquire, and William Smith (*Smyth*) quer.; Elizabeth Harrison (*Haryson*) widow late wife of Thomas Stanshawe esquire and daughter and heir of Alice daughter of James Berkeley knight late lord of Berkeley def. The manor of Elberton (*Aylberton*) and 24 messuages, 24 gardens, a mill, 700 a. of land, 272 a. of meadow, 208 a. of pasture, 54 a. of wood, and rents of 2*d.*, 2 red roses, 1 lb. of

cumin, and a clove in Elberton, Ingst (*Inste*), Cote (*Cotes*), and Olveston (*Wolston*). Right of John. Remise and quitclaim to John, Arthur, William, and William and John's heirs. (Warranty.) Cons. £100.

79/96/33

[Cf. above, no. 785.]

800. Morrow [25 May] of Ascension. John Parmenter (*Permyter*) and Isabel his wife quer.; John Walsh (*Walshe*) esquire and Elizabeth his wife def. A messuage, 28 a. of land, 24 a. of meadow, and 23 a. of pasture in Tockington (*Tokyngton*). Grant and render to John Parmenter and Isabel. To hold to them and their heirs in tail, of John Walsh and Elizabeth and John Walsh's heirs, paying a rose a year at St. John the Baptist and doing service to the chief lords. Contingent remainder to John Parmenter's heirs in tail. (Warranty, specifying Elizabeth's heirs.) Contingent reversion to John Walsh and Elizabeth and John Walsh's heirs.

79/96/34

[It appears anomalous that, while the tenure is to be of John Walsh's heirs and the contingent reversion specifies his heirs, the warranty specifies Elizabeth's.]

801. Morrow [25 May] of Ascension. William Sandys knight, John Kingsmill (*Kyngesmyll*), William Tistead (*Tistede*), and Henry Horn (*Horne*) quer.; John Giffard (*Giffard, Gyffard*) and Mary his wife def. Five hundred and ninety acres of land, 80 a. of meadow, and 400 a. of pasture in Weston (*Weston*). Right of Henry, as those which Henry, William, John Kingsmill, and William had by gift of John Giffard and Mary. Remise and quitclaim, specifying Mary's heirs, to William, John Kingsmill, William, and Henry and Henry's heirs. (Warranty.) Cons. 400 marks.

79/96/35

802. One week [17 June] from Trinity. (Made the morrow [25 May] of Ascension in the said year.) William Fream (*Freme*) and Alice his wife quer.; John Lovegrove (*Lovgrove*) and Anne his wife def. Twelve messuages, 60 a. of land, 20 a. of meadow, 40 a. of pasture, 4 a. of wood, and 20s. rent in Berkeley (*Berkeley*), Wanswell (*Wanneswell*), Hinton (*Hynton*), Saniger (*Sevanger*), Halmore (*Halmer*), and Ham (*Homme*). Right of William, of which he and Alice had 5 messuages, 8 a. of land and 5 a. of meadow by gift of John and Anne. Remise and quitclaim, specifying Anne's heirs, to William and Alice and William's heirs. And grant to William and Alice and William's heirs of the reversion of 7 messuages, 52 a. of land, 15 a. of meadow, and the said pasture, wood, and rent held by Eleanor Usher (*Ussher*) widow for term of life, of Anne's inheritance. (Warranty.) Cons. £100. *Endorsed with note of proclamations.*

79/96/36

803. One week [1 July] from St. John the Baptist. Thomas Machin (*Machyn*) and Agnes his wife quer.; John Hawkeslowe of Winchcombe (*Wynchecombe*) in the county of Gloucester (*Glouc'*) 'gentilman' and Joan his wife def. Half of a messuage, 100 a. of land, 6 a. of meadow, and 12 a. of pasture in Bromsberrow (*Bromesberowe*). Right of Agnes, as those which Thomas and Agnes had by gift of John and Joan. Remise and quitclaim, specifying Joan's heirs, to Thomas and Agnes and Agnes's heirs. (Warranty.) Cons. 40 marks. *Endorsed with note of proclamations.*

79/96/37

14 Henry VII

1498

804. One week [6 Oct.] from Michaelmas. Philip Ryngstone quer.; Richard Forster def. A messuage in Bristol (*Bristoll'*). Right of Philip by Richard's gift. Remise and quitclaim to Philip. (Warranty.) Cons. £20. *Labelled* Villa Bristoll'. *Endorsed with note of proclamations.*

294/82/25

805. One month [27 Oct.] from Michaelmas. William Warham clerk, Thomas Woodington (*Wodyngton*) clerk, Matilda Baker widow, William Greville (*Grevyle*), Walter Rowden (*Rowdon*), William Huntley, and Ralph Leigh (*Legh*) quer.; John Wright and Elizabeth his wife def. The manor of Eastleach Turville (*Estlecch Turvile*) and 8 messuages, 400 a. of land, 40 a. of meadow, 300 a. of pasture, and 60 a. of wood in Eastleach Turville. Right of Thomas. Remise and quitclaim, specifying Elizabeth's heirs, to the quer. and Thomas's heirs. (Warranty.) Cons. £100.

79/97/38

806. One month [27 Oct.] from Michaelmas. John Walsh (*Walshe*) esquire quer.; Richard Forster son and heir of Richard Forster late of Bristol (*Bristoll'*) esquire def. Sixteen messuages and a garden in Bristol. Right of John. Remise and quitclaim to him. (Warranty.) Cons. £100. *Labelled* Villa Bristoll'. *Endorsed with note of proclamations.*

294/82/26

807. One month [27 Oct.] from Michaelmas. John Walsh (*Walshe*) esquire quer.; Richard Forster son and heir of Richard Forster late of Bristol (*Bristoll'*) esquire def. Ten messuages and a garden in Bristol held by Alice Wickham (*Wykeham*) widow who was wife of the said Richard Forster late of Bristol esquire for term of life. Right of John. Grant to him of the reversion, of Richard's inheritance. (Warranty.) Cons. 100 marks. *Labelled* Villa Bristoll'. *Endorsed with note of proclamations.*

294/82/27

1499

808. Two weeks [14 April] from Easter. (Made one week from St. Martin in the said year [18 Nov. 1498].) Richard Boket clerk, Robert Higgs (*Hygges*) clerk, and John Brown (*Broun*) quer.; John Bodefaunt (*Bodyfaunte*) and Joan his wife who was wife of Robert Stanshawe def. The manor of Alderley (*Alderley*), the advowson of the church of Alderley, and 18 messuages, 4 tofts, 2 mills, 1,000 a. of land, 100 a. of meadow, 100 a. of pasture, 60 a. of wood, and 10*s*. rent in Alderley, Kilcott (*Kylcot*), Hillesley (*Hillisley*), and Tresham (*Tresham*). Right of Richard, as those which Richard, Robert, and John Brown had by gift of John Bodyfaunte and Joan. Remise and quitclaim, specifying Joan's heirs, to Richard, Robert, and John Brown and Richard's heirs. (Warranty.) For this, grant to John Bodyfaunte and Joan of a rent of £28 a year during Joan's life, payable at Michaelmas, Christmas, Easter, and St. John the Baptist from the manor and holdings, with right of distraint for non-payment. *Endorsed with note of proclamations.*

79/97/39

809. Two weeks [14 April] from Easter. (Made one week [9 Feb.] from the Purification in the said year.) Robert Isham clerk, Robert Hitchman (*Hucheman*) clerk, and Edmund Tame quer.; Thomas Woodington (*Wodyngton*) def. The manor of Eastleach Turville

1499

(*Estlecch Turvile*) and 8 messuages, 400 a. of land, 40 a.of meadow, 300 a. of pasture, and 60 a. of wood in Eastleach. Right of Edmund, as those which Edmund, Robert, and Robert had by Thomas's gift. Remise and quitclaim to Robert, Robert, and Edmund and Edmund's heirs. (Warranty.) Cons. 200 marks.

79/97/40

810. Two weeks [14 April] from Easter. (Made the morrow [3 Feb.] of the Purification in the said year.) William [Smith] bishop of Lincoln (*Lincoln'*), Reynold Bray knight, William Hody knight, John Shaa knight, Hugh Oldham (*Oldom*) clerk, Humphrey Coningsby (*Conyngesby*) serjeant at law, Richard Empson (*Emson*), William Cope (*Coope*), John Cutte, and Nicholas Compton quer.; Richard Pole esquire and Elizabeth his wife and Thomas Keble (*Kebell*) one of the king's serjeants at law def. The manor of Great Rissington (*Broderysyngdon*), the advowson of the church of Great Rissington, and 6 messuages, 4 ploughlands, 40 a. of meadow, 100 a. of pasture, and 40*s*. rent in Great Rissington and Notgrove (*Nutgrave*). Right of the bishop, as those which the bishop and the other quer. had by gift of Richard Pole and Elizabeth and Thomas. Remise and quitclaim, specifying Elizabeth's heirs, to the quer. and the bishop's heirs. Warranty against John [Eastney] abbot of St. Peter's, Westminster (*Westm'*), and his successors.) Cons. £300. *Endorsed with note of proclamations*.

79/97/41

[John Eastney had ceased to be abbot of Westminster in 1498: *V.C.H. London*, i. 455.]

811. One month [28 April] from Easter. William [Smith] bishop of Lincoln (*Lincoln'*), Reynold Bray knight, William Hody knight, John Shaa knight, Hugh Oldham (*Oldom*) clerk, Humphrey Coningsby (*Conyngesby*) serjeant at law, Richard Empson (*Emson*), William Cope (*Coope*), John Cutte, and Nicholas Compton quer.; John Greville (*Grevyle*) esquire and Joan his wife def. Ten messuages, 10 yardlands, 30 a. of meadow, 200 a. of pasture, and 100*s*. rent in Great Rissington (*Magna Resyngdon* otherwise called *Broderysyngdon*) and half the manor of Great Rissington. Right of the bishop. Remise and quitclaim, specifying Joan's heirs, to the quer. and the bishop's heirs. (Warranty.) Cons. £200. *Endorsed with note of proclamations*.

79/97/42

812. One week [2 June] from Trinity. (Made the morrow [10 May] of Ascension in the said year.) Roger Capes quer.; William Limerick (*Lymeryk*) def. A messuage, a toft, 20 a. of land, and 6 a. of meadow in Brimpsfield (*Brymesfeld*). Right of Roger. Remise and quitclaim to him. (Warranty.) Cons. 20 marks.

79/97/43

813. One week [2 June] from Trinity. (Made the morrow [10 May] of Ascension in the said year.) Robert Isham clerk, Roger Porter, Edmund Tame, and Robert Hitchman (*Hycheman*) quer.; Thomas Mimms (*Mymmes*) def. Two messuages, 40 a. of land, 30 a. of meadow, and 40 a. of pasture in Frampton on Severn (*Frampton super Sabrinam*). Right of Edmund, as those which Edmund, Robert, Roger, and Robert had by Thomas's gift. Remise and quitclaim to Robert, Roger, Edmund, and Robert and Edmund's heirs. (Warranty.) Cons. 40 marks. *Endorsed with note of proclamations*.

79/97/44

1499

814. One week [2 June] from Trinity. (Made the morrow [10 May] of Ascension in the said year.) Edmund Tame, Robert Isham clerk, and Robert Hitchman (*Hicheman*) quer.; William Limerick (*Lymeryk*) def. The manor of Tetbury Upton (*Upton*) and 16 messuages, 12 tofts, 300 a. of land, 40 a. of meadow, 100 a. of pasture, and 20*s*. rent in Upton, Doughton (*Dovton*), Charlton (*Charleton*), and Tetbury (*Tettebury*) held by Henry Ketelby and Elizabeth his wife for term of Elizabeth's life. Right of Edmund. Grant of the reversion, of William's inheritance, to Edmund, Robert, and Robert and Edmund's heirs. (Warranty.) Cons. £200. *Endorsed with note of prcolamations.*

79/97/45

15 Henry VII

1499

815. One week [6 Oct.] from Michaelmas. (Made the morrow of Ascension 14 Henry VII [10 May 1499].) Giles Bridge (*Brugge*) knight and John Jones 'gentilman' quer.; Philip Smith (*Smyth*) and Agnes his wife def. A messuage, 20 a. of land, 6 a. of meadow, and 40 a. of pasture in Cirencester (*Cirencestr'*) and Chesterton (*Chesterton*). Right of Giles, as those which Giles and John had by gift of Philip and Agnes. Remise and quitclaim, specifying Agnes's heirs, to Giles and John and Giles's heirs. (Warranty.) Cons. 40 marks.

79/97/46

816. Morrow [12 Nov.] of St. Martin. John Makernes and Edward Heritage (*Erytage*) quer.; Thomas Saunders (*Saundres*) and Elizabeth his wife sister and heir of Edward Epwell (*Ipwell*) def. A messuage and 1⅝ yardland in Broad Marston (*Brodmerston*) and Pebworth (*Pebworth*). Right of John, as those which John and Edward had by gift of Thomas and Elizabeth. Remise and quitclaim, specifying Elizabeth's heirs, to John and Edward and John's heirs. (Warranty.) Cons. 20 marks. *Endorsed with note of proclamations.*

79/97/47

817. One week [18 Nov.] from St. Martin. Matthew Catchmay (*Cachmay*) quer.; William Rogers def. Five messuages and 8 gardens in Bristol (*Bristoll'*). Right of Matthew by William's gift. Remise and quitclaim to Matthew. (Warranty.) Cons. £20. *Labelled* Bristoll'.

294/82/29

818. One week [18 Nov.] from St. Martin. John Vaughan quer.; Robert Young (*Yong*) and Agnes his wife def. A messuage in Bristol (*Bristoll'*). Right of John. Remise and quitclaim, specifying Agnes's heirs, to him. (Warranty.) Cons. £20. *Labelled* Villa Bristoll'. *Endorsed with note of proclamations.*

294/82/30

1500

819. Morrow [3 Feb.] of the Purification. Robert Ricardes (*Rycardes*) quer.; Richard Alynde def. A messuage, 20 a. of land, 3 a. of meadow, 30 a. of pasture, and 2 a. of wood in Ham (*Hamme*), Hamfallow (*Hammesvolowe*), and Hinton (*Hynton*) in the parish of Berkeley (*Berkeley*). Right of Robert by Richard's gift. Remise and quitclaim to Robert. (Warranty.) Cons. 40 marks.

79/97/48

820. Two weeks [3 May] from Easter. (Made two weeks from St. John the Baptist 14 Henry VII [8 July 1499].) Thomas Lane and Thomas Codyll quer.; John Langley esquire and Joan his wife def. Three messuages, 290 a. of land, 6 a. of meadow, and 8 a. of pasture in Turkdean (*Turkeden*). Right of Thomas Codyll, as those which the same Thomas and Thomas Lane had by gift of John and Joan. Remise and quitclaim, specifying Joan's heirs, to Thomas and Thomas and Thomas Codyll's heirs. (Warranty.) Cons. 40 marks.

79/97/49

821. Two weeks [3 May] from Easter. (Made two weeks from St. Martin in the said year [25 Nov. 1499].) Thomas Lane quer.; John More (*Moore*) the younger def. A toft, 40 a. of land, 2 a. of meadow, and 40 a. of pasture in Up Hatherley (*Uphatherley*) in the county of the town of Gloucester (*Gloucestr'*). Right of Thomas by John's gift. Remise and quitclaim to Thomas. (Warranty.) Cons. £20. *Labelled* Villa Glouc'.

294/82/31

822. Three weeks [10 May] from Easter. John Fryce quer.; Walter Denis (*Denys*) knight and Agnes his wife def. Seven messuages, 106 a. of land, 12 a. of meadow, 12 a. of pasture, and 6 a. of wood and half of 1 yardland in Williamstrip (*Williamsthorp*), Hatherop (*Hathorp*), Eastleach Martin (*Estlache*), Fairford (*Feireford*), and Eastleach Turville (*Letcheturvyle*). Right of John by gift of Walter and Agnes. Remise and quitclaim, specifying Agnes's heirs, to John. (Warranty.) For this, grant back and render to Walter and Agnes. To hold during Agnes's life. Remainder to John Mimm (*Mymme*) and his heirs in tail. Contingent remainder to the heirs of Walter Mimm.

79/97/50

823. One week [1 July] from St. John the Baptist. John Fryce and John Mimm (*Mymme*) quer.; Walter Denis (*Denys*) knight and Agnes his wife def. The manor of Swinbrook (*Swynbroke*) and 4 messuages, a mill, 160 a. of land, 30 a. of meadow, 40 a. of pasture, 20 a. of wood, and 10*s*. rent in Swinbrook, OXON., and 2 messuages, 60 a. of land, 10 a. of meadow, and 40 a. of pasture in Frampton on Severn (*Frampton super Sabrinam*), GLOS. Right of John Mimm, as those which the same John and John Fryce had by gift of Walter and Agnes. Remise and quitclaim, specifying Agnes's heirs, to John and John and John Mimm's heirs. (Warranty.) For this, grant back and render to Walter and Agnes. To hold during their lives. Successive remainders to Thomas Mimm during his life and to his son William Mimm and his heirs in tail. Successive contingent remainders to Thomas's heirs in tail and to the heirs of Walter Mimm. *Labelled* Oxon', Glouc'.

294/80/89

16 Henry VII

1500

824. Morrow [3 Nov.] of All Souls. Thomas Russell, Thomas Mullins (*Moleyns*), William Hall (*Halle*), and Thomas Wharnby quer.; Henry Strangeways (*Strangways*) and Katherine his wife def. Rent of £4 in Harry Stoke (*Herryestoke*) and Filton (*Felton*). Right of Thomas Russell, as those which the same Thomas, Thomas Mullins, William, and Thomas Wharnby had by gift of Henry and Katherine. Remise and quitclaim, specifying Katherine's heirs, to Thomas, Thomas, William, and Thomas and Thomas Russell's heirs. (Warranty against John [Islip] abbot of St. Peter's, Westminster (*Westm'*), and his successors.) Cons. 100 marks.

79/97/51

825. Morrow [3 Nov.] of All Souls. (Made two weeks from Trinity 15 Henry VII [28 June 1500].) Edmund Tame quer.; Thomas Pavy and Katherine his wife def. Ten messuages, 2 dovecots, 180 a. of land, 20 a. of meadow, 14 a. of pasture, 4 a. of wood, and £4 13*s.* 4*d.* rent in Gossington (*Gosyngton*), Slimbridge (*Slymbryge*), and Arlingham (*Erlyngham*). Right of Edmund. Remise and quitclaim, specifying Katherine's heirs, to him. (Warranty.) Cons. 200 marks.

79/97/52

1501

826. Morrow [3 Feb.] of the Purification. Philip Green (*Grene*) quer.; William Marshall (*Marchall*) def. Three messuages, 2 gardens, a dovecot, 20 a. of land, 10 a. of meadow, 40 a. of wood, 12*d.* rent, and a certain fishery in the water of Severn (*aqua Sabrine*) in Ruddle (*Rudhill*) and Newnham (*Newenam*). Right of Philip by William's gift. Remise and quitclaim to Philip. (Warranty.) Cons. £20.

79/97/53

827. One month [9 May] from Easter. Walter Rowden (*Roudun*), John Cook, and Thomas Teylowe quer.; Gerard Van Eck and Margaret his wife def. Two messuages, a toft, 506 a. of land, 11½ a. of meadow, and 2 a. of pasture in Ripple (*Rypyll*), WORCS., and a messuage and a garden in Gloucester (*Gloucestr'*). Right of Walter, as those which Walter, John, and Thomas had by gift of Gerard and Margaret. Remise and quitclaim, specifying Margaret's heirs, to Walter, John, and Thomas and Walter's heirs. (Warranty.) Cons. 100 marks. *Labelled* Wygorn', Villa Gloucestr'.

294/80/97

17 Henry VII

1501

828. One week [18 Nov.] from St. Martin. Richard [Fox] bishop of Durham (*Dunolm'*), Oliver [King] bishop of Bath and Wells (*Bathon' et Wellen'*), John [Arundel] bishop of Coventry and Lichfield (*Coventr' et Lich'*), John [de Vere] earl of Oxford (*Oxon'*), Giles Daubeney of Daubeney knight, Reynold Bray knight, Thomas Lovell knight, Christopher Urswick (*Ursewyk*) clerk, Hugh Oldham (*Oldom*) clerk, and Richard Empson (*Emson*) pet.; John Bassett esquire and Elizabeth his wife def. The manors of Heanton Punchardon (*Heaunton Punchardon*), Ashford (*Assheford*), Parkham (*Parkeham*), Bulkworthy (*Bulkworthy*), East Hagginton (*Esthagyngton*), Saunton (*Sampton*),

1501

Umberleigh (*Womberlegh*), Huntshaw (*Hundshawe*), Beaford (*Beauford*), Riddlecombe (*Redilcombe*), Landcross (*Lancarsse*), Langley (*Langlegh*), Uplowman (*Uplomen*), Gittisham (*Giddesham*), Lambert (*Lamford, Lampford*), Belstone (*Belston*), Tattiscombe (*Tottescombe*), Lyn (*Lyne*), Shirwell (*Shirwill*), Loxford [Loxhore?], Stoke Rivers (*Stokeryvere*), Holcombe (*Holcombe*), Hoccombe (*Hoccombe*), *Wyke, Borebagge, Ledyard*, Marsh (*Mersshe*), Curtisknowle (*Courtesknoll*), and *Yolston* [Youlston *or* East Youlstone], 500 messuages, 10,000 a. of land, 1,000 a. of meadow, 3,000 a. of pasture, 1,000 a. of wood, 20,000 a. of moor, 1,000 a. of furze and heath, and rents of £40, 20 lb. of pepper, 20 lb. of wax, 20 lb. of cumin, 20 cocks, and 40 hens in the same places [*the names are repeated*], Stockey (*Stokkehay*), Goveton (*Godeton*), Knighton (*Knyghton*), Hele, Rew (*Roustokhays*), Tedburn St. Mary (*Tettesbourne*), Torridge (*Torigge*), Widefield (*Wydefeld*), Peters Marland (*Petirismerland*), Upcott (*Uppecote*), *Snellard*, Ashridge (*Aysherigge*), Dodscott (*Dodecote*), Ashmansworthy (*Aysshemannesworthy*), Stroxworthy (*Estrokesworthy*), *Wyke* [again], *Borebagge* [again], *Lydyard* [again], Friars Hele (*Hele Pour*), Putford (*Putford*), Westcott (*Westcote*), Allercombe (*Allercombe*), Bratton (*Bratton*), Morthoe (*Mourthehoo*), Pilton (*Pylton*), Litchaton (*Lycheton*), *Barneford*, Gorrel (*Gorehill*), Buckland Dinham (*Bokeland Dynham*), Buckland Brewer (*Bokeland Bruer*), and Caffyns Heanton (*Coffenesheaunton*), and the advowsons of the churches of Heanton Punchardon (*Heaunton*), Churston Ferrers (*Chircheton*), Parkham, Stoke Rivers (*Stokeryvers*), Atherington (*Adryngton*), High Bickington (*Bygynton*), Huntshaw, Beaford, Uplowman, Landcross, Tedburn St. Mary (*Tettysbourne*), and Gittisham and of the chantries of Umberleigh and Beaford, DEVON, the manors of Lanteglos (*Lantegles*), Polruan (*Polruan*), Fawton (*Foweton*), and Trevillis (*Trevilias*) and 60 messuages, 2,000 a. of land, 200 a. of meadow, 500 a. of pasture, 100 a. of wood, and 2,000 a. of furze and heath, and £10 rent in those places [*the names are repeated*], CORNW., the manors of Brompton Ralph (*Brampton Rauff*), Hoccombe (*Hoccombe*), Oare (*Ore*), Withycombe (*Wythecombe*), Elworthy (*Elworthy*), Willett (*Welott*), Plaish (*Plasse*), Bradney (*Bradney*), Burbage (*Burbage*), *Wyke*, and Pyleigh (*Pylegh*), 100 messuages, 5,000 a. of land, 1,000 a. of meadow, 2,000 a. of pasture, 200 a. of wood, 1,000 a. of marsh, 2,000 a. of moor, 1,000 a. of furze and heath, and £20 rent in the same places [*the names are repeated*], Langley (*Langlegh*), Knighton (*Knyghton*), Westcott (*Wescote*), Allercombe (*Albercombe*), Friars Hele [again], Lydeard (*Lydeyard*), Upcott [again], Fawton [again], and Morthoe [again], and the advowson of the church of Brompton Ralph, SOM., the manors of Shrivenham (*Shirevenham*) and Stallpits (*Stalpitte*), 20 messuages, 1,000 a. of land, 100 a. of meadow, 1,000 a. of pasture, 100 a. of wood, and £12 rent in Shrivenham and Stallpits, and the hundred of Stallpits, BERKS., the manors of Frampton Cotterell (*Frampton Cotell*), Yate (*Yeate*), Sandhurst (*Saundhurst*), Poulton (*Pulton*), Westonbirt (*Westonbritte*), and Ablington (*Ablynton*), 100 messuages, 3,000 a. of land, 100 a. of meadow, 3,000 a. of pasture, 200 a. of wood, and £20 rent in the same places [*the names are repeated*], and the advowsons of the churches of Frampton Cotterell, Yate, and Westonbirt, GLOS., and the manors of Calstone Wellington (*Calston*) and Asserton (*Asserton*), 500 messuages, 1,000 a. of land, 40 a. of meadow, 1,000 a. of pasture, 20 a. of wood, and 100*s*. rent in Calstone and Asserton, and the advowson of the free chapel of Asserton, WILTS. (Plea of warranty of charter.) Right of the bishop of Coventry and Lichfield. Remise and quitclaim, specifying Elizabeth's heirs, to the quer. and the heirs of the bishop of Coventry and Lichfield. (Warranty against George

1501

[Fascet] abbot of St. Peter's, Westminster (*Westm'*) and his successors.) Cons. £1,000. *Labelled* Devon', Cornub', Somers', Berk', Glouc', Wiltes'. *Endorsed with note of proclamations.*

294/80/104

[Cf. *Wilts. Fines, 1377–1509*, pp. 171–2, no. 754. Like nos. 835, 842, below, this fine appears to have been carelessly drafted, with apparent repetitions and the assignment of places to the wrong counties. George Fascet had ceased to be abbot of Westminster in 1500.]

829. One week [18 Nov.] from St. Martin. Richard [Fox] bishop of Durham [*etc., as no. 828, above*] pet.; Hugh Beaumont (*Beaumount*) and Elizabeth his wife def. [*The wording of the fine is the same as no. 828, with a few minor variations in the spelling of place-names; where* Wyke, Borebagge, *and* Lydyard *are repeated they occur as* Wyke Ledyard Borebagge Lydyard.] *Labelled* Devon', Cornub', Somers', Wiltes', Berk', Glouc'. *Endorsed with note of proclamations.*

294/80/105

[Cf. *Wilts. Fines, 1377–1509*, p. 172, no. 755.]

830. One week [18 Nov.] from St. Martin. Richard [Fox] bishop of Durham [*etc., as no. 828, above*] pet.; John Beaumont (*Beaumonte*) clerk def. [*The wording of the fine is the same as no. 828, with a few minor variations in the spelling of place-names; where* Wyke, Borebagge, *and* Lydyard *are repeated they occur as* Wyke Borebagge Ledyarde.] *Labelled* Devon', Somers', Glouc', Cornub', Berk', Wiltes'. *Endorsed with note of proclamations.*

294/80/106

[Cf. *Wilts. Fines, 1377–1509*, p. 172, no. 756.]

1502

831. One week [20 Jan.] from Hilary. (Made two weeks from St. Martin in the said year [25 Nov. 1501].) Nicholas Brown (*Broun*) quer.; John Choke (*Chok*) knight def. A messuage in Bristol (*Bristoll'*). Right of Nicholas by John's gift. Remise and quitclaim to Nicholas. (Warranty.) Cons. £40. *Labelled* Villa Bristoll'. *Endorsed with note of proclamations.*

294/82/34

832. One month [4 April] from Easter. William Austin (*Austyn*) the younger, Thomas Austin the elder, Thomas Austin son of William Austin, Richard Austin, John Austin, Robert Baker, Richard Baker, Thomas Austin son of John Austin, Hugh Blanchard (*Blauncherd*), Thomas Hawarden (*Hawardyne*), and Richard Hill (*Hyll*) quer.; George Davies (*Davyes*) late of Tetbury (*Tettebury*) in the county of Gloucester (*Glouc'*) and Agnes his wife def. Two messuages and a garden in Woodmancote (*Wodmancote*) and Dursley (*Durseley*). Right of William, as those which William and the other quer. had by gift of George and Agnes. Remise and quitclaim, specifying Agnes's heirs, to the quer. and William's heirs. (Warranty.) Cons. 40 marks. *Endorsed with note of proclamations.*

79/97/54

833. Morrow [25 June] of St. John the Baptist. Reynold Bray knight, Thomas Cornish (*Cornysshe*) clerk, Hugh Oldham (*Oldom*) clerk, John Baker, and John Brooke (*Broke*) quer.; James Veal (*Vyell*) and Joan his wife def. Half of the manor of Shenington

1502

(*Shynnyngdon*) and half of 10 messuages, 100 a. of land, 10 a. of meadow, 40 a. of pasture, 4 a. of wood, and £8 rent in Shenington. Right of Thomas, as those which Thomas and the other quer. had by gift of James and Joan. Remise and quitclaim, specifying Joan's heirs, to the quer. and Thomas's heirs. (Warranty.) Cons. £100. *Endorsed with note of proclamations.*

79/97/55

18 Henry VII

1502

834. Morrow [3 Nov.] of All Souls. Elena Reed widow and Henry Whittingham (*Whittyngham*) quer.; John Morris (*Mores*) and Elizabeth his wife def. A messuage and 2 gardens in the town of Gloucester (*Gloucestr'*). Right of Elena, as those which she and Henry had by gift of John and Elizabeth. Remise and quitclaim, specifying Elizabeth's heirs, to Elena and Henry and Elena's heirs. (Warranty.) Cons. £20. *Labelled* Villa Gloucestr'.

294/82/38

1503

835. Two weeks [30 April] from Easter. (Made one week [9 Feb.] from the Purification in the said year.) Richard [Fox] bishop of Winchester (*Winton'*) late bishop of Durham (*Duneln'*), Oliver [King] bishop of Bath and Wells (*Bathon' et Wellen'*), John [Arundel] bishop of Exeter (*Exon'*) late bishop of Coventry and Lichfield (*Coventr' et Lich'*), John [de Vere] earl of Oxford (*Oxon'*), Giles Daubeney of Daubeney knight, Reynold Bray knight, Thomas Lovell knight, Christopher Urswick (*Ursewyke*) clerk, Hugh Oldham (*Oldom*) clerk, and Richard Empson (*Emson*) quer.; John Chichester def. The manors of Brompton Ralph (*Brampton Rauff*), Hoccombe (*Hoccombe*), Oare (*Ore*), Withycombe (*Wythecombe*), Elworthy (*Elleworthy*), Willett (*Wellott*), Plaish (*Plasse*), Bradney (Bradney), Burbage, *Wyke*, and Pyleigh (*Pylegh*), and 100 messuages, 5,000 a. of land, 1,000 a. of meadow, 2,000 a. of pasture, 200 a. of wood, 1,000 a. of furze and heath, 2,000 a. of moor, 1,000 a. of marsh, and £20 rent in Brompton Ralph, Hoccombe, Oare, Withycombe, Elworthy, Willett (*Welot*), Plaish, Bradney, Burbage, *Wyke*, Pyleigh, Langley (*Langlegh*), Knighton (*Knyghton*), Westcott (*Wescote*), Allercombe (*Albercombe*), Friars Hele (*Hele Poure*), Lydeard (*Lydeyard*), Upcott (*Uppecote*), Fawton (*Foweton*), and Morthoe (*Mourtehoo*) and the advowson of the church of Brompton Ralph, SOM., the manors of Calstone Wellington (*Calston*) and Asserton (*Asserton*), 7 messuages, 1,000 a. of land, 40 a. of meadow, 1,000 a. of pasture, 20 a. of wood, and 100s. rent in Calstone and Asserton, and the advowson of the chapel of Asserton, WILTS., the manors of Lanteglos (*Lanteglez*), Polruan (*Polruan*), Fawton (*Foweton*), and Trevillis (*Trevylyas*), 60 messuages, 2,000 a. of land, 200 a. of meadow, 500 a. of pasture, 100 a. of wood, 2,000 a. of furze and heath, and £10 rent in Lanteglos, Polruan, Fawton, and Trevillis (*Trevilias*), CORNW., the manors of Heanton Punchardon (*Heaunton Punchardon*), Ashford (*Assheford*), Parkham (*Parkeham*), Bulkworthy (*Bulkworthy*), East Hagginton (*Esthagynton*), Saunton (*Sampton*), Umberleigh (*Womberlegh*), Beaford (*Beauford*), Riddlecombe (*Redylcombe*), Landcross (*Lancarsse*), Langley (*Langlegh*), Uplowman (*Uppelomen*), Gittisham (*Gyddesham*), Lambert (*Lampford*), Belstone (*Belston*), Tattiscombe (*Cottescombe*), Lyn (*Lyne*),

1503

Shirwell (*Shirwell*), *Loxford* [Loxhore?], Holcombe (*Holcombe*), Hoccombe (*Hoccombe*), *Wyke*, *Borebagge*, Lydeard (*Lydyard*), Marsh (*Mersshe*), Curtisknowle (*Courtesknoll*), and *Yolston* [Youlston *or* East Youlstone], 500 messuages, 10,000 a. of land, 1,000 a. of meadow, 3,000 a. of pasture, 1,000 a. of wood, 1,000 a. of furze and heath, 20,000 a. of moor, rents of £40 and 20 lb. of pepper, 20 lb. of wax, 20 lb. of cumin, 20 cocks, and 40 hens in Heanton Punchardon (*Heaunton Puncherdon*), Ashford, Parkham, Bulkworthy, East Hagginton, Saunton, Umberleigh, Beaford, Riddlecombe, Landcross, Langley, Uplowman, Gittisham, Lambert, Belstone, Tattiscombe (*Tottescombe*), Lyn, *Loxford*, Holcombe, Hoccombe, *Wyke*, *Borebagge*, Lydeard, Marsh, Curtisknowle, *Yolston*, Stockey (*Stokehay*), Goveton (*Godeton*), Knighton (*Knyghton*), Friars Hele (*Hele*), Rew (*Roustokhay*), Tedburn St. Mary (*Tetteborne*), Torridge (*Torygge*), Widefield (*Wydefeld*), Peters Marland (*Peterysmarland*), Upcott (*Uppecote*), *Snellard*, Ashridge (*Ayssherigge*), Dodscott (*Dodecote*), Curtisknowle [*again*], Ashmansworthy (*Aysshemanesworthy*), Stroxworthy (*Estrokesworthy*), *Wyke* [*again*], *Bowrybage* [*apparently repeating* Borebagge], and Lydeard [*again*], and the advowsons of the churches of Heanton, Churston Ferrers (*Chircheton*), Parkham, Stoke Rivers (*Stokeryvers*), Atherington (*Adryngton*), High Bickington (*Bygynton*), Huntshaw (*Hundshawe*), Beaford, Uplowman, Landcross, Gittisham, *Yolston*, Shirwell (*Shirwyll*), Marsh, Upper Loxhore (*Overlokkysore*), Lower Loxhore (*Netherlokkysore*), Smythapark (*Smythespathe*), Holcombe, East Hagginton, Dodscott, Curtisknowle, Tattiscombe (*Tettescombe*), Lyn, Braunton (*Brampton*), Beaumont, Friars Hele (*Hele Poure*), and Tedburn St. Mary (*Tettebourn*) and of the chantries of Umberleigh and Beaford, DEVON, the manors of Shrivenham (*Shirevenham*) and Stallpits (*Stalpitte*), 20 messuages, 1,000 a. of land, 100 a. of meadow, 1,000 a. of pasture, 100 a. of wood, and £12 rent in Shrivenham and Stallpits, and the hundred of Stallpits, BERKS., and the manors of Frampton Cotterell (*Frampton Cotell*), Yate (*Yeate*), Sandhurst (*Saundhurst*), Poulton (*Pulton*), Westonbirt (*Westonbritte*), and Ablingon (*Ablynton*), 100 messuages, 3,000 a. of land, 100 a. of meadow, 3,000 a. of pasture, 200 a. of wood, and £20 rent in Frampton Cotterell, Yate, Sandhurst (*Saundhurste*), Poulton, Westonbirt, and Ablington and the advowsons of the churches of Frampton Cotterell, Yate, and Westonbirt, GLOS. Right of the bishop of Exeter. Remise and quitclaim to the quer. and the heirs of the bishop of Exeter. (Warranty against John [Islip] abbot of St. Peter's, Westminster (*Westm'*) and his successors.) Cons. £1,000. *Labelled* Somers', Devon', Wiltes', Berk', Cornub', Gloucestr'.

294/81/116

[Cf. *Wilts. Fines, 1377–1509*, pp. 175–6, no. 766. Even more than nos. 828–30, above, this fine appears to have been carelessly drafted, with repetitions, the assignment of places to the wrong counties, and reference to the advowsons of places without churches. The names of the counties with which the document is labelled are, unusually, not in the same order as in the body of the fine.]

836. One month [14 May] from Easter. John Easterfield (*Esterfeld*) quer.; Richard Tytherley (*Tyderley*) and William Tytherley def. A messuage in the town of Bristol (*Bristoll'*). Right of John by gift of Richard and William. Remise and quitclaim, specifying William's heirs, to John. (Warranty.) Cons. 20 marks. *Labelled* Villa Bristoll'.

294/82/39

1503

837. Two weeks [25 June] from Trinity. (Made the morrow [26 May] of Ascension in the said year.) William Harding (*Hardyng*) quer.; William Warner def. A messuage, 2 gardens, 30 a. of land, 4 a. of meadow, 20 a. of pasture, 12*s.* 10*d.* rent, and one quarter of a messuage, 72 a. of land, 4 a. of meadow, 13 a. of pasture, 4 a. of wood, and 27*s.* 6*d.* rent in Cam (*Camme*), Coaley (*Coueley*), and Arlingham (*Arlyngham*). Right of William Harding, of which he had the 12*s.* 10*d.* rent and one quarter of 4 a. of wood in Cam, Coaley, and Arlingham by William Warner's gift. Remise and quitclaim to William Harding. And grant to him of the reversion of the messuage, 2 gardens, 30 a. of land, 4 a. of meadow, and 20 a. of pasture held by William Oliver (*Olyver*) for term of life, and of the one quarter of a messuage, 72 a. of land, 4 a. of meadow, 13 a. of pasture, and 27*s.* 6*d.* rent held by Thomas Tailor (*Taillour*) for term of life, of William Warner's inheritance in Cam and Coaley. (Warranty.) Cons. £20. *Endorsed with note of proclamations.*

79/97/56

838. Two weeks [25 June] from Trinity. William Seymour (*Seyntmaure*) knight, William Ayloff, Richard Rowden (*Roudon*), John Payn (*Payne*) clerk, William Goldsmith (*Goldsmyth*), and John Arnold quer.; Hugh Croft esquire, Agnes Croft widow, and Lionel Croft def. The manor of Stanley Pontlarge (*Stanley Pountlarge*) and 9 messuages, 2 tofts, 400 a. of land, 60 a. of meadow, 300 a. of pasture, 20 a. of wood, and 1*d.* rent in Stanley Pontlarge and Greet (*Grete*). Right of Richard, as those which Richard and the other quer. had by Hugh's gift. Remise and quitclaim, specifying Agnes's heirs, to the quer. and Richard's heirs. (Warranty.) Cons. 300 marks. *Endorsed with note of proclamations.*

79/97/57

19 Henry VII

1503

839. One week [18 Nov.] from St. Martin. William Tracy, William Rudhall (*Rudhale*), William Denis (*Denys*), Edward Greville (*Grevyle*), and Roger Porter quer.; John Westby (*Wesby*) and Margaret his wife def. The manor of Rendcomb (*Rendcome*) and 12 messuages, 1,200 a. of land, 120 a. of meadow, 800 a. of pasture, and 250 a. of wood in Rendcomb, Calmsden (*Calmesden*), North Cerney (*Cerney*), Woodmancote (*Wodmancote*), Eycot (*Eycote*), Withington (*Wythyngdon*), and Hilcot (*Hilcote*). Right of William Tracy, as those which the same William and the other quer. had by gift of John and Margaret. Remise and quitclaim, specifying Margaret's heirs, to the quer. and William Tracy's heirs. (Warranty against John [Islip] abbot of St. Peter's, Westminster (*Westm'*), and his successors.) Cons. 500 marks. *Endorsed with note of proclamations.*

79/97/58

1504

840. Morrow [25 June] of St. John the Baptist. Edmund Tame quer.; William Dogett and Elizabeth his wife def. Two messuages, 300 a. of land, 20 a. of meadow, and 100 a. of pasture in Compton Abdale (*Compton Apdale*), Upper Hampen (*Overhampden*), and Lower Hampen (*Netherhampden*). Right of Edmund by gift of William and Elizabeth. Remise and quitclaim, specifying Elizabeth's heirs, to Edmund. (Warranty against John [Islip] abbot of St. Peter's, Westminster (*Westm'*), and his successors.) Cons. 100 marks.

79/97/59

1504

841. Morrow [25 June] of St. John the Baptist. William Wigston (*Wyggeston*) the younger, Richard Gillot, and Roger Wigston quer.; Thomas Everdon and Alice his wife def. Three messuages, 180 a. of land, 70 a. of meadow, and 60 a. of pasture in Lower Slaughter (*Nether Sloughter*) and Upper Slaughter (*Over Sloughter*). Right of William, as those which William, Richard, and Roger had by gift of Thomas and Alice. Remise and quitclaim, specifying Alice's heirs, to William, Richard, and Roger and William's heirs. (Warranty.) Cons. £40.

79/97/60

20 Henry VII

1505

842. One week [25 May] from Trinity. (Made two weeks from St. Martin in the said year [25 Nov. 1504].) Richard [Fox] bishop of Winchester (*Wynton'*), John [de Vere] earl of Oxford (*Oxon'*), Giles Daubeney (*Daubney*) of Daubeney knight, Hugh Oldham (*Oldam*) clerk, Thomas Lovell knight, Christopher Urswick (*Ursewyke*) clerk, and Richard Empson (*Emson*) knight quer.; John Chichester (*Chechester*) esquire and Margaret his wife and John Crocker (*Crokker*) and Anne his wife def. The manors of Heanton Punchardon (*Heaunton Puncherdon*), Ashford (*Assheford*), Parkham (*Parkeham*), Bulkworthy (*Bulkworthy*), East Hagginton (*Esthagyngton*), Saunton (*Sampton*), Umberleigh (*Womberlegh*), Huntshaw (*Hundeshawe*), Beaford (*Beauford*), Riddlecombe (*Rydylcombe*), Landcross (*Lancarse*), Langley (*Langlegh*), Uplowman (*Uppelomen*), Shirwell (*Shirwyll*), Stoke Rivers (*Stoke Ryvers*), Holcombe (*Holcombe*), *Wyke*, Marsh (*Mersshe*), Curtisknowle (*Courtesknoll*), and *Yolston* [Youlston *or* East Youlstone], 500 messuages, 10,000 a. of land, 1,000 a. of meadow, 3,000 a. of pasture, 1,000 a. of wood, 20,000 a. of moor, 1,000 a. of furze and heath, and rents of £40 and 20 lb. of pepper, 20 lb. of wax, 20 lb. of cumin, 20 cocks, and 40 hens in Heanton Punchardon, Ashford, Parkham, Bulkworthy (*Bulkeworthy*), East Hagginton (*Esthagynton*), Saunton, Umberleigh, Huntshaw, Beaford, Riddlecombe (*Redylcombe*), Landcross (*Lancarsse*), Langley, Uplowman, Shirwell (*Shirwell*), Stoke Rivers (*Stoke Revers*), Holcombe, *Wyke*, Marsh, Curtisknowle, *Yolston*, Stockey (*Stokehay*), Goveton (*Godeton*), Knighton (*Knyghton*), Hele, Rew (*Robstothaye*), Tedburn St. Mary (*Tetteburne*), Torridge (*Torygge*), Widefield (*Wydefeld*), Peters Marland (*Peterysmarland*), Upcott (*Uppecote*), *Snellard*, Ashridge (*Assherigge*), Dodscott (*Dodecote*), Curtisknowle [*again*], Ashmansworthy (*Asshemaymesworthy*), Stroxworthy (*Estrokesworthy*), *Wyke* [*again*], *Bowrybage*, Lydeard (*Lydeard*), Friars Hele (*Hele Pour*), Putford (*Putford*), Westcott (*Wescote*), Allercombe (*Awercombe*), Bratton (*Bratton*), Morthoe (*Mourtehoo*), Pilton (*Pylton*), Litchaton (*Lycheton*), *Barneford*, Gorrel (*Gorehyll*), Buckland Dinham (*Bokelond Dynham*), Buckland Brewer (*Bokelond Bruer*), and Caffyns Heanton (*Cofynyshaunton*), and the advowsons of the churches of Heanton Punchardon, Churston Ferrers (*Chircheton*), Parkham, Stoke Rivers, Atherington (*Adryngton*), High Bickington (*Bygynton*), Huntshaw (*Hunshawe*), Beaford, Uplowman, Landcross, Tedburn St. Mary (*Tettesbourne*), and Gittisham (*Gyddesham*) and of the chantries of Umberleigh and Beaford, DEVON, the manors of Brompton Ralph (*Brampton Rauff*), Withycombe (*Wythycombe*), and Wick (*Weke*), 100 messuages, 5,000 a. of land, 1,000 a. of meadow, 2,000 a. of pasture, 200 a. of wood, 1,000 a. of marsh, 2,000 a. of moor, 1,000 a. of furze and heath, and £20 rent in Brompton Ralph, Wick,

1505

Langley (*Langlegh*), Knighton (*Knyghton*), Westcott, Allercombe (*Albercombe*), Friars Hele, Lydeard (*Lydyerd*), Upcott, Fawton (*Foweton*), and Morthoe, and the advowson of the church of Brompton Ralph, SOM., the manors of Calstone Wellington (*Calston*) and Asserton (*Asserton*), 20 messuages, 1,000 a. of land, 40 a. of meadow, 1,000 a. of pasture, 10 a. of wood, and 100*s.* rent in Calstone and Asserton, and the advowson of the free chapel of Asserton, WILTS., and the manors of Frampton Cotterell (*Frampton Cotell*), Yate (*Yeate*), Sandhurst (*Saundhurste*), Poulton (*Pulton*), Westonbirt (*Weston Britte*), and Ablington (*Ablyngton*) and 100 messuages, 3,000 a. of land, 100 a. of meadow, 3,000 a. of pasture, 200 a. of wood, and £20 rent in Frampton Cotterell (*Frampton Cotelle*), Yate, and Westonbirt, GLOS. Right of Giles. Remise and quitclaim, specifying Margaret's and Anne's heirs, to the quer. and Giles's heirs. (Warranty by John and Margaret, specifying Margaret's heirs, against John [Islip] abbot of St. Peter's, Westminster (*Westm'*), and his successors.) For this, grant back and render to John Chichester and Margaret of the manors of Saunton, Brompton, Stoke Rivers, Huntshaw, Shirwell, and *Yolston*, of all the messuages, cottages [*not previously mentioned*], tofts [*not previously mentioned*], land, meadow, pasture, wood, and rent in Saunton, Brampton, Stoke Rivers, Huntshaw, Shirwell, and *Yolston* and the advowsons of the said manors [*sic*] of Saunton, Brompton, Stoke Rivers, Huntshaw, Shirwell, and *Yolston*. To hold to them and their heirs in tail, of the quer. and Giles's heirs, paying during the life of Hugh Beaumont esquire £86 13*s.* 4*d.* a year, at Christmas, the Annunciation, St. John the Baptist, and Michaelmas, with right of distraint for arrears, and after Hugh's death paying a rose a year at St. John the Baptist and doing service to the chief lords. Contingent reversion to the quer. *Labelled* Devon', Somers', Wiltes', Glous' [*sic*]. *Endorsed* Exempl' [sc. 'It is to be exemplifed'].

294/81/129

[Cf. *Wilts. Fines, 1377–1509*, p. 178, no. 778. Like nos. 828–30, 835, above, this fine has repetitions and places assigned to the wrong counties.]

843. Morrow [25 June] of St. John the Baptist. William Austin (*Austen*) quer.; George Davies (*Davyse*) and Agnes his wife def. Seven messuages, 6 gardens, and 1 a. of meadow in Dursley (*Durseley*) and Woodmancote (*Wodmancote*). Right of William. Remise and quitclaim, specifying Agnes's heirs, to him. (Warranty.) Cons. 100 marks. *Endorsed with note of proclamations.*

79/97/61

844. Morrow [25 June] of St. John the Baptist. Edmund Tame esquire quer.; Ralph Latham (*Lathum*) and Elizabeth his wife def. The manor of Dowdeswell (*Dowedeswell*), the advowson of the church of the same manor, and 5 messuages, 300 a. of land, 120 a. of meadow, 400 a. of pasture, 240 a. of wood, and 40*s.* rent in Dowdeswell and Withington (*Withyngdon*). Right of Edmund by gift of Ralph and Elizabeth. Remise and quitclaim, specifying Elizabeth's heirs, to Edmund. (Warranty against John [Islip] abbot of St. Peter's, Westminster (*Westm'*), and his successors.) Cons. £200. *Endorsed with note of proclamations.*

79/97/62

21 Henry VII

1505

845. Two weeks [13 Oct.] from Michaelmas. John Davies (*Davys*) quer.; William Fream (*Freme*) and Alice his wife def. Two messuages, 28½ a. of land, and 8½ a. of meadow in Ham (*Hamme*) and Hamfallow (*Hammesvalowe*) in the parish of Berkeley (*Berkeley*), Slimbridge (*Slymbrigge*), and Hurst (*Hurst*). Right of John by gift of William and Alice. Remise and quitclaim, specifying Alice's heirs, to John. (Warranty.) Cons. 40 marks. *Endorsed with note of proclamations.*

79/97/63

846. One month [27 Oct.] from Michaelmas. Henry Shoyer and John Chadwell quer.; William Bridge (*Brugge*) of Longdon (*Longdon*) and Alice his wife def. A messuage, 36 a. of land, 6 a. of meadow, and 6*d.* rent in Quedgeley (*Quedesley*). Right of Henry, as those which Henry and John had by gift of William and Alice. Remise and quitclaim, specifying Alice's heirs, to Henry and John and Henry's, heirs. (Warranty.) Cons. 40 marks. *Endorsed with a note of proclamations.*

79/97/64

847. One month [27 Oct.] from Michaelmas. William Henshaw (*Hanshawe*) and Alice his wife quer.; Christopher Throckmorton (*Throgmerton*) esquire and Richard Buckland (*Bukland*) and Eleanor his wife def. A messuage, a dovecot, a garden, and 1 a. of land in Gloucester (*Gloucestr'*) and Kingsholm (*Kyngeshome*). Right of William, as those which William and Alice had by gift of Christopher and Richard and Eleanor. Remise and quitclaim, specifying Eleanor's heirs, to William and Alice and William's heirs. (Warranty.) Cons. £40. *Labelled* Villa Gloucestr'. *Endorsed with note of proclamations.*

294/82/46

848. One month [27 Oct.] from Michaelmas. Walter Rowden (*Roudun*) quer.; John Style and Margaret his wife def. A dovecot and 3 gardens in Gloucester (*Gloucestr'*). Right of Walter by gift of John and Margaret. Remise and quitclaim, specifying Margaret's heirs, to Walter. (Warranty.) Cons. 10 marks. *Labelled* Villa Glouc'. *Endorsed with note of proclamations.*

294/82/47

849. Morrow [3 Nov.] of All Souls. Thomas [Savage] archbishop of York (*Ebor'*), John Savage knight, William Greville (*Grevyle*) serjeant at law, Roger Savage clerk, John Brereton, and Roger Cotton (*Coton*) quer.; John Stanley esquire def. The manors of Chipping Campden (*Chepyng Campden*), Berrington (*Buryton*), Westington (*Westyngton*), Aston Subedge (*Aston subtus Ege*), Ullington (*Ulyngton*), and Norton Subedge (*Norton subtus Ege*) and 30 messuages, 1,000 a. of land, 100 a. of meadow, 500 a. of pasture, 10 a. of wood, and 100*s.* rent in Chipping Campden, Berrington, Westington, Aston Subedge, Ullington, and Norton Subedge. Right of the archbishop, as those which the archbishop and the other quer. had by John Stanley's gift. Remise and quitclaim to the quer. and the archbishop's heirs. (Warranty.) Cons. £600. *Endorsed with note of proclamations.* [*Worn.*]

79/97/65

1505

850. Morrow [12 Nov.] of St. Martin. Roger Porter and Richard Spenser (*Spencer*) quer.; Geoffrey Griffith (*Griffyth*) and Joan his wife def. A messuage and a garden in Newnham (*Newenham*). Right of Richard, as those which Richard and Roger had by gift of Geoffrey and Joan. Remise and quitclaim, specifying Joan's heirs, to Roger and Richard and Richard's heirs. (Warranty.) Cons. 20 marks. *Endorsed with note of proclamations.*

79/97/66

851. Morrow [12 Nov.] of St. Martin. John Brooke quer.; Thomas Talbot esquire def. Four messuages and 3 gardens in Bristol (*Bristoll'*). Right of John by Thomas's gift. Remise and quitclaim to John. (Warranty.) Cons. £40. *Labelled* Villa Bristoll'. *Endorsed with note of proclamations.*

294/82/48

1506

852. Three weeks [3 May] from Easter. William Rudhall (*Rudhale*), Robert Ford (*Forde*), Richard Hartland, and John Keys quer.; William Hartland and Cecily his wife def. A messuage, 80 a. of land, 2 a. of meadow, and 10 a. of pasture in Malswick (*Malleswyke*) in the parish of Newent (*Newent*). Right of William Rudhall, as those which the same William, Robert, Richard, and John had by gift of William Hartland and Cecily. Remise and quitclaim, specifying Cecily's heirs, to William Rudhall, Robert, Richard, and John and William Rudhall's heirs. (Warranty.) Cons. £20.

79/97/67

853. One month [10 May] from Easter. John Maddock (*Madok*) the elder and John Maddock the younger quer.; John Chalver and Joan his wife def. A messuage, 60 a. of land, 10 a. of meadow, 20 a. of pasture, and 4 a. of wood in Hewelsfield (*Hewellesfeld*). Right of John Maddock the elder, as that which John Maddock the elder and John Maddock the younger had by gift of John Chalver and Joan. Remise and quitclaim, specifying Joan's heirs, to John Maddock the elder and John Maddock the younger. (Warranty.) Cons. £20. *Endorsed with note of proclamations.*

79/97/68

854. Morrow [22 May] of Ascension. Thomas Bush (*Busshe*) and Peter Reynolds quer.; Richard Hall (*Halle*) and Milicent his wife def. A messuage and ½ a. of meadow in Northleach (Northelecche). Right of Thomas. Remise and quitclaim, specifying Milicent's heirs, to Thomas and Peter and Thomas's heirs. (Warranty.) Cons. £20.

79/97/69

855. Morrow [22 May] of Ascension. Edmund Tame and Robert Hitchman (*Hicheman*) quer.; Henry Ketelby and Isabel his wife def. The manor of Tetbury Upton (*Upton*) and 16 messuages, 12 tofts, 300 a. of land, 40 a. of meadow, 100 a. of pasture, and 20*s.* rent in Tetbury Upton, Doughton (*Dowton*), Charlton (*Charleton*), and Tetbury (*Tetbury*). Grant to Edmund and Robert. Remise and quitclaim to them of whatever Henry and Isabel had in the manor and holdings for term of Isabel's life. (Warranty against John [Islip] abbot of St. Peter's, Westminster (*Westm'*), and his successors during Isabel's life.) Cons. £100. [*Worn.*]

79/97/70

1506

856. Two weeks [8 July] from St. John the Baptist. John Seabourne (*Seborne*) and John Chadwell (*Chatwell*) quer.; Henry Eden and Margaret his wife def. The manor of Elmstone (*Elmeston*) and 5 messuages, 400 a. of land, 20 a. of meadow, and 100 a. of pasture in Elmstone, Uckington (*Okyngton*), Hardwicke (*Harwyke*), and Leigh (*Lye*). Right of John Seabourne, as those which the same John and John Chadwell had by gift of Henry and Margaret. Remise and quitclaim, specifying Margaret's heirs, to John and John and John Seabourne's heirs. (Warranty.) Cons. £100.

79/97/71

22 Henry VII

1506

857. One week [18 Nov.] from St. Martin. John Jones quer.; William Warner def. Two messuages, a dovecot, 70 a. of land, 8 a. of meadow, and 20 a. of pasture in Cowley (*Coweley*). Right of John by William's gift. Remise and quitclaim to John. (Warranty.) Cons. 40 marks.

79/97/72

23 Henry VII

1507

858. One month [27 Oct.] from Michaelmas. Thomas Poyntz esquire, John Davies (*Davys*) and Thomas Trolley quer.; John Walsh (*Walssh*) def. Half of the manor of Nympsfield (*Nymsfeld*), half of 20 messuages, 400 a. of land, 100 a. of meadow, 400 a. of pasture, 300 a. of wood, and rents of 40*s*. and 3 lb. of pepper in Nympsfield, and the advowson of the free chapel of St. Anthony in Kinley (*Kynley*) in the parish of Nympsfield. Right of Thomas Poyntz, as those which the same Thomas, John Davies, and Thomas Trolley had by John Walsh's gift. Remise and quitclaim to Thomas, John Davies, and Thomas and Thomas Poyntz's heirs. (Warranty.) Cons. £200. *Endorsed with note of proclamations*.

79/97/73

[Where John Davies is first named his surname is omitted, and after the acknowledgement of right Thomas Poyntz's name is omitted from the clause saying that the premises were held by John Walsh's gift.]

859. One month [27 Oct.] from Michaelmas. Richard Spenser (*Spencer*) and Richard Peere quer.; John Roberts (*Robertes*) and Matilda his wife def. The manor of Okle Clifford (*Ocle* otherwise called *Ocleys Court*) and 3 messuages, 200 a. of land, 100 a. of pasture, 20 a. of meadow, 20 a. of wood, and 100*s*. rent in Okle and Newent (*Newent*). Right of Richard Spenser. Remise and quitclaim, specifying Matilda's heirs, to Richard and Richard and Richard Spenser's heirs. (Warranty.) Cons. £200. *Endorsed with note of proclamations*.

79/97/74

[Spenser and Peere were evidently acting on behalf of the prior and convent of Llanthony: *Llanthony Priory Regs*. pp. 86–8, no. 217. The pasture and meadow are not listed in the usual order.]

1508

860. Two weeks [7 May] from Easter. Simon Harcourt esquire, John Horn esquire, Edmund Bury, and Robert Egerley quer.; Richard Harcourt esquire and Agnes his wife def. The manor of Hampnett (*Hamptenet*), a messuage, a mill, a garden and 30 a. of meadow in Hampnett, Northleach (*Northleche*), and Chedworth (*Chaddeworth*), and the advowson of the church of Hampnett. Right of Robert, as those which Robert, Simon, John, and Edmund had by gift of Richard and Agnes. Remise and quitclaim, specifying Agnes's heirs, to Simon, John, Edmund, and Robert and Robert's heirs. (Warranty.) For this, grant back and render to Richard and Agnes. To hold to them and Agnes's heirs.

79/97/75

[The fine is endorsed *Glouc* and, upside down at the bottom, *Pedes*, i.e. Feet, part of labelling on what was once the back of a bundle of feet of fines.]

861. Morrow [2 June] of Ascension. Thomas Babington (*Babyngton*), Anthony FitzHerbert, Thomas Moleyns, and John Strange (*Straunge*) quer.; Sampson Norton knight and Elizabeth his wife and Ralph Shirley knight and Anne his wife def. The manor of Hambrook (*Hambroke*) and 6 messuages, 2 tofts, 300 a. of land, 40 a. of meadow, 200 a. of pasture, 10 a. of wood, and 3*s*. 2*d*. rent in Hambrook, Earthcott (*Erthecote*), Westbury-on-Trym (*Westbury*), and Coombe (*Combe*) in the parish of Westbury, GLOS., and 5 messuages in Bristol (*Bristoll'*). Right of Thomas Babington, as those which the same Thomas, Anthony, Thomas, and John had by gift of Sampson and Elizabeth and Ralph and Anne. Remise and quitclaim, specifying Elizabeth's and Anne's heirs, to Thomas, Anthony, Thomas, and John and Thomas Babington's heirs. (Warranty.) Cons. £300. *Labelled* Glouc', Bristoll'.

294/81/158

24 Henry VII

1508

862. One month [27 Oct.] from Michaelmas. Robert Byng (*Bynge*) quer.; John Tymbrell otherwise called John Tymburhill def. A messuage, a toft, 70 a. of land, 12 a. of meadow, and 20 a. of pasture in Edgeworth (*Eggeworth*). Right of Robert by John's gift. Remise and quitclaim to Robert. (Warranty.) Cons. £20.

79/97/76

863. Two weeks [25 November] from St. Martin. Robert Ricardes (*Rycardes*) quer.; Thomas Ricardes def. Half of a messuage, 30 a. of land, 6 a. of meadow, 44 a. of pasture, and 2 a. of wood in Ham (*Hamme*), Pedington (*Pedyngton*), and Stone (*Stone*) in the parish of Berkeley (*Berkeley*). Right of Robert by Thomas's gift. Remise and quitclaim to Robert. (Warranty.) Cons. £20.

79/97/77

INDEX OF PERSONS AND PLACES

References are to entry-numbers. Separate references to the same surname and forename, which may or may not relate the same person, have not normally been separated.

advowson, 828–30, 835, 842; manor, 429, 828–30, 835, 842

Bromsberrow, 265, 318, 803; advowson, 26, 72, 245, 469; manor, 26, 72, 245, 469

Bromsgrove (Worcs.), manor, 443, 539

Bromsgrove, John, 153

— Walter, 153

Bromwich, Castle (Warws.), manor, 635

Bromwich, Joan wife of Thomas, 469

— John, 72, 245

— Katherine wife of John, 245

— Thomas, son of Walter, 469

— Walter, 469

Brooke, Elena wife of Henry, 474

— Henry, 474

— Joan wife of Thomas, 250, 275, 432

— John, 781, 833, 851

— John, clerk, 429

— John atte, 265

— Richard, 461, 780

— Thomas, 250, 275, 432, 562

Brooms manor (Sussex), see Chilgrove

Brothercross (Norf.), hundred, 66

Broughton (Northants.), manor, 795

Broughton Gifford (Wilts.), manor, 278, 593

Brounflete, Edward, 481, 618

— Joan wife of Edward, 481

— Thomas, 481

Brown, Joan wife of John, 559

— John, 369, 559, 808

— Laurence, 339

— Margaret wife of Walter, 226

— Nicholas, 831

— Thomas, 773

— Walter, 226

— William (otherwise Brome), 353, 377, 631, 641, 657

Browning, Agnes wife of John, the younger, 264

— Alice wife of John, the elder, 264

— Cecily brother of William, see Whittington

— Elizabeth wife of Walter, 119, 174

— John, 119, 134, 393

— John, the elder, 264

— John, the younger, 264

— John son of John, 393

— Thomas, 60

— Walter, 119, 174

— William, 546, 559

Bruce, John, and Elizabeth his wife, 485; and see Braose

Bruet, Thomas, 239

Bruton (Som.), 250

Bruton, Richard, and Joan his wife, 83, 114

Brymerton (Worcs.), 557

Bryther, Maurice, and Agnes his wife, 352

Buck, Thomas, 733

Buckby, Long (Northants.), manor, 676, 750

Buckingham, John de, 18

— John de, clerk, 225

Buckinghamshire, Crown office in, 18; and see Ashridge; Ason Clinton; Biddlesden; Claydon, Steeple; Datchet; Ditton, Thames; Dorton; Hanslope; Lancaster, duchy of; Leckhampstead; Linslade; Marlow; Medmenham; Milton Keynes; Olney; Quarrendon; Ravenstone; Southcott; Thorpe, Castle; Twyford; Westcott; Whaddon

Buckland (Surrey), manor, 607

Buckland, West (Devon), advowson, 618; manor, 481, 618

Buckland Brewer (Devon), 828–30, 842

Buckland Dinham (Devon, recte Som.), 828–30, 842

Buckland-tout-Saints (Devon), see Goveton

Buckland, Agnes wife of Edward, 263

— Edward, 263

— Eleanor wife of Richard, 847

— John de, 55–6, 538

— Richard, 847

Bucknell (Salop.), manor, 607

Buckworth (Hunts.), manor, 222

Budleigh, West (Devon), hundred, 429

Bugbrooke (Northants.), manor, 635

Bughbrigge, William de, 66

Builth (Radnors.), 443, 539

Buktoft, John, 464, 507

Bulidge, in Kington St. Michael (Wilts.), 669

Bulkington (Wilts.), manor, 607

Bulkington, William, 269

Bulkworthy (Devon), 828–30, 835, 842; manor, 828–30, 835, 842

Bull, Richard, and Margaret (Cadel) his wife, 704

Bulley, 61, 337; manor, 255, 450

Bullingdon (Oxon.), hundred, 631, 641, 657

Bullock, John, 380

Bulmyng, William, and Agnes his wife, 13

Burbage (Som. recte Wilts.), 828–30, 835; manor, 828–30, 835

Burbage, Elena wife of John, of Malmesbury, 164

— John de, vicar of Hilmarton, 9

— John, of Malmesbury, 164

Burches, Geoffrey de, 48

Burdens Ball, in Wilton (Wilts.), manor, 473

Bures (Suff.), 595; Nether Hall manor, 595; Over Hall manor, 595

Burford (Oxon.), 131, 133, 218, 251, 283, 323, 378, 691; manor, 567, 750

Burford, John, 381

Burgess, John, 390

Burgh, Margaret wife of Thomas, see Botreaux

— Thomas, 670, 713

Burghill (Herefs.), 61

Burghill, William, 468

Cowbridge, Agnes wife of William, 378
— William, 342, 378
Cowley, 857; *and see* Birdlip
Cowley, Nicholas, 630
Cox, Alice wife of John, 609, 632
— James, 305, 328
— John, 609, 632
Cranborne (Dorset), manor, 443, 539
Cranford (Northants.), 304; FitzRanes manor, 304
Cranleigh (Surrey), advowson, 18
Cray, Thomas, 55
Credenhill (Herefs.), advowson, 245; manor, 245
Crediton (Devon), 582
Creech, East, in Steeple, or West, in Church
    Knowle (Dorset), manor, 443, 539
Crese, Richard, 150
Cressingham, Little (Norf.), manor, 750
Cresson, Henry, and Elizabeth his wife, 524
Crichel, Moor (Dorset), manor, 477
Cricklade (Wilts.), 309; *and see* Chelworth, Great
Cricklade, Robert, 288
Cripps, Isabel, 250
Crocker, John, and Anne his wife, 842
Croft, Agnes, 838
— Hugh, 838
— Lionel, 838
— Richard, 717
Crofton, in Great Bedwyn (Wilts.), manor,
    582
Cromhall, 459, 594, 616, 659; advowson, 7, 134,
    659; manor, 7, 134, 659; *and see* Bibstone
Cromwell, Matilda sister of Ralph, *see* Stanhope
— Ralph, 499, 607, 614, 716
— Robert son of William, 499
— William, 499
Crook, Alice wife of William, 70
— Henry, 460
— William, 70
Crooks Marsh, in Henbury, 787
Croome, Earl's (Worcs.), manor, 676, 750
Croome, Hill (Worcs.), manor, 631, 641
Crounok, William, 76
Croust, Robert, and Edith his wife, 108
Crowder, Agnes, 83
— Agnes sister of Agnes [*sic*], 83
— Juliana sister of Agnes, 83
Crowell (Oxon.), 55–6; vicar, 267
Croxton (Cambs.), manor, 607
Croys, John, 386
Crudwell (Wilts.), parson, 302, 309; *and see*
    Chedglow; Chelworth, Great; Eastcourt
Crumme, Thomas, vicar of St. Leonard's, Bristol,
    52
Crump, Thomas, 249, 334
Cruwe, Thomas, 349
Cubbington, Richard son of Roger de, 82
— Roger de, 82

Cuckfield (Sussex), *see* Legh
Cucklington (Som.), manor, 607
Cudlow, in Climping (Sussex), manor, 607
Cullompton (Devon), *see* Langford
Culver, William, 465
Cumberford, William, 635
Cumberland, *see* Carlisle
Cumberwell, in Bradford on Avon (Wilts.), 365;
    manor, 365
Cumberworth, Thomas, 184
Cumnor (Berks.), *see* Botley
Curdworth (Warws.), 410
Curry Mallet (Som.), advowson, 370, 397; manor,
    370, 397
Curson, Richard, and Isabel his wife, 676
Curtisknowle, in Diptford (Devon), 828–30, 835,
    842; advowson, 835; manor, 481, 618, 828–30,
    835, 842
Cusaunce, Peter, and Margaret his wife, 9
Cutte, John, 810–11
Cwmwd Deuddwr, in Llansantffraid Cwmdeuddwr
    (Radnors.), 443, 539

Daa, Alice wife of John, 783
— John, 780, 783
d'Abernon, *see* Abernon
Daglingworth, 62, 277, 433, 523, 540, 571, 577;
    manor, 571
Dalby, Mary wife of Richard, 778
— Mary wife of William, 788
— Richard, 778
— William, 788
Daldene, Robert, 220
Dallaway, William, and Joan his wife, 30
Damsel, Ralph, and Matilda his wife, 315
Danby, Robert, 698
Danvers, Edmund, 361
— Richard, 666
— Thomas, 707
— William, 666
Darcy, Richard, 452
Darling, Isabel, daughter of William Scott, 661
Dartmouth (Devon), manor, 595; *and see* Clifton
Datchet (Bucks.), 713; manor, 713
Daubeney, Agnes wife of Ellis, 7
— Ellis, 7
— Giles, of Daubeney, 828–30, 835, 842
— Richard son of Ellis, 7
Daunsepront, John, and Katherine his wife, 392
Daunt, Nicholas, 580
Dauntsey, Edward, parson of Yate, 306
— John (de), 152, 189
Daventry, Thomas (clerk, vicar of West Harptree),
    465, 505
Davers, Thomas, 716
— William, 716
David ap Yeuan, and Margery his wife, 366

SELECTIVE INDEX OF SUBJECTS

References are to entry-numbers.

257

BIBLIOGRAPHY OF C. R. ELRINGTON

This listing revises and extends that compiled by the late Patricia A. Tattersfield and C. R. J. Currie, and published in *English County Histories, A Guide*, eds. C. R. J. Currie and C. P. Lewis (1994).   J. D. H.

1954

'John of Salisbury's *'Entheticus de dogmate philosophorum'*: the light it throws on the educational background of the twelfth century', M.A. thesis, University of London.

1959

'The Fitzwilliam Museum', *V.C.H. Cambs*. iii. 326–7.

'The University Archives', *V.C.H. Cambs*. iii. 327–9.

'The University Seals and Insignia', *V.C.H. Cambs*. iii. 333–1.

'Index', *V.C.H. Wilts*. iv. 461–86.

1962

'Woodford', *V.C.H. Wilts*. vi. 221–7.

'Sir Robert Atkyns and Lower Swell Church', *Trans. Bristol and Glos. Arch. Soc.* 81 204–7.

'Open Fields and Inclosure in the Cotswolds', *Proc. Cotteswold Naturalists' Field Club* 34 (1-2) 37–44.

1963

The registers of Roger Martival, Bishop of Salisbury, 1315–30. Vol. 2, The register of divers letters (first half), ed. C. R. Elrington. (Canterbury and York Soc. lvii)

1964

'The Survey of Church Livings in Gloucestershire, 1650', *Trans. Bristol and Glos. Arch. Soc.* 83 285–98.

'The City of Birmingham: Growth of the City', *V.C.H. Warws*. vii. 4–25 (with P. M. Tillott).

'The City of Birmingham: Communications', *V.C.H. Warws*. vii. 26–42.

'The City of Birmingham: Local Government and Public Services', *V.C.H. Warws*. vii. 318–39, 350–3.

'The City of Birmingham: Churches', *V.C.H. Warws*. vii. 354–96.

1965

Victoria County History of the County of Gloucester, vi, ed. C. R. Elrington.

'Topography', *V.C.H. Glos*. vi. 1–258 (with Kathleen Morgan and Helen O'Neil).

1966

'Records of the Cordwainers' Society of Tewkesbury, 1652–1941', *Trans. Bristol and Glos. Arch. Soc.* 85 164–74.

1968

Victoria County History of the County of Gloucester, viii, ed. C. R. Elrington
'Topography', *V.C.H. Glos.* viii. 1–249, 262–90 (with Kathleen Morgan and N. M. Herbert).
'Index', *V.C.H. Glos.* viii. 291–310

1969

Review of W. E. Tate, *The English Village Community and the Enclosure Movements* (1967): *Antiq. Jnl.* xlix. 175–6.

1970

Handbook for editors and authors [of the Victoria History of the Counties of England], revised ed. C. R. Elrington (Institute of Historical Research, University of London).

1972

The Registers of Roger Martival, Bishop of Salisbury, 1315-30, Vol. 2 (bis) : The register of divers letters (second half) ii (2), ed. C. R. Elrington (Canterbury and York Soc. lviii).
Victoria County History of the County of Gloucester, x, ed. C. R. Elrington and N. M. Herbert
'Newnham', *V.C.H. Glos.* x. 29–51.
'Frampton on Severn', *V.C.H. Glos.* x. 139–55.
'Fretherne and Saul', *V.C.H. Glos.* x. 155–69.
'Hardwicke', *V.C.H. Glos.* x. 178–88.
'Longney', *V.C.H. Glos.* x. 197–205.
'Moreton Valence', *V.C.H. Glos.* x. 205–15.
'Standish', *V.C.H. Glos.* x. 230–42.
'Wheatenhurst or Whitminster', *V.C.H. Glos.* x. 289–99.

1973

Victoria County History of Cambridgeshire and the Isle of Ely, v, ed. C. R. Elrington.
'Great and Little Eversden', *V.C.H. Cambs.* v. 59–68 (with Celia B. Clarke).

1974

Abstracts of Feet of Fines relating to Wiltshire for the reign of Edward III, ed. C. R. Elrington (Wilts. Rec. Soc. xxix).
'The Wiltshire Record Society', *British Studies Monitor*, iv (2), 19–23.

Review of P. J. Fowler, *Archaeology and the Landscape* (1972): *Trans. Bristol and Glos. Arch. Soc.* 93 189–90.

1976

Introduction to James Bennett, *The History of Tewkesbury* (reprint of 1830 edn.). [reprinted 2002 with a new foreword by Susan Nuttall]

Introduction to William Hutton, *An History of Birmingham* (reprint of 1783 edn.).

Obituary: Kathleen Edwards, *Archives*, xii (56) 185 (with Susan Reynolds).

1978

Victoria County History of Cambridgeshire and the Isle of Ely, vii, ed. J. J. Wilkes and C. R. Elrington.

1980

'Fishersgate Half-Hundred', *V.C.H. Suss.* vi (1), 131.

'Kingston by Sea', *V.C.H. Suss.* vi (1), 132–8.

'Old and New Shoreham', *V.C.H. Suss.* vi (1), 138–73.

'Southwick', *V.C.H. Suss.* vi (1), 173–83.

1981

'Ralph Bernard Pugh: an Appreciation', *Wilts. Coroners' Bills, 1752–1796*, ed. R. F. Hunnisett (Wilts. Rec. Soc. 36), pp. xiii–xvii.

1982

'Our First Charter', *Antiq. Jnl.* 62 (2) 347–55 by R. B. Pugh; article seen to publication by C. R. Elrington after Pugh's death.

1983

Review of *Hampshire Studies*, ed. J. Webb, N. Yates, and S. Peacock (1981): *Southern Hist.* v. 281–2.

1984

Review of *Rolls of the Fifteenth of 1225 and the Fortieth of 1232*, ed. F. A. and A. P. Cazel (Pipe Roll Soc. new ser. xlv, 1983): *Wilts. Arch. and Natural Hist. Magazine*, lxxix. 266.

The Middlesex Victoria County History Council 1955-1984: an account of its work and a guide to the contents of volumes I-VII of the Middlesex history, I. W. Davies and C. R. Elrington.

1985

'Presidential Address: Assessments of Gloucestershire: Fiscal Records on Local History', *Trans. Bristol and Glos. Arch. Soc.* 103 5–15.

1986

'Index', *V. C. H. Suss.* vi (2), 219–39.

Review of *The World of John of Salisbury*, ed. M. Wilks: *Wilts. Arch. and Natural Hist. Magazine*, lxxx. 253–4.

Review of *The English Rising of 1381*, ed. R. H. Hilton and T. H. Aston: *Southern Hist.* viii. 160–1.

1987

'Wyndham Half-Hundred', *V.C.H. Suss.* vi (3), 169–70.

'Cowfold', *V.C.H. Suss.* vi (3), 171–89.

'Shermanbury', *V.C.H. Suss.* vi (3), 189–98.

1988

'One Hundred Years of Somerset and Dorset Notes and Queries', *Notes and Queries for Som. and Dors.* xxxii (328), 689–94.

'National Record Societies', *The Blackwell Dictionary of Historians*, ed. J. Cannon, 297–9.

Review of Philip Riden, *Record Sources for Local History* (1987): *Jnl. of the Soc. of Archivists*, ix. (3), 159–60.

1989

'Index', *V.C.H. Cambs.* ix. 421–51.

'Lordship and Lineage: the Descent of Manors in the Victoria County History', *Genealogists' Magazine*, xxiii. 41–7.

'Particular Places', *History Today*, xxxix. 61–2.

1990

The Victoria History of the Counties of England: General Introduction: Supplement 1970–90, ed. C. R. Elrington.

'Review of *A Professional Hertfordshire Tramp: John Edwin Cussons, Historian of Hertford-shire*, ed. A. Deacon and P. Walne (Herts. Rec. Ser. Iii, 1987): *Hist. and Arch. Review*, v. 33–4.

1992

'The Victoria County History', *Local Historian*, xxii (3), 128–37.

Review of Victor Belcher, *The City Parochial Foundation 1891–91: A Trust for the Poor of London* (1991): *London Topographical Soc. Newsletter*, xxxiv. 7–8.

1993

Review of Kate Tiller, *English Local History: an Introduction* (1992): *Jnl. of Educational Administration and Hist.* xxv (1), 105.

1999

Michael Greenslade: an appreciation, by C. R. Elrington, in Morgan, Philip Joseph; Phillips, A. D. M. (ed.), Staffordshire histories: essays in honour of Michael Greenslade (Collections for a History of Staffordshire, 4th ser., 19) (Staffordshire Record Soc., 1999) 1–4.

2001

Carr, D. R. (ed.), *The first general entry book of the city of Salisbury 1387-1452* (Wilts. Record Soc. 54, 2001). The preface notes: 'The translation and interpretation of this difficult manuscript have been immeasurably improved by the painstaking labour of Professor Christopher Elrington … who has not only examined the text in its entirety, but has also prepared the index of persons, and contributed to the index of places and subjects and the introduction.'

2003

Abstracts of feet of fines relating to Gloucestershire, 1199–1299, ed. C. R. Elrington (Glos. Record Series 16).

2004

'William Hutton (1723–1815), historian', article in Oxford Dictionary of National Biography.

'Roger Martival (*c*.1250–1330), bishop of Salisbury', article in Oxford Dictionary of National Biography.

Review of Nigel J. Tringham, ed., The Victoria History of the County of Staffordshire, ix, Burton-upon-Trent: *Midland Hist.* vol. 29, 150–1.

2005

A Village in London: An historical walk in the New River Conservation Area (The Amwell Soc.); ed. D. Sulkin and D. Cross; textual revision by C. R. Elrington of 1974 version (ed. I. Gray).
'Feet of Fines', article in *Hornsey Historical Soc. Bulletin* 46, 7–10.

2006

Abstracts of feet of fines relating to Gloucestershire, 1300–1359, ed. C. R. Elrington. (Glos. Record Series 20).

'Hungerford Cartulary, Part 2: The Hobhouse Cartulary', article in *The Recorder: the annual newsletter of the Wilts. Record Soc.* 5, 3–4.

'Music and Murder', article in *The Recorder: the annual newsletter of the Wilts. Record Soc.* 7, 4–5.

2007

Women land-owners in medieval Gloucestershire as seen in the feet of fines, by C. R. Elrington, in Bettey, Joseph Harold (ed.), Archives & Local History in Bristol & Gloucestershire: Essays in Honour of David Smith (Bristol and Glos. Arch. Soc. 2007) 7–16.

Kirby, J. L. (ed.) *The Hungerford Cartulary part 2: a calendar of the Hobhouse Cartulary of the Hungerford family* (Wilts. Record Soc. vol 60, 2007). Published after the editor's death; the preface acknowledges 'Professor Christopher Elrington for filling the gaps in Mr Kirby's work and compiling the introduction and the indexes'. He also typeset the volume.

2008

Review of *The Manors of Norton St. Philip and Hinton Charterhouse 1535–1691,* ed. Colin J. Brett, *Southern Hist.* vol. 30 152–5.

2009

'Angmering', *V.C.H. Suss.* v (2), ed. C.P. Lewis 29-59.

'Burpham', *V.C.H. Suss.* v (2), ed. C.P. Lewis. 60-75.

'Life and Death in Thirteenth-Century Wiltshire', article in *The Recorder: the annual newsletter of the Wiltshire Record Soc.* 8, 1–2.

2010

List of sheriffs of Gloucestershire, by C. R. Elrington, Trans. Bristol and Glos. Arch. Soc. 128 207–227.

2012

Crown Pleas of the Wiltshire Eyre 1268, ed. Brenda Farr and Christopher Elrington; revised and with an introduction by Henry Summerson (Wiltshire Record Soc. 65).

2013

Abstracts of feet of fines relating to Gloucestershire, 1360–1508, ed. C. R. Elrington (Glos. Record Series 27).

As Series Editor of the Victoria County History, and as General Editor of the Gloucestershire Record Series and of Wiltshire Record Society volumes, Christopher Elrington also contributed in greater or lesser measure to each of the editions prepared under his supervision; some significant instances are noted above. His help is also acknowledged in the introductions of many other volumes and articles on historical subjects, beyond those listed here.